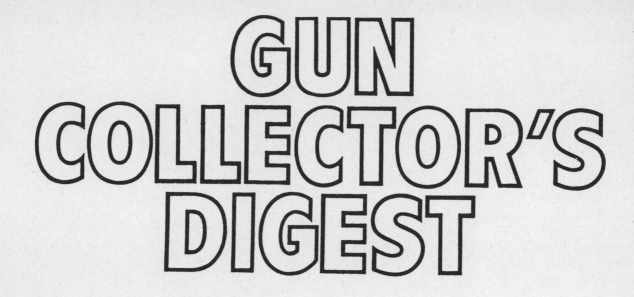

GUN COLLECTOR'S DIGEST

5th Edition

Edited by
Joseph J.
Schroeder

DBI BOOKS, INC.

Gun Collector's Digest Staff

EDITOR
Joseph J. Schroeder

SENIOR STAFF EDITOR
Harold A. Murtz

PRODUCTION MANAGER
Jamie L. McCoy

PRODUCTION ASSISTANT
Adam J. Newman

GRAPHIC DESIGN
Jim Billy
Steve Johnson
Mary MacDonald

COVER PHOTOGRAPHY
John Hanusin

MANAGING EDITOR
Pamela J. Johnson

PUBLISHER
Sheldon L. Factor

The Guns On Our Cover

The guns pictured on our cover include, from top, a Model 1904 Navy Luger with pre-WWI U-Boat markings, a Mauser Model 1906/08 pistol, and an early Soviet-era Nagant revolver. (Editor's collection)

ISBN 0-87349-037-1   **Library of Congress Catalog Card #73-83406**

CONTENTS

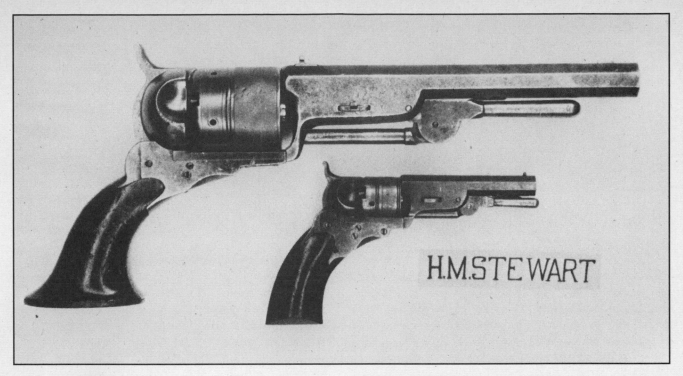

Two of Stewart's many Patersons. Top, a unique experimental, serial 1, in 54-caliber. Above, a 28-caliber Baby Paterson, serial 350.

A Gun Collector's Legacy

Henry M. Stewart, Jr.'s memory lives through a new major arms technology museum.

by WILLIAM B. EDWARDS

THERE IS a time to live and a time to die. A fatal heart attack in October, 1988 was not the time to die for gun collector Henry Stewart, who was in the midst of planning a major arms museum for his alma mater, the Virginia Military Institute. But after a first heart attack in 1966, he had cheated Death for 22 years. I knew "Hank" Stewart since 1948. Death was the only one he had ever cheated . . .

Hank's primary collecting interest was Colt arms, and inevitably he came across fakes. Collecting, study-

Stewart at a gun show, this one in Pennsylvania in the mid-1970s, glowing behind a table laden with rare Paterson and other Colt goodies. Son HMS III shared his travels with youthful enthusiasm.

ing, writing, and sharing his hard-won and immense knowledge with fellow collectors, he was often called on by enthusiastic but incautious "advanced collectors" to pass judgement on a rare piece. He was death on fakery; his collection today holds only one fake — a breech-loading conversion of, improbably, a U.S. 1842 horse pistol, the stubby breech suggesting the little-known but strictly modern 22 Tompkins target pistol of the 1950s. He put up with that instead of suggesting it be destroyed, after showing its once-happy buyer what it really was.

As president of the American Society of Arms Collectors, Hank had the opportunity to learn of fakes bought by the rich and famous. Along with other members of that exclusive society, such as Harry Knode and Col. Leon "Red" Jackson, he collected data on fakes and fakers to warn others and help unwary buyers get their money back. He put the "honor code" of his grand old school, the Virginia Military Institute of Lexington, the school of "Stonewall" and of Crozet, into everyday use. He had gone to VMI hoping to be commissioned in the U.S. Army Air Corps. There, while earning his wings and barnstorming through nearby valleys in a shared "Jenny" World War I biplane, he dug into the Institute's precious collection of military relics. Cleaning one of VMI's Colt revolving rifles confirmed a bent he had acquired as a student at Haverford Boy's School, where a classmate with a small collection of guns had first sparked his interest.

Truly the child was father to the man. This childhood curiosity about arms eventually matured into the world's major collection of Colt revolving rifles, as well as other arms contemporaneous with Colt. Studying arms history and the some 300 patent models he had accumulated showed him the ideas, systems and methods conceived by the designers and merchants of the past that he would later be able to apply in his adult career. He became a highly successful sales engineer, moving from work in water systems design to association with pioneers like Reynolds of ballpoint pen fame and groups of venture capitalists who revived failing companies. In WWII he did not fly — the Army considered him too useful for designing factories to manufacture TNT.

I first met "Hank" in 1948 when I was researching my standard biography of Col. Samuel Colt. John E. Parsons had told me about Stewart, and we made an appointment to meet at 8 PM in a Washington hotel. I then lived in Connecticut and hitchhiked south, arriving about 5 minutes early. I had forgotten the incident, but Stewart didn't. We often met thereafter in various places across the U.S., and every get-together enriched me in spirit and encouraged me by fact. While recently reviewing our correspondence, I discovered that I offered him special "old buddy" discounts, selling him rare arms at what today would be ridiculously low prices! He once lamented selling his serial No. 1 Paterson revolver to Bob Sutherland, so I offered him two New Service revolvers, serials 0 and 4, which he bought in consolation. Years later, he was to have the happy but unacknowledged chore of preparing Sutherland's monumental "Colt" collection book for the printer.

Hank and I collaborated on running down some of the 16 fake silver and gold "Tiffany" grips that were turned loose on collectors in the 1960s. I once spotted one fitted to a "Best of Show" award-winning revolver glittering under its protective bell jar. I saw that the inscription pad, a polished flat place on the back of the grip, had two tiny blow holes. I knew a 19th century goldsmith would never let bad work like that leave his hands; he would have simply tapped in a gold pin to close up the hole. Investigation later revealed the gun's recent finishing of gold inlay and blue had cost $1200, and the engraver remarked that, "It did not have the Tiffany grip on it when it left here. . ."

As a "Tiffany grip" expert, Stewart once certified as genuine a grip which a noted gun dealer had just declared a "fake." I tend to believe Stewart's opinion, for I also knew that this particular dealer had been ready to certify as genuine a Paterson Colt which a modern gunsmith in the Midwest had made from "whole cloth."

Stewart was orphaned as a youth and made his own way through life. He had been born into a good, but not rich, Philadelphia family. Yet, through life, he put his

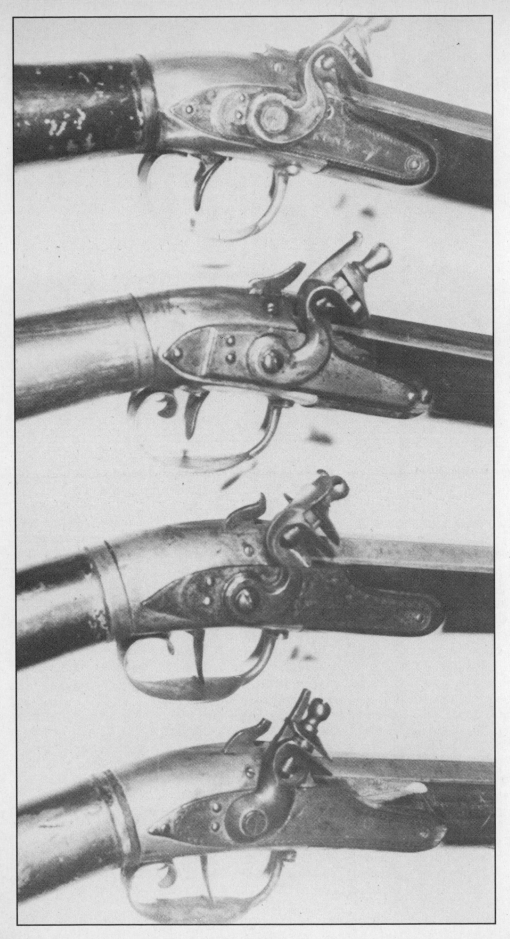

Four air guns, from Stewart's collection, display pseudo-flintlocks, introducing new designs in traditional forms for conservative 18th century sporting gentlemen.

(Above and below) Super rare U.S. Pistol M1799 by North & Cheney was snared by Henry as a kid. Found in a pawn shop for $5, it remained in collection for years.

money where his hobby led him, from spotting a North & Cheney in a pawnshop window for $5, to paying the top going price of $10,000 for a Paterson he needed to prove a point in his theme of arms development. He invested in guns not only to show the Colt story, but also the various arms surrounding and influencing the Colt designs. He was deeply hurt, as if by a personal injury, when he was called in to consult in the investigation by the Connecticut attorney general of the deaccessioning into private hands of over 300 guns from the Colt collection in the Connecticut State Library.

This amazing group of experimental, developmental, and test pieces had been donated by the Colt management to the people of Connecticut back in the 1950s. Included were arms from the beginning of Colt's work through some of John Pearson's experimental pieces, to post-WWII rifles, pistols and machineguns. By the mid-1980s, it came to official notice that the collection had been gutted by what was to be termed by some collectors, "the deal of the century." VMI Museum Director Keith Gibson, who accompanied Henry to Connecticut when officials sought his advice on whether they had been traded fakes or junk for their Colt collection, called it "more insidious than a simple theft" because the collection's dispersal had destroyed a unique technological archive that told, in hard metal, the story of an idea and a company. One pair of pistols, among eight items traded for 290 arms from the Colt collection, was a rare set of revolvers a dealer had bought in 1960 and was allowed to appraise at $1 million in 1980. Connecticut could not actually prove it had lost value in terms of dollars and cents. . .

Learning from this sad experience, Stewart, in bequeathing to VMI dozens of his Paterson pistols, scores of accessories, many cased sets, several dozen revolving Paterson and other Colt and competitive long arms, as well as single shots of merit, made sure that deaccessioning would not be a future hazard to his collection. And VMI's new museum, to be housed in a new building targeted to open in 1990, will be available to anyone interested.

This will be a student's museum where any qualified researcher will be welcome. The collection holds not just rare Colts, but also cadet arms from VMI's 1851 muskets to Nazi-era German 22-caliber training rifles. It also has air guns, from early pseudo-flintlocks to modern target models, showing the evolution and engineering of non-powder systems.

Hank apparently never threw away a scrap of paper. Randomly opening an envelope I found in his files, I came across his 1935 letter of acceptance to his application for his first job on leaving VMI. Surely his files on fakes and forgeries will provide many piquant revelations for generations to come.

Stewart the orphan became a sort of "Daddy Warbucks" of gun collectors, working hard and saving while running with the rich. But he remained ever a blunt, warm, if outspoken, person. He shunned sham, and was in collecting as in life, always a "straight shooter." This, as much as his bequest of his magnificent gun collection to the VMI Arms Museum, is his legacy. ●

The Peter Moucka specimen appears to be a rather ordinary pinfire revolver with the ejector rod missing.

The Pinfire/Centerfire
REVOLVER

Left view of the Moucka revolver shows the hammer back to reveal the centerfire striker. The grip was left smooth, uncheckered. Note the high rear sight.

by GRAHAM BURNSIDE

Several years ago when visiting my friend Peter Moucka at his home in Wisconsin and viewing his gun collections, he handed me what appeared to be a rather normal, common, 12mm pinfire revolver. Now Peter is not only a very serious collector and gunsmith of great talent, he also has a knack for coming up with things no one has ever seen before! I was about to give him back the pistol when I noticed a twinkle in his eye. Here we go again! At second glance, the darned thing was still just another military-size ordinary pinfire, but Peter doesn't get a twinkle in his eye without good reason.

I carefully checked the cylinder—it wasn't loaded. I drew back the hammer and stared in amazement. The blasted thing had a centerfire striker! I'm sure there must be several people out there who have seen one of these, but I've been around the block once or twice and have never seen this hermaphrodite!

Peter kindly loaned me the piece so I could do some research, take photographs, and store the information in some dusty corner. As for the revolver itself, stamped on the left barrel flat just forward of the cylinder is: LEFAUCHEUX B^{te}/ACIER FONDU.

This means it was manufactured by the famous gun-making house of Lefaucheux and made of cast steel. The B^{te} following the Lefaucheux name is an abbreviation for the French word *brevete*, which loosely translates as "registered" or "protected."

Engraved on the top of the barrel is: A FRANCOTTE A LIEGE. This is the mark of Auguste Francotte who operated a retail gun store in Liege, Belgium from

This close-up of the Moucka shows that the centerfire striker is staked in place through the face of the hammer. It struck the cartridge through an aperture in the rear of the frame.

The markings of the Moucka are common marks of the famous firearms firm of Lefaucheux.

about 1844 until well into the 20th century. Francotte was a retailer and dealer who sold all kinds of firearms and specialized in fowling pieces. Long after our Civil War, Francotte offered fine quality percussion shotguns. I don't know what he actually manufactured, but he had many sources of supply and even traded with wholesale dealers in other countries. His pecuniary success was such that he opened another gun shop in London, England in 1877 which stayed in operation until 1893.

So, we have an unusual pinfire/centerfire revolver that was manufactured in France and retailed in Belgium.

Now we come to the problem of ammunition. Everyone is familiar with the pinfire cartridge, but what did

the centerfire round look like? Because I had the revolver in my possession, we went to the cartridge collection. The tray holding the early European centerfire cartridges contained at least a dozen varieties of the 12mm French so-called "thick rim" cartridges. These rounds are known by a variety of names including "Galland," "Perrin," and "Franzos."

Galland was an early designer and inventor of an interesting French revolver system and the Perrin revolver was used in the American Civil War (probably by both sides). It is known that the Union bought at least 200 of them. These "thick rim" cartridges vary greatly and I'm sure they were intended for at least a few different chambers.

After great care and deliberation, I found that none

Three examples of the 12mm European centerfire cartridge. On the left is the inside primed type with the raised Gevelot head-stamp. Center is the common 12mm pinfire as made by Sellier and Bellot of Prague, Czechoslovakia. Cartridge on the right was made by Societe Francais des Munitions, a firm that succeeded the Gevelot organization.

The Mud Island revolver displays a different style of grip, a variant trigger guard and simpler frame design. This example has the ejector in place. The rear sight is a notch cut in the top of the hammer.

of those cartridges fit into the chambers of the strange revolver. Wait a minute! What about that unknown, inside-primed centerfire that dealers puzzled over for years? It's right here, and the rim is so thin it's almost not there. Sure enough, you couldn't have asked for a more perfect fit! Actually, this unknown, inside-primed 12mm is nothing more than an early version of the 12mm European centerfire cartridge which when tried, also fit perfectly.

Some cartridge collectors confuse the 12mm European centerfire cartridge with the fairly common 450 English revolver round. They do look alike, but the case length of the 450 English round is noticeably longer. And, incidentally, the rim of the 450 is large enough that the round will not chamber in our pinfire/centerfire.

The inside-primed 12mm cartridge is a rather scarce item these days. There was a time, as mentioned above, that cartridge dealers didn't know what it was and because of the raised "GD" headstamp, referred to it with a rather blasphemous pair of words.

Many years ago, Lewis Winant, author of *Firearms Curiosa* asked me what the "GD" stood for. This "GD" is encountered not only on cartridges, but also on percussion cap boxes and even on the percussion caps themselves. At that time I told him that in my opinion, it stood for "Gevelot Deposé," which means Gevelot's patent or protected product. M. Gevelot, a Parisian, was very active in the development of early priming and cartridge design. He held four French car-

Left view of the Mud Island gun with the slightly different Lefaucheux mark. Both revolvers bear a five-digit serial number on the lower left frame. (Photo courtesy of the Mississippi River Museum/Mud Island)

tridge patents that were issued between 1854 and 1861—a period when much progress was made in the field. M. Gevelot's patents covered features that other designers used when making their products. Consequently, Gevelot's finances were thus enhanced.

Sometime later I was conversing with some of the collectors at a Memphis, Tennessee gun show and brought up the subject of the pinfire/centerfire. I described the revolver, and I think it was Dave Dermon who said, "There's one of those out on Mud Island." I said, "What is it doing in the mud?" They then explained to me that Mud Island is the site of the Mississippi River Museum, and what a museum it is! Anyone going within 100 miles of Memphis would do well to go out of their way and take in this museum. It is not only

an outstanding collection of river memorabilia, but everything is beautifully displayed. I contacted the people at Mud Island and in time they supplied me with photographs of their specimen. It also bears a Lefaucheux mark, but in this case the marking is: E. LEFAUCHEUX/BREVETE. This tells us that Eugene Gabriel Lefaucheux had something to do with this second revolver. Eugene Gabriel was the son of the Lefaucheux who founded the well-known French gun house. (See *Gun Collector's Digest*, 3rd edition, p. 26.)

In viewing the photographs, some features prove interesting. In the Peter Moucka specimen, the centerfire striker is staked in place from front to back. The pistol at Mud Island has the striker pinned in place from side to side. The Moucka piece employs the external lock-

The right side of the Mud Island revolver clearly shows that the centerfire striker is pinned in place. Note the Liege proofmark of an "E.L.G" over a star is discernable on the cylinder. (Photo courtesy of the Mississippi River Museum/Mud Island)

ing spring feature, which is absent on the Mud Island revolver. Other style and design features are visibly different, which is totally understandable. Those people manufactured firearms to sell to the trade and make a profit. If one idea was better than the other, they used it; if one feature was expensive and not really necessary, they eliminated it. This process continued throughout Lefaucheux's production. The firm employed probably the best European workmen of the day, and many times their ideas were incorporated and utilized.

It's been a long time in grinding this article through the think, learn, and write procedure, but it has been very enjoyable and hopefully we all learned a thing or two.

●

Bibliography

Bartlet, W.A., and D.B. Gallatin. *Digest of Cartridges for Small Arms*. Ottawa, Canada: Reprint.

Burnside, Graham. *Gun Collector's Digest*, 3rd ed. Northbrook, Ill.: DBI Books, Inc., 1981.

Gardner, Robert Edward. *Five Centuries of Gunsmiths, Swordsmiths, and Armourers*. Columbus, Ohio: Walter F. Heer, 1948.

White, H.P. and B.D. Munhall. *Cartridge Headstamp Guide*. H.P. White Laboratory, 1963.

White, H.P. and B.D. Munhall. *Cartridge Identification*, Vol. I. Infantry Journal Press, 1948.

White, H.P. and B.D. Munhall. *Cartridge Identification*, Vol. II. Infantry Journal Press, 1950.

Russian Military Firearms:

A Rapidly Growing Collector's Field
The Imperial Era

by FRED A. DATIG

Nagant's Model 1895 "Gas-Seal" revolver, caliber 7.62mm/.30-inch. This example was made at Tula in 1899, the first year of Russian manufacture.

Berdan II, Russia's first bolt-action rifle, quickly replaced the Berdan I in Russian service.

THE SUBTITLE of this article is far from frivolous. When *The Luger Pistol* was being compiled some 35 years ago, less than a dozen of us were serious collectors of that marque; today the Luger fraternity is at least 100-fold larger. Personal interest in Imperial and Soviet military small arms goes back still further, to the late 1940s, and, once again, the number of enthusiasts known in the field today is still relatively limited, but definitely on the increase. Not only is this a collecting sector long neglected, it is one of extreme historical value and potentially great collector interest. It is one of the few remaining, relatively untapped, collectors' fields in which the beginning and/or less affluent enthusiast has the potential of uncovering true rarities at a reasonably affordable price.

With almost unlimited potential, detailed in the following pages are Russian arms types and variations which are most readily available at today's average gun show. Some of these are more common, while "sleepers" of a scarce, even rare, nature await discovery by the sharp-eyed and knowledgeable. Still better, such specimens — including rarities — are to be found in all types from flintlocks to self-loading pistols, early breechloaders to semi-automatic rifles, bayonets, edged weapons, accoutrements and accessories.

Having once attempted to catalog the variations in martial Russian muzzle-loading pistols, we were astounded when we uncovered a potential of *some hundreds* of variants! One historical type alone was encountered repeatedly — the handsome Model 1809 of Napoleonic Wars vintage. Specimens are almost always dated "1813" and bear the brass escutcheon engraved, A I (Tsar Alexander the First) on the top of the wooden stock. As our illustration indicates, the pistol is stocked

Flintlock Cavalry Pistol Model 1809, caliber 17.78mm/.70-inch, made in various Russian factories, 1809-1818. Foremost Russian handgun of the Napoleonic Wars.

Percussion "Soldier's (Enlisted Man's) Pistol" Model 1848, caliber 17.78mm/.70-inch. Possibly the largest, bulkiest martial percussion handgun ever issued. Saw extensive service in Crimean War, 1854-55. Rifled version has nomenclature "Model 1854."

Percussion "Soldier's (Enlisted Man's) Pistol" Model 1849 System Delvigne, caliber 17.78mm/.70-inch. Four variations made: short barrel, smoothbore; same, rifled; long barrel, smoothbore; same, rifled. Rifled versions especially for officers were designated Model 1854.

to the muzzle (full-stocked). The lockplate is not only dated, but also carries in Russian Cyrillic lettering the name of the factory of manufacture, usually Tula, Russia's most important arms plant, which appears as Мула ("Tula" written in Cyrillic longhand). Sometimes the full-stocked Model 1809 may be encountered in a half-stocked version. This is an official alteration and a pure collector's item, not necessarily a "butchered" martial handgun, and even scarcer than the full-stocked original. The half-stocked type was adopted as the Model 1839 and older pistols were altered to meet the later specifications.

Martial Russian flintlock muskets and rifles are seldom seen in the United States and are uncommon even in Europe. The many known models, of which there were some 38 different ones between 1700 and 1839, are easily identified by the ever-present Cyrillic lockplate marking and date. Most types are similar to those of contemporary nationalities, usually French or German.

While many variant flintlock pistol models were later officially transformed to the percussion system, only a few were originally produced as such. One of those is the large, bulky "Soldier's Pistol," Model 1848. This half-stocked giant is possibly the most massive martial percussion handgun ever officially adopted, nationality notwithstanding. It was used extensively in the Crimean War of 1854-1855 and almost invariably bears the brass escutcheon of Tsar Nicholas I who reigned from 1825 to 1855. The crowned H I actually translates to "N I," the Cyrillic "N" being written as "H." It was later introduced with a rifled barrel and given the designation "Model 1854."

Reported to be for the "Detached Cossack Corps," in service during the Crimean War, the long, slim, ball-butted pistol illustrated here was made in Belgium as a wartime expedient. Specimens may or may not carry a "crown-over-V" proofmark or have blued metal, and the wood of the ball butt is lighter in color than the stock. These pistols, while not martial arms, may be considered official Secondary Martials. They are frequently found for sale at reasonable prices relative to their availability and collector's importance. The "button trigger" and absence of a trigger guard are features typical to cossack firearms, long or short.

A scarcer official percussion pistol is the Model 1849, which may be found in both long- and short-barreled versions, either rifled or smoothbore. Of the four variations, the range of scarcity runs from the rare, rifled, long-barreled type to the same model smooth-bored, to the short-barreled rifled, and the same model smooth-bored. While all are scarce, the last is the one most often encountered. All of these are easily recognized by three distinctive features: **1.)** the downward-sloping back-action lockplate; **2.)** the swivel ramrod which is non-detachable; and **3.)** the "hooked" finger extension trigger guard. Numerous commercial variants, sizes and calibers of these 17.78mm/.70-inch unusual "Delvigne Patent" pistols of Belgian origin will be encountered, but those falling into the martial Russian category will bear Cyrillic lockplate markings with dates of manufacture and the H I ("N I") brass escutcheon. Those *not* having the Russian inscriptions have no known military significance, Russian or otherwise. Both rifled versions, long and short, were adopted in 1854.

The Russian military percussion rifle most often encountered in the U.S. is the attractive and desirable "Belgian Stutzer," Model 1843. With its two-groove rifling, grooved muzzle, brass patchbox and bayonet bar, it is the Belgian-made Russian-contract version of the famed Brunswick rifle, which was also adopted by and produced in England. Unlike domestic small arms, the place of origin, Malherbe or Liege, appears in Western lettering on the back-action lockplate which, also con-

Percussion Secondary Pistol of Belgian make reportedly for Russia's Crimean War "Detached Cossack Corps." Note typical cossack features of ball butt and lack of trigger guard for "button" trigger. Almost never found Russian marked.

trarily, is undated. Reportedly procured for the Russian tsar's (Nicholas I) Finnish Guards Regiment, the imperial double-headed eagle is evident on the upper tang of the brass buttplate. Serial numbers are usually four digits, despite the fact that some 15,000 were said to have been the contract's total. Specimens in original unaltered condition have the aforementioned two-grooved muzzle (sometimes removed by cutting off the front of the barrel) and a beautiful plum brown, Damascus-patterned striped barrel. The brass-hilted double-edged bayonet, itself a greatly desired collector's item, is unusually long, fairly heavy and quite striking with its short sword appearance. While similar, it is *not* identical to its British counterpart, being Belgian-prooved. The rare combination leather and brass scabbard is unique in that it bears an accommodation for a wooden rod bullet starter. Not only is the Model 1843 a desirable collector's item, but both rifle and bayonet — separate or combined — make exceptionally attractive decorations of antique high-art quality and beauty.

In 1867-1868, the U.S. entered the Russian scene with the sale by Colt's Patent Firearms Manufacturing Company of 30,000 Berdan I "trapdoor" single shot breech-loading rifles, which was possibly intended to keep the Finnish Guards equipped with the best available arms. These are of historical importance as they are chambered for the Russian redesign of Hiram Berdan's experimental caliber .45-inch straight-cased round to a bottlenecked brass cartridge case. Unlike the cartridge, which led the contemporary field for over a decade, the rifle itself left something to be desired. Finely made and finished, the tops of the barrels bear a long Cyrillic legend (Colt's, etc.), though some carry the barrel markings in English. Due to its origin as well as scarcity, the Colt-Berdan I Russian-contract rifle is expensive when compared to many other rare rifles.

Colonel Berdan, of U.S. Civil War "Sharpshooter"

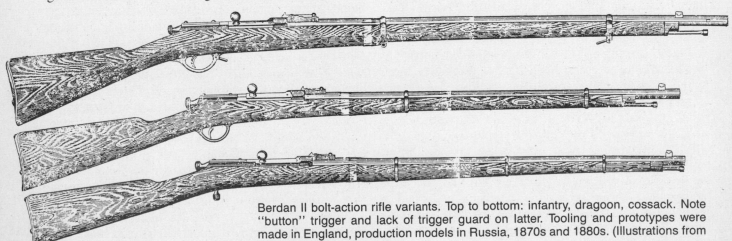

(Above) Belgian-made Brunswick two-grooved rifle by "Malherbe, Liege" known in Russia as "Littich Stutzer Model 1843." Over 10,000 made. Saw use in Crimean War. (Illustration from a Russian text)

(Above and below) U.S.-made Berdan I "trapdoor" infantry rifle, caliber 10.66mm/.42-inch. Thirty thousand made for Russia by Colt's in 1868. Specimens with English barrel markings are scarce.

fame, continued his lucrative relationship with Russia which, 3 years later in 1871, adopted the bolt-action Berdan II single shot rifle chambered for the same 10.66mm/.42-inch cartridge introduced with the Berdan I. Tooling and early pre-production examples were made in England by Birmingham Small Arms (B.S.A.) and are usually marked as such and often dated. Four basic types were officially adopted in the early 1870s. These were an infantry rifle; a somewhat shorter and lighter dragoon rifle; a "button trigger" cossack type; and a short cavalry carbine. The Cyrillic barrel markings indicate manufacture by one of Russia's three major arms factories — Tula, Izhevsk or Sestroretsk. As usual, the date, anywhere from the early 1870s to the late 1880s, was also included. The infantry rifle's original sighting setup proved inadequate for the high ballistic performance, so sometime during the Russo-Turkish War of 1877-78, or shortly thereafter, an alteration was made. This consisted of adding a grooved arm to the rear sight leaf and affixing an inverted cone to the front barrel band. Specimens without these sighting alterations are scarcer than those with them, as rifles of earlier manufacture were included in the modification program.

Until quite recently, the Smith & Wesson revolvers made on various military contracts for Imperial Russia in the 1870s claimed relatively little collector interest. At best they were broken into three basic groups: 1.) Old Old Model; 2.) Old Model; and 3.) No. 3 New Model. These were the loose designations given by the manufacturer for what amounted to Cyrillic-marked examples of 1.) First Model American with 8-inch barrel; 2.) Second Model American with 7-inch barrel and 3.) No. 3 or New Model with 6½-inch barrel. The two latter types were distinguished by the addition of a trigger guard finger rest extension, or "hook." Such specimens became known as the Russian Model, whether barrel markings were in Cyrillic or English. The Russians assigned their nomenclatures chronologically, Model 1871, Model 1872 and Model 1874, respectively.

Berdan II bolt-action rifle variants. Top to bottom: infantry, dragoon, cossack. Note "button" trigger and lack of trigger guard on latter. Tooling and prototypes were made in England, production models in Russia, 1870s and 1880s. (Illustrations from Russian book by Fedorov)

Smith & Wesson Russian Contract Model 1871 (above) and Model 1872 (below), caliber 44 S&W Russian with 8-inch and 7-inch barrels, respectively. M1874 is similar to M1872 but with 6½-inch barrrel. All have Cyrillic barrel markings and Russian proofmarks. (Illustration from Soviet book by Zhuk)

For the past century details of the Russian models and their variants were of little interest to even the most advanced researchers, authors and collectors. To further complicate matters, succeeding Russian orders for types already delivered were marked and serial numbered in a manner not consistent with the previously received identical revolvers. To make matters worse, especially from the standpoint of collectors unable to decipher the Cyrillic barrel markings, foreign-made copies of the Smith & Wesson New Model (Model 1874) were produced under further contracts. These included something over 100,000 examples produced by the German firm of Ludwig Loewe in Berlin, and domestically at the Tula Ordnance Factory from 1886 to 1896 in quantities exceeding 30,000. The latter became known in Russia as the Model 1880, though it was essentially identical to examples of the Model 1874 made by both Smith & Wesson and Ludwig Loewe. From the foregoing statistics, it becomes obvious that only 30 percent as many Tula-made revolvers were produced as those manufactured by Loewe; thus the Tulas are scarcer than the Loewes. Some 41,000 identical New Models were delivered by Smith & Wesson, making that variant slightly more available than the Russian-made version. Due entirely to its origin, the American-made specimen is, however, of greater value and collector interest despite being more common.

As is true in all collector fields, condition greatly influences value. Most specimens of Russian-contract Smith & Wesson revolvers which were actually delivered to Russia are usually found in a condition which leaves much to be desired. This is due mainly to their history of extended usage. As a consequence, a Smith & Wesson-made New Model Russian-contract revolver in excellent condition would be a prize find, and even the same in less desirable condition would undoubtedly be more coveted than, for example, a Loewe-produced specimen in much better condition. In such circumstances, a smart collector should obtain a reasonably-priced specimen in decent condition in hopes of future "upgrading" (acquiring a better example).

It is important to point out that some revolvers of the Russian type bear barrel markings in English or German. While, except for markings, such revolvers are identical in appearance, they are not in the Russian-contract military collector's category. The first type (Old Old Model, First Model Russian or Model 1871) is considered the most desirable by collectors, as only 20,000 were produced. The Model 1872 (Old Model), while 60,000 were delivered, seems to be the type least often encountered and rarely in better than "good," or average, condition. With three basic, obviously different appearance models and a dozen variations, collecting Russian-contract Smith & Wesson revolvers is not only of historical and mechanical interest, but also a field, as yet untapped, in which many values will continue to rise considerably as collector interest grows and competition becomes keener. While not plentiful, specimens of all variations can be seen at most major gun shows, so the initiated enthusiast has many opportunities to acquire a "sleeper"; at the least, they make a solid financial investment.

As with the Berdan rifle cartridge, the Russians also redesigned the caliber .44-inch Smith & Wesson American revolver round into the ballistically superior 44 Smith & Wesson Russian cartridge. This round was especially popular in the United States and many other countries for use in championship shooting competi-

Original Model 1891 Mosin-Nagant infantry rifle and bayonet. Note finger rest at rear of trigger guard, magazine-housing sling swivel, flat rear sight leaf, no stock crossbolt or upper handguard. (Illustration from contemporary European text)

tions. The American Ira Paine and the Russian-born Walter Winans both achieved worldwide fame with their recordbreaking performances achieved with their Smith & Wesson revolvers and high performance loadings. Trick shooters, too, found them to be of such accuracy that special target loadings, including many containing birdshot, were made with extremely successful results. For decades, the 44 Smith & Wesson Russian revolver cartridge was undoubtedly the most popular and highest result achiever of any handgun round worldwide. Though seldom seen in the U.S., Cyrillic-headstamped 44 Russian cartridges exist in a number of variations, dates, etc. and are much sought after by cartridge collectors. Those of American make with, for example, self-lubricating bullets and other scarce variations, box labels, etc. are also cartridge collector prizes.

Without question, the most common of all Imperial Russian military small arms to be found on the U.S. collectors' market is the bolt-action Mosin-Nagant five-shot repeating rifle. Originally designated the Model 1891, minor alterations were undertaken before true mass production began in 1894. In 1908, a new pointed bullet replaced the original round-nosed version. Both were loaded into a rimmed bottlenecked brass case of 7.62mm/.30-inch which the Russians designated "3-line" (a "line" is a measurement equalling .1-inch).

A delay in the original Russian tooling resulted in a French contract to supply 500,000 units. The earliest of these were of the true Model 1891 configuration and were marked over the chamber of the rifle's receiver with the date, 1893 or 1894, and the name of the French arsenal of manufacture, Chatellerault, in Cyrillics. Many specimens of this type are seen in the United States today but all, without exception, have been modified as described below.

Beginning about 1894, the three Russian factories — Tula, Izhevsk and Sestroretsk — began domestic production. Most of these rifles were of infantry length with the shorter, lighter dragoon version also produced in lesser quantities. A variant of the latter was the cossack type which was basically identical (no longer with a "button trigger" and lack of trigger guard). These carried slightly different sight graduations and were stamped with the Cyrillic КАЗ, indicating "kazachya," or "cossack."

In 1907, not 1910 as most sources have erroneously reported, a short, full-stocked carbine was introduced.

With the adoption of the new pointed bullet in 1908, modifications of the Mosin-Nagant's basic design were necessary. This amounted mainly to the addition of a metal cross bolt running from left to right through the wooden stock above the magazine, and a convex rear sight leaf which replaced the original flat leaf. The Model 1907 became a great rarity since it was produced in its original form for only 1-year before the initiation of these modifications. Finding any specimen of a Mosin-Nagant infantry, dragoon or cossack rifle or cavalry carbine without both of these modifications is extremely difficult, though on rare occasions one may be seen which incorporates only one of them.

With the outbreak of World War I, production of the cavalry carbine was discontinued; 1914 was the last year of its production. During that war, manufacture was concentrated on the infantry rifle and to a lesser extent on the shorter dragoon version. From the foregoing, it becomes clear that some specimens are rare, some scarce and others relatively common. All are to be found by collectors armed only with knowledge and perseverance for the modest prices still being asked.

Of special interest to American collectors are the hundreds of thousands of Mosin-Nagant infantry rifles and bayonets made under wartime contracts by the New England Westinghouse and Remington Arms companies. The dates of manufacture, in the 'teens, lie over the chambers together with the producer's name; there are two variant inscriptions in the case of the Westinghouse specimens. A number of these American-made Mosin-Nagant rifles never left the U.S. due to the beginning of the Russian October Revolution in 1917. As a consequence, it is possible to find both the rifles and their bayonets in new, unused condition. Some were, in fact, rechambered for the U.S. 30-06 Government rifle cartridge and sold commercially on the American market. While not necessarily rare, specimens in as-new condition have become scarce and may certainly be considered desirable collector's items.

Of still greater value are the Winchester Model 1895 lever-action military "muskets" (rifles) and corresponding bayonets made for Russia by that famous American firm. Chambered for the Mosin-Nagant's 7.62mm rimmed cartridge, specimens of this near 300,000-unit contract may also be identified by the Russian Cyrillic proofmarks found on them. Two different lengths of knife-blade-type bayonets and metal scabbards were made for the Winchesters, one with an

Presentation Model 1872 Smith & Wesson Russian Contract revolver. Gold washed and with elaborately carved ivory grips, it also bears a crest indicating it probably was done for a member of the Czar's court.

8¹/₂-inch/215mm blade and the other with a much longer 16-inch/400mm blade. The former is considered rare and the latter scarce. Their "white" (non-blued) blades or crosspieces are clearly marked with the Winchester logo.

In 1895, Imperial Russia adopted a revolver unique in military small arms history. This was Nagant's "Gas-Seal" system, and cocking the hammer also moved the cylinder forward to form a "seal" of the aligned chamber with the rear of the fixed barrel. The designer, Nagant of Liege, Belgium, was the same who co-designed the Model 1891 Mosin-Nagant, Mosin having been military director of Russia's Tula Ordnance Factory. The first examples of the "Gas-Seal" revolver were produced in Belgium and are so marked.

As with the rifle, the caliber was 7.62mm/.30-inch ("3-line"), but the rimmed brass cartridge was unusual in that the bullet was positioned entirely inside the case and did not protrude beyond its mouth (top) in the conventional manner. These revolvers were supplied in both single-action and double-action versions, the former being much scarcer than the latter. Both variations were continued after Tula took over the production in 1899, continuing until the end of World War I in 1918. Beginning in 1913, the name Peter the Great was added to the Imperial Tula(n) Ordnance Factory markings which appeared in Cyrillic, along with the date of manufacture, on the left sideplate of each revolver. The addition was made to commemorate the 200th anniver-

sary of the founding of the Tula arsenal by that famous monarch in, paradoxically, 1712. Because specimens bearing the date 1903 have proven scarce, one might assume many revolvers of that year's production could have been lost, perhaps sunk with the Russian navy during the course of the Russo-Japanese War of 1904-05.

It is estimated that over 1 million Nagant "Gas-Seal" revolvers were produced by Tula in the 20 years between 1899 and 1918. Literally thousands of specimens from this period can be found in the U.S. today. Outside of the aforementioned date, 1903, those made in 1907, 1910, 1911 and 1918 appear to be the scarcest. Examples dated 1899 are also of collector interest because that was the first year of domestic production. With the exception of 1898, all specimens produced in Belgium are scarce, the years 1895 and 1896 being considered rare. It should be noted that the Belgian-made Russian-contract revolvers carry a Russian proofmark consisting of a double-headed eagle over a Cyrillic letter "P." Those made for commercial sales to other markets will *not* bear Russian proofs.

An interesting martial-edged weapon not uncommon in the U.S. is the Imperial Russian artillery kinzhal (dagger). Its darkened wood handle is unprotected by any type of guard and the slightly curved blade is invariably dated 1917, 1918, etc., carrying a proofmark or Cyrillic inscription.

Sabers of an unending variety, called "shashkas,"

can be seen at even the most basic gun enthusiast gathering. Those most often noted are of the cossack type, being somewhat of a larger kinzhal. Also stamped and dated, some are unusual in that a provision for carrying a bayonet has been included. This simply amounts to a pair of rings having been added to the black leather-covered wooden scabbard's retaining bands.

Bayonets, either singly or together with their corresponding rifles, are also a collector's field with a widespread following. As was true in all countries, Russian flintlocks, along with most of their percussion rifles and muskets, used socket bayonets. These were simple triangular or quadrangular tapering spikes with a tunnel-shaped "socket" which fitted over the firearm's muzzle. Beginning with the Colt-Berdan I rifle, Russian bayonets were usually quadrangular (four-edged) and had a screwdriver tip instead of the usual sharp point. The bayonet for the Berdan II was similar. Though slimmer and lighter, this antiquated form was continued for use with the Mosin-Nagant rifle. An unusual fact is that Mosin-Nagant rifles were sighted for use with the bayonet attached, eliminating the necessity for a bayonet scabbard — also a holdover from Berdan days. While they are sometimes found, scabbards for Mosin-Nagant rifle bayonets are of Finnish or German origin, not Russian. The only official manner in which the bayonet was carried when not affixed to the rifle was by the previous mentioned attachment to the dragoon and cossack sabers (shashkas).

Of importance to collectors is the proven fact that all issue martial Russian small arms and edged weapons are invariably well marked with dates and Cyrillic letters, and usually bear the imperial crowned double eagle. Specimens reputed to be Russian and *not* in some manner Russian marked have almost always been proven to be of some nationality and/or origin other than Russian.

As the foregoing has indicated, Russian military small arms exist in a large variety of categories. This field is rich in mechanical and historical specimens manufactured not only in Russia but also in Belgium and the United States. Imperial police and gendarmerie units were sometimes equipped with Browning self-loading pistols Models 1900, 1903 and 1905, and even Model 1911 Colt pistols of caliber .45-inch are found with official Russian markings.

We have reviewed some of the various types of Russian small arms most often encountered at the average gun show. Prices can range from $20 for a common bayonet, to as high as several thousand for the scarce and most desirable examples, such as a Smith & Wesson Model 1871 or a Colt-Berdan I in excellent condition. A complete collection of the former would amount to some 15 or 20 variations, Mosin-Nagant rifles perhaps a dozen, and edged weapons somewhere in the hundreds. Souvenirs from historical wars could include the Napoleonic, Crimean, Russo-Turkish, Russo-Japanese, World War I and some lesser campaigns such as Khiva and the Balkan Wars. Mechanical variations include rifled flintlocks, blunderbusses, wall guns, percussion Colt revolvers, needlefire rifles, the "trapdoor" Colt-Berdan, the strange "pull-apart" Galand revolver, Nagant's "Gas-Seal" revolver, bolt actions, self-loading pistols and all of the more conventional forms. Pick your preference; the specimens are out there and a substantial bank balance is not necessarily a prerequisite. The Germans have a word for it — Weidmannsheil, or Good Hunting! ●

Nagant Model 1895 with issue holster, ramrod and 14-round cartridge packet. A scarce left-hand holster also exists.

Russian Military Firearms:

ANOTHER Rapidly Growing Collector's Field

The Soviet Era

by FRED A. DATIG

Tokarev's TT-30 (Tula-Tokarev) self-loading pistol, caliber 7.62mm Tokarev. It was made only from 1933 to 1935, with 1933-dated specimens rare. The slightly simplified TT-33 version was produced in Russia from 1935 to 1953, when it was replaced by the Makarov in Soviet service.

Tokarev's SVT-38 replaced the selective-fire Model 1936 Simonov in Russian service. Note the cleaning rod on the side of the stock. The SVT-40, which replaced it, had its cleaning rod in the conventional under-the-barrel location.

HISTORICALLY and chronologically, the Russian October Revolution took place in 1917. The *marked* (literally) influence of the new Soviet government did not begin until 1919; however, despite the fact that imperial forces were no longer operating the major small arms factories, markings such as Imperial Tula Ordnance Factory for example, continued to be used on weapons produced through the calendar year 1918. Consequently, the collecting of *Soviet* Russian small arms should correctly begin with those 1918-dated specimens, full imperial markings notwithstanding. Arms from this year are scarce.

Beginning in 1919, the Tula Ordnance Factory simply deleted the second line of markings on the Nagant "Gas-Seal" revolvers. As that line contained the abbreviation, "Imperial Peter the Great," all that remained was, Tula Ordnance Factory, and the date, 1919. Markings on Mosin-Nagant rifles carried the same modified logo, which was continued on both rifles and revolvers through 1920. These dates may also

This early Nagant "Gas-Seal" revolver, dated 1912, has had its imperial markings defaced by early revolutionaries.

The first factory marking found on Nagants made after the revolution was simply, "Tula Ordnance Factory" with the date of manufacture, which is in this example, 1919.

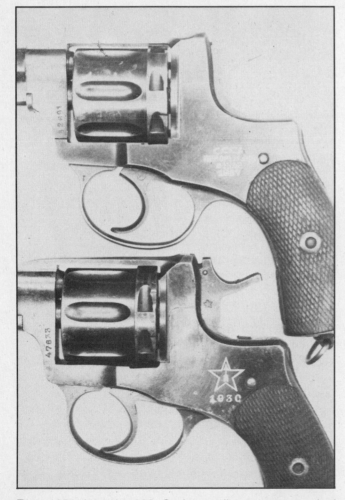

From 1921 through 1923, Soviet small arms were marked with the Cyrillic initials for "R.S.F.S.R." (Russian Socialist Federated Soviet Republics). In 1924, the marking was changed again to "C.C.C.P." (Cyrillic for "U.S.S.R."), as seen at top, for a few more years; then it was changed to the Russian star with the date of manufacture, as above.

be considered uncommon on Soviet weapons.

In 1921, a new name for Russia, Russian Socialist Federated Soviet Republics, was initiated. (It was abbreviated R.S.F.S.R.) Both rifles and revolvers, the only individual small arms in production at that time, were marked in Cyrillic Р.С.Ф.С.Р. for R.S.F.S.R. Quite possibly, only the Tula installation was in operation during this post-war period, as specimens marked for the Izhevsk and Sestroretsk arsenals have not been reported this early. Probably because Tula was, indeed, the most important of the three factories, and had been singled out as "imperial" under the tsars, that title was replaced by the official "First" ("Foremost"). This added the Cyrillic abbreviation Пер. to the marking, Туπ Ор. 3 аВ. About that time, the other factories resumed production of rifles, mainly of the shorter dragoon version, as many infantry-length examples survived World War I. The R.S.F.S.R. marking and title survived only through 1923. Both revolvers and rifles manufactured during that period are also difficult to acquire.

From 1924 through 1928 yet another new national name and marking came into use — the now familiar C.C.C.P. (S.S.S.R.), for "Union of Socialist Soviet Republics"; Nagant revolvers made in this period are so marked. With rare exceptions, only double-action types were made in the Soviet-controlled factories, but variant modifications and reworks will be encountered. Revolvers made in the period between 1918 and 1929 include many interesting, sometimes scarce, variations.

Mosin-Nagant Rifle Model 91/30 and its bayonet (above). Full-length infantry rifles and cavalry carbines were discarded soon after the revolution and the dragoon-length rifle modernized as the Model 91/30. Below is the sniper version with 2.5x PU scope and elongated, turned-down bolt handle. Earlier sniper rifles used 4x PE scopes, either top or side mounted.

The 1920s was a decade of experimentation and development, during which prototype work led to the eventual adoption of a new series of small arms. The earliest of these was the slightly altered Mosin-Nagant dragoon rifle, adopted as the Model 91/30. Infantry-length rifles and carbines were both discontinued. The old hexagonal Model 91 receiver was replaced by a round one, a hood was installed over the front sight, and a spring-loaded lock-catch was added to the quadrangular bayonet.

In 1929, the manufacturer's insignia on Nagant revolvers and Tula-made rifles was changed once again, the fourth time in a decade. The new logo consisted of a large five-pointed star with an upward-pointing barbed arrow in its center. The revolver's front sight was altered by notching the old "half-moon" blade at the same time.

Sometime in the 1920s, reportedly 1926, a small-caliber self-loading pistol was introduced in the Soviet Union. Chambered for Browning's 6.35mm/25ACP cartridge, this pistol was named the Tula-Korovin, or "TK." Rather large for its cartridge, early versions of this simple blowback carried finely-checkered wooden grip plates. Of importance to collectors is the fact that the original, not the more common replacement, grip plates had a smooth diamond-shaped section which framed the grip retaining screw on both sides. TK pistols of this early type are very scarce. In about 1930, the grip plates were changed to black hard rubber which carried a stylized, TO3 ("Tula Ordnance Factory" in Cyrillics), on each side near the top. Because these were somewhat fragile, many were replaced with wooden variants which were not as finely checkered as the originals and which did not feature the smooth frame around the retaining (grip) screw. Although serial numbers indicate production totaled some half-million units, TK pistols are not common in the U.S.

TKs were not martial military handguns, but were intended for police and gendarmerie use. Their frames are marked with Tula's "commercial" trademark — a T

Korovin's TK (Tula-Korovin) self-loading pistol, caliber 6.35mm Browning (25 ACP). Observed serials indicate more than a half million were made, a figure contradicted by its scarcity in the U.S. The "T03" logo indicates Tula manufacture.

in a circle in a triangle. This marking may also be found on a very few 22-caliber Nagant revolvers (rare) and most rifles which Tula made from the 1930s onward. Holsters for TK pistols are smaller versions of the larger and much more common Tokarev "TT" variants, and may or may not have accompanying brass-handled ramrods and/or spare magazine pockets. It should be of interest for cartridge collectors to note that *not one* specimen of a Soviet-made, Cyrillic-headstamped caliber 6.35mm/25ACP cartridge has ever been reported! From this, one may assume that TK cartridges were either not headstamped at all or were imported from foreign sources; the latter is highly improbable.

The introduction of Soviet Russia's first martial self-loading pistol, the domestic Tula-Tokarev "TT-30,"

Top to bottom: Imperial Russian Model 1907 cavalry carbine, Soviet Model 1938, Model 1944 with folding bayonet. (Illustrations from a Polish arms book)

was in 1930. This modified Browning design bore features of both the Colt Model 1911 and Browning's Model 1903. The corresponding cartridge was a minor alteration of the famous German caliber 7.63mm/.30-inch Mauser pistol round dating back to the 1890s. Now, rifle, revolver and pistol were all chambered for different rounds of the same "3-line"/.30-inch caliber, a "line" being a Russian measurement equalling $1/10$-inch. For a military handgun, the TT was unusual in that it carried no safety device other than a half-cock position on the hammer. The only 100-percent TT-30 pistols were produced in and dated with the year 1933, because in 1934 and 1935, slight, though important, mechanical changes were made. These led to the introduction of the modified "TT-33" Tokarev pistol in 1935. With less than 7000 produced, the original 1933-dated TT-30 may be considered quite scarce and a prized collector's item. Even specimens dated 1934 and 1935 are also uncommon. Probably due to the changeover to pistol production, Nagant "Gas-Seal" revolvers dated 1934 are among the most difficult to find. Small quantities of these revolvers were also made with military markings in caliber 22 Long Rifle, a desirable item for both collectors and shooters.

Also in the early 1930s the Mosin-Nagant sniper rifle was introduced. The first types used the 4x PE adjustable telescope mounted on the left side of the rifle's receiver with a relatively heavy, expanded U mount. Concurrently, the same optic was mounted on the top of the receiver ring by means of a less cumbersome mount. Early versions of the latter were fitted to the older prc-1930-type hexagonal receiver ring, whereas later production was for the rounded 91/30 receiver. Slight alterations were also made in the telescopes themselves; all types are normally dated with the year of manufacture. Either type of Mosin-Nagant sniper rifle is a sought-after collector's item on today's market, but may be encountered from time to time at major gun shows.

After experiments dating from the turn of the century, automatic fire mechanisms began production in the mid-1930s. Tokarev, the semi-automatic rifle expert who had taken time out to design the TT pistol, was, along with Simonov, among the foremost specialists. The latter made a selective-fire rifle which, though adopted in 1936, was produced mainly in a slightly modified form in 1938 to 1939. Of great interest to U.S. collectors are the rare and unusual bayonets for Simonov's rifles. The earlier 1936 type is one seldom seen, and even the later version is considered a rare and desirable collector's item — especially if accompanied by its correct steel scabbard. Only the most advanced collectors can boast of having one or both models of these knife-bladed rarities, which have no cross piece or barrel ring.

Tokarev's first semi-automatic rifle to be adopted was introduced in 1938, along with its special bayonet. Both were modified in 1940, the late model bayonet being substantially shorter. The cutting edge faces upward on both types, but the Model 1940 versions were changed during World War II to a downward-facing edge. At least five variant scabbards may be found, but the longer Model 1940 bayonet and scabbard remains the scarcity. The two Tokarev semi-automatic rifles are

(Above) Simonov's semi-automatic carbine SKS-45, caliber 7.62x39mm, sectional view. Note that this early version had a blade rather than four-sided bayonet. (Drawing from Soviet Army manual)

The world-famous AK, Kalashnikov's "Avtomat" (Assault Rifle), caliber 7.62x39mm M43. It is erroneously called "AK-47," an American misnomer. This Soviet book's illustration shows the AKM version with wire-cutter bayonet.

easily distinguishable, since the cleaning rod (ramrod) of the Model 1938 lies in an inletted groove on the right side of the wooden stock and the Model 1940's is more conventionally located under the barrel. The metal gas-piston housing at the front of the upper handguard is also shorter and has fewer (four) round cooling holes on the Model 1938 than the Model 1940 (seven).

A wartime version of the Model 1940 has a two-vent muzzlebrake, whereas all Model 1938 and most Model 1940 versions have six vents.

Official Soviet nomenclature for the two variants are "SVT-38" and "SVT-40," meaning "Semi-automatic Rifle Tokarev" plus the respective model years. While they probably exist, no specimens of the SVT-38 sniper rifle have been personally examined. On the other hand, the SVT-40, with its bifurcated (two-prong forked) sight mount and 2.5x optic, while expensive, are sometimes seen. These mounts slide onto grooves on both sides of the rifle's rear metal receiver. Some wartime rifles will not have these grooves, though such variants are scarce.

In 1938, an updated version of the old tsarist Model 1907 and 07/08 cavalry carbine was introduced as the Model 1938. This was simply a shortened version of the 91/30 all-purpose rifle, not full-stocked like the earlier type. Collectors should note that specimens produced in 1938 are slightly different than those of later manufacture. As a consequence, they may be considered very desirable collector's items with a somewhat greater value than Model 1938 carbines made between 1939 and 1945.

In the 1930s, the Soviets experimented with folding versions of the basic Model 91/30 quadrangular socket bayonet for that rifle. One type was folding but detachable; another was solidly affixed. Because sighting with the bayonet attached (no bayonet scabbards having been made or issued) was a long-time standard of the Russians, it was logical to allow the ever-present at-

tached bayonet to be folded beneath the barrel. The Italians had this feature on their carbines, as did the Japanese. Therefore, the Soviets introduced still another new firearm at the height of World War II, the Model 1944 carbine with folding quadrangular bayonet. A spring-loaded button acted as the bayonet release/locking catch; the result was a short, muzzle-heavy gun of questionable practical ability — a true wartime expedient which was short-lived. Many of these are to be found on today's market, but the majority are of Polish or Chinese manufacture; true Soviet-made wartime specimens, dated 1944 or 1945, are not too common.

Also during World War II, a new type of telescope and mount appeared on the 91/30 rifle. This consisted of a much lighter side mount with a 2.5x PU telescope, similar, but not identical, to that used on the Tokarev SVT-40 rifle. Most specimens will be dated 1944, and while neither rare nor common, are not as scarce as the earlier side- or top-mounted 4x versions.

With German armies posing a threat, Soviet small arms factories were completely disassembled and relocated far to the east in 1942. This brought about a further change in markings on small arms. Beginning in 1942, Tokarev TT pistols appeared with coarsely-checkered wooden grip plates and a marking consisting of an arrow in a triangle, instead of the earlier, simpler five-pointed star. In 1943, Nagant revolvers were marked with the familiar star, but now housing an "upright hammer" insignia. In 1944, a large upward pointing arrow inside a triangle inside a circle came into use. It is assumed that the existence of the two variant markings indicted that revolvers were then being produced at two different relocated factories. It is interesting to note that some specimens of this vintage have been examined which have been rechambered to take the 7.62mm Tokarev pistol cartridge! Whether or not these were factory alterations, field expedients or post-war

Makarov's PM self-loading pistol, caliber 9x18mm Makarov, has also been made in several Soviet sphere countries.

Stechkin's APS is a selective fire and so it comes under U.S. controls on machineguns. Supplied with a Mauser-type shoulder-stock/holster, the Stechkin is chambered for 9x18mm Makarov and has a 22-round magazine.

conversions in some other country has not been determined. Such alterations may be detected only at the rear of (and inside) the cylinder; no special markings were added to the gun's outer surfaces. As a collector's item they are certainly scarce and of historical/technical interest, whether or not they might be true official modifications.

The Soviets have a history of tenacious perseverance in the continued development, testing and modernization of small arms. The World War II era was no exception. In 1943, a revolutionary new assault rifle cartridge was officially adopted by the Soviets, prior to adoption of a gun chambered for it. This was the caliber 7.62x39mm M43 round, which was to become the most widely-used assault rifle cartridge in the world today. It was not until 1945 that the Simonov semi-automatic rifle chambered for this round was made official. Known as the "SKS-45," the Soviet translation means, "Simonov Semi-automatic Carbine Model 1945." Its folding bayonet now employed a knife blade rather than the old four-edge quadrangular form. It is assumed that the Soviets had hoped to see the SKS in mass production before the end of the war, but that did not transpire. The exact reason for its official adoption is not otherwise clear, but it, as with the folding-bayonet Model 1944 carbine, also appears more of a wartime expedient. Wartime production probably never reached mass production, and even the post-war Soviet-made specimens must be sorted from the many Chinese-produced examples found on today's market.

It soon became obvious why one might consider the SKS a stopgap weapon. This was brought into focus by the introduction of the "Avtomat Kalashnikov (AK)" in 1949, a true selective-fire assault rifle which eliminated the necessity for both the 91/30 rifle and the various types of Soviet submachine guns (machine pistols) employed in huge quantities throughout World War II. (From a strictly historical/academic standpoint, it should be underlined that no official Soviet military document refers to the AK by the U.S.-concocted misnomer, AK-47! Developed from 1942 to 1949 and adopted officially in 1949, still not in the final design stage, we see absolutely no logical reason for the fictitious nomenclature, AK(19)47!) In its numerous forms, the AK is well known to U.S. enthusiasts in semi-automatic versions of the "AK," "AKM," "AKMS," etc. The M represents "modernized," not

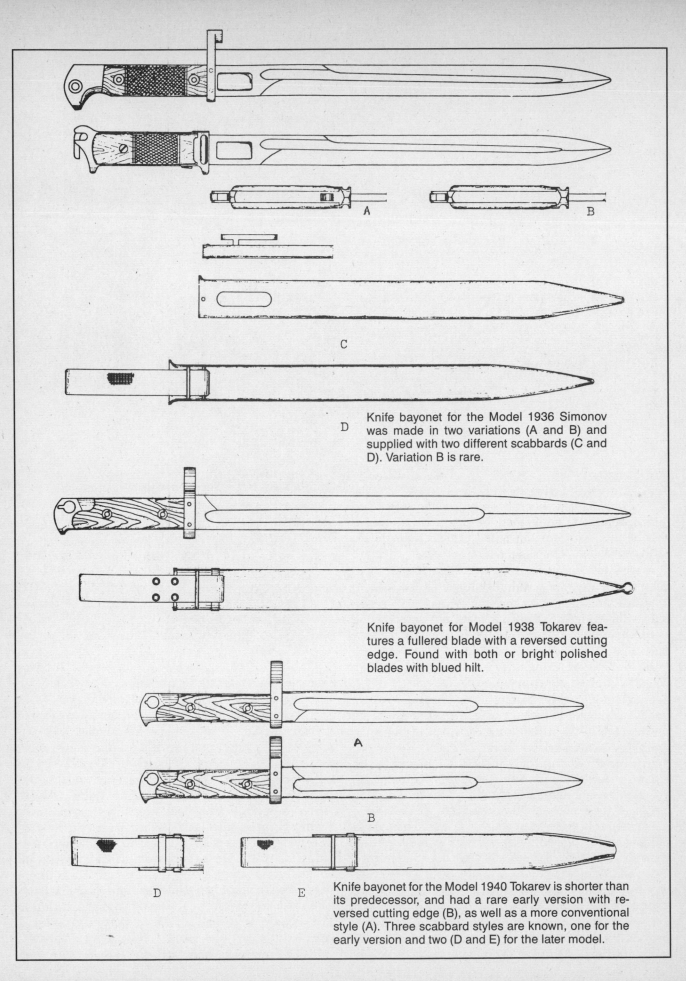

Knife bayonet for the Model 1936 Simonov was made in two variations (A and B) and supplied with two different scabbards (C and D). Variation B is rare.

Knife bayonet for Model 1938 Tokarev features a fullered blade with a reversed cutting edge. Found with both or bright polished blades with blued hilt.

Knife bayonet for the Model 1940 Tokarev is shorter than its predecessor, and had a rare early version with reversed cutting edge (B), as well as a more conventional style (A). Three scabbard styles are known, one for the early version and two (D and E) for the later model.

The Soviet PSM self-loading pistol, caliber 5.45mm, was introduced in 1974 but is very rare in the U.S.

"modified," and the S designates it as a folding-stock version. Therefore, AKMS means "Avtomat Kalashnikov Modernized with folding stock." None of the AK variants found on today's U.S. collector's market are identical to those actually issued to Soviet armed forces throughout the world, though the basic mechanism and most of the other major features are the same. If imitation is the sincerest form of flattery, then the AK is a superstar as the most widely modified and copied small arm in the entire world; even the name of its designer usually is correctly spelled and pronounced by the international news media!

The "AK-74," a small-caliber version intended for special troops, appeared in 1974. Having only four basic parts which are different from the AK, the caliber is 5.45mm/.215-inch with its own special cartridge, not a necked-down version of the 7.62x39mm M43 round. AK bayonets are available to collectors in several types. These variations are of the AKM combination wire-cutter version as well as the more conventional trench knife type. Many variants are available, but those of Soviet manufacture are the scarcest and most desirable.

Soviet Russia's post-war handgun field was brought up to date with the introduction of Makarov's "Pistol Makarov" (PM) in the late 1940s. While superficially a copy of the German Walther Model "PP," the Makarov is the result of a serious domestic design and development effort too involved to include here. Even more clever than this blowback, self-loading pistol's design is the unique cartridge which it chambers. In short, the caliber 9mm/.354-inch Makarov cartridge gives the highest performance possible when used in conjunction with the pistol's simple, unlocked breech mechanism, close to the ballistic performance of much more powerful rounds in more complicated and expensive pistols. Soviet-made specimens of the PM are relatively uncommon in the U.S. and are often priced out of balance with the production figures due entirely to supply and demand. Identical copies of other origins are more easily purchased, however, and original holsters are sometimes available at sensible prices.

While few, if any, have been, and are not likely to be, available to U.S. collectors, another exceptionally interesting Soviet handgun was introduced about 1951. This was the Russian designer Stechkin's APS, or "Automatic Pistol Stechkin," automatic meaning fully, not semi-automatic, although a selective-fire handgun. With a large 22-round magazine capacity, the APS also has a detachable holster stock, a la Mauser C.96.

The latest Soviet handgun to appear is the controversial "PSM" in caliber 5.45mm. This matches the caliber, though not the cartridge, of the AK-74 also introduced that same year. Unlike Makarov's PM, the PSM is mechanically an almost identical copy of the Walther Model PPK. Outside of its tiny caliber, the PSM is strange in that it is extremely flat, measuring only 7/16-inch at its thickest point. It is also the only Soviet small arm of any official nature whose nomenclature gives no indication as to the identity of the designer, in this instance a team of three. The corresponding new cartridge was designed by a fourth, a woman! PSM simply means, "Pistol, Semi-automatic, Small," though perhaps "flat" might more accurately describe it. Like the AK-74, the PSM was not intended as a successor, but rather a supplement to existing Soviet handguns.

As has been noted, there are a large number of historical, technical and otherwise collectable types and variations of Soviet military small arms and accessories. These await discovery and assimilation into comprehensive collections of both general and specialized natures. Of unquestionable historical value and much more than passing technical interest, collecting these relatively little-known small arms and accessories is a field still wide open to even the beginning collector. Indeed, Soviet small arms may represent the last frontier of collecting in which rarities can be found at prices that are a fraction of their ultimate potential. Long experience has taught that such situations have practically ceased to exist, and that today's passed possibility will surely prove to be tomorrow's lost opportunity. Is a word to the wise sufficient? ●

The Smith & Wesson "Escort" Model 61

by DONALD M. SIMMONS

THE SMITH & WESSON CO., one of the most, if not *the* most, prestigious handgun manufacturers in the world, has unfortunately had a bad record in the field of pocket automatic pistol design. It all began in 1909 with Joseph Hawes Wesson's purchase of the U.S. rights of a Belgian automatic pistol from Charles P. Clement. This innocent transaction led to the unhappy S&W 35 Automatic Pistol.

Starting with the Clement auto in caliber 25 Automatic Colt Pistol (ACP), Smith & Wesson in 1913 came up with their first automatic pistol—the S&W 35 Auto. It went into production, but only 9 years later, in 1922, despite many modifications, the manufacture of this automatic pistol was halted with only 8353 guns having been made during that long period.

In 1924, rising from the ashes of the 35 Auto, a greatly improved pocket automatic pistol was offered by the company. This time the caliber was 32 ACP, a well thought of and known cartridge. However, this pistol failed to establish itself for two reasons — it was too expensive, and it came too late, with the Great Depression just around the corner. Only 960 of the 32 S&W Auto pistols were sold by 1937, when it was dropped from the S&W catalog. Thus ended S&W's pre-World War II venture into pocket automatic pistols.

After World War II, S&W developed the highly successful high-powered 9mm Parabellum Models 39 and 59 and their specialized target pistols, Models 41 and 46, in 22 Long Rifle. With this success, it was logical that S&W decided to give the pocket automatic one more try. Starting as early as 1963, S&W was working on a 25 ACP auto pistol and by 1969 went into production with one, but in the more desirable caliber of 22 Long Rifle. Again, the design was very reminiscent of a Belgian pistol. This new S&W pistol looked like the Belgian Bayard Model 1908, as made by Ancien Etablissements Pieper (AEP), of Herstal, Belgium. It had the same recoil spring over the barrel, the same front sight used in takedown, the breechblock under the slide proper, the European-style magazine catch at the

Typical S&W Escort Model 61-3 (last type), right side (above) and left side (opposite page).

bottom of the grip, and the recoil spring housing a tube, mounted on and above the frame. There can be little doubt that S&W peeked at the Bayard before producing their Model 61 "Escort" automatic pistol. Though I have called the Model 61 a pocket automatic, it's more properly a vest pocket auto. The published specifications are shown nearby.

Nickel-plated finish was soon added as an option, but

S&W Model 61 Escort Specifications

Caliber:	22 Long Rifle
Magazine Capacity:	5 rounds
Barrel Length:	2¹/₈"
Overall Length:	4¹³/₁₆"
Overall Height:	3¹¹/₁₆"
Weight:	Airweight 14 ozs. with magazine
Finish:	Blue
Sights:	Fixed; ramp front, square-notch rear
Stocks:	Checkered impact-resist-ant plastic
Safety:	Manual, hammer indicator

was never shown on the specification sheets. The price blued was $47.50 when the pistol was first announced in 1971. When nickel was added in 1972, at $55.50, the cost for the blued gun dropped to $46.50.

The basic idea of this pistol was a low-cost defense firearm for a woman to carry in her purse, hence the name Escort. The grip only allows the normal male hand to wrap his middle finger around it, which is hardly conducive to accurate shooting. At the date of the Model 61's baptism, the only other available small, inexpensive 22 LR handguns were the single shot Colt derringer at $19.95 and the High Standard Model D-100 two-shot derringer at $42.95. Certainly, the Model 61 represented an advantage over its peers in that it offered five shots, and the inexperienced person using it just might understand how to get those shots off. After all, the 22 Long Rifle hollowpoint cartridge is generally agreed to be a better defense caliber than the 25 ACP. One must also remember that the odious Firearms Act of 1968 was now in force and no small concealable handguns could be imported to the U.S.; this made a Valhalla for domestic manufacturers.

Field-stripping this pistol is very easy and requires no tools at all. From the S&W instructions:

1. Remove magazine from gun.
2. Pull slide back to check that chamber is clear.
3. Holding the gun firmly in the hand, press down disassembly button (the recoil spring guide) on the front of the slide with the index finger. Lift out front

One of the virtues of the Escort was the ease of disassembly and its simplicity. The gun is shown stripped for cleaning.

In designing the Model 61 (bottom), S&W engineers probably remembered the Belgian Bayard Model 1908 pistol in 25 ACP (top), this one from the Len Hunter collection. There is some similarity between the two guns!

sight while holding the button depressed.

4. Slowly let disassembly button out, relieving pressure on recoil spring.
5. Remove spring and rod from slide.
6. Pull slide to extreme rearward position and lift straight up removing slide from frame. Reverse procedure to reassemble.

That's all there is to it and it takes a lot less time to do than it does to tell. My time is 9 seconds for disassembly and 25 for reassembly — not bad! Incidentally, the Escort came only with one magazine, the owner had to purchase an extra one if he felt it was needed. Most other Smith & Wesson autos come with two magazines.

So much for why the Smith & Wesson Model 61 should have been a success. The nitty-gritty is that it wasn't, even with all this going for it. Basically the fault, dear Brutus, was in the boxy look of the pistol — there seemed to be too much slide at the back of the gun and, conversely, too little grip. The pistol also had none of the modern safeties like a hammer-dropping device, and a blocked or locked firing pin. Initially, there was only an awkward manual safety and, of course, a disconnector to avoid firing more than one round with each pull of the trigger. Lastly, Smith & Wesson added a needed safety indicator which tells the user if the pistol's concealed hammer is cocked or not. This hammer-cocked indicator is a small plunger that protrudes from the upper rear of the left grip; it can be felt by the shooter's thumb in daylight or dark.

Much more desirable is a loaded chamber indictor, which tells the shooter not only that the pistol is cocked, but more importantly, that it is loaded. The hammer-cocked indicator must have been an afterthought, because on early pistols its mounting hole is machined into the frame, not part of the original casting. Almost immediately, S&W added a good safety feature that all their recent autos have — a magazine safety. This device makes it impossible to fire the pistol with the magazine removed. When someone unfamiliar with an automatic pistol removes the magazine during a firing session, the deadly forgotten round in the pistol's chamber can't be accidentally fired.

Unfortunately, the magazine safety also came as an

(Above) S&W's first automatic pistol was their 35 Auto that was in production only 9 years. Only 8353 guns were made, albeit with many modifications. This one was made about 1915. (Len Hunter collection)

(Left) This field-stripped Bayard Model 1908 exhibits a number of similarities to the Model 61.

afterthought, and in order for purchasers of the early non-magazine-safety pistols to have it installed, the gun had to be returned to the factory. Model 61 autos that were equipped with the safety were designated Model 61-1, whether as issued from the factory or modified by the factory. The original instruction sheet printed in October, 1969 reads as follows:

Important:
 The design of this pistol permits hand feeding of cartridges should your magazine become damaged or lost. Care should be exercised, however, to keep hands away from in front of the barrel.

In a way, this statement is a copout because as previously stated, Smith & Wesson was far seeing enough to have equipped all their modern autos with a magazine safety. After the safety was added, the instruction sheet printed in April, 1970 read:

Important:
 This pistol has been designed so that it will not fire when the magazine has been removed. This is done as a safety feature but care should be exercised to keep the gun pointed in a safe direction and to keep hands away from the front of the muzzle when operating the slide.

The collector will be interested in just how many plain Model 61s were made. The answer from Roy Jinks' excellent book, *History of Smith & Wesson,* is 6800 pistols from March to May, 1970. Serial numbers ranged from the first gun produced, B 1001, to B 7800. How many were sent back to the factory to have the magazine safety added? Jinks has no records, but if it is like most firearm recalls, less than 50 percent would be my guess. When a modified pistol was returned to its owner, the model designation at the bottom of the pistol grip had a "− 1" added.

Smith & Wesson continued to manufacture Model 61-1s from May to September, 1970. Those pistols left the factory with the magazine safety installed. There were only 2050 of them, so they are quite rare; serials ran from B 7801 through B 9850. There was also a group of presentation guns made as Model 61-1s, and they were in their own serial series of B 1 through B 500. The overall total of all original type 61-1s, with

(Right) In 1924, S&W tried again with an auto in 32 ACP, but it, too, failed. When it was dropped from the catalog in 1937, only 960 pistols had been sold. (Len Hunter collection)

(Left) One of the changes made to the Model 61 was the addition of a barrel bushing. The 61-1 (left) didn't have it. the 61-2 (right) did.

the exception of the modified 61s, is 2550. These are by far the most collectible of all Model 61 variations.

Starting in September, 1970, a bushing visible from the outside was added to the barrel to secure it to the pistol's frame. The bushing, or as the factory called it, barrel nut, was threaded on both its inside and outside; its use made the positioning of the barrel much more secure. Also, now at the chamber end of the barrel was a steel yoke that held both the barrel and the recoil spring housing. Heretofore, the barrel and the housing were force-fitted to the frame and to all intents and purposes was integral with it. Even the parts list gave no part number for the barrel, either as it was originally or with the bushing added. The bushing was started at serial number B 9851 and continued in use until the pistol was dropped. These pistols were called Model 61-2s.

In February, 1971, the story of Smith & Wesson's Model 61 began coming to an end. At that time, the United States government contracted H.P. White Laboratory of Bel Air, Maryland to test a group of handguns for reliability and endurance, and to come up with some yardsticks of safety and durability that could rea-

sonably be expected from a firearm, and more importantly, whether cost was any measure of quality — and it wasn't! While even H.P. White admits that their test program was breaking new ground, it was nonetheless a faltering step in the dangerous direction of legislated gun safety. Unfortunately for Smith & Wesson, H.P. White included in their testing two S&W Model 61-2s serials B 17324 and B 17391. The reliability test was performed on B 17391 and after a proof load was fired, that pistol was fired 4600 times with the following results. The firing pin broke and prevented further firing after the 4600th round (5000 was the goal). There were 28 failures to eject, 18 failures to feed and, finally, eight misfires. The gun's disconnector was found not to function before any testing. H.P. White recommended that the design and/or the hardness of the firing pin be modified; they also suggested that the assembly of the disconnector be improved.

The endurance test was next performed on B 17324. This test consisted of one proof round and an inspection; then 100 standard rounds plus one proof round. This was intended to be repeated until the pistol had

(Below) The Model 61 (top) was without a magazine safety, but this feature was added on the 61-1 (arrow).

(Above) The frame of the Model 61-1 (top) was of die-cast aluminum, but was changed to forged, machined aluminum on the 61-3 (bottom).

fired 5000 rounds and 50 proof rounds. The S&W 61-2 lasted for 600 rounds (seven proof rounds). The testing was then stopped because the seventh proof round ruptured. The damage to the gun was extensive — the sideplate broke, the left grip broke, the disconnector and the ejector bent. In addition, the pistol malfunctioned 23 times and the rear sight was found broken at the initial inspection. The gap between the barrel and bolt face, at which the hammer would still fall, had increased from .120- to .130-inch. This last point, of course, was the reason why the proof load ruptured. H.P. White recommended that cartridge head support be increased and that a metallurgical change in the material of the sideplate be considered, for more shooter protection.

The final test was with an overload cartridge, and was performed on B 17391 with the firing pin from B 17324. For the results of the test I quote directly from the H.P. White report:

1st firing (35,600 CUP) — The cartridge case head ruptured and the escaping gas fractured the sideplate, broke the disconnector, broke the extractor, deformed the ejector, and deformed the manual safety lever. The cartridge case remained in the chamber.

Smith & Wesson was informed of the results and were justifiably horrified, even though the proof loads and the overload cartridges were much higher than any shooter would ever use. The frame and sideplate of the gun were an aluminum die casting and undoubtedly would have been strong enough except that the S&W design had weakened the frame by the bolted-on sideplate. The company went to an expensive, forged, machined aluminum frame and sideplate to strengthen this area. In the same pistols, the disconnector was changed from two pieces to a one-piece riveted assembly to reduce the play in the disconnector-to-slide engagement.

In my own testing and measuring, I found that the distance from the bolt face to the barrel was .136-inch on a Model 61; on the other hand, on a 61-3, this space had been reduced to .084-inch. In the examination of various fired cartridge cases, I found that there was a swelling immediately under the rim that represented an increase of .008-inch when fired in the tightened up

(Above) An extractor cut was added to the Model 61-3 (arrow), giving another variation to the series.

The disconnector of both the 61 and 61-1 was a two-piece affair, but was changed to a riveted one-piece assembly on the 61-2 and 61-3 guns.

Model 61-3. S&W also added a clearance slot in the ejection port of the slide, for the extractor. These pistols were Model 61-3s, and if you sent in any other Escort pistol for repairs, a Model 61-3 was sent back to you. One can see that S&W, knowing their reputation was at stake, was trying to make good, regardless of the cost to them. Model 61-3s started at serial number B 40001 and continued to the terminal serial number of the Escort, B 65438. In March, 1973, production stopped and the Model 61-3 was dropped from S&W's catalog. The price of the pistol had risen only modestly during its sales period to $53.50 blued and $63.50 nickeled. Following is the model data in tabular form. In the whole run of Escort pistols, about 6600 were nickel-plated, which makes this easily recognizable feature a fairly scarce variation.

How does the Escort shoot? Well, I found that except for the already mentioned shortness of the grip, it does just fine. With a Model 61-3, I was able to hit beer cans at 25 feet with boring consistency. I used both regular and high-velocity 22s and only once had a failure to feed and one misfire, which fired when rechambered. I

Escort Automatic Pistol Variations

MODEL	DATE	SERIAL RANGE	QUANTITY	PERCENTAGE
61	Mar., 1970 — May, 1970	B 1001 — B 7800	6800	10.5
61-1	May, 1970 — Sep., 1970	B 7801 — B 9850	2050	3.2
61-1	1970	B 001 — B 500	500	0.7
61-2	Sep., 1970 — July, 1971	B 9851 — B 40000	30150	46.4
61-3	July 1971 — Mar., 1973	B 40001 — B 65438	25438	39.2

was really pleased and can say that as a protection pistol for a person with little or no knowledge of firearms, the Escort will get the job done.

Why, then, did Smith & Wesson decide to drop the Model 61 Escort? Well, Jinks says it was decided that this small pocket pistol was not in keeping with their image as the manufacturer of the highest quality handguns in the world. This is undeniably true, but why

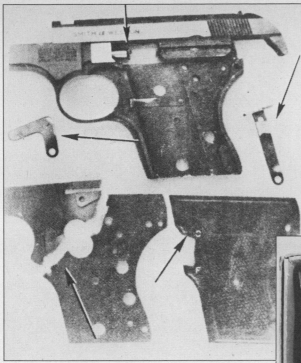

H.P. White Laboratory managed to destroy two Model 61s in the course of government contract testing. This copy of a page from their report shows the damage done by an over-pressured cartridge. Note the broken sideplate, cracked grip, bent disconnector, bent ejector and ruptured cartridge case.

A rare nickel-plated Model 61-3, new in the box, complete with the factory "rug." (Len Hunter collection)

wasn't that brought out when the idea of the Model 61 was first put on the table? If the idea was so repugnant why the Model 422 of today? The 422 is certainly another low-cost 22-caliber pistol, and not in the class with S&W's other 22 auto, the Model 41. The Model 422 also has a distinct family resemblance to the ill-fated Escort. The Escort pistol had one slightly doubtful honor given it. It is pictured on the cover of the Berkley book edition of Lawrence Sanders' story of Hollywood in the 1920s, *The Dream Lover.* One wonders if the cover designer thought the pistol looked like one from the '20s, or if he wanted a Bayard and by mistake got a S&W.

We will probably never really know the whole story behind both the appearance and the disappearance of this auto, but collectors will grow more interested because of the relative rarity of some of the variations. Even today, as this is being written, the value of a S&W Escort is much above its original cost; a composite value in excellent condition would be about $230 blued, and $275 or more nickeled. In collecting pistols, each new model with its variations is fascinating;

to be able to see how different arms designers face the same engineering and production problems, and each solve them in a different manner. The fact that a gun was or wasn't a success in the marketplace does little to enhance that piece to the collector. In fact, to be brutally honest, the less a gun model sells, the more rare and valuable it becomes. We live in a strange new design world in which individuals in general no longer design whole weapons. Instead, teams of designers backed by teams of production people are used, all of whom are overseen by a boogie man called the sales department. This is a far cry from John Moses Browning of 100 years ago, working on any gun idea that took his fancy, and who, after working out all the bugs and handmaking a working sample by himself, would sell it to the arms manufacturer. Lone genius is gone and in its place is a monstrous group of "experts" tripping over each other and designing things for a momentary market that may or may not work, but the guns are cheap to produce. In the case of Smith & Wesson, the committee that was to design a horse came up with a camel. ●

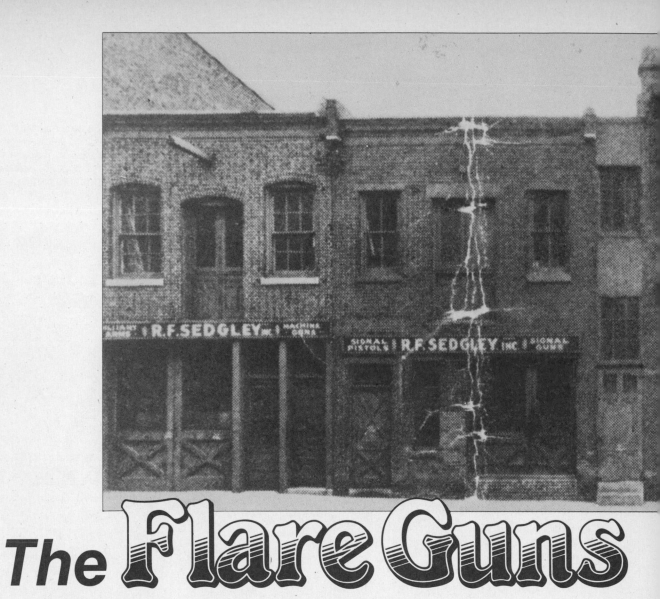

The Flare Guns

by HOWARD RESNICK

ARMS collectors have long noted that a few manufacturers are more successful than the majority of their competitors, and in the process produce a wide range of models and variations. In the limited field of flare gun collecting there are only a few such companies: Webley, Harrington & Richardson, Walther, and the subject of this article, R.F. Sedgley, Inc.

Reginald F. Sedgley founded his arms company in Philadelphia in 1897. Though it is best known today for its high-quality sporter conversions of military rifles such as the 1903 Springfield, Sedgley also manufactured firearms such as the "Baby Hammerless" revolvers and even a submachine gun, as well as pyrotechnics. Figure 1 shows the Sedgley plant as it appeared in the late 1920s; a stone in the building on the right is dated 1902.

Sedgley's first flare guns were probably just reworks of World War I Mk IVs in 25mm, as shown in Figure 2. This example is solid brass, nickel-plated, and has wood grips. It is marked R.F. SEDGLEY INC./ PHILA. PA. U.S.A. on the barrel. The original manufacturer is not known.

Though Sedgley had been issued a U.S. patent for a flare pistol in 1913, the war had apparently interrupted its development. It wasn't until 1929 that Sedgley actually introduced its Model 1929, based on the 1913 patent, but also marked OTHER PAT'S PEND'G. Figure 3 shows serial number 8 of the Model 1929; its blued steel barrel is marked 25 MM and MODEL 1929 along with the Sedgley name.

The 1913 patent covers the unique breakdown, in which the button just forward of the trigger releases the barrel, which can then be unlocked from the breech by rotating it 90 degrees. The barrel is then pulled forward and tilted down, opening the breech for loading. The firing mechanism is double action only. Probably less than 4000 Model 1929 Sedgleys were made.

Variations of the Model 1929 bearing the 1913 patent

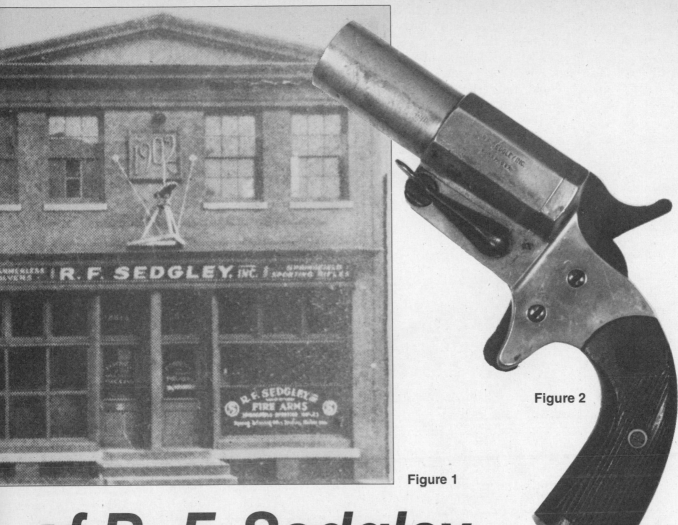

Figure 1

Figure 2

# of R. F. Sedgley

date include U.S. martials marked 25 MM U.S. (Figure 4) and commercial contract models marked LAKE ERIE CHEMICAL CO./CLEVELAND OHIO, a retailer. Another example of the Model 1929 bears the later patent date of 1-13-31, while another carries the marking GENERAL PROTECTIVE LAB. INC./ PITTSBURGH PA on its barrel. A Model 1929 in its original box is shown in Figure 5; some Model 1929 barrel marking variations are shown in Figure 6.

Following the Model 1929, Sedgley introduced a simplified version which featured a much simpler loading system. In this model the earlier rotating/sliding barrel was replaced with one that simply pivoted down when the barrel catch was released. A prototype of this model, marked simply MOD. #1 and without serial number, is shown in Figure 7. Another prototype, serial number 1001, is shown in Figure 8; Figure 9 shows either another prototype or a very early production example that has a heavily copper-plated steel barrel. Its serial number is 180.

Regular production examples include the Finnish contract bearing the SA marking (Figure 10) and the U.S. Navy contract (Figure 11) — note the USN embossed in its grips. Some Navy pistols have been noted with the "U" and "N" scratched out, leaving only the "S" for Sedgley. Whether these are overruns from the Navy purchase or later military surplus is not known.

Following the success of their 25mm flare guns, Sedgley came out with a line of 37mm flare arms. These proved quite popular, as the 37mm flare cartridges shot higher and burned brighter than the smaller bores. They were also usable for tear gas and line throwing, as well.

The first 37mm Sedgley flare gun is probably the Model H, shown in Figure 12. It has a unique muzzle-loading action; the odd lever on its left side expands the spring-steel split barrel, permitting a rimmed cartridge to be inserted from the muzzle. When the lever is released, the barrel retracts to its normal diameter, trapping the cartridge by its rim. Very few of these appear to have been made; the example shown is serial number T113.

Coston-Sedgley flare guns incorporate the name of the inventor of the signal flare, Benjamin Franklin Coston. It is not known if the Coston family had any connection with Sedgley or received any compensation for the use of their ancestor's name; the Coston Supply Company was in existence until the early 1960s. The unique feature of the Coston-Sedgley-marked flare guns is their trigger guard.

The long (8¹/₂-inch) barreled Coston-Sedgleys were produced first, and variations abound. The early prototype shown in Figure 13, serial number 104, is marked COSTON-SEDGLEY/PARACHUTE SIGNAL PISTOL/PAT 1-13-31 on its white metal grips; its receiver and the rear portion of the barrel are brass. Later ver-

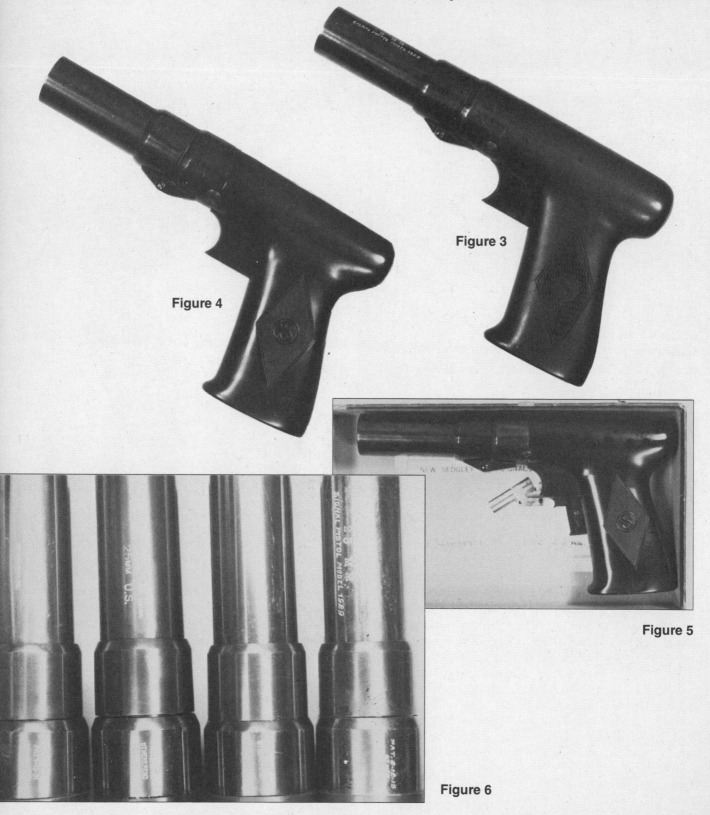

Figure 4

Figure 3

Figure 5

Figure 6

sions such as serial 2647, shown in Figure 14, are all steel and blued, and those in the 5000 serial range such as serial 5046 shown in Figure 15 have a one-piece barrel. Figure 16 shows a line-throwing version, complete with projectile, that has a barrel liner and a steel stud for attaching the line. Its serial is 5784.

Sedgley also made short (4½-inch) barreled Coston-Sedgleys such as serial 3809, shown in Figure 17. Principle variations in these pistols are in the marking location and legend.

In the late 1930s, Sedgley developed a simplified 37mm model. These were designated Mark I or Mark IV; no Mark II or Mark III marked Sedgleys have been reported. These are characterized by their lack of trig-

Figure 7

Figure 8

Figure 9

Figure 10

ger guard and Bakelite grips.

One example that may be a prototype is shown in Figure 18. It is marked COSTON-SEDGLEY/PARACHUTE SIGNAL PISTOL/PAT. 1-13-31 and is serial number 18. Note the long trigger, which may be the reason for eliminating the trigger guard.

Commercial Mark IV examples such as serial number 8905, shown in Figure 19, are marked R.F. SEDGLEY INC./SEDGLEY SIGNAL PISTOL/ MARK IV and Pat 8-22-32. The Bakelite grip is marked with the circle S Sedgley trademark. Examples made for the U.S. Navy are marked in the same way except for the grips, on which the Sedgley "S" was replaced with the Navy's USN logo such as serial

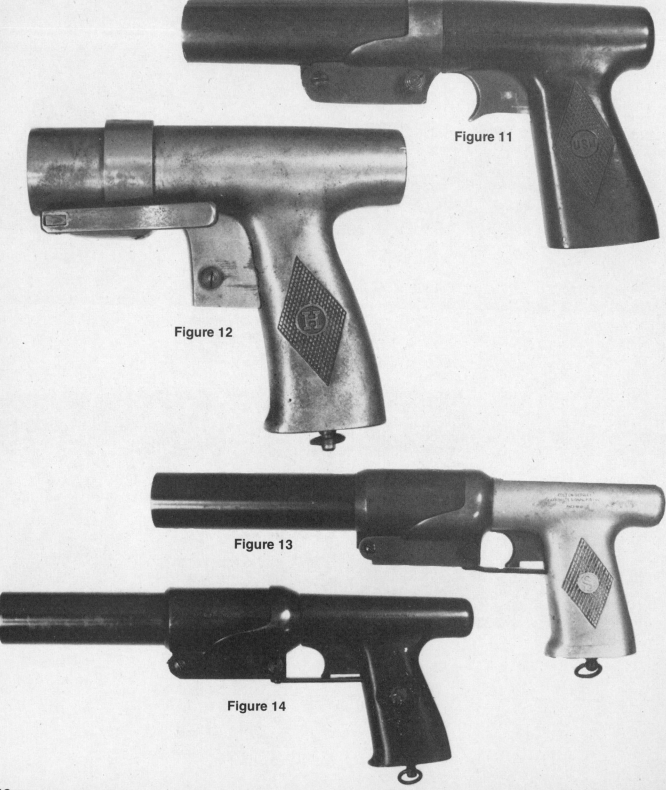

Figure 11

Figure 12

Figure 13

Figure 14

18131. Serial 14484, Figure 20, has had the "U" and "N" scratched out, either for surplus sale or as Navy contract overruns.

A pistol with the Mark I marking is shown in Figure 21; its barrel bears the unusual marking R.F. SEDGLEY INC./SUBMARINE ROCKET SIGNAL/ PISTOL MARK I and the 8-22-32 patent date. Only

two examples with the "submarine signal" marking have been reported.

In addition to the 37mm models, Sedgley also produced a number of 10-gauge flare pistols for military use during World War II (Figure 22). Designated the Mark V, they are mechanically the same as the Mark IV but have an aluminum barrel and receiver. Mark Vs are

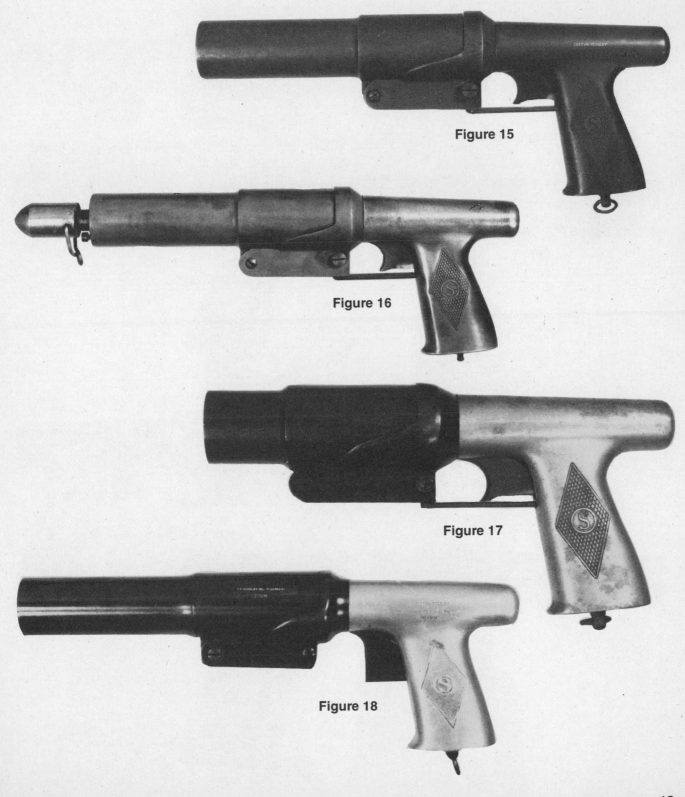

Figure 15

Figure 16

Figure 17

Figure 18

generally found dated 1942, 1942-43, 1943 or 1944. No Sedgley Mark Vs have been noted; it appears all 1945 Mark Vs were made by Vulcan Manufacturing Company.

A few — probably less than 500 — 10-gauge flare pistols similar to the Sedgley design were made by Van Karner in New York City. Not as sturdy as Sedgley's products, these are easily identified by their brass barrels and wood grips. The example shown in Figure 23, serial 266, is marked VK-M-24 on one side, VAN KARNER N.Y. USA on the other, and U.S. AND FRGN. PATENTS on the rib.

Shoulder-stocked Sedgley flare guns are quite scarce. These were made primarily for police, fire and

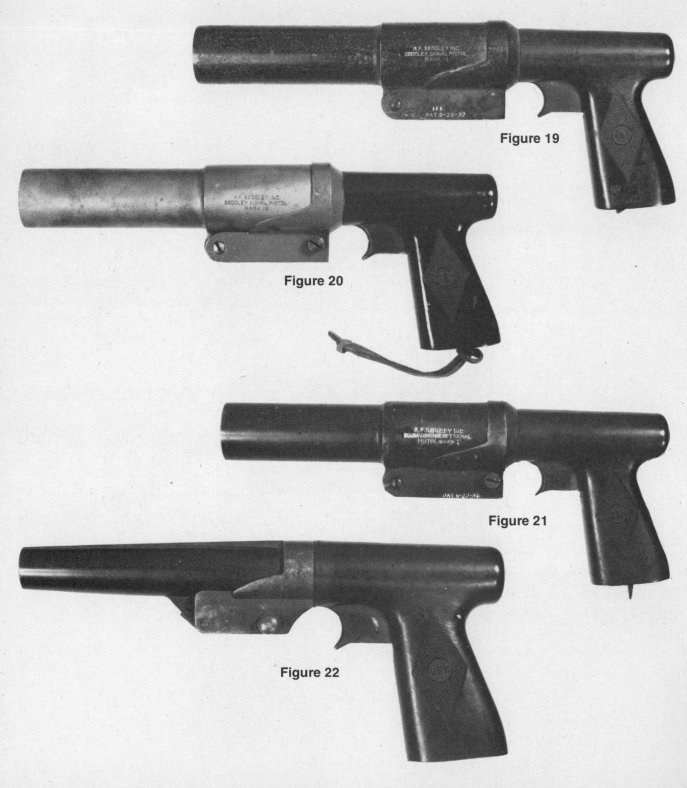

Figure 19

Figure 20

Figure 21

Figure 22

Marine use where they were used for line throwing and tear gas as well as flares. All are 37mm. The example shown at the bottom of Figure 24 is a prototype with an aluminum receiver that cracked during testing. This very gun hung above the desk in Sedgley's office for many years; it has a break-open lever that allows the barrel to unscrew for loading.

The early production example shown at the top of Figure 24 has a blued steel barrel and receiver and a button release to permit the barrel to unscrew for loading. It is marked LAKE ERIE CHEMICAL COMPANY and PAT 8-12-13 OTHERS PENDING. The serial number is 1072.

The line thrower shown in Figure 25 is marked R.F.

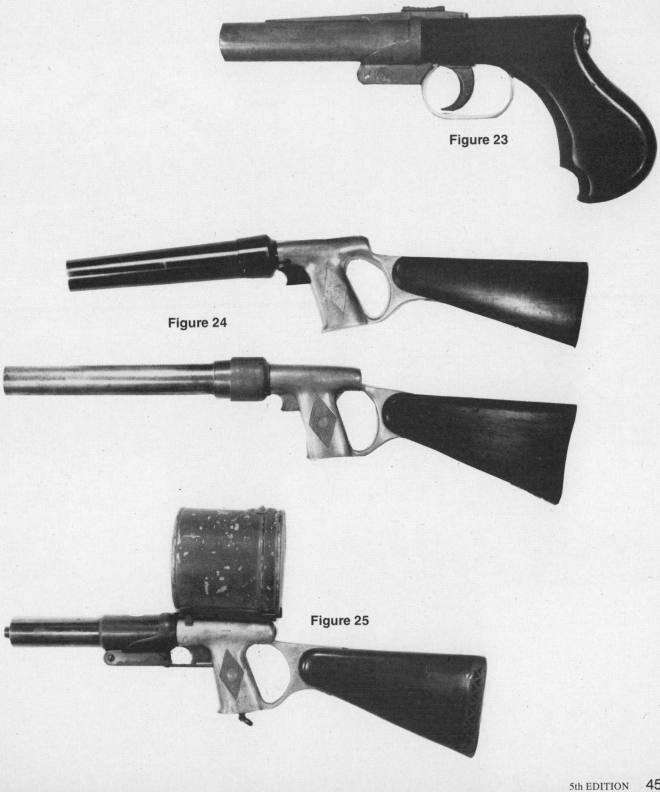

Figure 23

Figure 24

Figure 25

SEDGLEY INC./PHILA. PA USA and PAT 8-12-13 and breaks open for loading by pushing the button on the side of the receiver. Its frame is drilled and tapped for the line-throwing canister.

From the number of flare gun models and variations the company produced, it is obvious that the R.F. Sedgley Company has been a major contributor to the U.S. flare gun market. Flare guns occupied two full pages of their 1937 catalog (Figures 26 and 27). Though the Sedgley name has been fairly well known to the gun fraternity for their other activities, Sedgley's deep involvement with flare guns has not received the collector attention it deserves thus far. It is hoped that this article will serve to remedy that omission and attract attention to a previously neglected collecting field. •

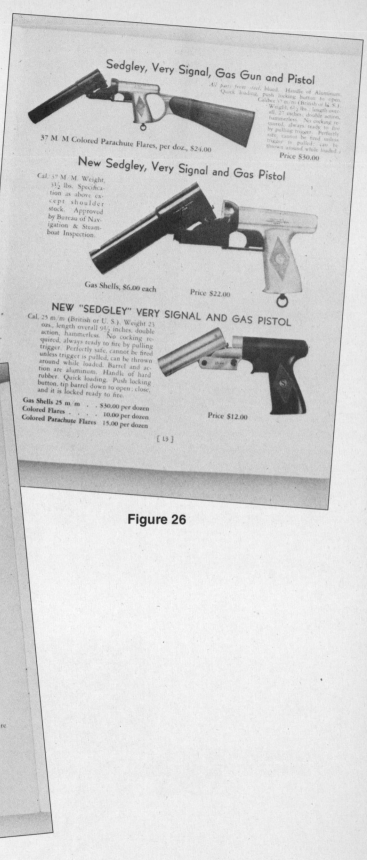

Figure 26

Figure 27

U.S. MILITARY HOLSTERS of World War II

by EDWARD S. MEADOWS

Model 1916 holster made by Boyt in 1944. Eighteen different contractors produced such holsters during the war, and about 3 million were made between 1942 and 1945.

WHEN THE United States entered World War II, the M1911/M1911A1 Colt 45-caliber automatic pistols were the regulation sidearms being issued to our military services, and the Model 1916 hip holster was the prescribed holster for use with them. This holster was officially designated the "Holster, Pistol, Model of 1916, For Automatic Pistol, Caliber .45, M1911 and M1911A1."

It is made of russet leather consisting of four component parts: the body/flap, belt loop/hook hanger, rest (inside) and bottom spacer or welt. A leg thong is attached to the bottom of the holster through two eyelets. The hanger, closing button, washers and eyelets are of brass and the flap is embossed with "US" in an oval. The maker's name or trademark and date (not always present) are on the back of the hanger.

Due to the large remaining inventory of Model 1916 holsters made during World War I, few were newly manufactured before 1942. Between 1942 and 1945, about 3 million were made by 18 private contractors. Boyt, Enger-Kress, Graton & Knight, Milwaukee Saddlery Co., Sears, Textan (Texas Tanning and Manufacturing Co.) and Warren Leather Goods Co. are the manufacturers most familiar to collectors. Other makers such as

Brauer, Crump, Fink, Harpham Brothers, Mosser and Walsh are less frequently encountered.

A specially-designed Model 1916 holster was also issued to General Officers. It is made of brown, lined calfskin consisting of five basic components: the body/flap, outer surface and inner lining, belt loop, rest and bottom spacer. The inner and outer surfaces are glued together, then stitched along the edges without reinforcing rivets. The belt loop/hanger assembly, called the "belt hook attaching piece," is stitched to the back of the body and reinforced with four brass rivets. The belt hook, closing button and drain hole finials on front and rear are also brass and all metal parts are gold-plated. There are no markings. A belt slide was issued with each holster for use with the General Officer belt and buckle, or it could be attached to the web belt by the hook.

As early as 1939, military experimentation had begun with shoulder holsters for the Model 1911/1911A1 pistol. By 1942, this had culminated in the introduction of the M3 shoulder holster for use by aircrews and mechanized cavalry. All M3 holsters were made by Boyt, Enger-Kress and Sears between 1942 and 1945.

The M3 is constructed of russet leather and consists of

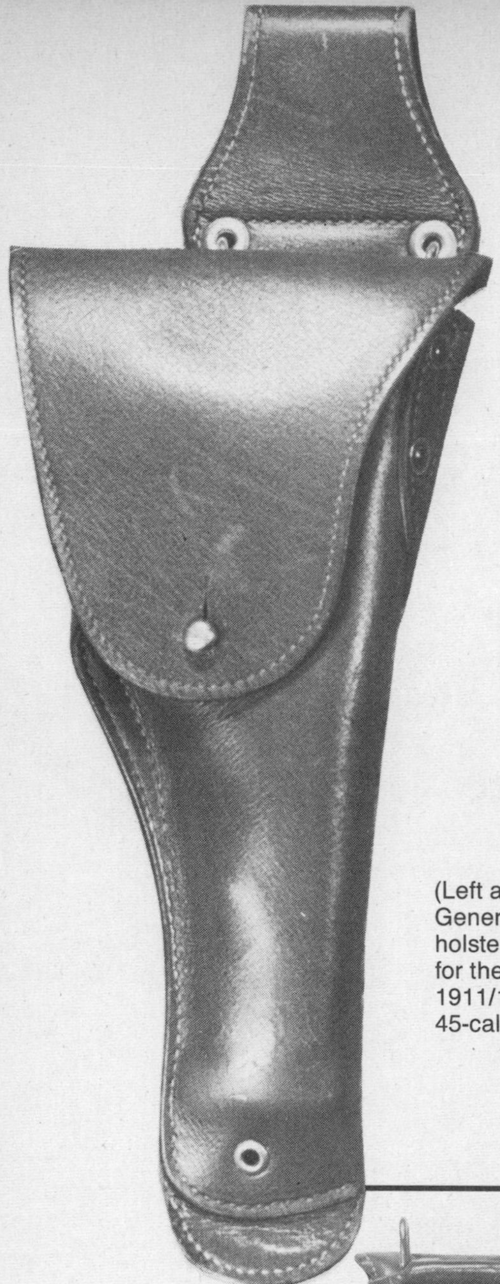

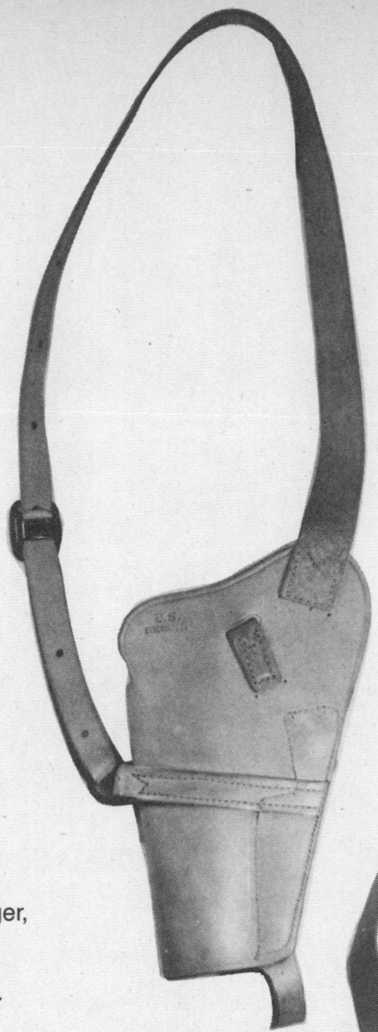

(Left and below)
General Officer
holster, with hanger,
for the Model
1911/1911A1
45-caliber pistols.

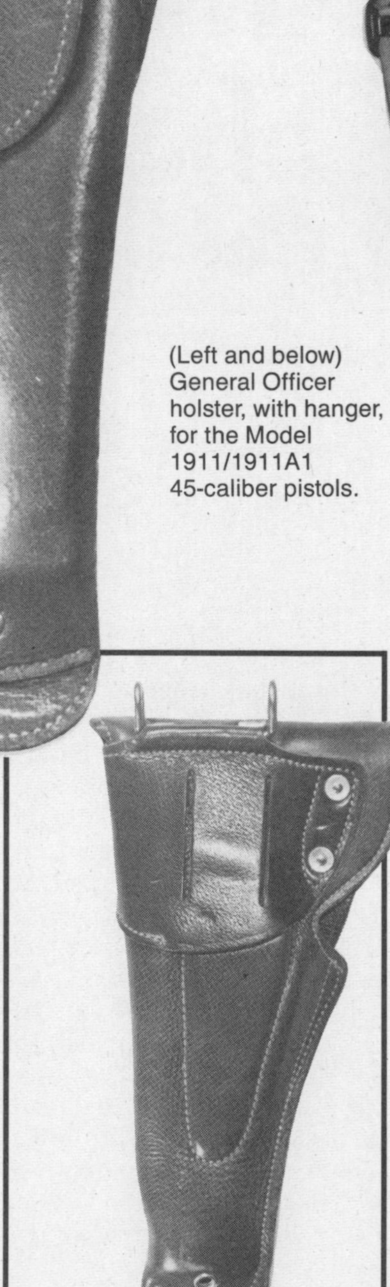

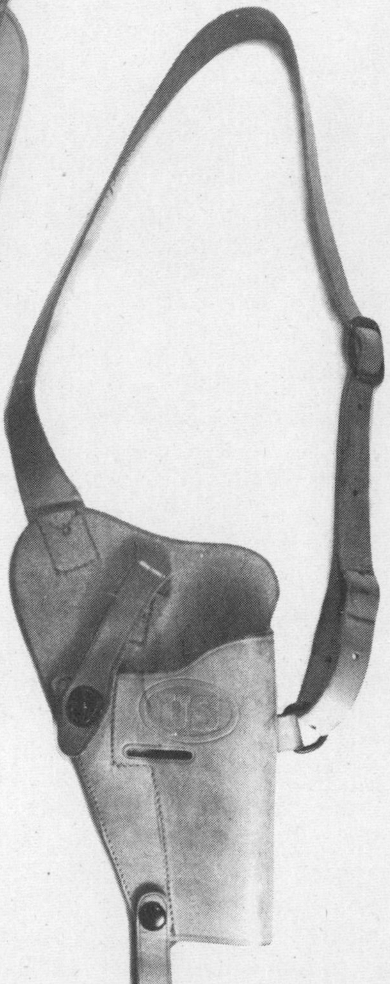

(Above and right) The
M3 shoulder holster
for the Model
1911/1911A1 pistols,
as made by
Enger-Kress during
WWII. The M3 was
also produced by the
Sears Saddlery Co.
and Boyt.

four component parts: the body, shoulder strap, closing strap and belt loop. The body is one piece of leather, folded over and stitched along the edge. The general outline of the pistol is also stitched for a secure fit. The closing strap passes though a slit in the upper portion of the body and is stitched to its back. The shoulder strap is stitched to the upper body on one end, attached to a D-ring on the other, and fitted with a buckle for adjustment. The belt loop is stitched between the folds of the holster bottom and the "Lift-The-Dot" fastener, belt loop snap, buckle and D-ring are all of blackened brass. The holsters are marked on the back "U.S.," "USN" or "USMC" and include the manufacturer's name and date. Not all are dated, however, but all are embossed with "US" on the front.

By 1944, an improved shoulder holster, the M7, had been introduced. It was designed to overcome criticisms leveled at the M3. Leaving the end of the shoulder strap of the M7 open for adjustment by lacing permitted it to be worn with greater flexibility by persons of various sizes. A shoulder pad was added to cut down on abrasion to the shoulder and neck, and the chest strap was added to keep the holster in position on the left shoulder, where it was designed to be worn, without the strap slipping off the shoulder.

The M7 was approved for use by Cavalry, Tank Destroyer, Armored Forces and the Army Air Forces in December, 1944. All World War II vintage M7 holsters were manufactured by Boyt and Enger-Kress.

The M7 is made of russet leather and utilizes six pieces in its construction: the body, shoulder strap and pad, closing strap, chest strap and belt loop. The body is one piece of leather, folded over and stitched along the edge. The

The U.S. Navy used the M3 shoulder holster with cartridge loops added.

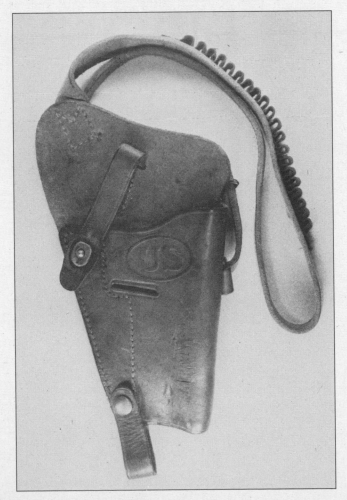

(Above and right) The M7 shoulder holster, which replaced the M3 in 1944. This example was made by Boyt for the U.S. Marine Corps and is dated 1945.

outline of the pistol is also stitched. The shoulder strap is attached to the holster through two brass D-rings, secured to the holster by straps stitched to the body. The shoulder pad slides on the shoulder strap for adjustment. The shoulder strap has a series of holes punched along its edges and in its center, which permit one end of both the shoulder strap and chest strap to be attached by lacing. Both shoulder and chest straps have a Conway buckle for length adjustment. A snap hook is attached to the front end of the chest strap and secured to the brass D-ring. The closing strap passes through a slit in the top of the holster, is stitched to the back of the body, and fitted with a "Lift-The-Dot" fastener. The belt loop is stitched between the folds of the holster bottom and has a snap fastener. A typical marking on the back is "US/BOYT/45" though some examples are marked "USMC."

Wartime demand far exceeded the ability of the Ordnance Department to supply 45-caliber automatic pistols, even though other manufacturers had geared up to supplement Colt's production. As a result, large quantities of Smith & Wesson "Victory Model" revolvers were pro-cured for issue, many going to Navy flight personnel. At the same time, both hip holsters and shoulder holsters were designed for issue with them.

The "Holster, Hip, Revolver, Caliber .38" was manufactured during WWII by Rock Island Arsenal, Boyt and Craighead. Three component parts, of russet leather, are used in their construction: the body, flap and belt loop/hanger extension. The flap is secured by a "Lift-The-Dot" fastener. The holster can be carried on either a web or leather belt, as it is provided with both belt loops and a wire hook. The rivets are of brass, the body is embossed with "US" in an oval, and the maker's mark and sometimes a date are on the back of the belt loop.

A slightly different style holster, constructed of two pieces of russet leather, was also made for issue to Navy shore personnel for use with the "Victory Model" revolvers. The body and flap are of one piece of leather, stitched along the edge. The hanger attachment is stitched to the back of the holster body. The hook hanger is iron, the closing finial brass, and there is no bottom plug. These holsters are usually unmarked.

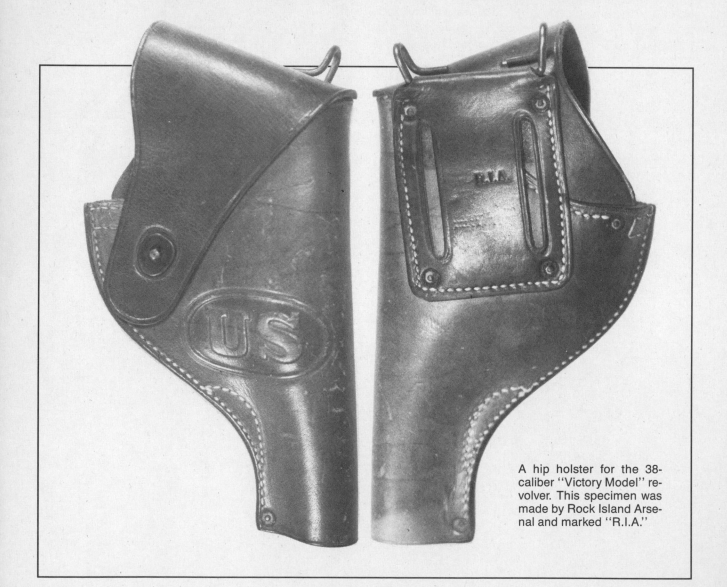

A hip holster for the 38-caliber "Victory Model" revolver. This specimen was made by Rock Island Arsenal and marked "R.I.A."

World War II examples of the "Holster, Shoulder, Revolver, Caliber .38" were made only by Boyt. They are of russet leather and consist of four component parts: the body, closing strap, shoulder strap and bottom strap. The body is folded over and stitched along the edge with a rivet reinforcement at the top. The closing strap is secured by a "Lift-The-Dot" fastener and the bottom strap has a snap. The shoulder strap has a Conway buckle for adjustment and is stitched to the holster body on one end and passed through a D-ring on the other. Manufacturer markings and the date are on the back of the holster, while the front is embossed with "US" in an oval. Many Navy holsters also had cartridge loops added to the shoulder strap.

A holster specially designed by Enger-Kress for Naval and Marine aviators and manufactured of russet leather as well was also issued. The six component parts are the body, shoulder strap, chest strap, closing strap, belt loop and cartridge carrier. The chest and shoulder straps are both fitted with iron buckles for adjustment, while the cartridge carrier slides on the shoulder strap for position-

A hip holster for 38-caliber revolvers made by Boyt in 1943 for the U.S. Navy, and is so embossed. This is a difficult variation to find.

(Right and far right) The so-called "Shore Patrol" holster made for issue to U.S. Navy personnel.

The M4 pattern holster dates from November, 1942 and is similar to the M2 except that the bottom plug and tie-down ring are omitted in favor of a closed end with eyelet. The Sears Saddlery Co. and Milwaukee Saddlery Co. manufactured all World War II M4 holsters.

The M4 is constructed of four component parts: the body, flap, belt loop and bottom spacer or welt. The belt loop is stitched to the body and reinforced with three rivets and the flap is also stitched and riveted. There are two eyelets in the belt loop through which a leather thong tied to an eyelet in the cartridge belt passes to prevent the holster from sliding on the belt. Another pair of eyelets are set into the bottom of the holster body which serve a dual purpose — as drains and for attaching the leg thong. The body is embossed with "US" in an oval, and the back of the belt loop is marked with the maker and sometimes, but not always, a date.

Shoulder holster for 38-caliber revolvers. Although designed for Naval aviator use, they were issued to other branches of service as well.

The USN/USMC aviator's shoulder holster was designed and made by Enger-Kress and is so marked. The design incorporated the cartridge loops which were also often added to other holsters.

ing. The closing strap and belt loop are equipped with snaps. All key points in the construction are rivet reinforced. The holster is marked on the back "Enger-Kress" without a date.

In addition to the 38-caliber revolvers, many Model 1917, 45-caliber revolvers were reissued during World War II. At first, the 1917/1918 Graton & Knight Model 1909 revolver holsters, with butt forward, were issued with them. In time, though, these stocks were depleted and two new holsters introduced for use with the Model 1917 revolvers, designated the M2 and the M4.

The M2, introduced in October, 1941, was simply a reversed version of the old Model 1909 pattern holster, designed so the pistol was carried butt to the rear on the right side. All M2s were made by Textan and Fink.

The M2 has four component parts: the body, flap, belt loop and bottom plug. The belt loop is stitched to the body and reinforced with three rivets and the flap is also stitched and riveted. There are two eyelets in the belt loop for a thong which secures the holster in position on the cartridge belt. A tie-down ring is affixed to the bottom plug. The finial, rivets and ring are of brass, and a drain hole is located at the bottom rear of the holster body. The front of the body is embossed with "US" in an oval, and the maker's name and date are stamped on the back of the belt loop.

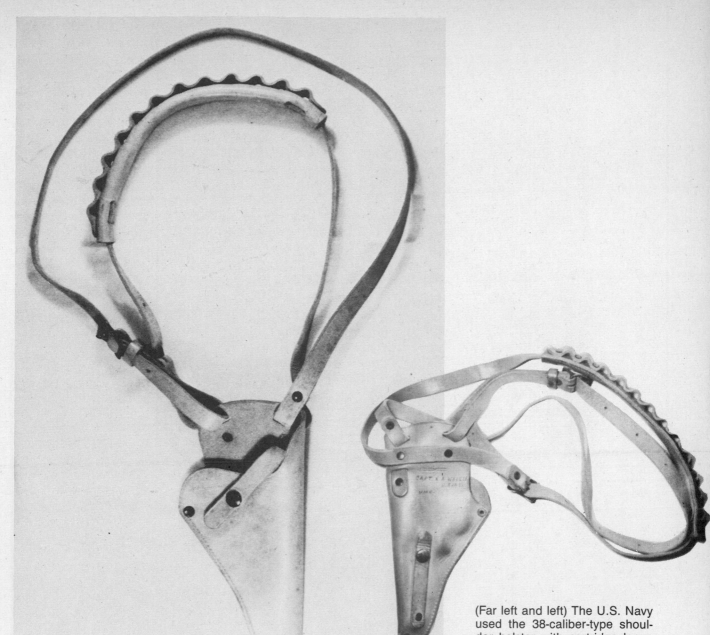

(Far left and left) The U.S. Navy used the 38-caliber-type shoulder holster with cartridge loops added to the shoulder strap, a common practice.

A small number of Colt Detective Special revolvers with 2-inch barrels were also procured by the Army during World War II, and both hip and shoulder holsters were designed in May of 1943 and subsequently manufactured specifically for use with them.

The hip holster is made of three pieces of russet leather: the body, flap, and belt loop. The flap is held closed by a "Lift-The-Dot" fastener. The wire hanger is iron and the rivets are brass. The holster can be carried on either a web or leather belt, as it is provided with both belt loops and a wire hanger. The body is embossed with "US" in an oval and the belt loop is marked "BOYT/43."

The shoulder holster for the Detective Special revolver is manufactured of russet leather with four component parts: the body, shoulder strap, closing and bottom straps. The closing and bottom straps are fitted with snaps for closure and are sewn to the body of the holster, as is the shoulder strap. The edge stitching is reinforced with a rivet at the top. Chest straps are sewn to the shoulder strap and the shoulder strap is adjustable by means of a leather thong which is passed through holes at various points on the strap. The body is embossed with "US" in an oval.

A number of 38-caliber Colt Official Police and Smith & Wesson "Victory Model" revolvers with 5-inch barrels

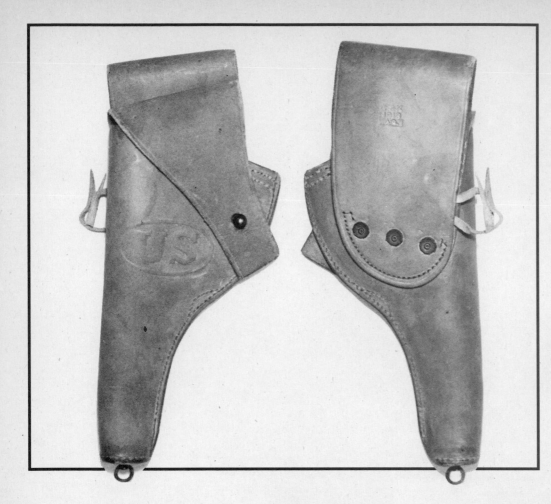

A Model 1909 holster for the 45-caliber revolver. This one was made during WWI by Graton & Knight for the Model 1917 Colt and S&W guns. These holsters were also issued with reconditioned Model 1917 revolvers during WWII.

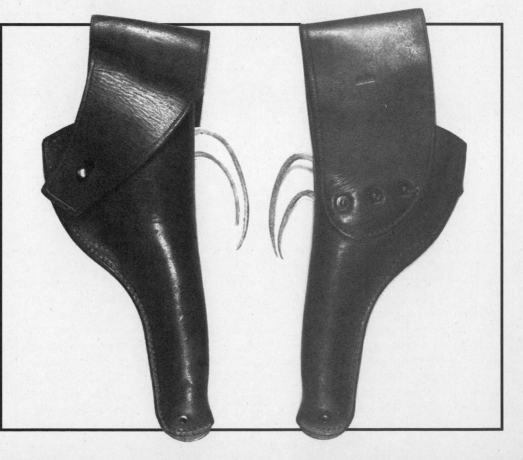

The M4 holster for the Model 1917 revolver, as made by Sears and Milwaukee Saddlery from November, 1942 until the end of the war. This example, by Sears, is undated.

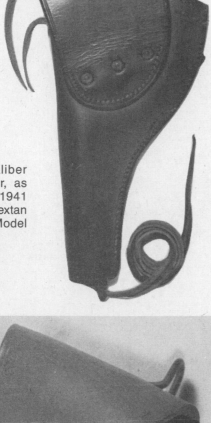

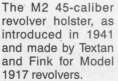

The M2 45-caliber revolver holster, as introduced in 1941 and made by Textan and Fink for Model 1917 revolvers.

were also procured, and another special holster designed and manufactured for use with them.

This holster consists of four component parts: the body, flap, belt loop/hanger and bottom spacer. The flap and belt loop are sewn to the back of the body and reinforced with four brass rivets. The body is sewn along the edge without reinforcing rivets, the flap secured by a "Star-*Pull" fastener. The wire hanger is iron. A leg thong is attached to the bottom of the holster; the holes through which it passes are not reinforced with brass eyelets as usually found. The body is embossed with "US" in the usual manner and the belt loop is marked "BOYT/43."

Several thousand Colt 32- and 380-caliber automatic pistols were also procured by the government during the war. These went largely to the Office of Strategic Services (O.S.S.), the U.S. Navy and to general officers. Both shoulder and hip holsters were made for them.

The hip holster is composed of three parts: the body, belt loop/lining and closing strap. The body and the belt loop/lining are laminated together and reinforced with stitching along the edges. The lining only goes down half-way inside the holster, as can be seen from the stitching line across the center, which is the point of termination. The belt loop is formed by a folded-over extension of the

Boyt made this holster for the Colt Detective Special revolver. This is a scarce item, as few of the guns were procured by the military.

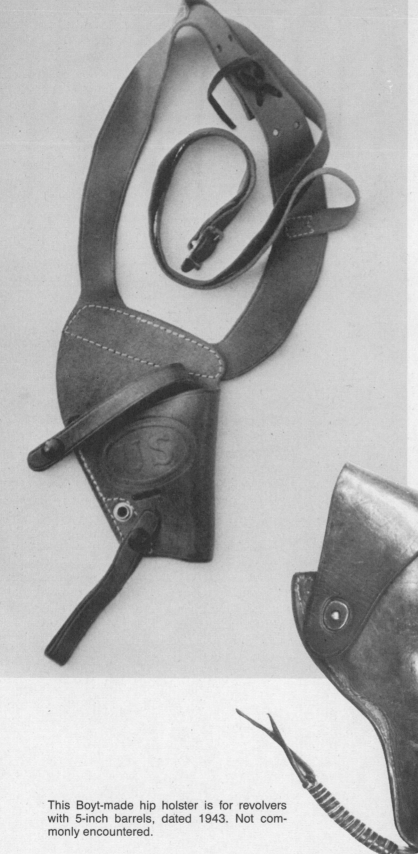

Another unusual holster is this shoulder rig for the Colt Detective Special.

This Boyt-made hip holster is for revolvers with 5-inch barrels, dated 1943. Not commonly encountered.

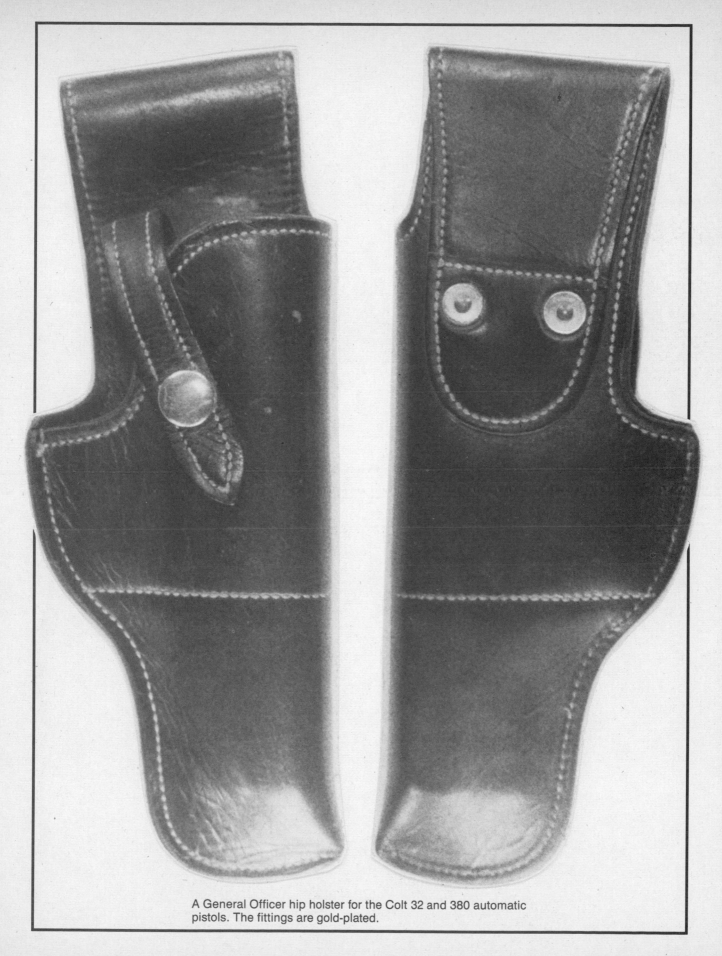

A General Officer hip holster for the Colt 32 and 380 automatic pistols. The fittings are gold-plated.

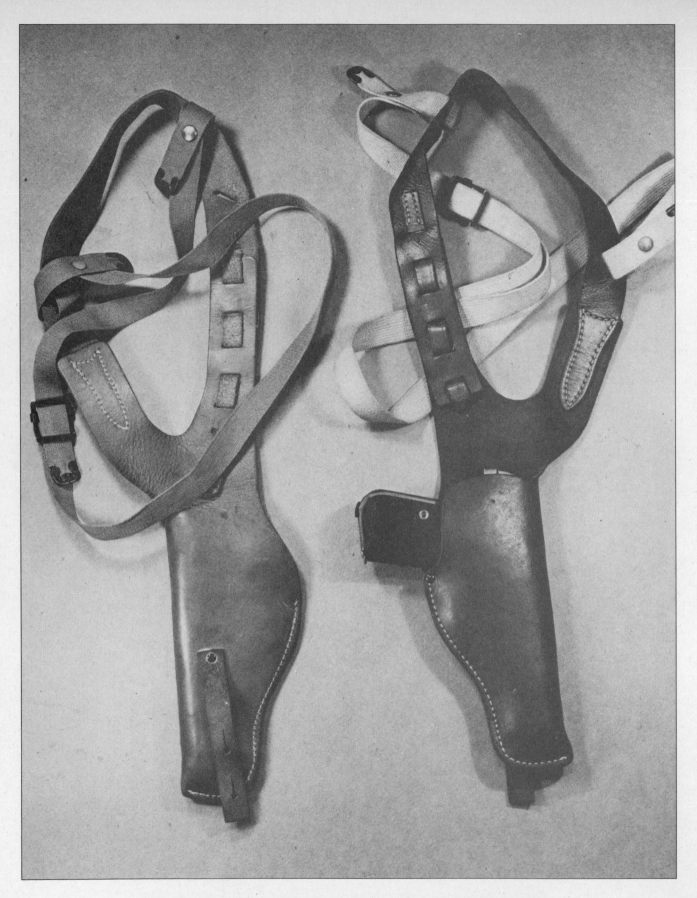

Shoulder holsters for the Colt 32 and 380 automatic pistols. The rig on the right has the issue white strap and a rivet at the top of the stitching on the holster body.

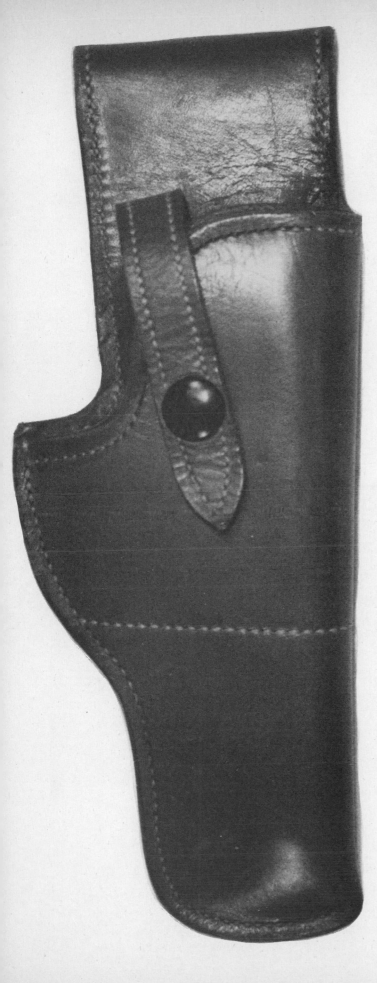

This is the standard-issue hip holster for the Colt 32- and 380-caliber automatic pistols.

liner, which is made of two pieces of leather with the smooth sides out. The top of the body portion ends at the curve in the belt loop. The belt loop is reinforced with two rivets, one of which also retains the lined closing strap. There are no markings. The holsters made for issue to General Officers are of calfskin, and their fittings gold-plated.

The shoulder holsters for the 32/380 automatics are made of five component parts: the body with extension for strap, shoulder strap, adjustment strap, belt strap and canvas chest strap. The body is stitched along the edge. Some holsters are reinforced with one rivet at the top. The shoulder strap is stitched to the extension on one side only; the other side is left loose and connected by the adjustment strap, which is laced in position. The belt strap is riveted to the back of the body. The chest strap, which may be olive drab (early) or white (later), is attached to the shoulder strap through two slits and retained by snaps. It has a sliding buckle for adjustment and metal tips. There are no markings.

In summary, 16 different holsters were made for the six primary sidearms issued during World War II. Of course, there were also a number of experimental or trial holsters developed during this period, but they are beyond the scope of this article, which encompasses only regulation, issue patterns. For a more expanded treatment of the subject, the reader is referred to the author's book *U.S. Military Holsters and Pistol Cartridge Boxes*. ●

WWII Holster Manufacturers' Names and Locations

Boyt — Iowa Falls, Iowa
Brauer Brothers — St. Louis, Mo.
Craighead — Denver, Colo.
Crump — Location unknown
Enger-Kress — Location unknown
Fink — Location unknown
Harpham Brothers — Lincoln, Neb.
Heiser — Denver, Colo.
Graton & Knight — Worcester, Mass.
Milwaukee Saddlery Co. — Milwaukee, Wis.
Joseph H. Mosser — Location unknown
Rock Island Arsenal — Rock Island, Ill.
Sears Saddlery Co. — Davenport, Iowa
Texas Tanning and Mfg. Co. (Textan) — Yockum, Texas
Walsh — Location unknown
Warren Leather Goods Co. — Worcester, Mass.
Western Manufacturing Co. — San Francisco, Calif.

MAKER

A rare Confederate side knife of unknown manufacture and in fine condition. The wooden handle bears a crude "JGG," probably the initials of the owner. The appearance of the stain on the blade indicates it may have been made by some viscous liquid, not water. (Photo by Michael Camacho, Dundee, IL)

by GRAHAM BURNSIDE

UNKNOWN

An unmarked 58-caliber bullet mould that casts the Minié ball with hollowed base. The insert formed the hollow base — the lead being poured into the top of the mould. With such short handles, one would have to use heavy gloves to avoid burns when casting bullets with this tool. (Photo by Michael Camacho, Dundee, IL)

EVERY once in awhile a collectors' item crops up that deserves more attention than the ordinary. It may be because of sheer rarity or because it forces us to explore a little-known field. Unfortunately, these interesting items are usually tucked away for future use because one item, however fascinating, usually does not lead to an article that will stimulate the average editor.

Well, if one interesting item will not do it, what about two?

Recently, my friend Al Zeigler purchased a small collection of edged weapons. It was mostly Nazi daggers and such, but one piece stood out that seemed to scream "Confederate!" At first chance, Al was at my door with a smile as wide as his head. Careful examination, and I mean *careful*, confirmed Al's suspicions. It suddenly dawned on me that I was holding the finest example of a Confederate side knife that I had ever seen.

Right from the start it should be understood that this piece is no woodshed rendering. This beautiful knife was made in some Confederate arsenal by a craftsman who knew his trade. The spearpoint-style blade is finely formed and polished, resulting in beautiful simplicity.

I probably have 100 books having to do with the Civil War, and more than a few of them are detailed studies of arms and equipment. Naturally, I quickly went to work with all the volumes that would most probably show examples of Confederate side knives. Many people call all of the larger knives of this type "Bowie knives." The term "Bowie knife," from Jim Bowie of Alamo fame, became very popular during the Civil War and has remained so to this day. I would prefer to call them all "side knives" (as did Confederate ordnance) and then describe them as having a Bowie-style blade with clipped point, as distinguished from the less-common spearpoint design.

I searched through many sources, even my complete bound editions of the *American Arms Collector*, and found blades like this one with guards that were quite similar and handles of the same construction, but I did not find this knife. Although somewhat disappointing, this last is very understandable. William A. Albaugh III, in his book *Confederate Edged Weapons*, lists about 150 sources for Confederate blades, and the term "Maker Unknown" is stated repeatedly.

The South was deficient in heavy ordnance, cannon

works and the lot, but they had many companies that could and did produce quality swords, pikes, and knives. When you think about it, there was a plethora of organizations that manufactured farming equipment and similar products in the southern states. Those companies could quite easily reorganize to a wartime functionary. The Nashville Plow Works (Sharp and Hamilton) and the Tredegar Iron Works of Richmond, Virginia are two examples of the above.

In 1861, when the Civil War started, side knives were extremely popular. Asby of Shelbourne Falls, Massachusetts gave a Bowie to every man and boy who joined the Union forces. The Federal soldiers abandoned their large knives early in the war because they were thought unnecessary and just one more burdensome thing to carry.

As the Northern boys discarded their side knives, the popularity of folding pocketknives increased. On the other side of the line, the soldiers of the South retained their big knives for a longer time during the war. The reason, probably, was that they lacked alternative equipment.

Again in the book *Confederate Edged Weapons*, pages 178 and 179, there is a knife described with a double-edged spear-type blade with a tin scabbard shaped to fit the spearpointed blade — "Maker Unknown." The specimen pictured here also has a "tin" scabbard, also shaped to closely fit the blade. Actually, the scabbard is made of sheet iron, not tin, and the seams of the folded sheath are soldered — again like the one described in the book. The side knife shown here is 15 inches overall when encased in the scabbard, 14³/₄ inches when removed, with a blade of 9¹³/₁₆ inches.

And now we must progress to our second rare and unusual Civil War item — also "Maker Unknown."

The bullet mould pictured nearby casts the 58-caliber "minney" ball, widely used by both sides in the Civil War. When the word "ball" is used, people automatically think that it has to be round or spherical. Not so! There are all kinds of balls of many shapes, and as long as they are round in one aspect or another, they're still balls. Our well-known football is a perfect example.

The "minney" ball should really be called the Minié, invented by a captain in the French army. He developed his bullet idea back in the 1840s. Captain Minié was not the first person to form a hollow-based bullet, but he patented the idea and that's what counts. The design of the hollow base is very sound and practical. The pressure of the expanding gases forces the soft lead base to expand to the full diameter of the bore, thereby insuring a minimal loss of pressure and excellent accuracy.

Minié's original design called for a wedge of iron in the hollowed base. (Wedges of wood and clay were tried as well.) After a time, it was realized that the wedges were an unnecessary feature because the gas pressure alone would do the job.

The Minié ball was adopted officially by the French military in 1846. Quite naturally, such a popular idea was bound to be tried by others. England wasted no time utilizing the idea, and they paid the good captain 20,000 pounds for the rights to manufacture his hollow-based design. By the time the American Civil War broke out, the Minié ball was old hat, and still the most successful system.

Here is a mould that was beautifully fashioned, complete with the insert, and devoid of any markings. You would think that anyone talented enough to make this mould would be proud enough to put his name on it.

It weighs 15³/₄ ounces complete with the insert and 12 ounces without it, and it's only 5⁵/₈ inches long. I haven't cast any bullets with this chunky little rascal, but if I do, I am going to use heavy welder's gloves.

In other moulds for this same 58-caliber ball, I have cast bullets that weighed from about 492 grains to 501 grains, and I found the heaviest ones were the most accurate. If you use railroad babbit, 58-caliber balls will drop down into the 470 to 475 range — a little too hard for my uses — and accuracy will suffer.

Included is a bibliography of my research sources for this article, but it is grossly incomplete. If I were to list *all* the books I perused, you'd just think that I was bragging about my library! I looked everywhere — books, magazines, you name it. Not only did I not find this mould, I did not find even one picture of *any* single-cavity 58 Minié ball mould of *any* design!

We know that the boys in the Civil War used the paper cartridge. The Union was rather proficient in supplying those paper cartridges, and considering the almost ridiculous array of rounds for the various and sundry carbines, the Federal ordnance people did a magnificent job.

I don't know who made this fine mould. I got it from a friend who had it since 1927. He got it from an aged man who had owned it for some untold years. As to its origin, my nod would go south of the Mason-Dixon line. We see 577 Enfield moulds from time to time and know they were used by the South, but there were a lot of captured Yankee Springfields down there, and this mould would have been mighty handy. ●

Bibliography

Albaugh, William A. *Confederate Edged Weapons*. New York: Harper and Brothers, 1960.

Albaugh, William A., and Edward N. Simmons. *Confederate Arms*. Pennsylvania: The Stackpole Co., 1957.

Edwards, William B. *Civil War Guns*. Pennsylvania: The Stackpole Co., 1962.

Logan, Herschel. *Cartridges*. West Virginia: Standard Publ. Inc., 1948.

Lord, Francis A. *The American Arms Collector*, ed. Hugh Benet. Vol. I, 1957; Vol. II, 1958.

Lord, Francis A. *Civil War Collector's Encyclopedia*. Pennsylvania: The Stackpole Co., 1963.

Lord, Francis A. *They Fought For The Union*. Pennsylvania: The Stackpole Co., 1960.

The MAUSER MODEL 1906/08 PISTOL:

Failure or Forerunner?

by JOSEPH J. SCHROEDER

AMONG SELF-LOADING pistol collectors, the Model 1906/08 is one of the most sought after of all the Mausers. Its exotic appearance and place in Mauser chronology — the first Mauser selfloader to follow the Model 1896 Broomhandle — assures its place at the top of any Mauser buff's "Most Wanted" list.

On the other hand, the '06/08 has pretty much been considered a "dead end" in Mauser pistol evolution; not only did it retain some of the Broomhandle's less desired features — in particular, the magazine in front of the trigger guard — but, if it was indeed supposed to

be an innovative new model, it was one that went nowhere. Fewer than 100 were made, undoubtedly all by hand in Mauser's experimental section, and there is no record of the '06/08 even being offered to any potential customer for evaluation. On reflection, however, this impression of failure is not entirely justified — the '06/08 really did represent a significant step forward in Mauser handgun development!

Before getting into the reasoning behind that conclusion, let's review Mauser pistol history prior to the 1906/08. Work on Mauser's first selfloader, the Model

The 1906/08 is a noticeably more compact pistol than a contemporary Model 1896, in this case another rarity — an early production 9mm Export C96.

The first production Mauser pistols to employ features of the Model 1906/08 were the 25-caliber Model 1910 (bottom) and the Model 1914 in 32 (top). Both incorporate the latching safety system, though the safety-lever itself is mostly concealed by the grip. Both are also striker fired and have wraparound grips. Missing in the early 1910s, such as this one, is the automatic slide release that was added when the Model 1914 and Model 1910/14 were introduced.

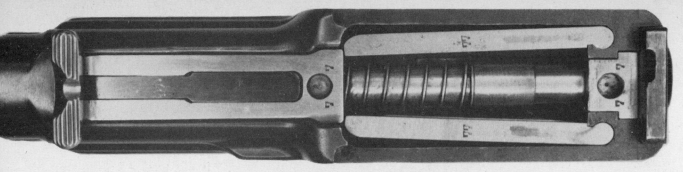

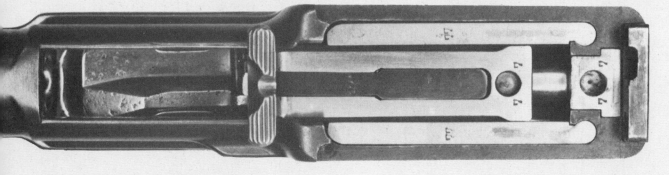

Breech-locking system of the 1906/08 shown with the action cover removed. At top, the action is closed and locked, ready to fire; below, the locking flaps have been cammed out of engagement and the bolt is open.

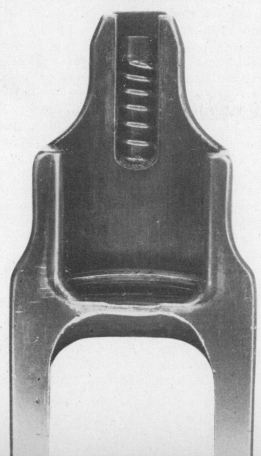

Detail of the '06/08's buffer spring, located in the front of the frame just forward of the magazine well. It is simply a group of leaf springs that cushion the rearward motion of the barrel extension. The coil spring visible at the very front of the frame returns the barrel to battery.

1896, probably began in 1893 or 1894, and by March of 1895, a well-made, functioning prototype (that still survives in a private European collection) was made and tested. Though some early examples were shown and demonstrated in 1896, widespread commercial distribution of the Broomhandle apparently didn't begin until 1897.

Though the pistol received favorable reviews and was tested extensively by various governments, the only quantity purchases that were forthcoming during the first few years of its existence were by Turkey (1000) and the Italian navy (5000). Disappointed, Mauser experimented with various minor modifications to the 1896, but real success in the form of a government contract still eluded them. By 1905, when most of their competitors were enjoying burgeoning sales in the self-loading pistol market, and the 1896 had been on the market for 8 years, it had sold fewer than 50,000 examples.

Obviously, something needed to be done. The answer had to be a totally new design — one incorporating features that would interest the serious potential buyers (particularly government commissions) who had thus far been unimpressed with the now aging Model 1896.

First a cartridge had to be selected. With few exceptions, the trend for service use had been to a minimum caliber of 9mm. Fortunately for Mauser, they already had a 9mm cartridge and a very good one at that. This was the so-called 9mm Export, which Mauser had already tested successfully in a few experimental Model 1896 pistols, and for which they would manufacture a

Mauser's only successful weapon that used locking flaps was the Model 1916 "Fliegergewehr," a rifle used in limited numbers by World War I German aviators.

limited number of production 1896 pistols in the 1906 to 1910 period.

The next question was the design itself. One of the on-going objections to the 1896 was that its bore was too high above the grip, leading to control problems during rapid fire. This was because its breech locking components and bulky firing mechanism were both mounted underneath the barrel breechblock assembly. A more compact arrangement than the 1896's was needed. The answer was found in an experimental Mauser self-loading rifle design, patented in 1906, which locked its action closed at the moment of firing with a pair of flaps behind and on either side of the bolt. When the barrel recoiled, these flaps were cammed aside, permitting the bolt to move to the rear between them.

Since size had been another objection to the 1896, the 1906's design offered yet another advantage. It was striker fired — a more compact arrangement than the 1896's outside hammer, and one that would result in a considerably smaller pistol, despite its powerful cartridge.

Once the basic design and choice of cartridge had been settled, all that remained was to mate them in a pistol that incorporated all the other features Mauser felt might interest potential buyers. The result was the Model 1906/08.

Perhaps most interesting about the 1906/08 are the number of those new features introduced with it that turned up again on later Mauser designs. In short, the Model 1906/08 was the first Mauser pistol to:

- be designed specifically for a 9mm cartridge;
- have a detachable magazine;
- have a bolt hold open independent of the magazine follower;
- have a "latching" safety-lever;
- be striker fired;
- have a wrap-around grip;
- incorporate a recoil buffer;
- have a flap-type locking system.

Without exception, every one of these features — all new with the Model 1906/08 — turned up on future Mauser pistols. Why then, wasn't the '06/08 itself a success? A significant problem, probably, was Mauser's fixation on placing the magazine in front of the trigger guard. After all, to a company that dominated the world's market in bolt-action rifles, that would certainly seem to be the logical place to put the magazine. Unfortunately, at a time when the rest of the pistol design world had adopted the grip to house the ammunition supply, Mauser's archaic approach was unacceptable. When eventually even Mauser realized this basic error, a few 1906/08 variants were made that mated a sharply slanted grip with a removable magazine to an 1906/08 upper half. Unfortunately, by then it was too late for the '06/08; new designs were on the drawing board.

Another problem plaguing the pistol was the choice of cartridge. The 9mm Export, essentially the bottlenecked 7.63mm Mauser case without the bottleneck, is very hot. Too hot, it seems, for the 1906/08, illustrated

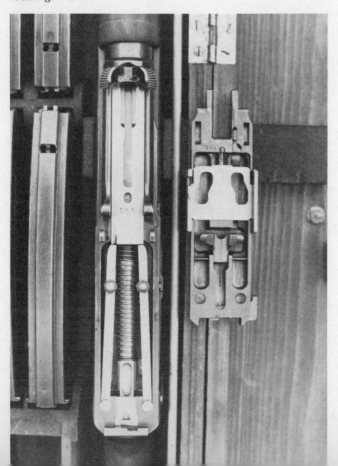

The Mauser Model 1912/14 — another large-caliber design that would probably have become a production pistol if World War I had not intervened. About 200 examples were actually produced. In addition to the '06/08 features used in the Model 1910 and 1914 pocket pistols, the 9mm 1912/14 also used flaps for breech-locking. Unlike the 1906/08, the 1912/14 had a fixed barrel so the locking flaps, located in the "box" in front of the trigger guard, had to be pushed aside by a stud on the bottom of the slide.

Action of the Model 1916 rifle with its protective cover removed. Like the Model 1912/14, the fixed-barrel Fliegergewehr required a release mechanism (located in the cover) to permit manual unlocking of the action for loading and unloading.

by one very early surviving example (one more accurately designated as a "Model 1906") that has a cracked frame. An ammunition problem might also explain that mysterious series of Mauser experimental cartridges based on the Mauser Export. The original DWM catalog number for the Export was 487; by the time Mauser finished trying to "perfect" it, they'd worked up DWM 487A, 487B, 487C, and 487D as well — each one a little different in case length, load and/or projectile. It seems very likely that those experimental cartridges were Mauser's attempts to provide ammunition that the 1906/08 could digest successfully. And the pistol's inability to handle a powerful cartridge might also explain why so few examples of the 1906/08 have turned up!

But what of those '06/08 features that did survive? How and where were they incorporated in subsequent Mauser pistols? Let's consider them in the order previously listed.

The detachable magazine was, of course, a feature of all later Mauser pistol designs. The staggered column '06/08 magazine is, however, closer in design to the "Schnellfeuer" magazines introduced in the 1930s with the full-automatic version of the 1896 than it is with other early Mauser pocket pistol magazines. Three different sized magazines were made for the '06/08 — a short one that held only six rounds, one slightly longer for 10 rounds, and an extended model that probably held about 15. What is most thought provoking about the '06/08's removable magazine is why Mauser didn't adapt it immediately to the venerable 1896 pistol!

A unique magazine-related feature the '06/08 introduced and one that became universal on all later Mauser pistols (except the vest pocket models) was the slide hold-open mechanism. Most contemporary self-loading pistols had some sort of hold open. Some, such as Mauser's own Model 1896, simply propped the bolt open with the magazine follower. When the follower

The Mauser Nickl pistol (above) was another experimental design that borrowed from the 1906/08 for safety, slide release and wraparound grip. The Nickl was an experimental design of the early war years, and actually went into production in Czechoslovakia as their Model 1922 pistol. Shown with it (below) is a very early Model 1914.

was moved out of engagement, by loading (integral magazine) or removal from the gun, the bolt closed. Others, such as the Colt 1902 and 1905 and the Luger, had a separate hold-open latch that required some sort of specific action by the shooter.

Mauser's unique approach was to make breech closing automatic. When the bolt was retracted on an empty magazine, the follower rose and held it in the full recoil position, just as with the Model 1896. However, when the empty magazine was withdrawn from the gun, a separate latch continued to hold the bolt open. Then, when the magazine — full or empty — was reinserted the hold-open latch was tripped and the bolt closed automatically. This feature was integral to Mauser's later pocket pistols, starting with the 1914 and continuing through the HSc, as well as all the experimental larger-caliber pistols such as the Model 1912/14 and Nickl. The one exception (other than the WTP vest pocket models, which were considered too small for a sophisticated hold-open mechanism) was the original 25-caliber Model 1910. When the 32-caliber Model 1914 was introduced, however, the Model 1910 was also upgraded as the Model 1910/14 and Mauser's engineers were able to find room for the added hold-open parts.

The "latching safety" of the '06/08 was another feature picked up on most later Mauser pistols. The safety on the Model 1896 was a lever that stuck out of the rear of the action. It was not particularly convenient, and not (especially in the early models) even very clear as to whether it was in the Safe or Fire position. On the '06/08, the safety was a pivoting lever above and be-

hind the trigger, with a push-button release latch that lay directly under the thumb of a right-handed shooter. Extremely convenient, unambiguous as well. Apparently, this safety mechanism really tickled the fancy of someone important at Mauser, as it was used in all subsequent Mauser pistols (again, with the exception of the WTPs) until the introduction of the HSc in the late 1930s.

The 1906/08 was Mauser's first striker-fired pistol. The 1896 was, of course, hammer fired, and the argument of external hammer vs. striker will probably never be resolved. The striker mechanism of the '06/08 is, like the rest of the pistol, overly complicated. Nevertheless, it is again true that all Mauser production pistols (and almost all experimentals) between the '06/08 and the HSc were striker fired.

Whether Mauser developed a fixation on the wraparound grip from the '06/08, or whether its use on that

In 1934, Mauser "modernized" its Model 1910/14 and 1914 pistols with an improved grip shape and high-polish finish, but both still used basic features introduced with the Model 1906/08.

It wasn't until the introduction of its totally redesigned HSc pistol that Mauser finally got away from the Model 1906/08 influence, and even then the departure wasn't quite complete. The HSc still utilized the automatic slide release of the '06/08 and its successors.

pistol was coincidental can be the subject of debate. Whatever the outcome of that argument, it is a fact that all subsequent Mausers until the WTP 2 had wrap-around grips.

The recoil buffer was still another new feature that Mauser introduced with the '06/08. This buffer was a multi-leaved spring mounted across the frame, just in front of the magazine housing, that cushioned the recoil of the barrel extension when it reached the end of its travel. Use of a buffer in the '06/08 may well have been an afterthought, trying to reduce the stress of the 9mm Export cartridge though Mauser's patent for the buffer was also granted in 1906. While Mauser never used the buffer in a production arm, it was used in a few experimental pistols of the 1909 to 1912 period.

The flap-type locking system was to become a feature of numerous experimental and limited production arms at Mauser for some years. In the pistol field it was

adopted (though in a fixed-barrel version) in the well known (but rare) Model 1912/14. It actually saw limited production — also with a fixed barrel — in a military rifle, the "Fliegergewehr," that was issued in limited numbers to German aviators in 1916-17.

Though Mauser's Model 1906/08 pistol never went beyond the experimental stage, it was certainly a test bed for a number of widely-used Mauser features. There can even be a legitimate question raised as to whether Mauser ever intended to offer the '06/08 to the market, as none of the few examples in collector's hands bear any proofmarks. Other Mauser pistols intended for outside testing and evaluation were, without exception, submitted to proofing! The '06/08 is today a highly-prized collector's item, but for Mauser, it provided an opportunity to evaluate a number of interesting new ideas before incorporating them in production guns. ●

"**A**BROAD they knight them, here they indict them," exclaimed Colonel George M. Chinn, United States Marine Corps, compiler of the monumental multi-volume study *The Machine Gun* for the Bureau of Naval Ordnance. Round-faced, almost oriental in appearance, a sort of all-wise Buddha of ballistics, Chinn was rapping from Washington with me long distance on the phone. From my Chicago office at *GUNS Magazine* back in 1957, I had called him for a quotable quote.

"Colonel, didn't you once tell me that the National Firearms Act (NFA) restricting machineguns was very damaging to the national defense of the United States?" I asked, and he erupted, "Damaging, hell, it's downright devastating." The line went dead!

When Chinn soon got back on the phone he said sheepishly, "That little gal tol' me that if I continued to use language like that she'd have to cut me off."

In retrospect, I realize that long-distance operators don't normally listen to conversations. Chinn's call was being monitored for Someone In Authority; Chinn was very likely being watched because he had become a director of the newly-formed American Automatic Weapons Association, the AAWA.

Soon, he called me to demand that his name be taken off the AAWA letterhead. "Boy, you have kicked up a hornet's nest in Washington; you're gonna lose me my pension," he exclaimed.

Although the AAWA had been founded to teach young Americans about the newest small arms and the new infantry assault rifles that were technically classified as machineguns, it was viewed with alarm by The Powers That Be. Within months of its formation, the AAWA was out of business.

The AAWA coordinated the hobby of collecting machineguns. In accordance with the National Firearms Act of 1934 in harmony with the laws of several states, the AAWA planned to provide interested citizens with the opportunity to fire fully automatic rifles and machineguns under safe range conditions. The AAWA and the machinegun hobby were logical developments of the prohibition-era NFA, which in 1934 theoretically "outlawed machine guns."

Actually, the NFA did no such thing. It simply used the taxing power of the government to place a heavy burden on the sale of machineguns, rifles, shotguns with "sawed off" barrels, and silencers.

For quick review, a "machinegun" is defined as any gun which fires more than one shot with a single pull of the trigger. "Sawed-off" guns included ordinary rifles and shotguns with barrels cut shorter than a legal limit, and later came to also include common pistols and revolvers when fitted with shoulder stocks.

The original purpose of the law was supposed to be "crime control." Its effect was to limit previously un-

Collecting Machineguns in America

by **WILLIAM B. EDWARDS**

regulated foreign commercial competition to the American arms makers. In the 1920s, mail-order dealers such as Pacific Arms Co. of San Francisco, run by John B. Mannerstam, offered imported Luger pistols with shoulder stocks with the grabby advertising pitch, "Combination Rifle, Pistol and Baby Machine Gun all in One."

In his 1924 catalog, Mannerstam introduced the Tommy Gun as "An efficient modern answer to unlawful violence." It was the Tommy Gun which would eventually put the end to mail-order machinegun sales with the National Firearms Act.

Collector rarity is exemplified by one of two handmade, German-type, 30-caliber MG42s built by Saginaw Gear Division of GM in 1944. The original mechanism was adapted to the 8x57mm case length so the gun jammed repeatedly in tests when adapted to the 7.62x61mm length case. Sights were styled after Browning LMG sights. Today, virtually identical guns are NATO-standard for firing the even shorter 7.62x54mm cartridge. Gun at right is shown with the barrel partially removed.

The original prohibitions against pistols of the NFA were struck down during its legislative history, but with the support of prominent Wall Street lawyer and former Secretary of War Elihu Root, the machinegun portion of the law was passed. Root was, at the time, counsel for the estate of Virginian Thomas Fortune Ryan, for whom the Tommy Gun was named. Ryan was born in Nelson County, Virginia in 1851. He died a multimillionaire, having built cathedrals and railroads but also leaving a somewhat somber legacy as part developer of the Belgian Congo.

In the Congo, labor problems with the native population inspired the adoption of the 9mm Browning pistol, designed according to the FN manual "for the use of colonial troops having to fight against uncivilized tribes." As a participant in colonial mining and timber development, Ryan supported the development of the light, portable, high fire-power weapon that now bears his name.

It is probably this uniquely American invention, very successful in a restricted sense, which has given a mystique, a sort of colorful character, to machineguns and has influenced the modern spirit of machinegun collecting.

The Thompson Sub-Machine Gun, as it is more formally known, evolved from Navy Commander John Blish's delayed-unlocking principle as applied to gun breeches. Army ordnance Brigadier General John Taliaferro Thompson, D.S.M., retired to take up at the end of WWI the task of developing the "Blish principle"—the adhesion of locking surfaces under pressure into a workable automatic gun.

The first 1919 gun was a sort of two-handed pistol that fired at the high rate of about 1200 caliber 45 pistol bullets a minute. A buttstock was added, and drum magazines for 50 and 100 cartridges were provided; the 20-shot stick clip proved over the years to be more practical.

General Thompson gave his name to the design, and guns were marked "Thompson Sub-Machine Gun." But the name "Tommy Gun" was quickly applied in token of Tommy Ryan's backing, and it stuck.

Much of the eventual mystique of the Tommy Gun ignored the original purposes of its developers. Tommy Ryan, deeply involved with New York politics, was sympathetic to the cause of Irish freedom. The first production run of 500 TSMGs was destined for Ireland, but might as equally well have been intended for control of labor in Virginia, where a 1919 program to develop the Blue Ridge iron ores and oil shales was planned, but which never came to pass because of a failure of cheap immigrant labor schemes of that time. The United States' steel industry vacillated between the heavily-armed Pinkertons with Spencer repeaters to put down its labor troubles, and the lament of Andrew Carnegie that breaking a strike was "not worth the loss of one workman's life."

Instead of quelling tribal troubles among African miners, cleaning the Brits out of Ould Eire, or suppressing labor riots in the Blue Ridge, the Tommy Gun

Experimental 22-caliber sub-caliber training device created by the MG Army by fitting a Colt Woodsman pistol to a M1917 water-cooled Browning. A five-cell hardware store flashlight with a five-cell extension was clamped on for night firing study. If this piece still exists, it is a vital historical link, one followed by Marsh Williams with his full-auto sub-caliber training insert device of the 1930s and by Howard Sarvis' "Trainfire" concepts of the Eisenhower years.

was Ping-Ponged between the U.S. Army, some British experiments, the U.S. Army Air Corps, the U.S. Navy and Marines, and Texas cowboys. One early catalog even pictured a fur-chapped cowpoke on the porch of a ranch house, blasting away at some nearby rustlers with his trusty 50-round drum-equipped Tommy Gun. At $30 a month and found, it certainly was beyond the ability of the average cowpoke to keep it fueled with ammo. One Tommy Gun would have taxed the resources of a cowboy western film company in a shoot-'em-up sequence.

A natty pintle rig mounted the Tommy on police motorcycle sidecars, but after a few state troopers were waylaid at faked auto accidents and relieved of their Tommy Guns, police came to view the arm with less enthusiasm. It was in the hands of Chicago prohibition beer runners and bootleggers that the Tommy Gun gained real prominence.

The Tommy Gun drew the attention of Alphonse Capone when compulsive killer Frank McErlane raked the Ragen Athletic Club with one, killing mobster Charles Kelly. Capone, the smiling, cigar smoking north-side Chicago businessman who gave free Christmas turkeys to the deserving and paid hospital bills for the needy, was fascinated by the new toy. His brother, John, and one Charlie Fischetti bought the first three for Capone from a dealer named Alex Korocek. At that time, the late 1920s, retail price on the various models ran from about $175 to $200. Compared to an L.C. Smith double shotgun at $37.50 and a Browning five-shot automatic shotgun sold direct to the consumer in 1931 at $49.95, this was a stiff price. But it realistically reflected the fact that only 15,000 Tommy Guns had been contracted for with the Colt Co., and of these, more than half were redesigned from the original Model 21 at 900 rpm to become the slower-firing Model 1928 at 600 rpm.

The slaughter of seven members of a rival gang, on St. Valentine's Day, 1929, "left the Capone-ites masters of the Chicago underworld," and gave to the gun that glamour that only gore can provide in the perceptions of the American public.

The U.S. Treasury Department came into the machinegun picture in 1934. By that time, repeated news stories had created an impression that the machinegun was the favorite weapon of criminals and that most such guns were in the hands of crooks. Actually, the U.S. Army had been selling to the public several models of obsolete machineguns as "surplus." Major Anthony Fiala, intrepid arctic explorer and outfitter of explorations, sold in his catalog aircraft machineguns priced at "$7.75 or $2 with order balance C.O.D. shipped by express." The air-cooled Colt-Vickers 11mm "balloon busters" and the 30-06 Marlin gas-operated fixed or flexible aircraft guns were new, "but rendered unserviceable by U.S. Government, to comply with law. (No parts removed and appearance unspoiled.)" Fiala said, "If you are a collector or interested, we would advise

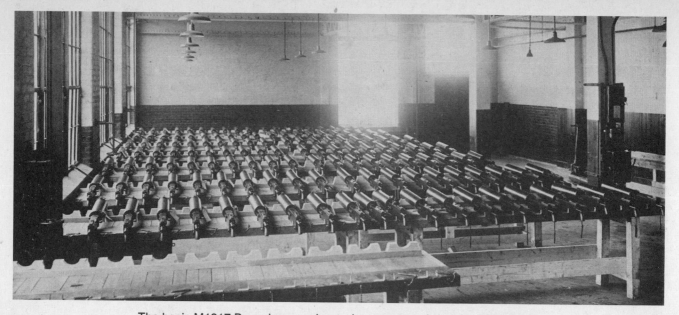

The basic M1917 Browning remains an important nucleus of any machine-gun collection. This photo taken at Remington Arms shows 140 guns in final production stages. Old Signal Corps photo caption alleges the guns are "complete in the photograph except for tripods" and ammo boxes, which are shipped separately, but magnifying glass examination of the old original photo reveals 68 guns are shells and incomplete, lacking front sight and interior parts, and all are lacking rear sights. These guns, pictured Friday, May 10, 1918, may be the first lot of Remington Brownings delivered as the firm completed only 11,000 of their 15,000 order by contract cancellation time at war's end.

you to place your order for one of these wonderful pieces of mechanisms (sic) before they are all gone."

I examined one of Fiala's Vickers guns, the air cooling for which consisted of ventilating the original water cooling jacket around the barrel. This jacket had been slightly dented, impeding the recoil function of the barrel. The gun would not function, but, of course, the jacket could be realigned and the gun made serviceable by a good gunsmith. I almost obtained one of those in 1943 when I offered in *Shotgun News* my Schmeisser MP40, the second one in the U.S. (Aberdeen's first example did not even have a magazine). I received a letter from a fellow in Detroit offering me one of the Vickers

guns with the original 50-round link belt of ammo. He explained that the government sold these "for about $7," and told me that the Schmeisser had cost the German government about $9 so he thought it was a fair deal. Feller's name was W.H.B. Smith, but I never made the trade . . .

Criminal use of machineguns, though statistically negligible, was always sensational. In New Jersey in 1926, police intercepted a Colt M1914 "potato digger" air-cooled gun before delivery to a road house. They believed it would have been used to "tie down" the police in the station house while the mobsters robbed a bank. Incidents like that were enough criminal activity

Russian-engineered PPSH-41 submachine gun made in Iran by Imperial Armament Factories was presented to General Lawton Collins and is now a choice display item in the West Point Museum Collection. Many similar guns returned to the U.S. with veterans from Korea and were lawfully registered during 1968 Amnesty, so may be legally bought and sold today.

Lineup of aircraft-style Browning 50s in final assembly at Colt's in 1940, probably for delivery to Britain's RAF. Goering said that if the Luftwaffe had used the 50-caliber Brownings, the Battle of Britain would have been over in a week. Japan also admired the Brownings. Here is a version with a hydraulic bolt-cocking cylinder on the side. The U.S.-design had reversible feed block so it could take the belt from either side. The Japanese copied one-side feed only, making Zeros tricky to balance as the ammo fed from unbalanced magazines to the wing guns.

to support the anti-machinegunners, and the National Firearms Act was created.

Because the Second Amendment to the Constitution preserved the "right to keep and bear arms," the taxing power of Congress was invoked. The Tommy Gun sold for $200, so the logical way to greatly limit its sale was to tax it out of existence with a $200 transfer or registration tax on every machinegun sale. All machineguns had to be registered. Those who already owned one also had to pay a $200 registration fee. Administration and enforcement of the new 1934 law was handed to the same agency which enforced the tax laws regulating liquor and cigarettes — the Alcohol and Tobacco Tax

Unit of the Internal Revenue Service of the Treasury Department.

An American, Hiram Maxim, had invented the recoil-operated machinegun in the 1880s and been knighted by Queen Victoria in appreciation for its civilizing influence on massed charges of Africans. American John Moses Browning had invented the gas-operated machinegun and been knighted with the Order of Leopold in token of his work. Americans Benjamin Berkeley Hotchkiss and Steven V. Benet had developed the Hotchkiss gun, acclaimed from the arid wastes of Africa during the Riff War to the icy hills of Manchuria in the Russo-Japanese War. Andreas Schwarzlose,

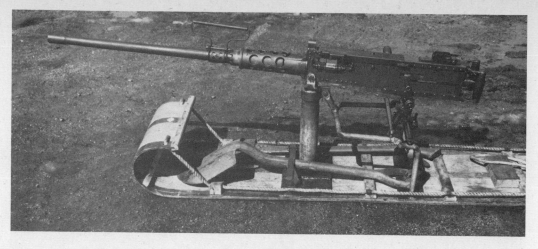

For outdoor sports and specifically cold-weather European fighting, this Browning 50 BMG was fitted to a toboggan at Camp McCoy, Wisconsin, in March, 1943. Shovel and axe are unusual but vital accessories to this rig in its tactical role, to get it there and dig it in.

Scotti, Revelli, Villar-Perosa, Bergmann, and the Schmeissers were among many at work on fully-automatic gun designs in Europe.

The NFA of 1934 pretty much finished off domestic U.S. machinegun invention. So small was the subsequent demand for the Tommy Gun that of the 15,000 original mechanisms contracted for, in 1957 there remained in U.S. ordnance stores — taken over at the beginning of World War II for possible military use — some 8000 M1921s and about 6000 M1928s. With so many unsold by 1940, the liquidation of the company was not surprising. With some simplifications, over 2½ million Tommy Guns were procured for Allied use during WWII, while an additional tens of thousands were made in China.

Gun collecting in America received its first formal boost in 1937, when some gun dealer/scholar/pioneers such as Miller Bedford and Ed Beard formed the Ohio Gun Collectors Association. Similar groups were formed in other states, but still, by 1940, the total enrollment of the National Rifle Association — reflecting the nation's population of "dedicated" gunners — was only about 40,000. By 1945 membership had risen to about 90,000, but then something important happened. Some 10 million Americans who had been in the Armed Forces began returning to civilian life. It has been said that the Frenchman fights for "glory," and the German fights for "the fatherland," but the American, ah the American, he fights *for souvenirs*. Along with Mausers, Lugers and P.38s, a variety of operating machineguns were sent home in duffel bags and in pieces by parcel post. Although the $200 tax still ap-

Eagle-eyed Rough Riders assemble in camp during the Spanish-American War (1899) displaying their handsome Colt-Browning M1895 "potato digger" gas-operated guns. Barrels are the early smooth, heavy type, later ribbed for better cooling in 1914 production. Buckles read "US" and bugler wears SAA Colt in his holster with two button holes, adapted to either Colt or heavy Smith & Wessons.

The Browning Auto Rifle (BAR) saw limited use in WWI. It is shown here being demonstrated by inventor John Browning's son, Lt. Val Browning, at Chaumont, France, November 9, 1918. Both Winchester (view in testing range showing racked guns) and Colt made them, the latter in the post-war period as a commercial "Police" model with Cutts Compensator and short barrel. It was dubbed the "Colt Monitor."

plied and registration was mandatory, the public had dealt with machineguns so little that few people really knew the law. If a feed pawl had been broken off to prevent belt feed in a Maxim, that was considered a "Dewat."

Λ "Dewat" is a *De*activated *War Trophy* firearm. To avoid the legal necessity of throwing half of America's citizen soldiers in jail because they brought home a captured machinegun or submachine gun as a souvenir, the Treasury Department established through regulation a class of firearms exempted from the registration and tax liability of the NFA. If a souvenir machinegun was welded up in the breech — for example, if the barrel was spot welded to the receiver and the chamber closed with weld — the gun would be considered an "unserviceable" firearm, a "Dewat," which could be owned and sold without tax liability.

In 1956, as editor of *GUNS Magazine,* I had been helping new gun firms get started in business. One such firm was International Armaments Corp., now Interarms, whose genial vice president, Sam Cummings, had been bird-dogging surplus arms around the world for resale to American collectors. Another kindred spirit was Valmore Forgett, Jr., who had just finished a stint in Army Ordnance at Aberdeen and was looking for some gun-collector related employment or business to enter. I had just refused the offer of a post with Cummings, preferring to stay at *GUNS.* But new business was in the air, and in discussion with Sam and Val in Alexandria, I asked if Sam knew that he could import machineguns, weld them up and sell them without paying the tax? He was astonished, but said he "had some Browning Automatic Rifles at the bottom of the pile in a

Rambo, eat your heart out! Snubbed M1917 BMG breech sports front as well as rear sights on top, has a mini tripod for super mobility in post-WWI tests using web belt from throw-away carton. Probably only one was made. Light weight sacrificed concealability, as muzzle flash must have lighted up the countryside.

Danish arsenal." I asked him their cost and he said "about $20." We all agreed that they could make money by being sold for $49.95. From that conversation the Dewat program was commercialized, with Forgett starting the "Service Armament Co."

There was a spirit of foolishness in the air, nobody was damning guns as "diabolical machines of death," and Forgett, in a spoof of Ma Barker, publicized the madame of mayhem with Tommy Guns. As a takeoff on Cummings' "Ye Olde Hunter" spoof of Hy Hunter, Forgett chose as his trade symbol "Ma Hunter, the loveable little old lady who sells machineguns." It may not make much sense reading about it today, but you have to be in the Spirit of '56 and know Forgett and Cummings to understand that even then it was merely good nonsense. But those were times of nonsense; the Communist Threat motivated governments to spend billions in blood and treasure and inspired many in civil life to build backyard atom bomb shelters and stock them with automatic arms for survival . . .

In that spirit of the times, the United States officially became "schizophrenic" with regard to automatic arms. On one hand, the U.S. sponsored programs for civilian training with military arms. The underpinning of the NRA was the annual military-style matches at Camp Perry, the Ohio National Guard range on Lake Erie. At the same time, the search for a fully-automatic shoulder-fired infantry rifle climaxed after much publicity on British EM-2s and FALs with the adoption in May, 1957 of the M-14 modified Garand-type rifle. Even as it was authorized for procurement, the M-14 was being replaced in Army R&D with the just-unveiled Armalite series, specifically the AR-15 which was to become the U.S. Rifle, M-16 in 5.56mm. While the military programs of the nation planned to wrap Young America up in olive drab and ship him off to war, there was no civilian plan to train the young rifleman in the use of the new fully-automatic arms. Into this breach, this vacuum of preparedness, stepped the American Automatic Weapons Association, Inc. of Grand Rapids, Michigan.

Founded by Arthur J. Hunt, a Grand Rapids heating contractor, the Association proposed to coordinate the mushrooming popular interest in automatic arms by establishing shooting clubs licensed under the NFA to deal in machineguns. Regular scheduled shoots were proposed, one designed after an existing Swedish pro-

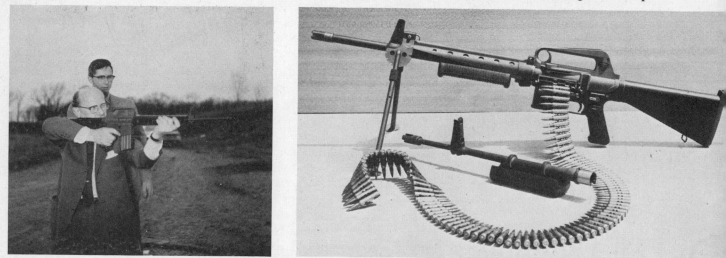

AR-15, serial number 00001, is fired full auto by Harry Light with the author looking on in 1956 test in Illinois gravel pit. Already in production in Holland at the time was the AR-10 in 7.62mm NATO caliber. (Right) Using interchangeable light and heavy barrels, this experimental variation NATO machinegun proved unreliable in feeding due to the light mass of recoiling parts, resulting in insufficient belt pull energy.

Colt-Maxim guns offered by Fiala Outfits in 1934 were government deactivated by a slight dent in the air cooling jacket; otherwise new and complete. Original 30-caliber ground guns had been modified to French 11mm Gras caliber for incendiary bullets against anti-aircraft barrage balloons and marauding bomb-dropping Zeppelins. Author was offered such a gun in 1950 by a Chicago shop, but referred the offer (at $25) to Frank Tallman of the Tal-Mantz Hollywood aviation firm. Fiala also sold Marlins.

gram using five-man teams variously armed with BARs, bolt-action rifles, and K-pist submachine guns. I knew of the varieties of automatic arms which were available as "surplus," and knew that many of these could be sold to such clubs. This would limit the tax liability and still make available on a secure controlled basis hands-on experience with automatic weapons.

In *GUNS Magazine* I had published an account of shooting the M-14 rifle, actually a T-44 by Matthewman Tool Co., which I had tested at Rock Island Arsenal courtesy of Captain George C. Nonte, then on active service as Rock Island's public information officer.

While I only fired a couple of hundred rounds, I had many years earlier fired my Schmeisser MP40 and also a buttstock-less Tommy Gun I had bought through *Shotgun News*. (A frantic phone call from the seller later persuaded me to return the gun to him, as no tax had been paid, which was probably just as well — I had ordered the gun because I saw a misprint in the ad and knew what it was anyway. When I got home to my garage apartment on Chicago's south side, I saw that Railway Express had left two packages outside my door. One contained the Tommy Gun, the other a 50-round drum magazine! No signature . . .) The Tommy Gun, fired offhand as a pistol, chugging along, had revealed to me some systems of holding which matured in the T-44 shooting test.

The AAWA initially enlisted some pretty high-power friends. Michigan Congressman Gerald Ford thought well of the program, and Art Hunt often spoke of what his representative would be able to do "for the Association" in Washington. Colonel Chinn initially agreed to be an advisor, as did Col. George Burling "Red" Jarrett, chief of Foreign Material at Aberdeen Proving Ground. Val Forgett was a director, as was Harvard lawyer and U.S. artillery reservist Leslie Field of MARS Equipment and Centennial Arms companies in Chicago. I was first vice president, and as editor of the official journal, *The Machine Gunner*, began laying out

The 9mm Parabellum United Defense Gun was built by High Standard in WWII as a commercial/military gun, and was sometimes used by the OSS. A solidly-built arm, it was sold cheaply as a "Dewat" in the late 1950s. It's a rare item today.

High Standard created this experimental belt-fed T10E3 gun in WWII, based on the BAR locking. The feed mechanism is similar to the Marriner A Browning of 1934. Variant and experimental guns are super rare in MG collecting.

Author about 1954, wearing Buffalo Bill Cody's jacket and hat on loan from museum, fits Accles drum feed onto experimental Colt 1890 Gatling "police gun" from the John Amber collection. Colt Navy revolver in the belt holster was "interchangeable test" parts gun used as the prototype in 1957 for replica gun production in Italy.

The horse, which they said would never get replaced, was replaced. Here, a Vickers Maxim in British service in WWI is shown in the pack harness. Forty years later, GIs met identical Maxims on Russian Sokolev wheeled mounts as used by North Korean and Chicoms in heavy fighting in Korea.

the first issue with stories on automatic arms. Dick Boutelle, then president of Fairchild and boss of the Armalite program, bought a full page ad, as did Frank Cowdrey of Harrington & Richardson. Col. Ellis Lea, then Army director of civilian markmanship, heartily endorsed our program to me in personal conversation. And then the roof fell in . . .

Powerful influences had caused the Treasury ATU to prepare a schedule of "Revised Regulations" in June 1957. These "revised regulations" are substantially the restrictions on imported surplus and interstate sales and against inexpensive guns, which eventually became law in the Gun Control Act of 1968.

When at the Treasury Revised Regulations hearings I announced that Col. Lea was in favor of helping the AAWA, the anti-gun forces took action. The Treasury was the active arm, threatening to indict the officers of the AAWA for violation of the NFA despite its registration as a "dealer" and the payment of the requisite taxes. Hunt, Field and I had pooled our personal machineguns, and *rewatted* several Dewats, that is, restored them to operating condition. These were to become the AAWA's museum group, for the study of systems and use by the directors to formulate training and range firing programs. Restoring a gun, rewatting, was considered "manufacturing, for sale or distribution," but these guns were not for sale nor were they to be distributed. All the guns were registered, and, according to law, taxes paid. But the ATU's enforcement chief, Oscar T. Neal, held otherwise.

With Neal ramrodding, and with the fullest approval of the Secretary of the Treasury, Colonel Lea was

The stalemate of the trenches bogged war and warriors down in years-long struggle over a few hundred yards of ground because heavy Maxims, dug in and massed along trenches, made bloody fire lanes against advancing troops. Most-used Maxim was the MG 08, on a sled mount and carried by two gunners with the sled flattened like a stretcher. Photo of the author, taken in the 1950s in a quiet grove south of Chicago, shows the gun in the lowest position.

forced to retract his support. The NRA even furnished a ready platform for the new restrictions by publishing a column against the AAWA, and Treasury lawyers whetted their knives to lay into us for 22 multiple violations of the NFA. Yes, with threat of thousands of dollars in fines and 44 years in jail, I felt a bit uneasy. And Art Hunt, we learned, was vulnerable.

Hunt was then in his mid 40s. Years earlier, when he was still a kid, he had acquired a number of machineguns. Some were Dewats, and some were veteran-post giveaways — "Get that thing out of here kid, it's cluttering up the place." Most of those went into his basement. When he was 15, his mother took up that same refrain, and young Art — unmindful of laws, which, after all, were only for criminals — cleaned out the basement. He gave some away, sold others to friends, and sold half of them to a gun dealer. He was "turned in." His lawyer, instead of citing his youth and mitigating circumstances, pleaded him guilty.

Faced with the inevitable, even the most generous judge is left with no choice but to inflict a penalty. The judge gave Hunt a suspended sentence, but it was a fed-

The British "Tommy Atkins" and his brother Johnny loaded down with everything but the kitchen sink and jammed into a motorcycle sidecar outfit for WWI-style Blitzkrieg. The Vickers Maxim water-cooled gun has the regular tripod folded and the barrel jacket sports an auxiliary stand which was little more than a camera tripod for low ground profile when dismounted. The sidecar is fitted with heavy armor plate to give protection during assault fire on the advance. Webley Mark III 38s are in left-side belt holsters of probably experimental but certainly unacceptable design as the sidecar passenger's holster has become detached from his belt. Tray over sidecar wheel held spare ammo can.

eral crime and it did make Art a convicted felon under the law. The ATU gleefully lost no time in telling those who were supporters of the AAWA of this fact, and we suspended business.

On advice of counsel we surrendered our 22 machineguns to the ATU. Not wanting to see them go into the smelter, I called my friend Col. Magruder of the USMC Museum at Quantico to "requisition" these arms for the Marine Corps Museum. I didn't regret losing my 1921 Thompson overstamped 1928, as it was returned to the Marines who had lost it in Nicaragua, and I was happy to see my Marlin-made Colt 1914 grasshopper gun on a landing carriage on display in the museum. Thus, the first American association of machinegun collectors and shooters passed into history . . .

Following those first Browning Automatic Rifles "at the bottom of a Danish Arsenal" came many more collectible machineguns. Martin B. Retting and Pasadena Firearms, retailing as "Golden State Arms Co.," had much to do with releasing machineguns to the collectors' market. Golden State brought in thousands of submachine guns, relics of the Chaco Wars in South America, and also a lovely assortment of Lewis Guns from Ireland, along with thousands of M1917 Enfields. Johnson LMGs by the hundreds were welded, sold to Fidel's agents, then turned up back in service in the Orient. From Canada, Cummings bought lots of 50-caliber M2 Brownings for $25 each, then teamed them up with state department-furnished Ground Gun Kits to go to Central American governments for $175 — still bargain-priced.

When Bill Sucher offered me some 3800 machineguns, including about 1000 MG-34s and about 900 MG-42s, I felt "something" could be done with them. We tried to

An instructor with the BEF in France removes the sixth round in the belt to prevent rookie gunner from blasting away more than five in a burst. MG collectors find shooting their hobby guns exciting and costly as a few minutes' rattle can exhaust a case of ammo. A Chinese ambassador once declined to buy Maxim guns, saying they would bankrupt his kingdom in a few minutes. Solutions to these problems have since been found, by collectors as well as war ministers.

sell the MG-42s to the state of Illinois as reserve or emergency arms for $25 each, since we could have had the whole lot in the Antwerp bonded zone for $10,000. But the Dewat program had just been shut off, and with that $200 transfer tax before us, we just didn't see much use for 3800 active machineguns in the U.S. in 1958 . . .

The mobile MG brigade met with success in a raid on German trenches at Contamaison, on the "western front," in WWI. Armor plates show bullet splashes but victorious Brits returned with souvenir "pickelhauben," defeating troops armed with M1888 Commission model rifles.

Val Forgett (now of Navy Arms) and the author admiring a like-new Johnson M1941 light machinegun fresh off the boat from Holland. Scene is in front of International Armaments Corporation's Alexandria, Virginia office in 1956, after Edwards had suggested Interarms import such collector machineguns and weld them into "unserviceable" Dewats so they could be sold without restriction. So welded, this gun retailed for $49 in the '50s, would bring several thousands today.

Times have certainly changed. Today there are about 125,000 registered operating machineguns in private hands in America. Not one registered gun has been involved in a crime. Recent changes in the law have prohibited the manufacture of machineguns for private sale, although existing guns may be legally sold as before by paying the taxes. Thus, there is no large-scale market for MG parts, as it is not now legal to "make a firearm" even if it is not for sale or distribution. Recent manufacturing often consisted of rebuilding, through rewelding and re-manufacturing, burned and scrapped guns. New parts are combined with old and when re-Parkerized and testfired, a gun equal to new, although restored, is again "on the firing line."

With the high tax and the restrictions on import and manufacture, one might think the interest in collecting machineguns is ending. Far from it. Restriction by limiting the numbers of guns does introduce an element of monopoly into the marketplace. Prices go up. Not so much the "forbidden fruit" lure, but the challenge of scarcity will prompt many who have no great need for a machinegun to buy one if they can pay the price. And what has happened to that price? The tax now has the same relation to many machinegun sales that the ordinary sales tax of 4 or 6 percent has to the price of a loaf of bread.

In Virginia, where machineguns must be registered "within 24 hours with the state police on a form to be supplied for that purpose," Dick Chandler, the energetic chief of Chesterfield Armament, will furnish you with a like-new 50-caliber Browning ground gun for the modest tag of $5000. If the sales tax is 4 percent, you'd expect to pay an additional $200 anyway! But these are probably signs of the times.

When the AAWA went to the Chicago ATU office to pay

taxes on its machineguns back in 1957, the special tax stamps received were crumbling, yellowing issues of 1934. With the transfers — hundreds of thousands of them — of legal machineguns to collectors in recent years, I suppose the Treasury has probably printed some new tax stamps. And from the kind of interest reflected in prices of $2000 for those "$20 BARs," and $5000 for those $49.95 Tommy Guns of yesteryear, I sure hope they printed enough of them . . .

Machinegun collecting has indeed come of age! ●

The man considered the "father" of the war surplus gun business, Lt. Col. G.B. Jarrett of the Foreign Material Branch, Aberdeen Proving Ground. He's holding one of his favorites, a WWI Villar Perosa dual submachine gun.

One of the most sought after of the "Tommy Gun" variants is the Model 1927 Thompson Semi-Automatic Carbine. Unfortunately, its barrel was still under the magic 16-inch minimum specified by the National Firearms Act of 1934, so ownership and transfer came under government supervision.

46   A. F. STOEGER, Inc., 509 Fifth Avenue, NEW YORK, N. Y.

Thompson Anti-Bandit Sub-Machine Gun

Model No. 21 (With Cutts Compensator)

Specifications: Caliber .45 Weight 9 pounds, 11 ounces. Length 33 inches. Length of Barrel 12½ inches. Equipped with Lyman sights and wind gauge. 20 cartridge capacity magazine. Ammunition caliber .45 Colt Automatic Pistol Ball Cartridges. Rate of Fire—600 shots per minute full automatically, or up to 100 aimed shots per minute semi-automatically firing single shots. Gun also with CUTTS COMPENSATOR (extra). This device stabilizes the gun when fired rapidly and reduces recoil to practically nothing. For Thompson Sub-machine Guns Model 1921, Cutts Compensators control the tendency of muzzle rising in full automatic machine gun fire.

The Thompson Anti-Bandit Gun is a new type of firearm combining the portability of a rifle with the effectiveness of a machine gun and was especially designed as an auxiliary to police departments and for the protection of Banks, Payrolls, Plants, Warehouses, Mines, Ranches, Railroads and Business Property of all kinds. Adopted and used by the U. S. Marine Corps, U. S. Navy Landing Forces, New York, Chicago, Detroit, Philadelphia, San Francisco, etc. Police Departments—Guaranty Trust Co., N. Y., and many Federal Reserve Banks. State Police, Texas Rangers, Northwest Mounted Police, National Guards and many other law enforcement bodies or business.

TAC Thompson Sub-machine gun complete with Cutts Compensator and one 20 Cartridge capacity box magazine.
Price .... $200.00 Each

TACC Thompson Sub-machine gun complete with 20 capacity box magazine but without Cutts Compensator.
Price .... $175.00 Each

TAC 1 20 shot magazine, ball cartridges, box model .... $3.00 Each
TAC 2 18 shot magazine for shot cartridges (special) .... $3.00 Each
TAC 3 50 shot magazine, ball cartridges, drum model .... $21.00 Each
TAC 4 Discontinued
TAC 5 Canvas web gun case (specify for TAC or TACC gun) .... $16.50 Each
TAC 6 Canvas web belt only for carrying magazines .... $2.00 Each
TAC 7 Canvas web base for 50 drum magazine .... $5.00 Each
TAC 8 Discontinued
TAC 9 Four pocket web case for four 20 shot box magazine .... $5.00 Each

Same prices for Carbine Model, shooting semi-automatically only.
All sales subject to State and Federal Laws.
SEND YOUR GUN TO STOEGER'S FOR REPAIRS

American Automatic Weapons Association
PUBLISHERS OF "THE MACHINE GUNNER"
517 EAST 32ND STREET   GRAND RAPIDS, MICHIGAN

ASSOCIATION OFFICERS
ARTHUR J. HUNT, Pres.
WM. B. EDWARDS, 1st Vice-Pres.
L. E. FIELD, 2nd Vice-Pres.
LT. COL. GEO. M. CHINN, USMC, RETD
3rd Vice-Pres.
L. A. HUNT, Treas.
ROBT. S. BROOKS, Sec't.

LEGISLATIVE BOARD
R. KEITH HUDSON, Ph.D.
L. E. FIELD
ROBT. S. BROOKS, Lt. Col., USAFR
S. B. SAXTON

TECHNICAL ADVISORY BOARD
VAL FORGETT, JR.
FRED A. DATIG
KENT BELLAH
STEWART E. RAUCH, JR., Lt. Cmdr. USNR
NILS KVALE, Sweden
LT. COL. G. B. JARRETT, USA, RETD

24 May, 1957

Mr Samuel M Cummings,
Vice President,
International Armaments Corp.,
5229 Manning Place NW
Washington DC 7

Dear Sam:

Please find enclosed check $40 in payment for one
TSMG 1921/28 "Nicaraguan" @ $27. and case 1200 rds
.45 ball ammo. I think I have included enough for
Express.

Please ship to my attention at:
        4923½ S Greenwood Ave.,
        Chicago, Ill. 37,
and notify me by separate Air Mail at time of shipment.
Thank you.

Sincerely,

William B. Edwards
1st Vice President

Page from Stoeger's 1929 catalog showing a typical "Tommy Gun" advertisement from the days before the NFA of 1934 clamped down on private machinegun ownership.

Author's 1957 order to Interarms for a Dewat "Tommy Gun" — for $27, plus shipping! Note the names on the AAWA letterhead.

WILLIAM H. BAKER: DOUBLE-BARRELED ENTREPRENEUR

by JIM C. COBB

AMONG the early pioneers in the American breech-loading shotgun industry such as Charles Parker, Dan Lefever, F.A. Holenbeck, William H. Baker and Ansley Fox, Baker stands out as the most influential. Though he perhaps did not have the inventive genius of Dan Lefever or even the corporate wisdom of Charles Parker, he did have entrepreneurship, the ability to see the need for a product and provide the services and the ability to bring together those individuals who could provide the services and their inventions to market. He knew how to get things organized. The Baker name, though not so widely known, is among the more important names in American shotguns. Baker helped form the L.C. Smith Gun Company, Ithaca Gun Company, Syracuse Gun Company and, of

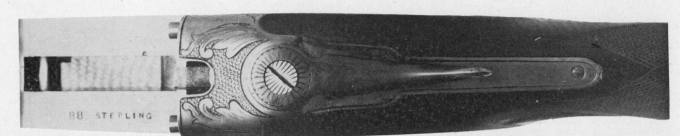

In 1909, Baker introduced a single-barrel trap shotgun in three grades: Sterling (shown), Elite and Superbra. Prices ranged from $65 to $160. These guns are scarce today as they were made in limited numbers.

A CARD.

—:o:—

Having many inquiries as to what distinguishes the "ITHACA GUN" from the original "Baker Gun," of which I was the inventor, and for a time the manufacturer, I will say: The "ITHACA GUN" has the top lever, instead of the trigger action, an entirely new arrangement of locks, and construction, making it more desirable in every respect; for which reason it was thought best not to have it conflict in name with the old gun.

Sincerely thanking my numerous friends for their liberal appreciation of my efforts to produce such work as our progressive shooting demands, and trusting that the "ITHACA GUN" will continue to merit their patronage and that the pleasant business relations formerly existing, may be continued with the Ithaca Gun Co. I am

Very Truly,

W. H. BAKER.

Ithaca, N. Y., May, 1885.

This note from W.H. Baker appeared in the 1886 Ithaca Gun catalog. Baker and L.H. Smith founded the Ithaca company in 1883.

course, the firm that later bore his name — Baker Gun & Forging Company.

William Baker was born in 1835, one of seven children. His younger brother, Ellis, who was later to become a most influential factor in William's career, was born in 1845. W.H. Baker became a gunmaker, while his younger brother pursued a career in medicine. It was this younger brother who, in Lisle, NY, first became associated with George Livermore and L.H. Smith (the founders of the L.C. Smith Gun Company). By 1878, William, his brother Ellis, L.H. Smith and Livermore had gravitated from Lisle to Syracuse, New York. At that time they came in contact with L.C. Smith (for Lyman Cornelius, L.H.'s brother) and persuaded him to join a new firm called the W.H. Baker and Sons Company of Syracuse, New York, located at 20 Walton Street.

The guns they produced were double-trigger, break-action, double barrel and combination rifle and shotgun drillings, which were made under the W.H. Baker patent of August 31, 1875. Under this partnership, guns were made for 2 years, until 1880. In 1880, L.C. Smith bought out the Baker brothers and his own brother, L.H. Smith, and formed his own company. The guns were of the same design and were marked on the rib **L.C. Smith and Com-**

This top view of the 1909 Sterling trap gun shows nice engraving and excellent wood to metal fit. Gun sold for $65.

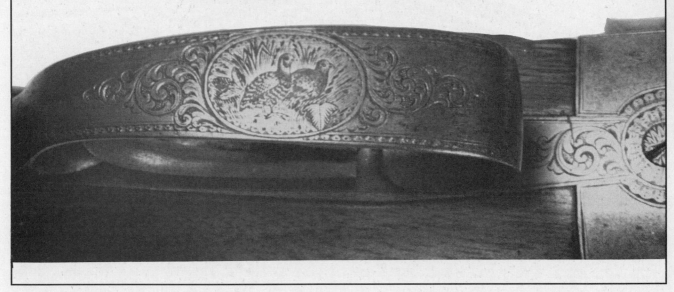

The trigger guard of this Paragon Standard Model shows fairly extensive engraving, it being the lowest grade. It was available in 10-, 12- or 16-gauge and sold for $82.50 in 1909.

pany, Makers of Baker Guns. The Baker patent dates also appeared on the lockplate.

After L.C. Smith bought out the partnership in 1883, L.H. Smith and W.H. Baker moved to Ithaca, New York to form a new gun company called the Ithaca Gun Company. Their guns were also of the Baker patent and design and were hammer boxlock guns, rather than the now familiar sidelock models which were also in production at that time. The design had an unusual feature; shotgun hammers were usually mounted on a detachable sideplate, but the Baker design was a boxlock with the hammers located in the rear of the assembly. The partnership, at that time, consisted of Baker, L.H. Smith, George Livermore, Lou Smith, J.E. Van Nita and Dwight McIntire.

W.H. Baker was again bought out and he left Ithaca, New York. Apparently, W.H. was never content with "status quo" and thus was continually on the move. In 1887, he moved back to Syracuse, New York, where he rejoined his younger brother to form the Syracuse Forging Company. This new company produced two hammer model guns and later a hammerless gun before fire destroyed the firm. The

company then relocated to Batavia, New York and formed the Batavia Gun & Forging Company to make guns under both the Baker and Batavia names.

In 1899, the company introduced its first hammerless sidelock gun, available at that time in grades A or B. These guns strongly resembled the L.C. Smith guns of that same vintage. The chief difference between the A and B grades was that the A Grade had Damascus barrels and the B Grade London twist barrels. The firm was very safety conscious and expressed concern in the catalogs for the safety of the then "new-fangled" hammerless guns.

Both A and B grades sported very nicely engraved hunting scenes featuring birds and dogs. It is very difficult to tell one grade from the other by examination. About the only way to accurately distinguish Grade A from Grade B is on the barrel lug, where the letter D indicates Damascus, and thus an A Grade. The B Grade sports a T on the barrel, indicating twist barrels. Both the A and B grade models met with success so the company then began marketing its new Paragon Grade, which actually was four different grades, though all were called Paragon.

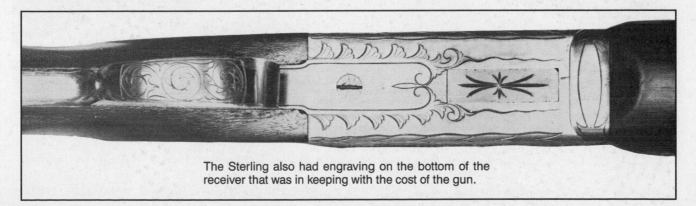

The Sterling also had engraving on the bottom of the receiver that was in keeping with the cost of the gun.

PARAGON GRADE
MADE TO ORDER ONLY

Paragon Grade, Ejector, 12, 16 and 20-Gauge, weights 6 to 8 lbs. $115.00
Paragon Grade, Non-ejector, 12, 16 and 20-Gauge, weights 6 to 8 lbs. 100.00
Single Trigger, extra.. 40.00
Soft Rubber Recoil Pad, extra... 5.50
34-inch Barrels on 12-Gauge, extra.. 16.50

    Barrels—Finest quality fluid steel, high tensile strength, bored and fitted with extreme care. Boring tested by shooting into 30-inch circle at forty yards.

Stock—Selected figured Walnut, beautifully checkered and polished. Straight, full or half pistol grip as ordered.

    Locks and Action—Regular Baker system with taper wedge fastening and extra cross-bolt, positively guaranteed never to shoot loose with standard loads of smokeless powder. Lock and action finely fitted and polished and special design of lock plates.

    Engraving—Elaborately engraved in beautiful artistic scroll and pictorial design.

The lowest Paragon Grade was the Standard. It featured either fine close Damascus or Krupp fluid-compressed steel barrels. The stock and forend were of fancy European walnut, beautifully finished, and could be furnished in full, half pistol grip, or straight grip. The metal was nicely engraved with scroll and pictorial designs, usually consisting of pointing bird dogs. Available in 10, 12, and 16 gauges, the Para-

The Baker Batavia Leader sold for $40 in 1915. The barrels were "Special imported 'Cockerel' steel, bored for black or nitro powders."

The Baker Paragon Grade of 1915 sold for $115 and was offered on a "made to order" basis only.

gon Standard Grade with automatic ejectors sold for $82.50 in 1909.

Next step up was the Paragon Ninety-Nine, which was very similar to the Standard Grade but more richly finished. It was offered with automatic ejectors for $95, also with choice between Damascus or Krupp fluid steel barrels. The next highest grade was the Expert, priced at $150 with automatic ejectors. It could be had with either Damascus or Hol-

BATAVIA LEADER

12, 16 or 20 Gauge $40.00

    The **BATAVIA LEADER** Grade is designed to give the greatest value at a moderate price. No more serviceable gun can be made at any price. These guns are made to standard specifications only. For special weights and specifications, see **Black Beauty Special Grade**. Weight of 12-gauge gun with 30-inch barrels, about 7¾ pounds. Other gauges and lengths in proportion.

    Barrels—Special Imported "Cockerel" steel, bored for black or nitro powders.

    Stock—Selected Walnut, full capped pistol grip. Drop at comb, 1¾ inches; drop at heel, 2⅞ inches; length, 14 inches.

    Locks and Action—Fitted with side lock plates which may readily be taken off for cleaning, etc. The 4-piece lock construction is simple and functions perfectly. Never shoots loose.

    Finish—The checkering, case-hardening, blueing, etc., is artistically done and surpasses that of other guns in this class.

BLACK BEAUTY SPECIAL

Weights: 12-Gauge, 6½ to 8 lbs.; 16-Gauge, 6¼ to 7 lbs.; 20-Gauge, 6 to 6½ lbs.
12, 16 or 20 Gauge $62.00
Automatic Ejector, extra 15.00

The BLACK BEAUTY SPECIAL. This grade is designed especially for those desiring a moderate-priced gun made up to their individual specifications and with finer finish than the Batavia Leader.

Barrels—Special steel, bored for black or nitro powders. All guns are carefully tested for targets at forty yards shooting into a 30-inch circle.

Stock—Selected Walnut, hand-fitted, and straight, full or half pistol grip, any reasonable length or drop, without extra charge.

Locks and Action—Regular Baker system with taper wedge fastening, guaranteed not to shoot loose with any standard loads of smokeless powder. Frame is case-hardened and action is richly finished.

Engraving—Top of frame is neatly matted; balance of frame, guard and lock plates are neatly engraved with line engraving making this an attractive model at a medium price.

Baker's Black Beauty Special sidelock gun retailed at $62 in 1915 and was available in 12-, 16- or 20-gauge. Automatic ejectors were $15 extra.

land fluid steel barrels, and was elaborately engraved and very highly finished. It could be finished to any reasonable specification or style of stock at no extra charge. The highest grade was the Deluxe model, priced at $300, and furnished with a choice of Damascus steel barrels or Sir Joseph Whitworth fluid-compressed steel barrels, which were supposedly the highest quality barrels obtainable in the world.

It should be noted here that both the Krupp and Whitworth fluid steel barrels were used by several different gunmakers, among them Lefever, L.C. Smith, Ithaca and Parker. The Whitworth barrels were used only in the top-of-the-line models of these gun companies: the Optimus Grade by Lefever; the Deluxe by L.C. Smith; the Grade 7 by Ithaca; and A-1 Special by Parker.

In Baker's mid-range grade guns, the Grade R was a popular choice. It was available in 12- and 16-gauge only and featured a choice of Damascus or Krupp fluid steel barrels. It was finished with European walnut, was not as elaborately engraved as the Paragon models and not quite as nicely finished. In 1909 it was priced at $58.75 with automatic ejectors.

The Grade S was Baker's next lower grade. It was furnished with flue-tempered steel only and had scroll-type engraving on the lock. It was available in 10-, 12- and 16-gauge in semi-pistol grip only. The lower end of the Baker gun grades consisted of the Batavia Ejector, Batavia Damascus, Batavia Leader and Batavia Special. All of these guns were very similar in appearance, the most significant difference between them being the type of barrel and/or use of automatic ejectors. The Batavia Ejector model was furnished with either Damascus or Homo-tensile fluid blue steel. Its price with steel barrels was $35, and with Damascus barrels $37. The Batavia Damascus was very similar to the Batavia Ejector, but did not have auto ejectors and was furnished only with Damascus barrels. It was priced at $28. The Batavia Leader was the next grade, furnished with London twist barrels, which were a type of Damascus steel, and priced at $25. The Batavia Special was fitted with Homo-tensile brown steel barrels, which were said to be as strong as any barrels of the day. That was the lowest priced hammerless gun of the Baker line in 1909. The Batavia line of guns are

the guns most frequently seen in used gun shops today. They are all very similar in design, and the only distinguishing difference is the type of barrel steel used.

In 1909, Baker introduced a trap model shotgun, a single barrel gun in three grades — the Sterling, Elite and Superbra. Prices ranged from $65 to $160. Those guns are rare as they were only made in limited numbers. During the years 1910 to 1915, Baker introduced a new boxlock gun available with either Krupp fluid steel or Nitro rolled barrels. They were of similar design to the early Grade C and Syracuse boxlock guns, and are also rare.

In 1919, the gun division of the Baker Forging Company sold out to the H. & D. Folsom Company of Folsom, New York. The Folsom Arms Co., the maker and importer of dozens of brands of firearms, continued to assemble Baker-made parts into Baker guns for several years from the existing parts in inventory. Folsom introduced the Folsom Batavia Leader, which was made in 12-, 16-, and 20-gauge, and a rather rare 410-gauge. The Folsom-made Bakers have the letter F as a suffix to the serial number which distinguishes the Baker Batavia guns from Folsom, New York guns. Generally, Folsom-numbered firearms are somewhat less valuable than Baker guns. Apparently, the last Baker guns were made around 1930.

Values of Bakers today are rather difficult to determine as they are generally little appreciated by collectors. The high-grade Bakers are not seen too frequently and command a much higher price, of course, than the low- or common-grade guns. The Paragons are seen infrequently; however I have seen one Grade Ninety-Nine priced at $1,250. The S and R grades would generally be priced between $500 and $750; the lower-grade Batavia ejectors and Batavia Leaders anywhere from $250 to $400. The later Folsom-made 20-gauge guns command a higher value, even though they were made by Folsom, while the 410s command a top price as they are relatively rare. Baker single-barrel trap models will bring from $600 for the lowest up to $1,500 for the highest grade, in excellent condition. All of the above values are for guns that are in excellent, original condition and have steel barrels. Damascus-barrel guns bring approximately 50 percent less. ●

A standard pre-1916 Gew.98. Note the old-style marking disc on the butt. (Author's collection)

The Guns of the GERMAN NAVY 1914-1918

by DOUGLAS BLACK

ASK MOST non-specialist collectors what firearms the German navy used during World War I and most will reply that the sailors carried a Mauser rifle or a "Navy Luger." However, though this contains an element of truth — Gewehre 98 and Pistolen 1904 were indeed issued in large numbers — the actual issues were far more complicated than supposed. The best way to introduce the German navy small arms is to consider the changes in the rifles ordered in the fiscal years 1905 to 1908.

Ordnance Revolver 79. Despite its length (14 inches) and weight (over 3 pounds, loaded), many of these antiquated old troopers continued to serve the Kaiser in both naval and land service through WWI. (Joseph J. Schroeder collection)

Captured Russian rifles were often used by the navy. Here, men of the fifth company of I.Matrosen-Division (Kiel) pose for a photo in 1918. (Engleman collection, via Anthony Carter)

Small Arms

1905

Gew.98: 26,925 were to be issued to I. and II.Matrosen-Division (16,100), I. and II.Seebataillone (7177), the Minenkompagnie (300) and I. and II.Torpedo-Abteilungen (3848).

Gew.71/84: 17,145 were issued to I.Matrosen-Division (6000), and a total of 9750 among the four Matrosen-Artillerie-Abteilungen. A total of 500 was issued to the two Torpedo-Abteilungen, on the scale of 250 apiece, while 895 went to the "Augmentationsschiffe" of III. and IV.Matrosen-Artillerie-Abteilungen.

Jägerbüchse 71: 6803 were issued to I.Matrosen-Division (1818) and the two Werft-Divisionen (4985). In 1905, therefore, a total of 50,873 rifles (plus 172 Revolvers 79) satisfied the needs of the active land-based navy units. In addition, approximately 15,000 guns (mostly Gew.98s) were carried aboard the ships.

1906

The distribution of the rifles was similar to the previous year's, except the additional issues of Gew.98s to the two Matrosen-Divisionen: I.M.D. had 8900 and II.M.D., 8200. A few hundred additional guns were issued to I.Torpedo-Abteilung, whose Gew.71/84s had been withdrawn for partial re-issue to I.Matrosen-Artillerie-Abteilung. The land-based rifle total amounted to 52,327: 28,729 Gew.98s, 16,795 Gew.71/84s and 6803 Jägerbüchsen 71, plus the same 172 revolvers.

1907

A considerable re-allocation had taken place, I. Matrosen-Division receiving additional Gew.98s in exchange for its Jägerbüchsen. The issues were:

Gew.98: I.Matrosen-Division, 10,544; II.Matrosen-Division, 8400; I.Werft-Division, 40; I.Torpedo-Division, 2548; II.Torpedo-Division[1], 2874; I.Seebataillon, 3906; II.Seebataillon, 3271; Minenabteilung, 598; and III.Matrosen-Artillerie-Abteilung, 289. Total: 32,470.

Gew.71/84: A total of 16,639 distributed among I. Matrosen-Division (6100); the four Matrosen-Artillerie-Abteilungen (9644); and the "Hilfschiffe" of III. and IV.Matrosen-Artillerie-Abteilungen (895).

Jägerbüchse 71: 4985 to the Werft-Divisionen.

The total number of rifles in land service amounted to 54,094, plus 331 Pistolen 1904 (Parabellums, or Lugers) replacing the obsolete revolvers.

1908

By 1908, with the modernization of the navy well underway, all the surviving Jägerbüchsen 71 had

[1]Enlarged and renamed versions of the Torpedo-Abteilungen.

A man and his ship: A sailor from *SMS Cöln* (see p. 92), a 4300-ton light cruiser built by Krupp's Germaniawerft shipyard in Kiel. The ship was launched in June, 1909 and commissioned on June 16, 1911. The back of the original photo is marked, "In commemoration of the days spent with the airship crews at Kiel, 1914" and is signed "Joseph Oberberger." He carries a Gew. 71/84.

been withdrawn from the active units. In addition, large numbers of the Gew.98s had also been withdrawn, counterbalanced by new issues of the Gew.71/84s. They are believed to have gone to the warships in exchange for the older Mausers.

Gew.98: The total issue was 18,349, only the two Seebataillone retaining their 1907 issue levels. The two Matrosen-Divisionen now only had 5292 Gew.98s, compared with about 19,000 the previous year, while the Werft-Divisionen inventory was increased to 3362. A few guns remained with the Matrosen-Artillerie-Abteilungen, but all rifles had been withdrawn from the Torpedo-Divisionen—who were subsequently to get pistols instead.

Gew.71/84: These were issued only to the two Matrosen-Divisionen—I.M.D. had 7397, II.M.D. 6306—and the four Matrosen-Artillerie-Abteilungen, which had 10,376. There were 24,079 Gew.71/84s in the

The *SMS Cöln* in the Kaiser-Wilhelm-Kanal sometime before 1914. *Cöln* was sunk at the battle of Heligoland Bight shortly after the outbreak of WWI. Was Oberberger on her at the time . . .? (Photo courtesy LPI archives)

active land-based units, making the 1908 rifle total only 42,428. The Pistole 1904 allocation remained unchanged from the previous year.

Rifles

Apart from their distinctive property marks (Table 1), the navy rifles were the same as the standard army issue.

The earliest single shot bolt-action Mausers presented a rather dated appearance. The army's Infanterie-Gewehr M.1871 (adopted on March 22, 1872) had a full stock, two spring-retained barrel bands and a sling swivel on the trigger guard. Its brass-hilted sword bayonet had a muzzle ring and a stud/leaf spring attachment mating with the lug on right side of the nose cap.

As far as is known, no army rifles reached the Kaiserliche Marine prior to 1918; instead, the sailors used the Jägerbüchse M1871, adopted on January 18, 1876. That was essentially similar to the infantry rifle, but was shorter and had differing sight graduations. Also, the trigger guard was spurred, the rearmost sling swivel lay under the butt, and a turned-down muzzle crown accepted the leather-gripped Hirschfänger M.1871.

The navy Jägerbüchse 71 (as it came to be known) had replaced the old Dreyse needle rifle of 1854. A single shot bolt-action rifle firing an obsolete 11mm-caliber (.433-inch) cartridge loaded with blackpowder, it

A member of the Marinekorps surveys the Flanders coast from a well-prepared position. He is armed with a Gew.98. (Photo courtesy LPI archives)

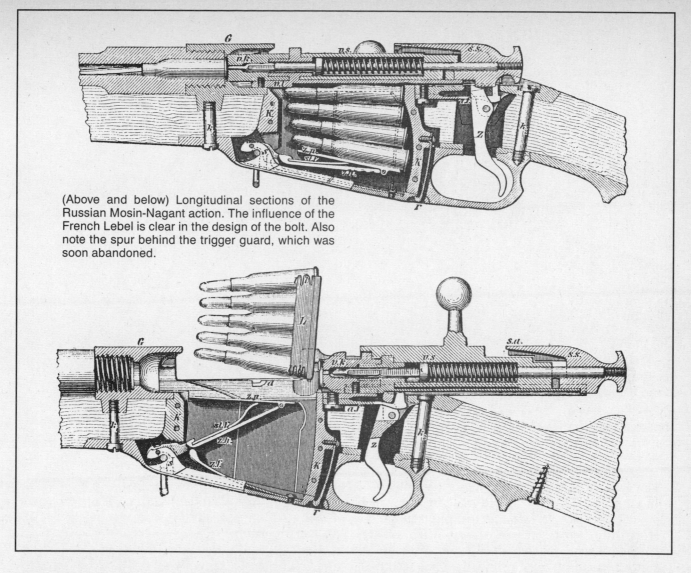

(Above and below) Longitudinal sections of the Russian Mosin-Nagant action. The influence of the French Lebel is clear in the design of the bolt. Also note the spur behind the trigger guard, which was soon abandoned.

measured 48.6 inches overall, had a 28.3-inch four-grooved barrel with an actual caliber of 11.15mm (.439-inch), and weighed about 9.7 pounds. The Patrone 71 was 3.07 inches long, weighed 1.53 ounces and was loaded with a round-headed lead bullet weighing 385 grains. The 77-grain charge of blackpowder generated a velocity of about 1410 fps at the muzzle. The standard rear sight had a fixed notch for 300 meters, a small hinged leaf for 400 and a large leaf-and-slider for distances between 500 and 1600 meters.

Preceded by an experimental "M.1882" rifle, the Infanterie-Gewehr M.1871/84 (adopted on January 31, 1884) was a modified 1871-type gun in which eight rounds could be placed in the tube magazine in the forend, beneath the barrel. A ninth round could be placed on the cartridge elevator and a 10th in the chamber. The Gew.71/84 was about 50 inches long and weighed something in excess of 5kg (11 lbs.) when loaded. Its sights were much the same as the Jägerbüchse 71, though the standing block and hinged leaf were for 200 and 300 meters, and the large leaf for 400 to 1600. Construction duplicated the M.1871, apart from the

magazine/elevator system and the addition of an ejector.

Prussian guns were made in the government arsenals in Danzig, Spandau and Erfurt; Bavarian guns in the state factory in Amberg; and Württemberg's by Gebrüder Mauser's successor — Waffenfabrik Mauser AG. Only Prussian guns will normally be encountered with navy markings. The Gew.71/84 was originally issued with a short knife-type bayonet with a 10-inch blade, a 17mm-diameter (.67-inch) muzzle ring on its short crossguard, an internal coil-spring press stud in the pommel and shaped-back wooden grips. The Patrone 71/84 was very similar to its predecessor, but had a flattened nose and a deepened primer pocket to guard against accidental magazine explosions.

In army service, the Gew.71/84 was quickly replaced by the 8mm Gew.88. However, the new rifle had a comparatively short front-line life and never seemed to have reached the Kaiserliche Marine. The short-lived semi-experimental Gew.88/97 was also soon found deficient, and was replaced by the Gewehr 98 on April 5, 1898. The most obvious differences between

The original Mondragon rifle, the Mexican M.1908, had a conventional box magazine. The guns purchased for German service in WWI, however, were issued with a special "snail" magazine made by Hamburg-Amerikanischen Uhrenfabrik. (Author's collection)

the Gew.88/97 and the Gew.98 were the omission of the former's barrel jacket, the adoption of what has become recognized as the standard German Mauser nose cap (rather than the simpler "Export" pattern that requires a bayonet with a muzzle ring), a refined Lange-pattern rear sight and an improved stock with a short handguard stretching from ahead of the rear sight to the single spring-retained barrel band.

The Gew.98 had a standard Mauser turnbolt action, with a third, or "safety," lug and an internal five-round charger-loaded box magazine. It measured 49.2 inches overall, had a 29.1-inch barrel rifled with four grooves, and weighed approximately 9.04 pounds depending on the stock wood. It was originally issued with the Seitengewehr 98, a slender sword bayonet with a "pipe back" or strengthening rib along the blade back and a very distinctive hilt. In an attempt to isolate the bayonet from the rifle barrel, the Gew.98 had a sturdy twin-band nose cap with an abnormally long attachment bar to give sufficient rigidity to the mount without needing a muzzle ring on the bayonet. The crossguard has nothing but a short curving quillon.

The standard cartridge was originally the 8mm Patrone 88, but that was replaced by the 8mm S-Patrone on March 3, 1903. The S-Patrone weighed 0.84 ounces, was 3.16 inches long and contained a flat-based round-nosed bullet weighing 154 grains. The charge of 49.4 grains of Gewehrblattchenpulver S enabled the bullet to reach a muzzle velocity of about 2935 fps. Converted guns generally display an "S" atop the chamber. A modified Lange sight was approved on June 2, 1905, appreciably taller than its predecessor and with a much modified slider. In addition, the extractors were greatly strengthened in effect on December 12, 1905 and an auxiliary sight (or "Hilfskorn") was adopted on December 22, 1914 to

correct the point-blank range settings — otherwise, the Gew.98 shot high at all ranges shorter than 400 meters. From 1915 onward, the marking disc inletted in the butt was replaced by a hollow tubular washer.

Until 1916, all rifles were stocked in walnut. However, supplies of properly-seasoned wood soon ran short and beech and birch substitutes were authorized on June 7, 1916, to be followed on January 10, 1917 by European maple (Ahornholz). Until the desperate days of 1918, those rifles were supposed to be restricted to second-line units. Their butts bore a large roman "B" or "A."

Navy units also carried the Karabiner 98AZ (adopted by the army on January 16, 1908), though distribution was limited; the first issues appear to have been made to the Maschinengewehr-Bedienungsmannschaften of III.Seebataillon (machinegun instructors of the third battalion of marines) in 1914. However, only 1700 of these short rifles were delivered to Kiel during World War I, compared to nearly 17,000 full-length rifles. According to a report from Flanders in July, 1917, the Gew.98 was carried by the Marine- and Matrosen-Infanterie, the coast and anti-aircraft artillery, and the Marine-Pionier-Kompagnien. Issue of the Kar.98AZ was restricted to the field and foot artillerymen, airmen and balloonists.

Once World War I began, however, navy authorities had to supply not only the ships of the battle fleets, but

(Above) The Mauser-Selbstladerkarabiner, shown here in the "Fliegergewehr" (flyer's rifle) version, was a complicated and expensive gun that required lubricated cartridges to function reliably. Accordingly, it was issued with a fitted case with eight magazines to assure an ample supply of properly-prepared ammunition. (Left) The trigger guard serves as the magazine release. (Joseph J. Schroeder collection)

also the land-based Marinekorps, which secured the coastal flank of the Western Front in Flanders. According to the 1909 Tirpitz Principles, the warships needed almost 20,000 Gew.98s even then — not including many of the vessels commissioned in 1910 to 1914 — while the budget for the fiscal year 1910 noted the requirements of the land-based naval units as 26,968 Gew.71/84s and 23,759 Gew.98s[2]. Consequently, the Kaiserliche Marine would have issued at least 50,000 modern Mauser rifles by the beginning of World War I. But virtually half of those were shipboard, and of no real use during a war.

It was soon clear that supplies of Gew.98s were insufficient to arm the ever-increasing numbers of men mobilizing for action. From May, 1915 until the end of the war, for instance, only 16,959 Gew.98s and 1700 Kar. 98AZs were delivered to the Kiel dockyard for the entire Baltic (Ostsee) district. Most of those had come from the Artillerie-Verwaltung Danzig, the artillery depots in Erfurt, Mainz and Spandau, and the Erfurt rifle factory (königlich Gewehrfabrik).

Fortunately for the navy quartermasters, the Germans were soon in the ascendant; on the Western Front, large quantities of French equipment were seized on the Marne, while even vaster stores were taken from the Russians in the East.

The simplest way of releasing Gew.98s for the Marinekorps (not to mention the army) was to issue the Kaiserliche Marine's warships and home-service units with "Beutegewehre," or captured rifles. The first guns — French Mle.86 and 86/93 Lebels — reached the navy in the middle of November, 1914, closely followed by Russian obr.1891g Mosin-Nagants. By November 6, 10,000 French and 7000 Russian guns had been received into navy stores. On November 25, the Baltic Station command reported the state of issue as:

Jägerbüchse 71: to the Baudivision.
Gew.71/84: to the Seewehrabteilung, Matrosen-Artillerie-Abteilung and I.Matrosen-Division.
Gew.98: to I.Ersatz-Seebataillon, recruits of I.Matrosen-Division and I.Matrosen-Artillerie-Abteilung, plus the guards at important military installations such as the Prinz Heinrich Bridge (over the Kiel Canal) and the locks at Holtenau.
French rifles: to I.Werft-Division and I.Flieger-Abteilung.

[2]This was the standard "Tirpitz" allocation (see p. 98); like all cruisers serving on overseas stations, *Emden* would have carried supplementary weapons authorized under Auslandzuschlag.

Russian rifles: to the dockyard and munitions-depot guards, as well as the Luftschiff-Detachment Kiel.

On October 1, 1915, Kiel's inventory of Beutegewehre stood at 9705, effectively releasing large numbers of Gew.98s for more important tasks. On April 14, machineguns had been withdrawn from U-Boats — which had been using them to destroy drifting mines — in return for two Russian rifles, with which the tasks were subsequently performed with much less ammunition waste. By September, three ex-Russian guns were being issued to patrol ships as anti-mine protection.

Surviving fragments of the dockyard inventories, which were submitted monthly from 1915 onward, indicate the diversity of rifle issue. In February, 1918, for example, Kiel reported its stocks of small arms as 3244 Gew.98s, 305 Kar. 98AZs, 566 Lebel-Gewerhe, 4405 "Russische Gewehre," two Jägerbüchsen 71, 484 Inf. Gew.71/84s, 200 FSK.15s (Mondragons), 13 Modell 79 revolvers and 2497 Pistolen 1904. Edged weapons included 1572 Seitengewehre 98/05, 261 S.98s, nine S.11 boarding cutlasses, 595 Hirschfänger 71, 13 S.71/84s, 40 S.84/98s and 46 Marine-Offizier-Säbel.

Automatic Weapons

The Kaiserliche Marine had acquired substantial numbers of Maxim-type machineguns prior to the army's standardization of the MG.08, the navy guns being identifiable by their brass barrel casing and simpler land mount. They are normally designated "MG.00," though the date year has never been authenticated. Most remained aboard the warships until the middle of the war — *SMS Emden* had four on her final cruise in 1914, the guns being stored under the forecastle — and then removed for land service.

However, the Kaiserliche Marine also made limited use of self-loading rifles, trials being undertaken with the Mauser and Mondragon patterns in 1915. A suitable gun was apparently being sought for the naval airmen (though, apparently, more for the ground-defense units than for aerial combat). Trials undertaken from September, 1915 on into the winter convinced authorities that the gas-operated 7mm Mondragon was more serviceable than the cumbersome, costly 8mm Mauser, even though to standardize the former would mean complicating ammunition supplies.[3]

Ultimately, the Mondragon was accepted as the "Flieger-Selbstlader-Karabiner M 15" (FSK.15) on December 2, 1915. The entire remaining stocks, about 3000 guns, were immediately purchased from Schweizerische Industrie-Gesellschaft in Switzerland.

---

[3]The ammunition was actually made in sequestered facilities in Belgium.

(Above) Early long-frame Pistole 1904. This example has the altered, restamped safety, and also bears the extremely rare pre-war U-Boat marking "U.A.5" (left) for "Unterseeboot Abteilung." (Joseph J. Schroeder collection)

Each Mondragon plus six 30-round box magazines cost RM 200, approximately one-sixth that of the Mauser. In addition, the Mondragons could be obtained in quantity at a time when monthly production of the Mausers could not exceed 15 guns.

Navy Mondragons were issued to the airmen, the airfield defense units, the observers' schools and Marinekorps storm troops. The guns were well liked and reasonably reliable, provided they were kept clean and fired good quality ammunition. Their "Achilles heel," however, was the capricious snail magazines manufactured by Hamburg-Amerikanischen Uhrenfabrik of Schramberg in 1916.

Toward the end of 1918, substantial numbers of Mondragon rifles were returned to Kiel, where the inventory stood at 429 in September with a further 35 serving in U-Boats. In addition, 13 Mauser-Selbstladegewehre, issued in limited numbers as the Modele 1916, had also been returned from naval air detachments.

The Mexican-designed Mondragon measured 45.3 inches overall, had a 24-inch four-grooved barrel and weighed 9.5 pounds empty. Its leaf sights were graduated to 2000 meters and the 7mm bullet attained a velocity of 2165 fps, 80 feet from the muzzle. Though the length of Mauser Selbstladekarabiner was similar, the gun weighed 10.6 pounds and had recoil-actuated "flap

A group of sailors from I.Torpedo-Division, Kiel, pose on completion of their basic infantry training on November 14, 1913. Note the fine array of Pistolen 1904 and the then-standard boarding cutlass, the Seitengewehr 1911. (Hartmut Kordeck collection, via Reinhard Kornmayer)

locks" rather than the gas-operated Mondragon's rotary bolt. However, it developed greater power — firing the standard (though the cases had to be lubricated) 8mm cartridge at 2725 fps.

Luger Pistols

The Germans flirted with many experimental pistols in the early 20th century. The Mauser C96 was initially favored until persistent jamming problems allowed other guns into contention. Testing undertaken in 1901 to 1903 proved that the Borchardt-Luger (by then renamed "Parabellum") had the greatest potential, and once the case mouth had been opened out to receive a 9mm-diameter bullet — straightening the previously bottlenecked case — it was sufficiently lethal. During the summer of 1904, the Imperial navy began trials of its own. Previously, obsolete 10.6mm-caliber revolvers (M.1879) had been carried in shipboard armories for some of the members of a landing party — officers, petty officers, signalmen, engineers, stretcher bearers and machinegunners.

The trial reports submitted to the Imperial navy office (Reichs-Marine-Amt) in the late summer of 1904 all agreed that the pistols were far superior to the revolvers, and much handier than rifles; consequently, 8000 guns were ordered from DWM on December 12, 1904. No deliveries of the perfected coil-spring guns were made until the Spring of 1906 and no issues to naval personnel were made until the following year. The first bulk deliveries of naval pistols were not what is now generally identified as the "1904 Navy Luger," but rather of what could be called the "9mm interim model." The *true* navy Pistole 1904 is the so-called Second Issue, with a coil mainspring but no toggle lock. Navy Lugers all had 15cm (6-inch) barrels, a unique two-position sliding rear sight on the back toggle link, and a standard grip safety mechanism. Their safety-levers were originally of the "up-safe" pattern. Internally, the mainsprings bore on the toggle through an intermediate lever.

The introduction of the Pistole 1904 coincided with an acceleration of German naval construction caused when the commissioning of *HMS Dreadnought* reduced the superiority of the Royal Navy by eclipsing the "pre-dreadnought" battleships and large armored cruisers. Estimates of September, 1905, calling for about 6900 navy Parabellums, were superseded by a new plan conceived in great secret. Initialed by Admiral von Tirpitz on June 4, 1909, this required about 12,675 guns.[4]

---

[4]This estimate, made by Joachim Görtz in 1985, omits the requirements of the detachments in the Kiautschau protectorate (China). These, however, are presumed to have been small.

Deliveries of first-pattern Pistolen 1904 continued until about 1913. From June 22, 1912, however, the operation of the safety catch was revised. Though the precise nature is not specified in the official papers, it concerned the reversal of the manual safety-lever recessed in the left rear of the frame. The work was entrusted to the dockyards, guns on overseas stations being substituted by modified guns.

Midway through January, 1914, however, the Reichs-Marine-Amt decided that the grip safety of the Pistole 1904 was to be eliminated altogether. Thus, there were to have been *two* changes to the guns with regard to grip

A standard Pistole 1904 of the last (or short-frame) pattern delivered from 1916 onward. Note the date — 1917 — on the frame rail ahead of the trigger plate and the inspector's mark on the front left side of the receiver. (Tom Knox collection, photo by Rod Stout)

Table I
Typical Navy Markings

The most commonly encountered mark is a distinctive squared imperial crown above ''M'' — the mark of the principal navy inspector responsible for the particular weapons. Unlike the army inspectors' marks, which were coded to the individual, all naval personnel used the same punch design. Unit markings also often appear on the buttplate of the rifles, or the backstrap of the pistol grip. The most common are:

A.D. — Probably ''Artillerie-Depot,'' rarely encountered as ''A.D.M.,'' for Artillerie-Depot Mainz, or ''A.D.E.'' for Artillerie-Depot Erfurt.

M.A. — Minen-Abteilung (unconfirmed).

M.A.A. — Matrosen-Artillerie-Abteilung. Often written simply as ''M.A.'' (see above), but distinguished by a prefatory roman numeral.

M.D. — Matrosen-Division (sailors' division — general personnel).

M.F.A. — Marine-Flieger-Abteilung (naval airmen detachment); mark unconfirmed.

M.L.A. — Marine-Luftschiff-Abteilung (naval airship detachment); mark unconfirmed.

S.B. — Seebataillon (marines).

St.S.B. — Stamm-Seebataillon.

T.A. — Torpedo-Abteilung (pre-1908).

T.D. — Torpedo-Division (post-1908, technical personnel).

U.A. — Unterseeboot-Abteilung (very rare).

W.D. — Werft Danzig (dockyard inventory); existence unconfirmed.

W.D. — Werft-Division (artificers, stokers, engineroom staff, etc.); prefaced by a roman numeral.

W.K. — Werft Kiel (dockyard inventory; probably issued for shipboard use).

W.W. — Werft Wilhelmshaven (see above).

Table II
Tirpitz Principles

The Tirpitz Principles list the small arms required by each ship, from the newest dreadnoughts to navy auxiliaries. For example, *SMS Friedrich der Grosse,* the fleet flagship at Jutland, carried 385 Gew.98s and 97 Pistolen 04 (excluding the extra guns carried by the admiral's staff); the armored cruiser *SMS Blücher,* sunk by the British at Dogger Bank in 1915, carried 280 rifles and 100 pistols; and the light cruiser *SMS Emden* carried 70 Gew.98s and 46 Pistolen 1904* before being driven aground on North Keeling Island in 1914. The gunboat *Jaguar* and the small destroyer *S90* each carried 20 pistols, though only the former was allocated rifles (60 Gew.98s); the large destroyer *V155* had 30 pistols, and a typical U-Boat had a surprising 24. Rifles were not carried aboard ships below destroyer size.

On the battle cruiser *von der Tann,* commissioned approximately contemporaneously with the Tirpitz Principles, 93 Pistolen 1904 were distributed among the officers (20), surgeons (3), midshipmen (8), petty officers of the nautical division (9), signalmen (9), dispatch runners (3), pioneers (9), stretcher bearers (22) and the remaining 10 to the 8mm machinegun crews.

*This was the standard ''Tirpitz'' allocation; like all cruisers serving on overseas stations, *Emden* would have carried supplementary weapons authorized under Auslandzuschlag.

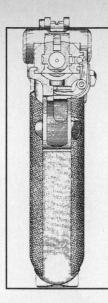

Drawings of the Pistole 1904 from the 1913 edition of the navy manual *Leitfaden betreffend die Pistole 1904*. (Courtesy of Joachim Görtz)

safeties — the mechanism was "revised" effective in June, 1912, and then "disengaged" altogether (a process finally prevented) in January, 1914.

At about this time, the "second pattern" Pistole 1904 appeared. It was mechanically identical to the Pistole 1908, but had a 15cm (6-inch) barrel, a navy rear sight and a long frame. The grip safety had been eliminated. Reversal of the safety movement appears to have occurred *prior* to the acquisition of these army-style Pistolen 1904.

No official order for these guns has yet been found, though a little less than 6000 navy pistols were delivered to Kiel between March, 1915 and August, 1916, when "orders were complete." No sooner had world War I begun than stocks of navy pistols declined dangerously; early in October, 1914 only six pistols remained in store at Kiel. The immediate reaction would have been to expedite work on the 1914 contract.

The Reichs-Marine-Amt subsequently ordered 8000 more guns from DWM on August 29, 1916. The manufacturer was asked to strive for a monthly delivery of at least 800 guns, starting in October. These third-pattern guns were similar to their predecessors, except that their short frames and chambers were dated 1916 or 1917.[5] For details of the controversy surrounding the production totals of these guns, see Görtz & Walter, *The Navy Luger*, pp. 58-64.

The Fate of the Pre-1918 Small Arms

Under the provisions of the Treaty of Versailles, the German armed forces were greatly restricted. Renamed "Reichsmarine," the Kaiserliche Marine was reduced to a sham of its former glory. Allowed only six old battleships, six obsolete small cruisers and a selection of smaller craft, the 15,000 men could scarcely have required more than 20,000 rifles and 4000 pistols even allowing for reserve stocks. Post-war Reichsmarine manuals indicate that Gewehre 98 and Pistolen 1908 — standard and long-barreled — were regarded as the post-1921 service weapons. Most original Navy

Lugers had been discarded[6] or, particularly in the case of third-pattern guns, converted to P.08 standards simply by changing the barrel and the rear toggle link. Only their original navy marks distinguished these pseudo-P.08s from the true pre-1918 army guns.

Weapons retained into the Reichsmarine period may be identified by the supplementary "1920" (more rarely, "1921") datemark struck into the chamber top or frame rail under the supervision of the Inter-Allied Military Control Commission.

Acknowledgements

Portions of this article have been adapted — with the permission of the authors — from material recently published in *The Navy Luger: a concise history of the 9mm Pistole 1904 and the Imperial German Navy* by Joachim Görtz and John Walter. A debt is also acknowledged to the Bundesarchiv, the Bayerisches Hauptstaatsarchiv, John Walter's book *The German Rifle* (London, 1979) and Hans Reckendorf's *Die Handwaffen der Koeniglich Preussischen und der Kaiserlichen Marine* (Dortmund-Schönau, 1983). ●

---

[5]Two guns have been reported dated "1914," one "1915" and one "1918." All four are believed to contain mismatched army and navy parts.

[6]Though most of the 6-inch-barreled Pistolen 1904 had been discarded by the mid-1920s, small numbers appear to have been held in reserve. During the occupation of Denmark during World War II, the Germans formed a guard of Danes willing to guard merchantmen laid up in Copenhagen harbor. Supervised by the Kriegsmarine, these men received 6-inch-barreled navy pistols in locally-made holsters marked OPLAGTE SKIBE I NORDHAVEN.

Gun Oil and Gun Grease

by GEORGE G. KASS

LOOKING for a unique gun-related item to collect? Something interesting? Something inexpensive? Something you can find at gun shops, gun shows and flea markets? Then take a good look at the gun oil and gun grease containers marketed by companies that made and/or make guns and/or ammunition.

Who would know better how to clean and preserve guns than the people who made the guns or the ammu-

Two old-timers — a Sears, Roebuck grease can and a Remington oiler.

Savage gun grease and powder solvent packages, showing different addresses on otherwise identical items.

Oil cans from Montgomery Ward (right) and Western Auto (left); both are of fairly recent manufacture, as indicated by their plastic tops.

nition used in the guns? In my collection of gun cleaners and lubricants, I have included products from companies that marketed guns or ammunition, as well as the manufacturers. These include Sears, Roebuck & Co., Montgomery Ward and Co., and Western Auto (Revelation Brand).

A unique feature of this kind of collecting is that once into it, you learn that companies love to change packaging and locations, and generally do whatever else they can to confuse future collectors. At times, I believe some of them never made two identical products. This certainly adds spice to collecting, as new and different variations crop up.

Take, for instance, Savage Arms Corp. Almost identical product packages exist at the Utica, New York and the Chicopee Falls, Massachusetts distribution loca-

(Left to right) Marble's gun oil packaging changed from a bottle early in the century through several can styles to today's plastic squeeze bottle.

A Savage gun oil can. Note the early all-metal spout and cap.

Winchester's Crystal Cleaner was still being sold in bottles like the one at left in the late '30s, while their gun oil came in cans. The early type can is in the center, a later version at right.

Winchester's gun cartons always contained a tag like this, extolling the virtues of its own cleaning materials.

Winchester gun grease (right) and rust remover (far right) packages underwent many changes over the years.

tions. Another such example is Marble's products— some containers have the name "Marble Arms & Mfg Co.," others simply "Marble Arms Corp."

Add this to the fact that the companies often produce introductory packages, samples for handouts at industry shows, and special packages for inclusion with guns, and the field becomes even more interesting. You like research? Great, there is plenty of opportunity to research when products were marketed. Such information can be found in gun magazines, manufacturer and distributor flyers and catalogs, as well as gun and ammo textbooks.

Packaging covers a wide range, from glass bottles to individual tear-open packages, squeeze tubes to aerosol cans and a little bit of everything in between. Glass bottles are one of the more interesting collectors' items. The early ones had cork stoppers and raised lettering. Pictured nearby are a Savage Red Gun Oil, a REM-UMC powder solvent, and a Winchester bottle.

Tins are another interesting packaging method; note

(Right, center) Two older versions of Remington powder solvent cans, shown with a modern (far right) Remington oil can styled to mimic an earlier type.

Foreign gun cleaning materials like this Birmingham Small Arms "barrel perserver" are rarely seen in the U.S.

An older "Rem Oil" package (top) shown with a modern counterpart, Revelation (Western Auto) gun oil carton (above).

Stoeger gun grease can, same size and design as a shoe polish can.

(Right) Rare early oil bottles from the turn of the century: (left) Savage "Red," (center) Winchester, and (right) Rem-Oil.

(Far left) Remington gun grease and (left) rust remover packages. Like Savage, Remington had a problem deciding which city, New York or Bridgeport, to call home.

Two pages from Remington's 1918-19 catalog showing their gun cleaning materials of the period.

the Stoeger Barrel Grease can, which at first glance looks like a package of shoe polish. Look carefully, as they come in all sizes and shapes.

OK, you're interested, but where do you start? First, try your own gun cleaning supply box or cabinet. You may be amazed at some of the unusual items you've

Page from a pre-World War I sporting goods catalog, showing cleaning materials from Winchester, Marble and Stevens.

"Cleaning Preparations" from Abercrombie & Fitch's 1940 catalog. Note that Winchester's "Crystal Cleaner" still came in a bottle.

Waffen Glaser in Zurich offered this variety of gun oils and greases in the mid-1930s.

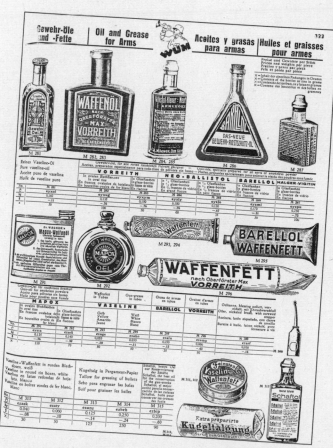

gathered over the years! Next try your local sporting goods outlet for more current items, followed by visits to your shooting or collecting buddies' gun rooms. Finally, visit local gun and antique shows and flea markets. What? It is only a month since first reading this article and you already have over a dozen items in your collection! Mother, clean out the kitchen cupboards—the gun room is expanding again! ●

Another wide range of gun maintenance material was offered in Adolph Frank's famous "WUM" catalog of the '30s.

The MANN

PISTOLS

The Mann 25 pistol, left and right sides. This is the late-production gun, number 25897-2.

by J.B. WOOD

IN the era of the Westen-Taschen Pistole in Germany, Fritz and Otto Mann made one of the smallest, slimmest, and strangest looking of the 25-caliber vest-pocket pistols. It was designed in 1919, and production began early in 1920 at the Mann Werkzeugfabrik in Suhl-Neundorf. Most of the 25 automatics of that time used some elements of the 1906 Browning-FN design, but not the little Mann. In many ways, the pistol has excellent engineering, but these factors are often missed by those who are put off by its odd appearance.

The blowback action uses a cylindrical internal bolt with a cocking piece at the rear of the frame. The recoil spring is mounted above the barrel, and its guide has a threaded end that screws into the knob. The internal front

left side to serve as a forward stop for the safety-lever. The magazine catch is located in the frontstrap on the frame, and its lever is tipped with a round checkered button. It is pushed inward to release.

The Mann is a true hammerless, with a cylindrical striker moving lengthwise in the bolt. The firing pin point at the front of the striker is unusually shaped, being conical rather than rebated to a slim tip. With this design, breakage would be very unlikely. The grip panels are made of moulded black hard rubber, and they are attached with a single screw on each side. An oval at the top of each grip contains the Mann name in overlapping letters.

During the production life of the 25 Mann, the markings and some mechanical features changed. On one very

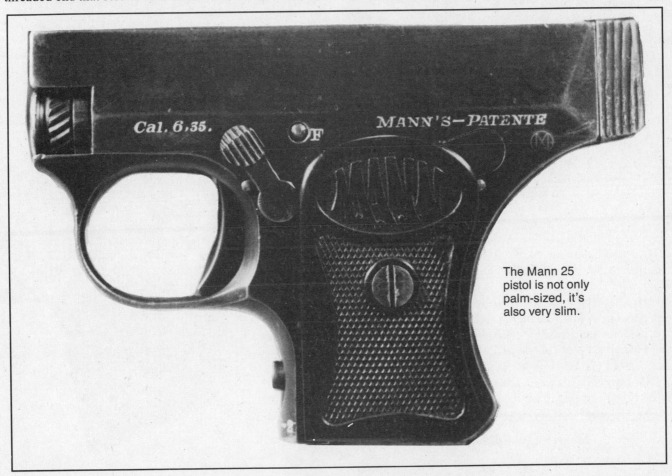

The Mann 25 pistol is not only palm-sized, it's also very slim.

portion of the bolt is larger in diameter than the rear opening in the frame, so there is no danger of bolt exit, even if the spring guide should break. There is no separate extractor; a flange on the recessed face of the bolt engages the rim as the cartridge is fed from the magazine. An ejector is mounted inside the frame on the left, and the rounded tip of its mounting post protrudes to provide the detent for the manual safety in the on-safe position.

The manual safety, a lever on the left side at the top front of the grip, directly blocks the trigger when moved rearward. The serrated button of the safety (on late pistols) alternately covers the letters "S" and "F" on the frame. The trigger pivot pin is slightly extended on the

early pistol (number 356-20; the "20" of the serial is probably the year of manufacture, 1920), the checkered button on the safety-lever is circular with a hole at the center, and the safety positions are marked with FEUER and SICHER. Marked on the front left of the frame is Cal. 6.35., and to the rear of the safety, above the left grip, Jn & Auslands Patente.

The magazine release on the early gun is a screw-headed push button on the left side at the rear terminus of the trigger guard. On the right side of the frame, a separate screw retains a spring-tempered bar that bears on the barrel as a turning catch. The grip panels have no screws, and as this pistol has been seen only in photographs, the

An unusual "re-marked" Mann 32-caliber pistol, left and right sides, with "Fabrica-cion Alemana" on the slide. Note that the Mann trademark is still present on the grips and the frame.

method of attachment is unknown.

On pistol number 2421-20, a double-ended arrow is arched between the FEUER and SICHER safety markings, and the magazine catch is now on the frontstrap of the frame. The grips are held by screws and the barrel-turning latch is present on the right side of the frame. The left side of the frame is marked Cal. 6.35. at the front, and Mann's Patent above the grip. Note that in this case the Patent marking is without a final "e."

My own very late pistol has no barrel-turning latch, and the oblong serrated safety-lever button covers the position

Mann Pistol Specifications

	25-caliber	32-, 380-caliber
Weight:	8.75 ozs.	12.35 ozs. (32), 13.23 ozs. (380)
Length:	4 1/8"	4 11/16"
Height:	2 3/4"	3 1/16"
Width:	11/16"	—
Barrel length:	1 3/4"	2 7/16"
Mag. capacity:	5 rounds	5 rounds
Lowest number noted:	356-20	40212
Highest number noted:	25897-2	51797
Estimated total production:	26,000	12,000

letters, as noted earlier. Marked forward on the left side is Cal. 6.35. and over the left grip and rearward Mann's - Patente — with a final "e." Directly under that "e," the circle-MW (for *Mann Werke*) trademark is lightly stamped; on the right side, the German crown-N proof is on the bolt, barrel, and frame.

With the bolt retracted slightly, turning the barrel anti-clockwise (front view) until it stops allows the barrel to be taken out toward the front. For the non-gunsmith, this is as far as takedown should go, and will be enough for routine cleaning. The amateur gunsmith might think you can simply unscrew the recoil spring guide, unscrew the handle from the bolt, and take the bolt out toward the front.

You can't. The sear will stop it, and it will break if force is used. It's best to leave complete takedown to a gunsmith who is familiar with the pistol.

I remember reading some years ago a remark by a writer that the Mann 25 probably failed because shooters were painfully injured when the lower edge of the bolt knob pinched the web of their thumbs against the frame. Actually, because of the long upsweep of the backstrap, this area is far removed from the thumb web, even during recoil. I have fired the little Mann 25, and the knob didn't even come close. The felt recoil is rather sharp, because of the light weight and an inadequate grip, but it's not unpleasant.

I think the reasons for the rather brief production time of the pistol were its odd appearance and the introduction of the excellent Walther Modell 9 in 1921. The total production of the Mann 25 pistol can only be estimated. Mathews notes that "serial numbers over 17,000 are known," and I can verify that — my own 25 Mann, pictured here, is numbered "25897-2." The reader may speculate on the significance of the "2" suffix, but if the suffix "20" on the previously discussed pistols does indeed indicate the year of manufacture, then the "2" no doubt is for "1922." I would estimate total production of the little Mann to be around 26,000 pieces. It was discontinued in 1923.

In 1924, Mann began production of a 32 and 380 pistol that had a more conventional external appearance. Internally, though, it was still quite different from other pistols of its time and also somewhat smaller than most guns of the same chamberings.

Like the 25 Mann, the larger gun also had an interesting barrel-mounting method. In this case, it was a square-section helical screw arrangement, with the barrel removable toward the front. The recoil spring surrounds the barrel and is visible in the ejection port in most pistols. One 32 pistol that has been seen in a photograph seems to have the rear of the spring covered with a sleeve, but that is unusual.

One notable feature of the larger Mann pistol is the manual safety, which is also the magazine release. The serrated button of the lever is in a good location — at the forward edge of the left grip panel. On the frame, just to the rear of the trigger, "S.," "F.," and "Mag.," are stamped in descending order. Aligning the lever with the "S." internally blocks the sear. The "F." is firing position, of course. If downward pressure is continued to bring the lever to "Mag.," the magazine is released. When the magazine is removed, spring tension moves the lever to the "S." position — in effect, a magazine safety.

The 32 and 380 Mann pistols are true hammerless guns, striker fired. The hard rubber grips are retained by pivoting bars mounted on the inside of the Mann-trademark medallions that are set into the panels at upper center. A wide band across the top of the panels has MANN marked in large block letters. On the left upper rear flat of the frame the circled "MW" monogram trademark is stamped, often rather lightly.

Three different slide marking have been observed. On an early 380 pistol (number 42012), the left slide flat has

A cutaway Mann 32, left side view, showing the safety-lever function. In the "safe" position, the hook on the safety's end, visible in the cut at the rear of the frame, blocks the sear from moving when the trigger is pulled. (Joseph Schroeder collection)

(Left) Right side view of the same cutaway, with the magazine retaining bar visible in the cut in the frame. Below, a closeup of the Mann logo, an "M" (for Mann) over a "W" (for Werke).

a two-line marking: Fritz Mann - Suhl and Mann's Patent. An early 32 also has two lines, but marked differently: Cal. 7.65m/m Mann-Werke A.G. Suhl, and Mann's Patent. On two later 32 pistols, numbers 50238 and 51797, there is a single line at the lower edge of the left slide flat: Cal. 7.65 Mann-Werke A.G. Suhl Mann's Patent. There may well be other marking variations.

There is one oddly-marked 32 Mann, pictured nearby, which was apparently "re-marked" by a later marketing firm for export to a Spanish-speaking country. Instead of the usual Mann markings on the slide, there is a single line at center, Fabricacion Alemana, which translates to "German Manufacture" or "Made in Germany." The Mann name at the top of the grips has been replaced with vertical lines, but the trademark medallion is still on each panel and the trademark is stamped on the left upper rear flat of the frame in its usual location. On the right side, the German crown-over-N proof appears on the frame, slide, and barrel. This pistol was unquestionably made by Mann in Suhl. The reason for the changed markings would probably be an interesting story in itself.

I have observed only four serial numbers for the 32 and 380 Mann: 42012, 42013, 50238, and 51797. (A cutaway, serial 45825, is in the collection of the GUN COLLECTOR'S DIGEST editor.) There will doubtless be others reported after this article appears, but the span of these can give us

an idea of the total production. My best estimate would be around 10,000 to 12,000 pieces, perhaps half the figure for the smaller pistol. In my experience, the larger gun has certainly not been seen as often. Production ended around 1928.

According to contemporary firearms articles in Germany, Fritz Mann originally intended to make a 32 pistol in the same pattern as the 25, just a little larger. This, apparently, was never done. Another news item of that time noted that he was experimenting with a bottlenecked 6.35mm round with the idea of making a more powerful 25-caliber pocket pistol. No examples of this cartridge or a gun in this chambering have been reported.

Mann pistols are sometimes found in general collections, or in those assembled by caliber, but usually only as individual guns. With all of the variations among the three calibers, though, a specialist could assemble a Mann collection of respectable size. If one could come across the prototype of the 25-pattern 32-caliber Mann, or one chambered for the experimental bottlenecked 6.35mm round, this would be quite a coup.

Overall, the Mann pistols were well made, and are mechanically interesting. Their history still has some blank spaces though. Perhaps this little essay will at least supply a starting point toward filling in some of those blanks. ●

A Luger Controversy

Proof and Inspectors' Marks

by JOACHIM GÖRTZ and JOHN WALTER

A typical DWM-made Pistole 1908, serial number 7716a, dating from 1909. Note that the proof and inspectors' marks lie on the *left* side of the receiver ahead of the trigger plate. (Rolf Gminder collection)

IT IS A popular pastime among collectors, researchers and authors to identify virtually all the major marks found on the receivers of Germany military Lugers as "proofmarks." In this article, we shall provide conclusive documentation that, insofar as the Pistole 1908 is concerned, the term "proofmark" refers *solely* to the displayed eagle found on the front right side of the receiver, the underside of the barrel and the side of the breechblock. Together with its later Reichswehr and Wehrmacht equivalents, this was applied after the assembled gun had successfully fired two super-power proof cartridges loaded to give a pressure 20 percent in excess of normal.[1] In addition to the displayed eagle, however, guns from the Imperial era also show several

---

[1] These proof cartridges were usually identifiable by the word "Beschuss" in the headstamp, green primer annuli or green case-mouth seals. The degree of overload has sometimes been claimed as 50 or even 75 percent.

The marking system was soon changed. This gun, serial number 6225a, was made by DWM in 1913. Note how the proof and inspectors' marks now lie on the front *right* side of the receiver. (Rolf Gminder collection)

An enlargement of the marks on gun 7716a, showing the proofmarks (2, 3, 6), inspectors' marks (4, 5), plus the caliber mark "8,83" (8.83mm, 1). At the time of this writing, it is not known precisely how these were applied.

crowned Fraktur ("gothic") letters alongside this *Beschusszeichen*. Reichswehr and Wehrmacht guns bear a selection of numbered and numbered-and-lettered eagles in much the same positions. But why were these applied? And should they be considered as an integral part of the proof?

Anonymous Offices or Responsible Individuals?

Marks such as a crowned Fraktur "B" are invariably identified as inspectors' marks when they appear on the magazine, dismantling lever or the trigger plate; all parts which needed to be passed as fit for service.[2] But, if this is so readily accepted among collectors, why should the similar marks accompanying the proofmarks have been applied by anyone other than inspectors?

The problem, then, becomes one of determining the significance of the individual marks. Prior to 1918, the Parabellums were made only in the government factory

in Erfurt and by the solitary private contractor, Deutsche Waffen- und Munitionsfabriken of Berlin. This clearly makes the theory that the letters represent "sub-offices" or "inspection areas" untenable. The *Vorschrift für die Untersuchung und Abnahme von Gewehren und Gewehrteilen 98* ("Instruction for the inspection and acceptance of Model 98 rifles and rifleparts"), which became effective in 1898-9, stated that:

> All pieces found acceptable during the inspection procedure . . . are to be marked with the dies held by the inspector . . . [note: the plural "dies" is due to each inspector being issued with several different sizes of "his die."] Each inspector is responsible for the acceptance of items certified by his mark. Consequently, his mark will also be applied to items accepted by assistant inspectors acting under his supervision . . .

In 1913, the instruction *Untersuchung und Abnahme von Pistolen 08 und deren Teilen* ("Inspection and acceptance of Pistolen 08 and their parts") was even more explicit:

---

[2] See, for example, John Walter, *The Luger Book*, p. 123-5, section G31; or Joachim Görtz, *Die Pistole 08*, p. 85-90.

An enlargement of the marks on gun 6225a. The "receiver hardened satisfactorily" mark (1) was applied first, followed by "pistol ready for testfiring" (2), the proofmark (4) and, finally, "testfiring satisfactorily negotiated" (3). Some guns will be encountered with mark No. 3 absent; many of these proof failures, which generally had headspace problems, were later accepted by the Revisions Commission and display additional "crown/RC" receiver stamps.

In order to identify an official by his mark [letter], even years later, his mark (die sizes 11.75, 4.2, 3.2 and 2mm) is to be struck by his senior [superior] inspector into a sheet of zinc, together with his name and date of posting to the rifle factory, the zinc sheet to be held in custody by the senior inspector. When the official retires, the senior inspector is to reclaim the dies and to mark his date of retirement on the said sheet.

It is clear, therefore, that the crowned Fraktur letter marks of the pre-1918 era served to identify an individual inspector rather than the office to which he was posted. The marks constituted personal liability, and a means of identifying they once existed. It seems unlikely that a true record of these marks will ever be retrieved (much less the zinc plate!), but there is a theoretical chance of gradually piecing together the story.

Most of the pre-1918 marks represented the initial letters of the individual officer's surnames. However, when two men with similar initials were serving concurrently—e.g., a Schmidt and a Schultz — some method of distinguishing the junior man would be needed. The collection of the Imperial War Museum, London, contains DWM-made pistols with (for example) the marks of acceptance officials "H" and "S." The former could be the mark of Oberbüchsenmacher Hoffmann, posted to Spandau in 1900, or his colleague Oberbüchsenmacher Hesshaus (1901 onward); the latter, the mark of Oberbüchsenmacher Schilling, who arrived at Spandau in 1905.

Other guns display the identifier "T," often with a short bar beneath the letter. According to Horst W. Laumanns, writing in the *Deutsches Waffen-Journal* but basing his work on information gleaned from the *Militär-Wochenblatt*, two Triebels may have served in the Spandau rifle factory during the period that interests us. As there is also an unusually high incidence of the letter "X" — which, together with "Y," is rare in German family names — the seniority sequence may have been a plain

letter for the most senior man, a barred letter for the next most senior inspector (or perhaps one with the same name) and then "X" for any others with the same initial. It has to be stressed, however, that this has yet to be proven.[3]

That the letters are always crowned simply indicates that the inspectors were acting on behalf of their sovereign, the king of Prussia.

Missing Proofs

Occasionally, guns are encountered with fewer than the standard three inspectors' letters alongside the displayed eagle proofmarks. Except for the undated early DWM guns, which only had two inspectors' marks on the left side of the receiver ahead of the trigger plate[4], most "two-mark" examples appear to have failed final inspection. This is implicit in the pronounced gap between the proof eagle and the remaining crowned letters. These guns were rejected after appearing to pass proof, probably because of unacceptable headspace. Many were subsequently accepted by the Revisions-Commission, whose mark, a crowned "RC," signified that no one should take individual responsibility for accepting them; others may have survived because they had been offered to officers at a reduced rate or sold commercially.[5]

---

[3] The effects of retirement and changes in seniority are unknown.

[4] Which of the three later inspection stages was omitted is uncertain but it seems possible that the "receiver hardened" and "pistol readied for proof-firing" stages were originally combined.

[5] Interestingly, during the Third Reich, some of the Krieghoff-made guns were sold commercially after failing final acceptance; the most common cause of failure, moreover, was headspace problems.

TABLE I

Inspectors active in the Erfurt and Spandau rifle factories in the Parabellum period. **Note:** Extracted largely from the articles by Horst W. Laumanns in the *Deutsches Waffen-Journal* (July and August, 1980; January, May and June, 1983), this contains information for 1908-14 only; for security reasons, detailed postings no longer appeared in the *Militär-Wochenblatt* once WWI began. A "Büchsenmacher" (literally, "gunmaker") was an armorer-artificer. The term was changed to "Waffenmeister" (literally, "weapons master") on July 3, 1910, when the old title of Fabriken-Kommissarius was dropped. An Oberbüchsenmacher was simply a senior Büchsenmacher.

Erfurt Inspectors:

AUSTEN — promoted Oberbüchsenmacher, January 1, 1905.

BETTIG — posted to Erfurt on July 1, 1878, retired on July 1, 1911.

BÜTTNER — promoted from Erfurt artillery depot to the rifle factory, December 1, 1906.

GEBHARDT — promoted to Oberwaffenmeister effective November 1, 1911.

HÖFLING — promoted to "Waffen-Revisor" ("inspector") from July 12, 1911.

KEMPF — promoted to Oberbüchsenmacher at the rifle factory, April 13, 1875; retired as Betriebsleiter (operations manager) on November 19, 1910.

KLOSE — two men, one promoted from the Danzig rifle factory to Erster Revisionsbeamter ("senior supervising inspector") at Erfurt effective April 1, 1908; and a second, an Oberbüchsenmacher, also posted to Erfurt on the same date.

KÖHLER — promoted to Oberbüchsenmacher at Erfurt effective from April 12, 1888, to Betriebsinspektor on July 1, 1905 and Erster Revisionsbeamter ("senior inspector") on March 14, 1906.

KUNZE — posted to Erfurt and promoted to Oberbüchsenmacher on February 1, 1902.

KUTZI — Zeughaus-Büchsenmacher seconded to Erfurt artillery depot from the rifle factory, where he was concurrently a Hilfsrevisor ("assistant inspector"). Promoted Oberbüchsenmacher on November 1, 1907.

LIEBERT — managing director of the Danzig rifle factory, transferred to Erfurt on August 29, 1911.

MATHESIUS — posted to Erfurt rifle factory on April 1, 1909, and promoted to Oberbüchsenmacher.

REIF — posted from Erfurt artillery depot to the rifle factory, as a "Waffen-Revisor," effective November 28, 1911.

SCHUCH — promoted to Oberbüchsenmacher and posted to the Erfurt rifle factory, July 1, 1905.

WALTHER — promoted to Oberbüchsenmacher and posted from Spandau to Erfurt rifle factories on April 1, 1907.

WIEBE — promoted from Oberbüchsenmacher to Betriebsinspektor in the rifle factory on April 1, 1909.

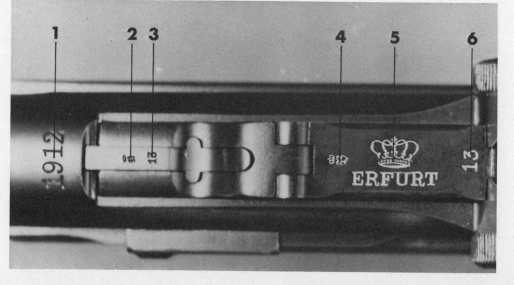

The receiver top of a standard Erfurt-made Pistole 1908, showing the date stamp (1), inspectors' marks (2,4) accepting individual components, the last two digits of the serial number (3, 6), and the maker's mark (5). (Rolf Gminder collection)

Spandau Inspectors:

BALLE — promoted to Waffen-Revisor at Spandau, October 1, 1910.

BALSCHMIETER — Oberbüchsenmacher; posted from Erfurt to Spandau rifle factory on November 1, 1903.

BARANOWSKI — promoted to Oberbüchsenmacher and posted to Spandau, effective September 1, 1900.

BARTZ — posted to the Spandau rifle factory from Danzig on June 12, 1901, and promoted from Oberbüchsenmacher to Erster Revisionsbeamter on April 1, 1908.

CESARZ — promoted to Oberbüchsenmacher and moved from Danzig to Spandau rifle factories on April 1, 1907.

DAHLKE — Oberbüchsenmacher, active in the first decade of the 20th century.

DOBCZYNSKI — Hilfsrevisor, promoted to Oberbüchsenmacher in Spandau, effective April 1, 1909.

GEBHARDT — promoted to Oberbüchsenmacher in the Spandau rifle factory on July 1, 1905, and then posted to the Infanterie-Konstruktionsbureau, Spandau, effective April 16, 1908.

GRONEBERG — Oberbüchsenmacher; transferred from the Danzig to Spandau rifle factories on October 1, 1909.

GRÜBER — Oberbüchsenmacher; posted to Spandau on April 1, 1908.

HESSHAUS — Oberbüchsenmacher transferred from the Erfurt to Spandau rifle factories on June 12, 1901.

KANSCHAT — Waffenmeister; promoted to Waffenrevisor in the Spandau rifle factory, January 22, 1912.

KELLNER — Oberbüchsenmacher; transferred from Erfurt to Spandau on October 11, 1902. Promoted to Waffenrevisor and then posted to the Infanterie-Konstruktionsbureau on October 1, 1910.

KÖRNER — Oberbüchsenmacher; transferred from Spandau ammunition factory to Spandau rifle factory on March 23, 1898. Promoted to Erster Revisionsbeamter on January 1, 1899 and retired on January 1, 1913.

KUHWALD — promoted to Oberbüchsenmacher while posted to the Spandau rifle factory, March 1, 1907.

MARQUARDT — promoted to Oberbüchsenmacher in the Spandau factory, effective July 1, 1905.

REINKE — Waffenrevisor, Spandau; posted to the Danzig rifle factory, 1912.

SCHILLING — promoted to Oberbüchsenmacher while serving in the Spandau rifle factory, July 1, 1905.

SCHMIDT — attached to the Spandau rifle factory as Hilfsrevisor, and promoted to Oberbüchsenmacher there on January 1, 1907.

SCHÖN — Oberbüchsenmacher; posted to the Spandau rifle factory from Erfurt, April 1, 1908.

TRIEBEL — Oberbüchsenmacher; posted to Spandau rifle factory on April 1, 1905. There were at least four inspectors with this name, but only one seems to have served during the Parabellum period.

ZEHNER — promoted Oberbüchsenmacher while serving in the Spandau rifle factory, April 1, 1908.

The Reichswehrzeit

The abdication of the Kaiser and the subsequent foundation of the Weimar Republic (1919-23) wrought considerable changes in the German army. The Treaty of Versailles restricted the Reichsheer to a mere 100,000 men, and the Inter-Allied Control Commission diligently supervised the confiscation and destruction of huge quantities of surplus weapons. The inspectors' marks applied during this period, though positioned somewhat similarly to the pre-1918 crowned letters, take the form of numbers surmounted by displayed eagles. The latter may be stylized to the point of being unrecognizable.

The pre-1918 instructions were amalgamated into the Heeresdruckvorschrift (H.Dv.) 464, *Vorschrift über die Stemelung und die Bezeichung von Waffen und Gerät bei der Truppe* ("Instruction how to mark and designate arms and equipment adopted for the service"). The introductory part of the H.Dv. 464, the 1923-vintage *Vorbemerkungen,* states:

1. Marking and designating equipment serves . . . to identify the source from which, and the year in which equipment has been procured, by whom said equipment has been accepted, in whose custody it is, and finally — if applicable — to distinguish between sizes. **2.** Consequently, four types of markings are to be found:

a. The manufacturer's logo, applied free of charge by (and identifying) the manufacturer, together with, if necessary, his location; the year of production; and, if necessary, the serial number. Without these identifying marks, no piece of equipment must be accepted by military authorities. The purpose is to . . . make manufacturers liable in succeeding years for defects that may have been over-looked by the accepting official.

b. The acceptance mark, indicating the authority and the number of the official in charge; the purpose being the same as described under **a.**

c. A size mark, only necessary for equipment made in differing sizes, with "1" signifying the smallest.

d. The unit or property marking, necessary for the prevention of theft and for the designation of the holder entrusted with the custody of the equipment in question.

Paragraph 2(b) of this extract is most important; it states unequivocally that the inspector of the Reichsheer period was now identified by a number rather than a letter, though his responsibility and accountability remained unchanged. Substituting a number for a letter freed the system from the problems of having several officers with the same family-name initials. The replacement of the crown by an eagle was simply a consequence of republicanism. H.Dv. 464 proves that attempts to link the number marks with contracts or delivery lots are mistaken (cf., Sam Costanzo, *World of Lugers, Proof Marks*, Vol. 1, p. 111, mark No. 158).

Paragraph 2(b) also called for the identification of the authority (Behörde) under which the equipment was accepted. It is suggested that this stipulation originally referred to procurement by local or regional military authorities, though all post-1920 Reichsheer firearms were accepted by the Inspektion für Waffen und Gerät (IWG) — easily identifiable as a "Reichsbehörde" or federal authority through the presence of the neue Reichsadler (federal eagle).

The Third Reich

On March 16, 1935, the Reichswehr was renamed "die Wehrmacht" and the previously clandestine ex-

---

TABLE II

A partial summary of the German army's ordnance inspection and acceptance facilities, 1939 (from *Heereseinteilung 1939,* edited by Generalleutnant a.D. Friedrich Stahl, published shortly after WWII by Podzun-Pallas-Verlag, Friedberg). The abbreviations (W), (E) and (z.D.) in the ranks denote an officer with special training in Waffen ("weapons"); an emergency (Ergänzung) appointment, usually someone who had been commissioned during World War I and recalled for duty in the 1930s; and a "zur Disposition" officer who had been placed on the inactive list with the proviso that he would be recalled when necessary.

East Zone (Berlin-Schöneberg)
Army acceptance official: Oberstleutnant Koenig
Local offices:
Berlin-Borsigwalde — Hauptmann (E) von Heyden
Berlin-Tegel — Hauptmann (W) Rulf
Spandau — Hauptmann (WE) Kampe
Unterlühs — Hauptmann (W) Rebeschiess
Zeithain — Major (E) Danneil

Central Zone (Erfurt)
Army acceptance official: Oberst z.D. Aufhammer
Local offices:
Erfurt — Hauptmann (E) Kamps

Freital — Major (W) z.D. Palm
Leipzig — Major (WE) Rieger
Reinsdorf — Oberleutnant (W) Büchmann
Sömmerda — Oberleutnant (W) Körner
Suhl — Oberleutnant (W) Körner

West Zone (Hannover)
Army acceptance official: Oberst Krech
Local offices:
Bochum — Oberleutnant (W) Liewert
Düsseldorf — Hauptmann (W) Reiner
Essen — Oberleutnant (W) Skorning
Hannover — Hauptmann (W) Heinrich
Magdeburg 1 — Oberleutnant (W) Lenker
Magdeburg 2 — Oberleutnant (W) Drescher
Magdeburg-Buckau — Hauptmann (W) Kufferath

South Zone (Nürnberg)
Army acceptance offical: Oberstleutnant (WE) Buschatski
Local offices:
Erlangen — Hauptmann (W) Paape
Nürnberg — Leutnant (W) Salzmann
Oberndorf/Neckar — Hauptmann (E) Krimer

South-East Zone (Wien)
Army acceptance offical: Oberst Arnold
Local offices:
Enzesfeld — Hauptmann (E) Richter
Felixdorf — Oberstleutnant Niederle
Hirtenberg — Oberleutnant (W) König

What is to be made of the handful of "Spandau" pistols? An enlargement of the markings on one such gun is shown here. Note that by the style of the proof eagle and the inspectors' marks, this was originally a DWM-made receiver; the bar under the T of the "receiver satisfactorily hardened" mark (3) is characteristic of many wartime DWM Pistolen 1908. The question is simply why the gun bears a "Spandau" toggle-link mark and two additional inspectors' marks (1, 2) on the receiver side. The answer is surely that the Spandau guns were cannibalized from damaged guns during a time of great stress — the great Spring Offensive of 1918, perhaps, or the near anarchy as the Armistice approached. (Jack Chappell collection, courtesy of Randall Gibson)

pansion of the German armed forces became more obvious. At this time, too, the style of the acceptance marks was revised after a brief flirtation with a pattern abstract enough to hinder identification of the eagle. The perfected marks comprised a simplified eagle with three straight pinions per wing, above "123" or "WaA 123." The abbreviation "WaA" simply represented the *Waffenamt* (weapons office), which had replaced the IWG in 1926. These marks are found on all types of German equipment: Mauser-made P. 08s display WaA 63, WaA 135 or WaA 655 depending on date of acceptance, while ERMA-made sub-caliber inserts ("Einsteckläufe") may display WaA 77 or WaA 280. These WaA numbers are generally identified with particular "sub-offices," an interpretation which is utterly contrary to military tradition of individual — not collective — accountability.

Of course, regional or local sub-offices did exist; many could even be found within the premises of the principal manufacturers. During the Imperial era, Parabellums made by Deutsche Waffen- und Munitionsfabriken in the Charlottenburg (later, Wittenau) districts of Berlin were accepted under the supervision of inspectors seconded from the Royal Prussian Rifle Factory in nearby Spandau; the manufacturer had to provide accommodation, furniture, heat, light and additional manpower free of charge.

There is no reason to suppose that the principle had changed by the 1930s; we know from the affairs of Fabrique Nationale[6] that the final Waffenamt inspectorate was established there under the command of Hauptmann (W) Dorn (see Table III). This applied the number "140," which will be found on many German-issue firearms made in Belgium during the occupation. The question is simply whether the number "140" was issued to Dorn personally, or to the office and staff he commanded. Though there can be no doubt that the former is correct, the latter is unaccountably preferred by many enthusiasts. No anonymous body would be held responsible for the acceptance of the weapons; this was not only contrary to German tradition (or the traditions of most other armies[7]), but it would also have hindered apportion of blame for faulty weaponry.

The principal German inspector did not undertake all the work personally — tasks for which assistants were employed — yet he still held the same personal responsibility to his superiors in 1939 as his predecessors did in the pre-1913 regulations quoted above. Thus, there is no truth in claims that the WaA mark was applied by a sub-office except in the very general sense that a well-established senior officer would be identified with the office he commanded.

When the senior inspector was posted elsewhere, however, he *took his numbered punches with him;* the sub-office continued to accept guns under the supervision of a new inspector, but marked them differently. This explains the differing numbers on the Mauser-made P. 08 (63, 135 and 655) much better than assuming that either different offices were used or Oberndorf's establishment was renumbered three times in 5 years! Several inspectors were sometimes employed concurrently in the largest firms, acceptance procedures being divided between them. This explains the use of separately-numbered punches — one inspector may have accepted guns in the white ("Weiss-Abnahme") while another supervised testfiring

---

[6] Previous inspectors had used 613 (Tennert, appointed on September 1, 1940) and 103 (name unknown); see Robert D. Whittington, *German Pistols & Holsters 1933-1945 . . .*, p. 105-6.

[7] Many instances of the fear engendered in Russian army inspectors by the prospects of failure have been documented; some men even believed they would face the firing squad for accepting defective guns on behalf of the Tsar!

TABLE III

Organization of the HWaA sub-bureau in "DWM Werk Lüttich" (the sequestered Fabrique Nationale d'Armes de Guerre factory in Herstal-lèz-Liége, Belgium) on August 1, 1944.

Source: CIOS Report XXXII-18

Leiter (chief): Oberleutnant (W) Zorn.
Geschäftszimmer (secretariat): Ia, Fräulein Büttner; Ib, Fräulein Stahl.
Gruppenleiter Gerät (section leader, equipment): Technischer Inspektor Tennert.*
Gruppenleiter Pistolen (section leader, pistols): Waffenmeister Porath.
Gruppenleiter Infanterie-Munition (section leader, small arms cartridges): Oberfeldwebel Pilz.
Lauf-Abnahme (barrel inspection): Feldwebel Hahn.
Gerät-Abnahme (equipment inspection): Wachtmeister Lehnen.
Karabiner-Teile-Abnahme (inspection of rifle parts): Unteroffizier Diekhöfer.
Pistolen-Anschuss (testfiring, pistols): Unteroffizier Pelzer.
Hülsen und Geschosse-Abnahme (inspection of cartridge cases and bullets): Unteroffizier Dreyer.
Hülsen-Beschuss (proof firing of cartridge cases): Unteroffizier Wittenstein.
Chemiker (chemical engineer): Feldwebel Opitz.

*Technischer Inspektor Tennert — a civil servant ranking as a Leutnant, graduate of an engineering college — was the first Leiter of the Werk Lüttich sub-bureau, apparently using the number 613. He was replaced by an unknown (probably military) official with the number 103, who in turn handed over to Oberleutnant Zorn.

Vorschrift
für die Untersuchung und Abnahme von Gewehren und Gewehrtheilen 98.

———

I. Allgemeine Bestimmungen.

and acceptance would grind to a halt in the original location. (In addition, analyzing thousands of the WaA inspectors' marks has failed to reveal a pattern that would make periodic renumbering seem feasible.)

The Men

In the German periodical *Deutsches Waffen-Journal*, Horst W. Laummans has listed names and short biographical data about many inspectors active prior to 1914.[8] Regrettably, there seems little chance of linking Fraktur letter punches and names with any degree of accuracy. At the Spandau rifle factory, which was responsible for accepting DWM-made Pistolen 08, three inspectors with the initial "K" were active in 1900 to 1914: Kellnar, Klose and Kuhwald. Who used a crowned "K," a similar mark above a bar, or the substitute letter "X" will never be known unless some seniority is established. And what happened when the first inspector retired? Were all punches recalled and reissued in accordance with the revised seniority? Or were all new inspectors with the initial "K" simply issued substitute punches . . . ? Only the zinc marking plate could solve these riddles.

No information of even this degree of clarity has yet been discovered from the periods of the Reichswehrzeit or of the Third Reich, apart from a tantalizing fragment from the *Heereseinteilung 1939* (the German order of battle) suggesting that the "eagle/63" mark found on contemporary Mauser-made small arms may have

———

[8] Specifically August, 1980, January and May, 1983, and June, 1986.

("Anschuss") — but this did not happen in Oberndorf.

"Mobile marks"

Many instances can be cited in which WaA marks appear on items made in more than one town. Discounting the obvious, if in the unlikely chance of a small firm standing on a railway junction and sending consignments in alternate directions to different inspectors, it is much more likely that the inspector controlling the fictitious "WaA 111" should be transferred from Thüringen in 1937 to occupied Czechoslovakia in 1940 (with, perhaps, his secretary and driver) than for the entire office to be moved. Otherwise, all inspection

(Opposite page, left, and above) The title pages of the three most important documents quoted in the text.

An example of the proofs observed on the receiver of a typical P.08. The numbers 1 through 4 indicate the order in which the marks were applied. **1** — "Receiver hardened"; the date was struck into the chamber top at the same time. **2** — "Pistol ready for testfiring"; the complete serial number was added at the same time. **4** — "Beschuss-Stemple"; the displayed eagle proofmark, indicating that the gun had fired the two super-power proof cartridges with no obvious damage. **3** — "Pistol accepted after testfiring"; an indication that the pistol had survived its post-proof inspection, whereupon the land diameter was marked on the under surface of the barrel in hundredths of a millimeter (e.g., "8,84").

identified Hauptmann (E) Krimer. This link initially seemed impossible to investigate until it was remembered that contemporary German law forced everyone to register with the local authorities. Changes of domicile may be checked if the records still exist. According to the Oberndorf registers, Hauptmann Max Krimer moved to Brno in occupied Czechoslovakia on December 12, 1939. Coincidentally, the "eagle/63" inspector's mark does not appear on post-1940 Mausers; but it *does* appear on post-1940 firearms made in Czechoslovakia . . .

We also know that "WaA 140" signified the senior inspector serving in the occupied FN factory in Herstal-lez-Liège in 1944 — Hauptmann (W) Dorn — and it may be a matter of time before others are identified from the *Heereseinteilung* list now that a procedure has been established. However, it will take painstaking research (and a much greater awareness of the accuracy with which punch marks must be read) before real progress can be made.

In conclusion . . .

This article, the substance of which first appeared in the *Deutsches Waffen-Journal*, has been based on the unimpeachable evidence of original German documents. However, we accept that there are still areas in which supposition is more evident than fact, and would welcome any comments or additional information through the editor's office. Anyone who may have made a detailed study of the output of individual manufacturers prior to 1939 — the only year for which we

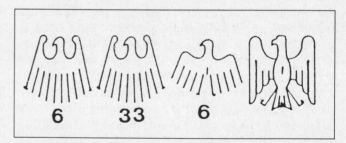

This example shows marks found on the pistols accepted during the Reichswehrzeit (1919-35). The royal crown has been replaced by the republican eagle, and the letters by numerals. The proofmark remains a displayed eagle, though its form has been simplified to lose the orb and scepter of the pre-1918 designs. The differences in the design of the individual eagles are simply due to the limited life of the dies and, therefore, regular replacement.

have definitive information — may have an important part to play.

Of course, it would be particularly thrilling to find the pre-1918 zinc inspectors' markplate or the lists that must have been its later equivalent! ●

CONFESSIONS of a YOUNG GUN COLLECTOR

by DONALD M. SIMMONS

Fourth of July 1933: The author with his sister and mother and his father's Colt 45 automatic Model 1911, the first time he ever fired a firearm. A big day in a 10-year-old boy's life.

As a gun collector, I go way back — I wasn't even 10 when I became interested in firearms. In all honesty, I don't remember when I first showed an interest in guns, but both my parents did and always took great relish in reminding me of it. When I was about 3 years old and sick one day, as a special get-well treat I was allowed my parent's double bed all to myself. During this therapeutic stay, I found my father's loaded Colt 45 Model 1911 automatic in the bedside table. My father was a young major on General Pershing's staff during World War I and, like all veterans from time immemorial, had "liberated" his sidearm when he was discharged. My mother walked into the bedroom to be confronted by a gurgling child waving a 45 at her. The pistol was loaded but locked, and my hands were too little to have pulled the trigger while depressing the grip safety anyway. However, at that point my mother was not as interested in Colt's design niceties as she was in wresting a loaded gun from a drooling kid. Incidentally, my father ended up as the villain of the incident, but I have gone on to demonstrate that as the twig is bent, so grows the tree.

I got my first real gun, an India matchlock, at a New York auction when I was still in short pants. In fact, I think the short pants may have helped because although my mother would take me to these Depression-day auc-

tions, she wouldn't bid for me. So, in order to be seen by the auctioneer, I had to stand on a seat and wave in my bid. The sight of a short "britched" kid bidding usually stopped all other potential buyers, and I got my gun. By the time I was 10, I had a pre-Revolutionary War flintlock musket, a cap-and-ball squirrel rifle, a Spanish-American War Mauser in 7mm and a 45-70 Springfield trapdoor, plus my original matchlock musket. All of them were bought at auctions, and all were in the $2 and $3 price range.

My first handgun, bought in Long Beach, California, was a Colt Model 1860 percussion revolver for which I had to save a couple month's allowance — it cost me $5 and I was all of 11 years old. I took apart every gun I owned and by then could do minor repairs, or more accurately, replacements.

Around that same time, my dad decided to introduce me to military rifle shooting. He rented a sporterized Springfield 1903 and bought a box of 30-06 cartridges. We went to an apparently deserted beach with a high inland bluff as a target. My dad particularly wanted to demonstrate how you heard a crack when a slug passed over your head at supersonic speed. Therefore, I was stationed behind a low dune while he fired into the bluff.

The area was a natural amphitheater and that one shot

The same air rifle 55 years later, very much user-modified.

August 13, 1933: The author on his 11th birthday with his first shooting gun, a Daisy Model 27 500-shot air rifle. The empty hip holster is for a cap pistol, which he was trying to outgrow.

reverberated all over, impressing not only me, but a man who was grazing sheep at the top of the bluff. It turned out that he had never taken the trouble to get permission to graze his woolly charges there. He begged dad to make that the first and last shot in that area, to which my father, somewhat taken aback by the multiple explosions himself, agreed. Thus, an old shepherd kept me from shooting a military rifle for a time, and also probably kept my 100-or-so-pound body from being blown right into the Pacific Ocean.

It was about that time that I found out from a schoolmate about Bannerman, which, living then in New York City, meant it was only a subway ride for me to visit the world's greatest collection of military equipment. Kids today just can't imagine what Bannerman was like. For one thing, they had a table of "Guns for Decoration," (what we now derisively refer to as "Decorators") but to a 12-year-old kid with little money and a big itch, it was heaven! I remember getting a pair of Sharps cartridge carbines, 50-70 caliber, for $1.50 each. My cap-and-ball slant-breech Sharps carbine, the now-called John Brown Model, was $3.50. I bought an old sporterized Swiss Vetterli 41 rimfire single shot rifle which was called a Chamois gun and was for years illustrated in Bannerman's catalog, our bible of that happy age.

In addition to arms, Bannerman had a whole island (literally!) of ammunition dating from the Civil War onward. It was in this period that I wanted to get a shooting gun and found that I already had two or three because Bannerman sold Spencer 56 rimfire carbine ammo at shooters' prices. They also had a huge supply of surplus 45-70 ammo. I started buying a little ammo without my parents' knowledge and during our summer vacation in Sewickley, Pennsylvania, started to shoot my old Spencer carbine, Springfield Trapdoor 45-70 and Peabody 50-70. When I was 14, my mother, tired of me begging for a 22 shooter, took me to a second cousin, in the absence of my father, and asked that worthy outdoorsman if he thought I was ready to own a 22. The good doctor said, "Of course." Ecstatic, I was allowed to buy a new Iver Johnson single shot rifle for $5. When my father was home on vacation, he and I would spend half a day shooting targets with my new 22 rifle. He was very surprised that, because of my secret training, I was a passable shot. The 22 was much more pleasant to shoot than my old charcoal burners, had less kick and you could see the target immediately after firing. Father next got me a Remington Model 41 with a Lyman 4x scope from Abercrombie & Fitch. This single shot 22 was very accurate and with the scope and a rest, we found we could literally drive a tack.

Was I now content? Well, as any good shooter would guess, I was not. At 14, I wanted a shooting handgun. I had found a mail-order house which would sell a new Iver Johnson "Sealed Eight" 22 revolver for $7. I bugged both my parents to let me get it and they finally agreed, out of desperation more than anything else. At this point in my shooting career, except for my bootleg sessions, I had to shoot with one of my parents as a supervisor, so I actually didn't get too much shooting in. Also, ammunition came out of my allowance, which wasn't too big. Sears, Roebuck had 22 Shorts for 14 cents for a box of 50, which sounds cheap today, but this was still the Depression and most of my 50 cents weekly allowance was saved to buy more guns for my collection.

Today, we hear so much about gun control that there is a tendency to think that it is a new phenomenon. Nothing could be less true — my first brush with anti-gun thinking came in 1936, or thereabouts. We had put up a shooting range on a 3-acre lot we owned that had once belonged to my grandparents. Our nextdoor neighbor, who built his house very close to the firing line of our range, called my

October, 1937: Away at boarding school in Tucson, Arizona. I'm shooting my new Iver Johnson 32 S&W Short revolver.

mother to complain about the noise. But mother, never liking the man anyway, couldn't understand his complaint about the little snap of 22s. She, of course, was unaware that most of the types of ammunition available from Bannerman had also been fired over that same range, and to protect my illicit shooting, I was forced to remain silent.

Her reaction to this attack on her first born's shooting was analogous to a mother tiger about to lose a cub. She told the complainer that she and her family had been there before he had moved in, that they would be there long after he was gone, and that they would shoot over this range as long as they wished. To add to her cause, she now encouraged me to shoot as often as I wanted to, and even on occasion bought extra ammo for me. It was too good to last, and it didn't. The gentleman whose audio purity I had invaded also was the head of our borough council, and at the next sitting of that august group, an anti-shooting ordinance was passed.

In those halcyon days, the right to bear arms was more highly regarded than it is today so the ordinance made it illegal to discharge any firearm which was legal under the federal law of 1934! In other words, you could fire a shotgun only if its barrel length was less than 16 inches, which, of course, made it illegal federally. This put an end to any more shooting on our ancestral acres. In retrospect, I think if I had been older, I would have offered to move my range a little farther away from the councilman's

property line and by my compromise, future shooters would possibly still be able to have a range in our small borough. However, in light of ordinances in Morton Grove, Illinois, San Francisco, California and the perennial New York City nightmare, maybe part of urbanization is losing some of our rural rights. It's comparable to people who move near an airport, then complain about the noise made by the airplanes.

Up until this period, I had lived at home with my family in New York City during the winter and returned to Pennsylvania for a long, lazy summer. After Christmas in 1936, my mother decided that I was getting too many colds in the severe New York winters and should go away to school in Arizona for my health (frankly, I was as healthy as a horse). At Greenfield School in Tucson we had very few rules about shooting, and at last, at 14, I was on my own. I had my Iver Johnson rifle and pistol out in cowboy country. As a rule of the school, I also had my own horse, Smoky, and my own saddle and bridle — what more could a boy ask for? We were also allowed to go into Tucson every Saturday afternoon on our own.

I soon found the local hock shops, and even the Western supply shops, like Porter's, which were a Valhalla for guns. One of the hardest things for today's new collectors to realize is that back then there were no books on gun collecting *at all*. Today there are literally hundreds of books on guns, covering almost every collecting spe-

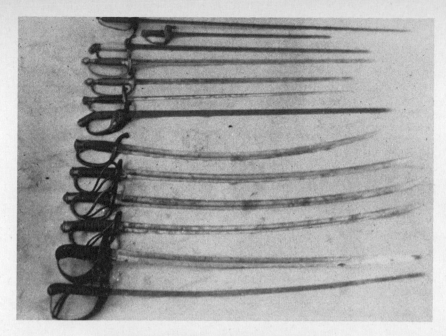

September, 1940, my sword collection, top to bottom: 15th century rapier, cabin boy's sword, War of 1812 ivory-handled officer's sword, Civil War NCO's sword, Civil War NCO's sword, Officer's dress sword, German WW I dispatch rider's sword, Mexican War saber, Civil War cavalry saber, Civil War cavalry saber, Civil War cavalry saber, Spanish American War Toledo blade saber, and a German Heidelberg student's fencing saber.

September, 1940, top to bottom: Indian matchlock musket (my first firearm), Spanish flintlock blunderbuss, French flintlock blunderbuss, Revolutionary War "Committee of Safety" rifle, cap and ball half-stock New York state-made squirrel rifle. The last two guns are now in my gun museum in "Old Tucson."

cialty. In the 1930s, though, the best references we had were Stoeger's, Hudson Sporting Goods Co.'s, Galef's and, most important, Bannerman's catalogs. The obvious reason for this lack of literature was that there just weren't that many people interested in gun collecting. For example, in the little town of Sewickley, Pennsylvania, where I grew up, there was a population of 5000 and to my knowledge only three gun collectors, of which I was the youngest. In those days, NRA meant National Recovery Act — the National Rifle Association was almost unknown.

I soon bought my first of many Colt single-action revolvers, 45-caliber, 4³/₄-inch barrel, with a thinning nickel plate. It was the old type with the screw-held cylinder pin. This prize set me back all of $5, and it was very expensive to shoot — we didn't know then that early ones really should be shot only with blackpowder cartridges. I don't think I shot too many boxes of ammo through it before I found my first S&W; it was a 4-inch barrel M&P 32-20. It cost me $15, but the guy threw in a 303 Ross straight-pull rifle to sweeten the deal. The Ross wouldn't eject unless I put the butt on the ground and jumped with all of my 115 pounds on the bolt handle. When the spent cartridge case was finally ejected, the case's shoulder had moved forward a good ¹/₄-inch. This, I was told, was because the chamber had been relieved to help the rifle extract. Well, even at 15, this fix scared me enough that I just relegated the Ross to my non-shooting collection.

The S&W, on the other hand, was my first modern qual-

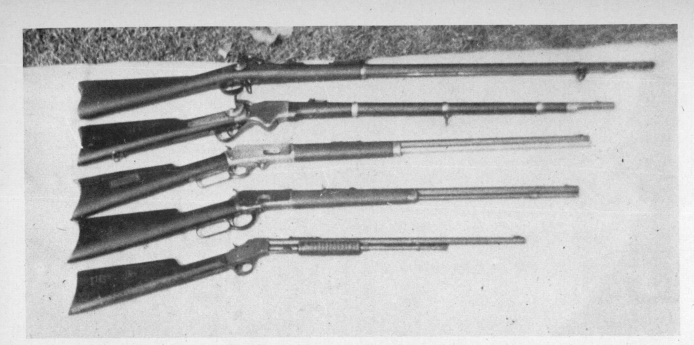

September, 1940, top to bottom: Springfield Trapdoor 45-70 rod-bayonet rifle, Spencer 56 rifle, Marlin 1893 32-40 rifle, Winchester 32-20 rifle, Stevens "visible loader" 22 pump rifle.

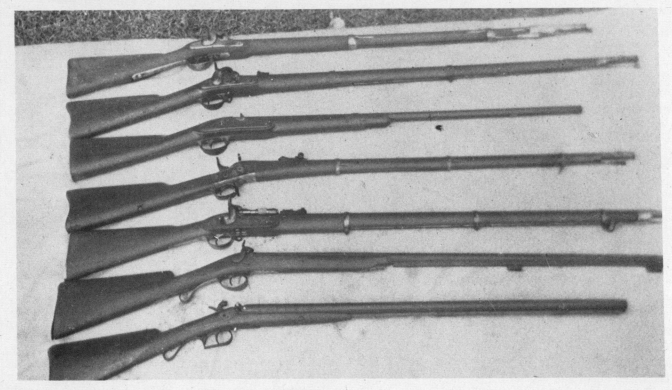

September, 1940, top to bottom: Imported Austrian Civil War rifle, Remington contract Civil War rifle Model 1863 with Maynard primer, S. North Musket (missing hammer), Remington 50-70 rolling block New York State rifle, Snyder-Enfield rifle, cap and ball fouling piece, percussion double-barreled shotgun.

ity handgun, and even if the 32-20 caliber wasn't too desirable, I found it excellent and very accurate. At Christmas time this same year I received a package from home while vacationing with a group of boys and a teacher at the Circle Z Ranch in Patagonia, Arizona. In this package was a weird looking gun called a Bullseye pistol. For those of you who came along later, a Bullseye pistol was really just a repeating slingshot. It used a big rubber band to drive #8 lead shot down a little trackway. That doesn't sound like much, but it was very accurate and cost next to

nothing to shoot. With a Bullseye it was easy to hit a fly at rest, 10 feet away. This was basically what I used mine for and each miss left a little dent in the wall instead of the fly, while a hit left a slight depression loaded with fly. Even today, if you are in a building where a Bullseye once held sway, you will find these little dents and, occasionally, a painted-over fly.

Around this time I bought my first automatic pistol, little dreaming that some day these would be my main interest in gun collecting. My first one was a total disaster — it was a well-worn, Spanish-made 25 ACP caliber. I couldn't get it to fire more than one shot. The former owner, a sensitive man, had made magazine lip corrections with a pair of gas pliers and possibly a 2-pound sledge hammer. He had also attempted to delicately unscrew the barrel with the same pliers. I sold it back and bought another much better looking Spanish 32 ACP.

I am sure some of you are laughing at my Hispanic faithfulness, but I was getting a little smarter, albeit a little poorer, each time. The 32 auto wouldn't even fire its first shot because, overlooked by me, its firing pin was broken. So here I was, stuck with a $2 gun that wouldn't even fire. On my next Saturday jaunt to Tucson, I hunted up a gunsmith and asked how much a new firing pin would cost. First, in all fairness, let me say that he expressed some pretty earth-shaking remarks about cheap automatics, which he seemed to feel were a blot on his trade. He

September, 1940, top to bottom: Swiss Vetterli "Chamois rifle" bought from Bannermans, Dutch Beaumont rifle, Spanish Mauser in 7mm, Krag-Jorgenson rifle, German WW I Mauser of 1898 in 7.9mm, Canadian Ross 303 straight-pull rifle, Remington 22 Model 41.

then went on, getting redder and redder in the face and suggesting to a wide-eyed 15-year-old where to put that same Spanish masterpiece. Suddenly in the middle of his tirade, he must have seen the disappointment in my face, he concluded by telling me to give him a week and $1 and he would make me a firing pin.

This gunsmith's specialty was making snubbies, or as we called them, "belly guns," out of all things, 1917 Colt and Smith & Wesson 45 ACP revolvers. He got the guns as military surplus and cut the barrels to only 2 inches long. He then ground the hammer spur off completely, and removed the front half of the trigger guard. Finally, he smoothed up the double action and, for all this work plus the original price of the gun, he got $25.

After having blown a whole buck repairing my Spanish auto, I didn't have enough money left to buy even a cheap box of 25 rounds of imported German 32 ammo. I decided to practice by dry firing it until I could get some money for cartridges. This was my second mistake; I broke my new firing pin, plus continued dry firing beat the inside of the slide around the internal hammer to a pulp. So much for the steel used in those Spanish autos.

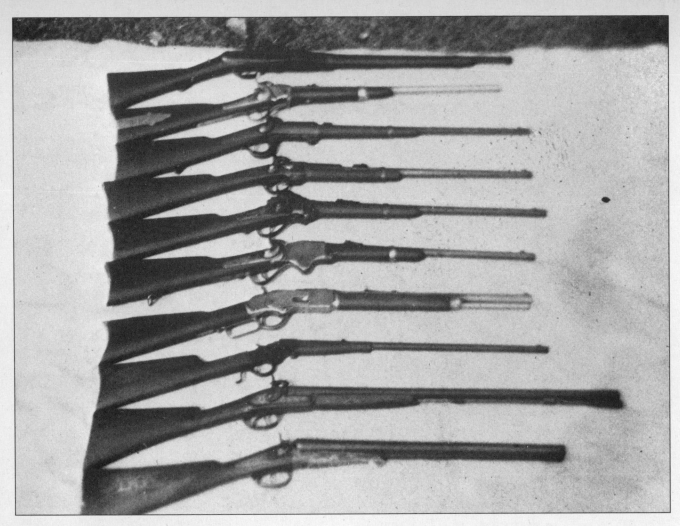

September, 1940, carbines, top to bottom: Hall "Harper's Ferry" carbine, Sharps "slant-breech" 52-caliber carbine ($3.50 at Bannermans), Burnside 52-caliber carbine, Ball 52-caliber carbine, Sharps 50-70 carbine (two for $3 at Bannermans "Guns for Decoration Table"), Spencer 56-caliber carbine, Winchester Model 1873 44-40 carbine, Stevens "Crackshot" 22 rifle, percussion double-barrel shotgun, 12-gauge Belgian double-barrel shotgun.

I decided my next auto would be American-made; I was torn between a $12.50 used Colt 1903 hammerless 32 ACP and a $14 Remington Model 51 in 380 ACP. You can see that I had really learned my lesson! Not so at all. In the middle of a 1/2-hour bargaining session between me and the owner of the pawn shop, during which I graphically described my current and future financial outlook, and he, on the other hand, laboriously droned on about how his family had to keep eating with some regularity, I looked away from what I was attempting to buy and saw a $7 auto called an "Infallible." With the brilliance of an older and wiser person, I saw a pleasant shape, a lot of fascinating levers whose purpose I could not even guess, and best of all, a much cheaper American-made pistol.

Just as the dealer was winding up his speech on home economics, I pulled a switch on him by casually saying, "OK, how much do you want for that one?"

Now, I could see I had him. He had spent so much time on me that he almost had to sell something, so he breathlessly allowed me to steal his Warner Arms "Infallible" for a paltry $6. When I got enough money to buy the 25 rounds of 32 ACP that required the dollar I had saved on the deal, I took my "Infallible" out to shoot. By then I did know what each lever did; the safety lever, the grips told me, "blocked the sear." The little button in the rear dropped a piece of steel, allowing the bolt to be removed after its cross pin was pushed in.

In a week I had found out a lot about my "Infallible"; now to shoot it. The first round was great, the second round a beauty, the third round — well, the bolt didn't get all the way back to battery. The hangup was obviously in the two spring-loaded recoil rods — they were bending upward. As my shooting session wore on, I learned a great lesson. With guns, like most everything, you get what you pay for, and cheap is cheap even if American-made. My Infallible had failed! I sold it without a tear in my eye and with the $2 bought a 44-40 Winchester Model 1873 lever-action rifle. It looked too long to me so I hacksawed off the barrel to about 18 inches, thus committing another

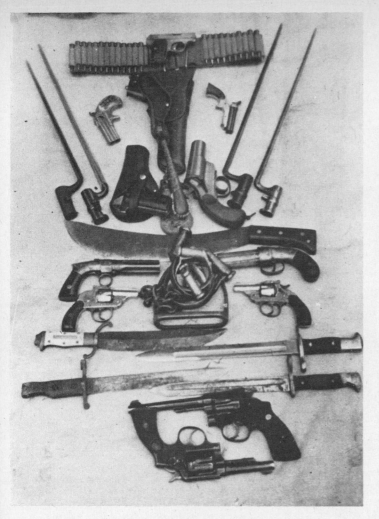

September, 1940, handguns, (top to bottom): 25 ACP Spanish vest pocket auto (junk), father's 45 Colt 1911 — later rebuilt by me when I was stationed at Aberdeen Proving Ground — Remington double derringer 41-caliber RF, Sharps 22 four-shot derringer, Spanish 32 ACP auto, British Webley 1-inch WW I Very pistol, Robins & Lawrence 32 percussion pepperbox, Allen 32 percussion pepperbox, a wonderful S&W K-22 (one of the best guns I've ever owned), S&W M&P Model 10 32-20 (to go with the Winchester of the same caliber), plus miscellaneous bayonets, etc.

little antique shop in New York City; the owner had a few guns, but was more into Louis Quatorze chairs. His name was Robert Abels — the same Bob Abels who became a great weapons dealer and, for my money, a good friend and one of the great contributors to my teenage gun collection.

Just as Bob was getting into guns, going to shows in Ohio and bringing goodies back to New York, I was getting into Remingtons as a specialty. In a very short period, I acquired from Bob a small but fantastic collection of Remington handguns — a cased First Model pocket Beals, a factory-engraved pearl-grip Rider magazine pistol, and a cased gold-plated and engraved Remington 41 double derringer. The only Remington to elude me was the 22 zig-zag derringer.

One vacation I strolled into Abels' shop and found him obviously excited about something; he told Bernie to bring out the new case of guns to show me. It was a huge 3- by 5-foot velvet-lined wooden case with 20 or more pistols in it, all of them in new condition. There was only one Remington, but what a Remington it was — Navy Model 36 cap-and-ball, silver-plated with ivory grips, *brand new*. The entire case of guns had been made up by Schuyler, Hartley and Graham of New York City as a gift to an Argentinean general who had helped dispose of our surplus guns after the Civil War. I knew I had to have that revolver so I asked the fateful question — the answer was $90, which sounds like a joke today but was twice as much as this not-too-diligent schoolboy had ever spent on a gun before. I bought it, and it was for years the focal point of my Remingtons.

My second year at Lawrenceville I had a pair of Swiss percussion dueling pistols as decorations in my room. I say decorations, but I could actually fire them as I had some powder and had cast a few balls with a Bannerman-

faux pas. Never alter a gun, because if you do, it will lose much of its value — even if when you come to sell it, you have the nerve to keep a straight face when you say, "That's just how I got it; I think it must have been shortened by a stagecoach driver years ago."

This Winchester whetted my appetite for another lever-action gun, and I found a Marlin Model 1893 in 32-40 caliber for only a paltry $2. When I got it back to school, I found that I had fallen for the old broken firing pin ploy again. This time, however, a letter to Marlin brought a replacement by return mail. This Marlin was one of my favorites for many years. Its only trouble came when I took up casting my own bullets; since the bore was so badly pitted it leaded up very quickly. It wasn't until just a few years ago, at a gun show in Girard, Pennsylvania, that I found a perfect mate — same caliber, same vintage, but with a very good bore — so I sold my old friend and now shoot its new brother.

In 1939, after the results of my less than brilliant performance on the college board exams, my mother decided that I had had enough Western fun and games and it was time to start my serious education. I was shipped to the Lawrenceville School in New Jersey with an Arizona tan and damned little else. I was immediately dropped back a year. During this traumatic period in my life I found a

July, 1941: Bonnie and Clyde Simmons, and their 1936 Ford V8, going out shooting for the afternoon. On my hip is my brand new Colt 44-40 "Frontier Six-Shooter" with stag grips, bought from Hudson's Sporting Goods for $27.50; one of the guns I had always wanted.

purchased 52-caliber bullet mould. On trips into the New Jersey countryside for a forbidden cigarette I would also bring and shoot my dueling pistols.

One day when a planned trip was canceled by rain, I thought it would be fun to fire one of the duelers in my room at school. It would be easy as I would just muffle the noise with a pillow and, of course, I wouldn't use a ball. That's what I thought! First, my sound proofing didn't work perfectly; there was an ominous muffled explosion, which for all I know might have been heard as far away as Trenton. But that wasn't all, as there was smoke — and I mean smoke! Sulfurous clouds drifted down the halls and into other rooms when startled students imprudently opened their doors to see what had blown up. As if this wasn't bad enough, the over-powder wad I used seemed somehow to have ignited the pillow. My first duty was to stamp out the conflagration — I owed this to my panicked fellow housemates.

Just as I got the fire under control, my housemaster, usually a smooth talking and unflappable gentleman, stuck his head in my door through the billowing smoke. "What in hell was that noise, Simmons?" "Oh, sir, I was just having a little trouble with a chemical experiment." Well, the rapid oxidation of a mixture of sulfur, saltpeter and charcoal, triggered by a detonated charge of fulminate of mercury is a chemical experiment, but it was the last such project I ever dared at Lawrenceville. I think it was only because I was the vice president of my house that kept me in the school.

That was the year I bought my first successful automatic pistol — successful in that it *worked*. A fellow student had both a 32 rimfire Smith & Wesson Model 3 spur trigger revolver and an Ortgies 32 ACP automatic, and I got the pair for a $5 bill. The Ortgies was indeed a neat pistol. I soon found how to remove the grips without breaking them, and I really liked the way the barrel locked to the frame. The trigger nose was broken, but Stoeger had parts for Ortgies so that was soon repaired. As I remember, for a pocket automatic that Ortgies was a good shooter. Today, I still have this fine, though inexpensive, German-made pistol. I also have my second Spanish 32 ACP automatic, which still has a broken firing pin, but it is safer that way. At W.S. Brown in Pittsburgh I bought a beautiful little Harrington & Richardson 25 ACP auto. This was so well made that, in my mind, it redeemed the negative memory of my first Spanish 25. It also represented my first shootable U.S.-made automatic.

About the time of the British retreat at Dunkirk, my father was transferred and put in charge of his company's Washington, D.C. office. This meant that we moved to Washington, which gave me a chance to look into a whole new group of gun-selling places. We lived in an affluent area of the northwest section, and when the cry went out for arms for Britain, it was answered by most of our generous neighbors. Barrels of guns and swords and even spears appeared before each house for collection. As this gun collector walked down the street past more different guns than I had ever seen before, I was tempted, oh Lord! was I tempted, but patriotism and honesty kept my hands in my pockets. The above vignette shows my good side; now let me tell of my bad side, or if not bad, at least show that I was becoming a crafty gun buyer.

In Washington, "D" street was where the pawn and hock shops were, and it was there that I usually visited when I was home from school. One day, I spied a Henry iron-frame rifle in the rack among a bunch of Winchester 94s in a dark shop. I asked the entrepreneur to let me see it, as I was thinking of going hunting in the fall. The gun looked almost new, and I worked the lever and saw that it still had its pair of rimfire firing pins and saw its serial number. Hiding my excitement, I next asked how much. The owner said he would part with it for $30.

Now even in those days $30 for an iron-frame Henry was a steal, but I had become so much a part of the gun collecting world that I felt it was my duty to offer $25. He said in no way would he let go a good hunting gun for only $25. I then slyly countered by asking if, at $30, he would throw in a box of ammo. He said he would, and handed me a broken box of centerfire 44-40 cartridges. Now I figured I had him; I showed the now abject shopkeeper how centerfire cartridges would not work in this rimfire

August, 1945: Taken just as the war ended in Okinawa. Corporal Simmons is firing a "borrowed" 45 Colt Model 1911-A1. The only target now is just floating debris in the Pacific. Getting ready to come home.

April, 1945: My collection of Remington rifles, pistols and revolvers, top to bottom: Two rolling block sporting rifles, rolling block pistols flanking two cased Beals pocket revolvers, (under cases) Elliot 32 rimfire derringer, cased 41 double derringer, second 41 double derringer, Rider 32 rimfire magazine pistol, (left to right) New Model Navy 36 revolver, New Model Army 44 revolver, same but dug up, New Model 38 rimfire conversion revolver, vest pocket single shot derringer 22 Short, New Line 38 rimfire revolver, New Model Navy 36 silver-plated and ivory grips (a gift from our government to an Argentinean general), New Model Navy conversion 38 rimfire revolver, Model 1875 44-40 single-action revolver. I'm in the service and this was a snapshot taken to remind me of some of my Remington collection while overseas.

Henry. He gave up and gave me the gun for $25. When he made up the receipt, he couldn't find the serial number because he wouldn't believe it was a single digit — 2! As I left the store, he could hardly suppress a smile at having hooked this smartass kid with a lever-action rimfire *hunting* rifle. That snookered kid had, however, walked out of his shop with one of the two trial guns used to demonstrate the Henry rifle to Abraham Lincoln during the Civil War — all for $25. Yes this kid *was* learning over the years.

This brings me up to World War II. I had some 40 guns in my collection, most of which I could, and had, shot. All were loved, especially my Remingtons, and one other that I have kept for the last. I may have left the West under a parental cloud, but the West never really left me. In my late teens, I wanted more than anything a matched pair of brand new Colt Single Action Armys. This required (including the two holster rigs) an outlay of close to $90 that I just couldn't swing. I settled for a Hudson Sporting Goods reduced "Frontier Six Shooter" in 44-40 caliber with a 4³/₄-inch barrel, blue and new for $23.50, plus a Lawrence-made, basket-weave, embossed holster and belt from Stoeger for another $10. This was it — as storm clouds began to spread over Europe, I would soon have to put away my playthings and take up a more serious-purposed weapon, but I was maybe a little better prepared than most because of my life-long hobby — gun collecting. ●

A FACE

This woodcut of Col. H. D. Capers is from the November, 1895 issue of the *Confederate Veteran*.

from the *PAST*

by
GRAHAM BURNSIDE

I GUESS we've all said several hundred times, "I wish that gun could talk." We can't help feeling that way. As I wrote this, I glanced at one of my gun racks that holds 14 Trapdoor Springfields dating from 1868 to 1888. Now, I have more Springfields than that, but just consider those 20 years — from the post-Civil War period to almost the end of the Indian conflicts — and think of

Serial number 10951 of the 1860 Army, probably manufactured at the Colt factory in late August of 1861. The cylinder bears the same number and the wedge appears to be original.

The 1860 Colt Army, serial number 10951, owned and carried during the Civil War by Col. Henry Capers.

the stories some of those rifles could tell. In my daydreaming I admire their graceful contours and silent dignity — I almost wonder if they compare notes.

That is just one of the rewarding aspects of collecting, and remember, we are not only collecting items, but gathering knowledge and history that becomes part of us as well. The truly fortunate collector is one who finds a piece that compels him to go into the past and shed light on some dusty archives. One of those so blessed is Frank Pangallo of Fort Wayne, Indiana, who, in 1988, found the 1860 Colt Army revolver pictured here.

Frank and his lovely wife, Eileen, attended a gun show in Louisville, Kentucky last April. Frank wandered about, looking over the varied displays, while Eileen "table-sat." An older gentleman appeared at the table and showed Eileen an 1860 Colt Army revolver with an engraved backstrap. Realizing the possible interest and value that could well be associated with an engraved Civil War revolver, Eileen quickly found her husband. Although the man with the Colt had left their table, they quickly found him and purchased the pistol for what one would consider a very nominal price. Values on such items can and do vary depending on several factors — the most important usually being the gun's owner. In this case, though, they paid the man the price he asked, no argument.

When Frank showed me the Colt, I carefully examined its features to form my own opinion as to its authenticity and originality. I've seen more than a few bad ones over the years! But from every angle, this one came up "pure quill."

I talked to Frank about contacting the National Archives and what photographs I wanted — this one should be shared with the collecting fraternity. How many times have you heard that "all the good ones are gone"? Hogwash! There are still thousands of rare fire-arms hiding in attics and closets gathering dust, unap-preciated and ill kept. If you can find a valuable piece in April of 1988, there will still be many more to be found in April of 1998!

Frank Pangallo did his homework, and here is the story.

First, we must examine the revolver itself. The piece has matching serial numbers, an even patina overall, and the engraving is typical of the style used in the Civil War period. The serial number, 10951, dates the revolver appropriate to the engraving. A fire at the Colt factory in February of 1864 destroyed most or all of the Colt records pertaining to production prior to 1861, but it has been estimated that Colt started 1861 with ap-proximately serial number 2000, and by the beginning of 1862, had passed the 25,000 mark. This would put gun number 10951 about halfway through 1861 — per-fect timing to have been engraved and presented in

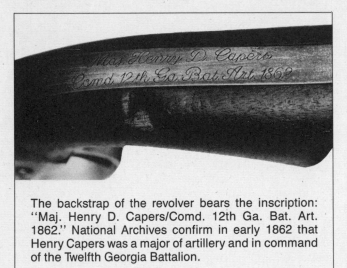

The backstrap of the revolver bears the inscription: "Maj. Henry D. Capers/Comd. 12th Ga. Bat. Art. 1862." National Archives confirm in early 1862 that Henry Capers was a major of artillery and in command of the Twelfth Georgia Battalion.

1862. The Pangallos learned from Colt's that this re-volver was shipped on September 14, 1861 to the arse-nal at Governors Island, New York. How the piece found its way south after that is not known but not at all surprising. Throughout the entire Civil War, arms manufactured in the North continued to trickle south by various channels. The engraving reads: Maj. Henry D. Capers/Comd. 12th Ga. Bat. Art. 1862.

When I got home from the gun show I tried to find some record of Henry Capers but failed. I did find ref-erence to one Brig. Gen. Ellison Capers of South Caro-lina in the book, *Confederate Soldier in the Civil War*, page 363. Subsequent research has revealed that Elli-son Capers was Henry's brother.

Henry D. Capers ended his military experience as a colonel. His varied and interesting career would fill a book, but for the purpose of this writing we shall move along with some alacrity. Col. Capers entered the South Carolina Military Academy in 1852. He then studied medicine and graduated from the South Caro-lina Medical College in 1856. It would appear that he was a very precocious young man, as he was already a faculty member of the Atlanta Medical College when South Carolina seceded from the Union. Henry Capers resigned his professorship and was promptly commis-sioned in the Confederate army. He was active in the Fort Sumter fight, and subsequently was the private secretary and chief clerk and disbursing officer of the Confederate State Treasury. When he left that position and was appointed a Lieutenant of Artillery in the regu-lar Confederate Army, he was presented with an en-graved "elegant dress sword." That sword was captured during Sherman's Georgia campaign, but was returned to him 25 years later. As of 1895, Capers' engraved sword was preserved in the Museum of the Barnard E. Bee Camp at Aiken, South Carolina.

Early in 1862, Henry Capers was promoted to Major of Artillery and commanded the Twelfth Georgia Bat-talion, which served under Generals Kirby Smith, Bragg and Beauregard.

On June 2, 1864, Col. Capers was severely wounded at Cold Harbor and was relieved of field duty. When the war ended, he taught school and entered law. His suc-cess as a lawyer was such that he was admitted to the bar of the Georgia Supreme Court in 1871, and the United States Supreme Court in 1873.

After the deaths of Jefferson Davis and Mr. C. G. Memminger, Col. Capers became, by the date of his commission, the oldest Confederate officer still living (1908).

Although this gun show "sleeper" has already talked enough to give us much historical information which has undoubtedly enhanced the value of the piece far above its April, 1988 purchase price, there remain some questions.

First, Henry D. Capers lived a long, successful life and was beloved by family and friends. How did his engraved revolver become separated from his family? What happened to it prior to its surfacing in Louisville, Kentucky in 1988?

Second, what of Capers' presentation sword? Does it still repose in some hallowed place — a museum?

Maybe we'll never know. But then again, maybe this article will trigger further inquiry, and we'll learn even more about one distinguished Southern gentleman — Colonel Henry D. Capers. ●

Bibliography

Amann, William Frayne, ed. *Personnel of the Civil War*, Vol. I. New York: Thomas Yoseloff, 1961.
The Confederate Soldier in the Civil War. New York: Fairfax Press. (Compilation of Confederate newspapers.)
Confederate Veteran Magazine. Vol. III, Nov., 1895. Vol XVI, June, 1908.

Researching the
BATAVIA

AUTOMATIC PISTOL...

...the more I learn, the less I know

Right side of the Batavia automatic pistol. The knob under the barrel near the muzzle, when it's pulled to the rear, operates the action. The knurled, slotted knob over the trigger guard is for takedown.

Left side of the Batavia. The small button just below the rear sight releases the action when the hammer is cocked.

MOST ARTICLES on gun collecting are neatly organized research exercises that lead the reader (along with the writer) down a logical trail in which the arm or arms under discussion neatly fit into some mutually satisfying, logical arrangement. If that's the only kind of article you like, *stop* reading *now* and turn the pages to the next offering. If, however, you enjoy mounting confusion and sharing a research effort that thus far has generated much heat but little light in the mind of the author, read on. Who knows, maybe you have the clue that will unlock the mystery of both the Batavia automatic pistol and rifle!

by JOSEPH J. SCHROEDER

A large, awkward, ugly automatic pistol caught my eye as I stalked the aisles of an Ohio Gun Collectors' Association meeting several years ago. "Batavia!" my memory cried. As a long-time auto pistol collector I had often studied the photo essay on pioneer collector

Aleck Montgomery's fine auto pistol collection in *World's Guns*, a paperback published by Golden State Arms in the late 1950s. A Batavia was pictured there.

I stopped to talk to the owner. Negotiations ensued, and soon I was the proud owner of another rare automatic. "Now," I thought, "one of these days I'll pick up a Batavia automatic rifle, note the differences and similarities, and then I'll know the story of this early and rare American pistol." Hah!

Initial study of the Batavia pistol was rewarding. First of all, careful comparison of my pistol with the picture in *World's Guns* showed it was not only identical — it was the same gun! That established its provenance back to the late '50s, at least. Though its grip frame is large and clumsy and the grip checkering rather crude, the strap is definitely original, not a reworking of the tangs of a rifle action.

The frame is marked BATAVIA AUTOMATIC RIFLE/ PATENTED DEC. 14TH AND 28TH.09/BATAVIA N.Y. in three lines on the left side and MODEL NO. 1 on the right. The barrel is marked only . . . ORT CTG as the original ".22 CAL. SH. . ." portion of the legend was removed when the barrel was tapered. The serial number, 525, appears inside the frame.

To load the Batavia, pulling the knob toward the front of the barrel rearward retracts the bolt and cocks the hammer; releasing the bolt permits it to return under spring tension, stripping a cartridge from the removable box magazine into the chamber. The operating knob and carrier are then locked in the forward position

Detail of the Febiger (top) and Batavia rifle actions, showing markings. Note that the magazine of the Batavia is located farther forward than it is on the Febiger.

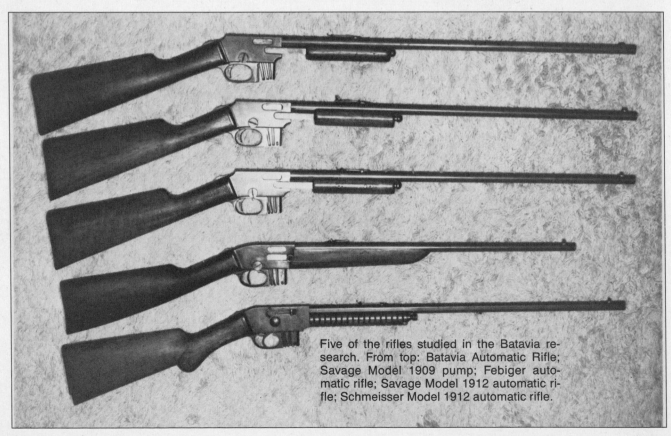

Five of the rifles studied in the Batavia research. From top: Batavia Automatic Rifle; Savage Model 1909 pump; Febiger automatic rifle; Savage Model 1912 automatic rifle; Schmeisser Model 1912 automatic rifle.

Right side view of the Savage Model 1909 pump (top), Batavia (center), and Febiger (bottom). Note the forearm release button on the Febiger.

Inside the action of the Febiger (top) and Savage (bottom). The magazine of the Savage is wider because it is chambered for 22 Long, while the Batavia is in 22 Short.

as long as the hammer is cocked; a button on the upper left side of the frame unlocks the carrier to permit unloading. Takedown is simple — unscrew the knurled knob on the right side of the frame above the trigger guard and the action breaks down into two pieces.

Time passed, and though I wasn't actively searching for that needed Batavia rifle, my desire for one was always in the back of my mind. Finally one day — at another OGCA show, of course — one caught my eye. It had a much higher serial number than my pistol, 4135, and the price was right so I bought it. A few minutes later I showed it to a friend who knew of my Batavia interest, commenting that with it I could now complete my research on the Batavia. His response: "That's nice, but did you see the Febiger on the other side of the room? The Febiger, you know, is a Batavia with different markings!"

No, I didn't know . . . but I soon found out. Not only did I find out, but research demanded that the Febiger

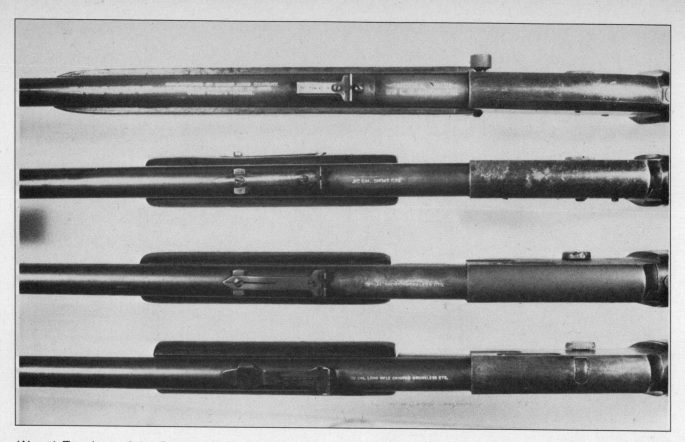

(Above) Top views of the Savage Model 1912 automatic rifle (top), Febiger (second from top), Batavia (third from top), and Savage Model 1909 pump (bottom). Note the locking block on top of the Savage pump.

(Below) Detail of the Savage Model 1912 (top) and Schmeisser Model 1912 automatic rifles. The actions are both very similar in design to the Batavia/Febiger guns, and their magazines are interchangeable.

Marking of the Schmeisser: "Automatic Rifle System Schmeisser Model 1912 For Rimfire Cartridges Cal. 22 Long, Smokeless."

be studied as well, so, naturally, I bought it — serial 221 — too. The waters were starting to muddy!

Back home, careful examination of the two Batavias showed them to be identical internally and with the same frame markings, though the barrel marking on the rifle is .22 CAL. SHORT SMOKELESS CTG. Mechanically, the Febiger is essentially identical to the Batavias, with the notable exception that its magazine well is positioned farther back in its frame; in both Batavias there is actually a spacer mounted in the front of the trigger guard and a corresponding cut in the inside front of the well, moving the magazine forward. This change could have been the result of early feeding problems, making the rash assumption that all three guns were serialed in the same series.

The Febiger also has a pushbutton release on the forearm that latches it to the operating lever. This must be pressed when shooting the gun or the forearm will cycle with the action; the Batavia's forearm is free-floating, so no special release is needed. The Febiger is marked on the left side of the frame FEBIGER ARMS CO. NEW ORLEANS LA./PATENTED JAN. 5. 09 in two lines, MODEL NO. 1 on the right, and — like the pistol — .22 CAL. SHORT CTG on the barrel.

Now, anyone who knows anything about Savage 22 rifles will recognize the similarity between the Batavia, Febiger, and early Savage pumps — the Savage Models 1903 and 1909. If, in fact, one of the early Savages is carefully compared with the Batavia/Febiger guns, the actions and most internal parts are absolutely identical! The only difference is that the Savage pumps, not being recoil operated, have a cammed locking block in the top of the action and no recoil spring.

This leads to a number of very interesting but as yet unanswered questions. As Jim Cobb mentions in his article "William H. Baker: Double-Barreled Entrepe-

nuer" starting on p. 85 of this edition of GUN COLLECTOR'S DIGEST, "Batavia Gun & Forging Company" as well as just plain "Batavia" were names used by Baker for his low-end shotgun business from about 1889 until he sold out to Folsom in 1919. Did Baker or someone in his employ convert a 1909 Savage to semi-automatic operation, and then did Baker contract with Savage to build semi-autos for him to market under the Batavia name? If so, why did Savage, a progressive company in its own right, make "state-of-the-art" semi-auto rifles for a competitor while waiting until 1912 to introduce its own first semi-auto? Though both are New York companies, Savage was in Utica, in the central part of the state, while Batavia is 150 miles or so farther west. And where did Febiger come in? Why the different patent dates on the Febiger and Batavia, and what features do they actually cover?

Finally, as one more contribution to this already hopelessly muddled stew, how about the German-made Schmeisser Model 1912? This uncommon rifle, though it has a somewhat different takedown than its American relatives, is most certainly a knockoff of the Savage/ Batavia/Febiger. So close a knockoff that it uses the same unique ribbed box magazine that the others use!

So many questions, so few answers. What started out as a simple research exercise to further authenticate a rare and unusual pistol has expanded into a major study effort with multiple paths yet to be followed.

One thing does seem likely in the midst of all these unanswered questions. The Batavia 22 pistol, if it is indeed the distinct model it seems to be and not simply a conversion of a rifle, is almost certainly the first 22-caliber self-loading pistol to be commercially offered. If so, the Batavia pistol is of immense historical importance — it sure will be nice when we finally figure out how it came to be!　●

"TRUST ME!"

You say it belonged to Jesse who?

A glossary of commonly-used arms collectors' terms that may be more true than you think.

by
GARY STRAUP
and
FRANK ZIKA

THE VARIETY of interests among arms collectors often requires the acquisition of specimens at a distance. This precludes pre-purchase examination, forcing the buyer to rely on the written or verbal description of the item by a fellow collector or the dealer.

After many decades of collecting with much study of arms advertisements and dealers' catalogs, we have come to regard many of the commonly-used descriptive terms with a certain degree of skepticism. While deliberate attempts to falsify a description seem relatively rare, there is a rather broad gray area composed of a mixture of ignorance, vagueness, stupidity and perhaps even cupidity.

Based on our observations over these years, and with apologies to the many astute and ethical traders in collector arms, we offer the following guide to the language of arms collecting.

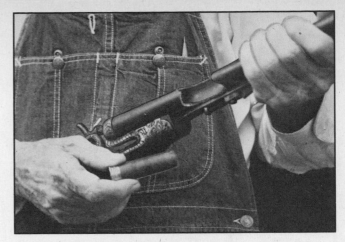

"Needs A Little Work"

Mint Condition — Condition as manufactured, with all original finish.

Minty Condition — As above, except for a few areas of deep pits.

Action Needs Tuning — Internal parts broken or missing; will never function as it should.

A Little Rough — Vaguely resembles a gun.

Good For Its Age — NRA poor to awful.

$350 Value For Only $250 — Now only twice what it's worth.

Genuinely Old — Assembled in the Far East before 1980.

Much Original Finish — In the deeper crevices.

Some Original Finish — Under the grips.

Shows Honest Wear — Used as a hammer by an early settler.

Very Good Bore — Traces of rifling among the pits.

Good Bore — Pits form a spiral.

Fair Bore — You can see light through it.

Poor Bore — You can't see light through it.

Needs A little Work — Beyond repair.

Tight — Thanks to epoxy cement.

Hairline Crack — You can see light through it.

Small Chip Out Of Stock — Enough wood missing to cook a campfire meal.

Nice Patina — Solid coat of rust.

Some Wood Repair — Stock replaced.

Representative Piece — Still resembles a gun.

Good Shooter — For the suicidal.

Pre-Revolutionary — Made before some revolution, but not the American.

Probably Confederate — Probably not.

Naval Variation — From a Portsmouth or San Diego pawn shop.

Worn Finish — Markings gone.

Needs Tightening — Everything's loose.

Some Parts Replaced — Some may be original.

Armory Reconditioned — Belt sander special.

All Numbers Match — They didn't used to, but they do now.

Reasonable Offers Considered — I'm desperate.

It may be "A Little Rough," but it's still a "Representative Piece."

The 12mm Scheintod Pistolen

by *HOWARD RESNICK*

As an avid collector of flare pistols of all types, I had accumulated over the years a variety of small-caliber (12mm or less) signal guns. Then, one day at a Columbus, Ohio gun show I picked up an unusual large-caliber, three-barreled repeating pistol. On its hard-rubber grip was a dancing skeleton with a cloud of vapor around its skull.

That was my first "Scheintod," a German-made pistol designed to fire gas cartridges and whose name translates to "appearance of death." This acquisition started me in yet another collecting direction and over the last 10 years (time flies when you're having fun!) I've picked up quite a few more 12mm gas pistols, single shots and revolvers, as well as the multi-barreled

Perhaps the most exotic of the Scheintod pistol family are the three-barreled models such as this one, probably made by the well-known German arms firm of August Menz in Suhl.

Figure 1: (Right) A very early, all-steel, single-barreled Scheintod pistol (bottom) and a later (probably late 1920s) version with a zinc alloy barrel. The early pistol is marked "Scheintod D.R.G.M. Pistol," while the later version bears "Scheintod Pistol D.R.W.Z." on the barrel and the Nico trademark on the bakelite grips.

Figure 2: (Left) Original box for the later Nico pistol in Figure 1. Note a Scheintod in use on the cover blowing a cloud of gas at an "attacker."

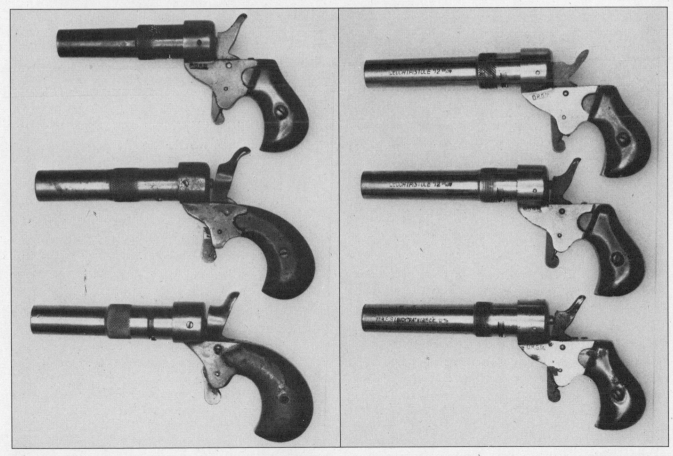

Figure 3: Six variations of the early single-barrel, all-steel Scheintod pistols. At left, top to bottom — short barrel with steel grips and flat hammer, marked only "D.R.G.M."; wood grips with only a "crown over U" proof; barrel marked "Leuchtkugel 12m/m," with an unusual proof showing an officer shooting a Scheintod pistol. At right, top to bottom — barrel marked "Leuchtpistole 12m/m"; same except for hammer shape; nickel finish, barrel marked "Nur Für Leuchtpatrone cal. 12m/m."

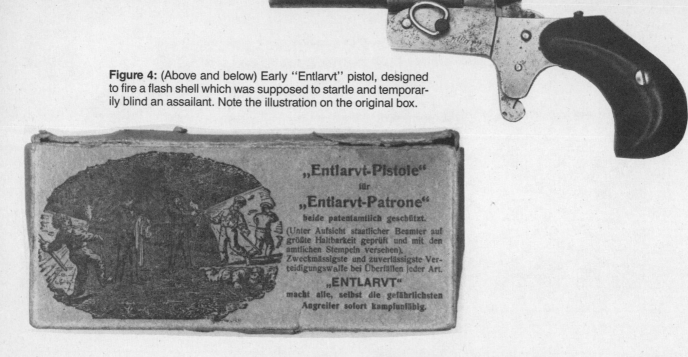

Figure 4: (Above and below) Early "Entlarvt" pistol, designed to fire a flash shell which was supposed to startle and temporarily blind an assailant. Note the illustration on the original box.

„Entlarvt-Pistole"

für

„Entlarvt-Patrone"

beide patentamtlich geschützt.

(Unter Aufsicht staatlicher Beamter auf größte Haltbarkeit geprüft und mit den amtlichen Stempeln versehen).

Zweckmässigste und zuverlässigste Verteidigungswaffe bei Überfällen jeder Art.

„ENTLARVT"

macht alle, selbst die gefährlichsten Angreifer sofort kampfunfähig.

Figure 5: Two more "Entlarvt" variations. The upper gun has a lever-type barrel release and stepped barrel without knurling.

variety. Some of these were also marked Scheintod and some even had the dancing skeleton trademark that had originally intrigued me.

A number of Scheintod pistols appear in the 1911 ALFA catalog of the Adolph Frank Company of Hamburg, Germany, which refers to them as "Scheintot-pistolen" and describes them (in four languages) as "Defensive arms non killing." Designed for self-protection, these turn-of-the-century gas pistols were chambered for a variety of 12mm gas and signal cartridges. Later, smaller caliber (down to 6mm) gas guns were introduced as well.

Although most Scheintod pistols bear no markings to indicate their purpose, some will be found marked (in German) either "Only For Gas Cartridges" or "Only For Flares" on the barrel or frame. Oddly enough, examples of otherwise identical pistols may be found with either marking, even though they are capable of firing both types of cartridges! In addition to gas and flare cartridges, blank and flash ("Entlarvt") cartridges

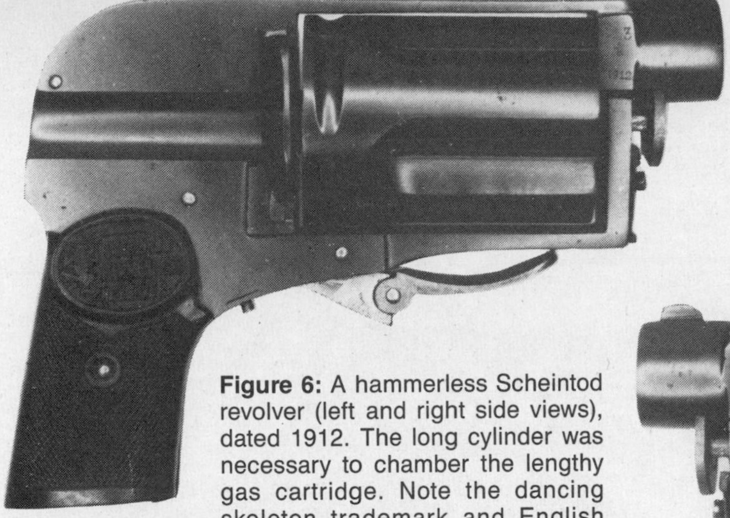

Figure 6: A hammerless Scheintod revolver (left and right side views), dated 1912. The long cylinder was necessary to chamber the lengthy gas cartridge. Note the dancing skeleton trademark and English marking on the grip, which reads "Schientod Hammerless Revolver."

Figure 7: Two Scheintod revolvers with the characteristic folding triggers. Note the difference in grip markings; the bottom pistol is dated 1912, the top is undated.

were also made to be fired from Scheintod pistols.

The earliest Scheintod pistols had a single barrel and were made in several variations. Probably the earliest type had a Flobert action and used a socket-bayonet-type catch which held the barrel to the frame. To load the chamber, the barrel was removed by rotating it a quarter turn and pulling it forward.

Figure 1 shows a very early all-steel example bottom marked Scheintod D.R.G.M. Pistol and a later — probably late 1920s — example with a zinc alloy barrel and bakelite grips marked Scheintod Pistol D.R.W.Z. and Nico. Figure 2 shows the original box for the later pistol — note the Scheintod in use! Other variations of the early all-steel models are shown in Figure 3.

"Entlarvt" pistols, though similar to the Schein-

tods, were originally designed to fire flash cartridges. When fired, flash cartridges produced a brilliant flash of light which was supposed to startle and temporarily blind an attacker. Apparently this proved unsuccessful, at least under some conditions, so gas and flare cartridges were later designed for them.

The original Entlarvt pistol was in 10mm and used a Flobert action. It was opened for loading by removing the rear barrel pin and tipping the barrel down. Figure 4 shows an early example with nickel finish, complete with original box. Two other Entlarvt variations are shown in Figure 5. An Entlarvt with a lever barrel release instead of the removable (and easily lost) pin, made in both 8 and 12mm, was a later improvement.

Scheintod revolvers were also popular around the

Figure 8: Right and left side views of a revolver dated 1920; note the wood grips and unusual loading gate.

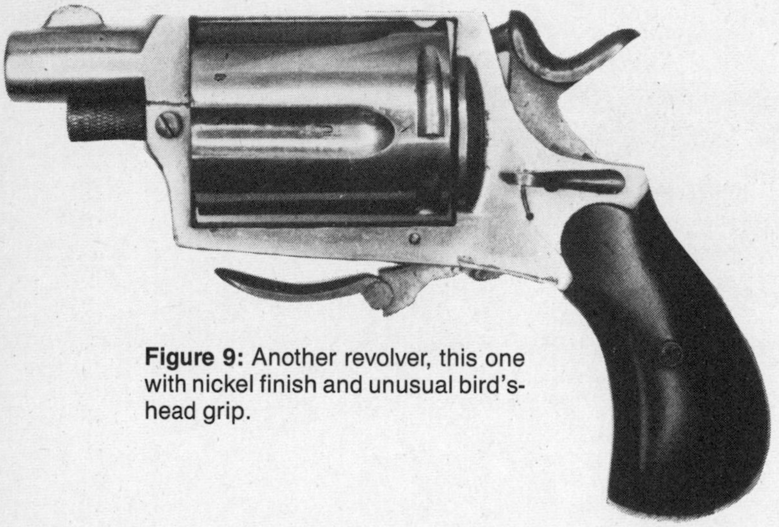

Figure 9: Another revolver, this one with nickel finish and unusual bird's-head grip.

Figure 12: The three-barreled Van Karner 60-caliber gas pistol is impressive in appearance. It was made in New York and is of all aluminum construction.

turn of the century. An obvious feature was their unusually long cylinder to hold the gas or signal cartridge; folding triggers were also the rule. The rarest is the hammerless version, dated 1912 and marked with serial (or assembly) number 13, shown in Figure 6. Note the dancing skeleton and English marking on the grip. Figures 7, 8 and 9 show four more variations.

The unusual three-barreled Scheintod pistols like the one pictured earlier were always attention getters. The August Menz firm was probably the producer of this type of Scheintod, which is very similar to the Regnum, a four-barreled 25-caliber repeating pistol. It

Figures 10 and 11: Pages from the Adolph Frank (ALFA) catalog of 1911, showing Scheintod pistols then available.

loaded by pulling the striated release rearward, then tipping the barrels down to expose the chambers.

Some of the range of Scheintod pistols available in pre-World War I Germany is indicated by the samples of pages from the classic Adolph Frank (ALFA) catalog, published in Bremen in 1911 (Figures 10,11).

Probably because European gun laws were more strict even in the late 19th century than those in the United States, gas pistols (which required no permit) were far more popular over there than here. Though tear gas pens and even billy club guns were made in some numbers in the U.S., the only Scheintod-type gas

Figure 13: A rare two-barreled Nico Scheintod pistol marked simply "D.R.G.M."

Figure 14: Four variations of the three-barreled Nico Scheintod pistol, made shortly after World War I.

Figure 15: Two original Nico Scheintod boxes. Some had rather "adventerous" depictions of the guns in use.

Figure 16: Single-barreled Perplex Scheintods, made in Zella Mehlis, Germany by Bernh Paatz in the late 1920s and '30s.

pistol made in this country was the Van Karner shown in Figure 12. Beautifully designed and made entirely of aluminum, the 60-caliber Van Karner was made in New York in very limited numbers; the few serial numbers noted all fall between 3700 and 4000.

After World War I, a new type of multi-barreled Scheintod, the "Nico," appeared. They were all of aluminum construction, and were loaded by pressing a small button on the side of the frame which permitted the barrel block to be lifted out. A rare two-barreled variation, marked simply D.R.G.M., is shown in Figure 13. Four three-barreled variations appear in Figure 14

Figure 17: Barrel marking of a single-barreled Perplex pistol. "Nur Für Leuchtpatronen" means "Only For Signal Cartridges"; an identical example is marked "Nur Für Gaspatronen," meaning "Only For Gas Cartridges," even thought the two are otherwise identical.

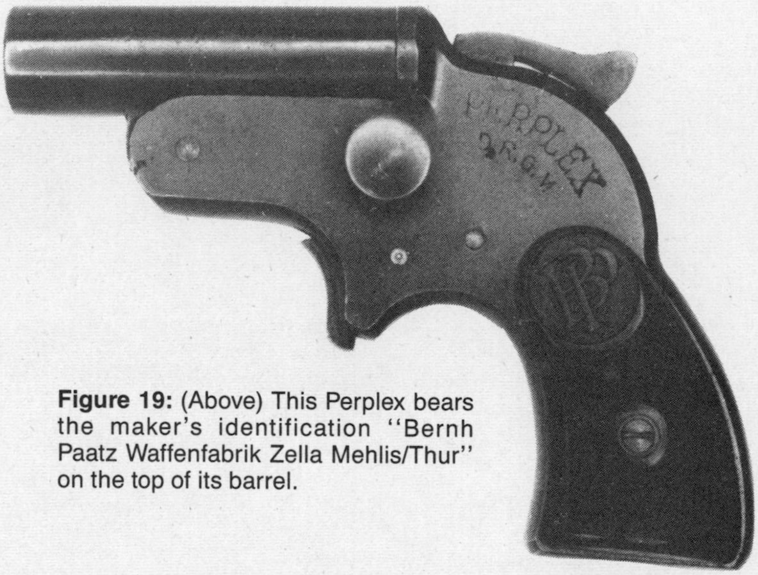

Figure 19: (Above) This Perplex bears the maker's identification "Bernh Paatz Waffenfabrik Zella Mehlis/Thur" on the top of its barrel.

Figure 18: (Left) Two variations of the double-barreled Perplex pistol. The one at top is early, with a pushbutton barrel release like the single-barreled Perplex. The barrel catch on the lower Perplex is pushed to the rear to release.

and two types of Nico boxes are shown in Figure 15.

The most popular Scheintod pistols of the late 1920s and '30s were sold under the "Perplex" name. These nicely made and finished blued steel pistols were made in both single- and double-barreled versions by "Bernh Paatz" Waffenfabrik, Zella Mehlis. Figure 16 shows several single-barreled Perplex variations, while Figure 17 shows one of the various barrel markings. Two variations of the double-barreled Perplex, officially termed the "Model-2," are shown in Figure 18.

The Scheintod represents a type of non-lethal defensive weapon that is still widely used in Europe. The pages of current German gun magazines such as *Deutsches Waffen-Journal* contain ads for a number of current 8mm gas and blank-firing pistols, mostly near-perfect copies of various current model Beretta, Colt, Walther and other "real" guns. Perhaps this current breed should be covered in a subsequent article. Though we've included a good number of the many 12mm Scheintod variations in these pages, there are undoubtedly many more that could be included. The author would be very pleased to hear of any additional variations the readers of *Gun Collector's Digest* may turn up.

Totschläger und Boxer

Nr. 865

Nr. 866

Nr. 865 **Lederbezogene Spiralfeder** mit Bleikugel und Handschlaufe an einem Stück, sehr zu empfehlen . . . . *(gusch)*

Nr. 866 Ausführung wie Nr. 865, jedoch ohne Handschlaufe, mit 2 Bleikugeln und angeknüpftem **Handriemen** . . . . *(hahan)*

Schlagringe
mit und ohne Zacken

Nr. 870 **Schlagringe** von Metall, blank gescheuert, gewöhnliche Qualität, **ohne** Zacken *(havec)*
mit Zacken . . . . *(hakar)*

Nr. 871 **Schlagringe** aus Rein-Aluminium, **ohne** Zacken . . . . *(heloc)*
mit Zacken . . . . *(holon)*

Nr. 872 **Schlagringe** „Modell Boxer", extra kräftig, mit guter Handlage und stumpfen Zacken, aus Aluminium . . . . *(heliu)*

Nr. 870/72

Scheintod-Pistolen

Nr. 900 **Scheintod-Pistole**, Modell III, fein polierter Lauf, mit Bajonettverschluß, welcher leicht abnehmbar ist und dann bequem in der Tasche zu plazieren
(helfr)

Nr. 900

Nr. 905 **Scheintod-Repetier-Pistole,** tiefschwarz, mit Sicherung, 3schüssig, mit 3 übereinanderliegenden Läufen. Kautschukschaft *(hagoa)*

Nr. 906 Luxusmodell, wie vor, aber hochfein vernickelt, mit verzierten Schalen . . . . *(hambu)*

Nr. 905

Nr. 908 **Original-Scheintod-Patronen,** in Kartons a 10, 25 und 50 Stück
(halar)

Nr. 908

Figure 20: Two Scheintod-Pistolen were marketed by Stotz & Goesel of Suhl, Germany, as shown on this page from their early 1920s catalog.

The Government Model COLT in British Service

by CHARLES W. CLAWSON

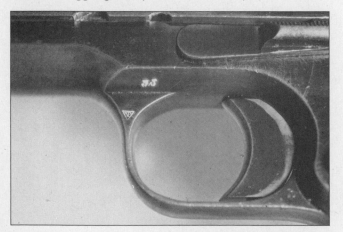

(Above and right) An early 45 Government Model (left and right side views) shipped to the London Armoury Company March 30, 1916. Also, (below) detail of the "JJ" marking above the trigger guard. (Author's collection)

THE THREAT of war existed in Europe as early as 1905. During the pre-WWI years, Colt's received many inquiries from representatives of foreign governments. Samuel M. Stone and Frank C. Nichols, both Colt officials, visited several European countries beginning in 1909. Negotiations with the Russian government that began in 1909 led to significant orders for machineguns and 45 ACP automatic pistols in 1915. The Turkish government placed an order for small

(Right) Webley "Pistol, Self Loading .455 Mark I," caliber 455, with the "N" marking for naval use. (Left) Also, 45 ACP (far left) and 455 cartridges.

arms in 1909. In 1910, Nichols met with officials of the Fabrique Nationale d'Armes de Guerre, in Herstal-Liege, Belgium — Colt's counterpart in Europe — to secure a joint arrangement for the two companies to meet the steadily increasing demand for firearms in Europe.

In 1912, those negotiations led to the sale of Colt automatic pistols on the European market and the sale of Browning automatic pistols in England, Ireland, and Canada. The brokerage firm of Frederick Peters, Amerikanische Waffen und Munition in Hamburg, Germany represented Colt's in continental Europe on a limited scale until 1912. From 1910 through 1914, five or six of Colt's salesmen traveled Europe.

After the closure of Colt's London Armoury at 14 Pall Mall, London, S.W. in 1857, a supply of small arms was maintained at their sales office in the same location under the official name of Colt's Patent Fire Arms Mfg. Co., London, England, commonly referred to as Colt's London Office, or Agency, their only outlet in Great Britain. In 1913, Colt's London Office closed and the London Armoury Company, Limited, became Colt's exclusive sales agent in the British Empire. In 1914, the Greek government placed an order for 10,000 caliber 38 Army Special revolvers, which was subsequently increased to some 50,000. Salesmen were also engaged in the South American trade, and one representative traveled in China and the Far East. As a result of these efforts, Colt's did considerable business in Great Britain, Russia, France, Greece, Norway, Spain, Sweden, Turkey, and the Argentine Republic. Prior to 1910, Colt's had never maintained an inventory of finished products, but from that time on they manufactured for stock and carried a surplus of about 15,000 completed firearms, with about 25,000 to 30,000 in continuous production.

The outbreak of hostilities, in July, 1914, caught many participants unprepared. President Wilson de-

clared the United States' neutrality, though American industry was free to trade weapons and war supplies with any of the belligerents. Foreign governments established purchasing commissions in the U.S. and competed for American munitions. On January 15, 1915, J.P. Morgan & Company of New York signed an agreement to act as purchasing agents for the British government with full authority to negotiate and sign contracts in the U.S. They also carried out the general supervision of contracts, and made all necessary arrangements up to and including the actual shipments. In the spring of 1915, Morgan also signed an agreement with the French government "exactly similar"[1] to the British agreement.

From 1915 to 1917, approximately 84 percent of the essential war materials to England and France were shipped through the export department of J.P. Morgan & Company, some $3 billion in value. The American government took control of all war supplies after the U.S. entered the war, at which time J.P. Morgan & Company withdrew as purchasing agents.

Colt 45 and 455 automatic pistols were well represented on the battlefields of Europe. From August, 1914 through April, 1919, more than 70,000 pistols were sold to foreign governments, all numbered in Colt's regular commercial serial range. There were 4900 pistols shipped to the government of Canada from September through November, 1914; France purchased 5000 pistols between November, 1915 and January, 1916; Norway received 400 pistols in June, 1915, and another 300 in May, 1917. The Netherlands purchased 50 pistols in February, 1917, and the Philippine government took delivery of 302 in May, 1917. In De-

---

[1] Contract language according to the statement of Mr. J.P. Morgan at the Hearings before the Special Committee Investigating the Munitions Industry, United States Senate, 74th Congress, pursuant to Senate Resolution 206, April, 1935, p. 7487.

cember, 1917, the French High Commission received 500 Model 1911 pistols and 1000 magazines from stores on hand at the Springfield Armory, by direction of the Adjutant General of the U.S. Between February 19, 1916 and January 18, 1917, 47,100 pistols were shipped to Russia. They were numbered between C23000 and C80000 and marked in Cyrillic (Russian) "English Order." Russia became the largest foreign purchaser with Great Britain the second largest.

Great Britain

More than 17,600 Colt "Government Model" automatic pistols were shipped to England prior to May, 1919. They were all produced and numbered in the commercial series, in calibers 45 or 455, with C or W serial number prefixes, respectively. Some were imported for commercial sales, others sold to the British government for military use. Colt's and various government records indicate the following distribution:

  5040 caliber 45 C prefix commercial sales[2]
   600 caliber 455 W prefix commercial sales
  2200 caliber 455 W prefix British War Office
   500 caliber 455 W prefix British Air Service/
    RFC
10,000 caliber 455 W prefix British Air Service/
    RAF

The designation GOVERNMENT MODEL was stamped on the right side of the frame above the serial number. Barrels were not marked, but the caliber was identified on the right side of the slides in the following manner for C prefix serial numbers: COLT AUTOMATIC/CALIBRE 45. Serial numbers with a W prefix were identified as follows: COLT AUTOMATIC/CALIBRE 455.

---

[2] In addition, innumerable small lots and individual pistols were shipped to England.

(Top left and above) Left and right side views of the Government Model in 455, serial W99858, that was inspected and proofed at Colt's by a British inspector. Also, (bottom) inspector and British property markings. The "C" behind the trigger (below) indicates Canadian use. (Julius T. Kosan collection)

45-Caliber

All Government Model pistols shipped to England prior to July, 1915 were in 45-caliber. They were all standard commercial pistols with highly-polished blue finish and conventional markings of the period. They were not normally shipped in numerical order; consequently, serial numbers in each lot were often scattered over a range of several hundred numbers or more. As a state of war existed in Europe at that time, it can be presumed that most of the sales were to military personnel. A British officer had the option of purchasing his service pistol or revolver from a civilian dealer, or from military stores.

Although sidearms were required to be in the service caliber (455), that rule was widely ignored during the war, with many officers carrying Colt 45 ACP pistols. Winston S. Churchill purchased a Colt 45-caliber automatic pistol from the London Armoury Company in 1915, serial number C15566, one of 200 pistols shipped from Colt's on July 19, 1915. His pistol was engraved WINSTON SPENCER CHURCHILL on the right side of the slide.[3]

455-Caliber

The official designation of the British automatic pistol cartridge was ".455 Webley Self Loading Pistol Cartridge, Mark I." It was an improved version of an earlier Webley & Scott cartridge, and featured a thicker extractor rim to ensure positive case extraction. Its designation was later changed to "Cartridge, Pistol, Self Loading .455 Inch Mark I"; nitrocellulose powder loading was designated "Mark I.z." The cartridge was adopted by the British Admiralty in 1912, and approved by the British Army for "Land Service" in 1916.

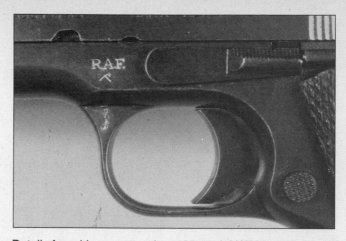

Detail of markings on another 455, serial W99811, that was shipped to the London Armoury Company November 2, 1917. In addition to the Royal Air Force markings, it also has the crossed split-tail pennant Enfield inspector's mark. (Paul M.R. Breakey collection)

Bullet diameter is .005-inch larger than the 45 ACP, and the cartridge case correspondingly larger and longer. In addition to the different barrel measurements, the 455 cartridge required a wider magazine and magazine well, along with other minor dimensional changes. As a result, 455 cartridges and magazines are not usable in caliber 45 ACP pistols. However, it is possible to fire 45 ACP cartridges in 455-caliber pistols, but they do not function satisfactorily due to excessive headspace.

Although the serial number prefix W indicates Webley, 455 magazines are marked CAL.455 ELEY, which is misleading. The so-called 455 Eley was the improved Webley cartridge manufactured by Eley Bros., Ltd. Colt's production ledger mentions "W-Webley" or

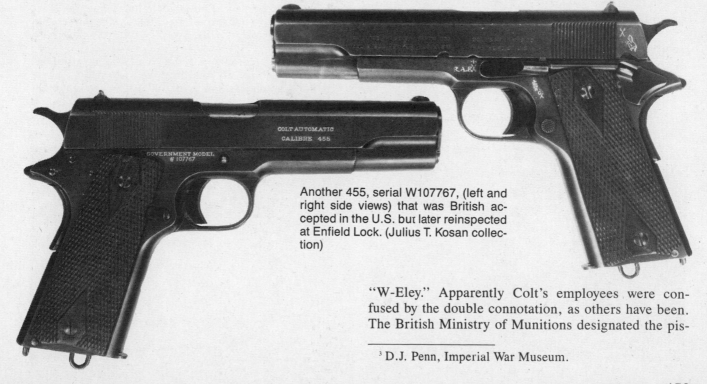

Another 455, serial W107767, (left and right side views) that was British accepted in the U.S. but later reinspected at Enfield Lock. (Julius T. Kosan collection)

"W-Eley." Apparently Colt's employees were confused by the double connotation, as others have been. The British Ministry of Munitions designated the pis-

---

[3] D.J. Penn, Imperial War Museum.

tols "Colt Automatic Pistol, Caliber .455 Webley."

Distribution of the first two shipments of 455-caliber pistols in England, totaling 600, is not definitely known. They were not listed in British War Office orders, details were not recorded at Colt's, and the records of the now defunct London Armoury Company are not known to exist. Therefore, the author presumes they were imported for commercial sales.

The first 200 pistols were shipped to the London Armoury Company on July 19, 1915. Serial numbers were mostly between W19001 and W19200, with a few in the W19700 range. Although the serial number prefixes on those pistols were not listed in Colt's records, the few actual pistols observed from that lot are W prefixed. The second shipment in 455-caliber, 400 pistols, was shipped to the London Armoury Company on January 10, 1916. They were all serial numbered within a specific lot of 444 consecutively numbered 455-caliber pistols extending from serial number W29001 through W29444, but were not shipped in serial order. They were listed as "Special Order" in Colt's production ledger. Also stated in the ledger was, "All 45 Autos[4] on this order will have the letter W before each number on each receiver."

Of the remaining 44 extra pistols, a few were sold to individuals in the U.S. and the others shipped to England in later orders.

All subsequent pistols in 455-caliber, through April, 1917, were ordered by the British War Office through Colt's agents at the London Armoury Company, and shipped as follows:[5]

Contract 94/P/952, dated May 16, 1916.

500 pistols and 1000 spare magazines:

Date Shipped	Qty.	Serial Range
Jun. 26, 1916	500	W40401-W41000

(including 10 pistols W29227-W29411)

Contract 94/P/1118, dated June 29, 1916.

1900 pistols at the rate of 200 per month, increased to 300 per month by January 1917, and 4000 spare magazines:

Date Shipped	Qty.	Serial Range
Sep. 7, 1916	200	W40500-W58200
Sep. 26, 1916	200	W56000-W65300
Oct. 31, 1916	200	W60800-W70500
Nov. 1916	200	W64000-W75000
Dec. 3, 1916	200	W70000-W78000
Jan. 19, 1917	200	W70000-W84500
Mar. 30, 1917	300	W91000-W95000
Apr. 6, 1917	200	W91600-W97000
Total	1700	

A grand total of 2200 pistols was delivered on British War Office contracts. Although there is no evidence that they were issued to any particular group, War Office orders were usually for the Army. Nevertheless, it is reasonable to assume that they were probably issued to units already using the 455 Webley Self Loading pistol cartridge, which included the Royal Flying Corps, Royal Horse Artillery, Royal Navy, and Royal Naval Air Service. However, general correspondence suggests that all or most of the pistols were procured for the Royal Flying Corps.

With the U.S.'s entry into the war, in order to meet the demands of the U.S. government, commercial manufacture at Colt's was drastically reduced. The highest Government Model serial number manufactured in 1917 was W100038, assembled on September 20, 1917 and shipped to the British government on November 2.[6] Due to Colt's job shop manufacturing practice, com-

---

[4] The phrase "45 Auto" was used as a general term for the Government Model in Colt's records.

[5] "Firms & Factories List, Orders for Machine Guns, Small Arms, and Small Arms Ammunition, 1 August 1914 to 31 March 1917," published by His Majesty's Stationery Office, April, 1917 (No. S.19).

[6] Conversely, according to Colt's records, some pistols serial numbered in the 80,000 range were shipped as late as 1919. For example, a shipment of 400 pistols was sent to the Argentine Republic on May 27, 1919, in the serial range of 86790 to 116000.

(Below and bottom right) Detail of the inspection and accepting markings of a 455, serial W107767.

mercial pistols were not manufactured or assembled in numerical order. The pistols in most shipments at that time were usually scattered throughout a few thousand serial number range, and routinely included the extra pistols left over from previous production runs. Specific production runs normally included a certain overrun to account for waste. For example, the special order for 400 pistols shipped on January 10, 1916 resulted in the manufacture of 444 pistols, an extra 11 percent overage.

By about March, 1917, the administration of small arms contracts was transferred to the British Ministry of Munitions of War. On September 7, 1917, R.H. Brand, Representative of the British Ministry of Munitions of War in the U.S. wrote General Crozier, U.S. Chief of Ordnance, to complain that Colt's was cutting off British deliveries in favor of U.S. government orders.

As a result of the Ministry's appeal, the U.S. War Department authorized Colt's to resume the British deliveries. On September 14, General Crozier sent a telegram to the Inspector of Ordnance at Colt's[7] that read: "Inform [Colt's] company that authority is granted to continue delivery of the minimum of three hundred pistols a month to British Ministry of Munitions of War."

Meanwhile, with regard to the minimum number of pistols required, the British Ministry of Munitions of War in the U.S. received a cablegram from London on September 11 stating that "400 (automatic pistols) per month is the absolute minimum required . . . in consequence of the largely increased establishment of flying services."[8]

On September 20, the U.S. War Department granted authority to Colt's for the increased delivery. Therefore, on October 2, Colt's advised the Ministry of Mu-

nitions of War in the U.S. that they were prepared to accept the British Government's order for a specified quantity of pistols to be provided at the rate of 400 per month.

On November 28, 1917, the British Ministry of Munitions of War placed a formal order with Colt's, No. U.S. 1139-MM67. The order was granted priority class "A1" by the War Industries Board on December 17, and the contract was formally signed on January 2, 1918 by Colt's Patent Fire Arms Mfg. Co. and His Britannic Majesty's Government calling for "5,000 automatic pistols of .455 calibre . . . exactly similar to the pistols furnished by the Seller to the Buyer under contract 94/P/1118."

The contract specified one magazine to be fitted to each pistol and 15,000 extra magazines, with delivery of at least 400 pistols and 1200 magazines per month, and final delivery no later than 12½ months after the date of the contract. The contract also specified that the ammunition necessary for testing the pistols would be furnished by the British government, and the British government had the right to have one or more inspectors at Colt's for the purpose of inspecting the pistols. The net price was $16.187 per pistol, and 67.5 cents per extra magazine. Payment was through J.P. Morgan & Company, 23 Wall Street, New York City.

As authorized by the U.S. War Department, two interim consignments totaling 500 pistols not covered by the formal contract, destined for the British Air Service, were shipped to the London Armoury Company in October and November, 1917. Serial numbers began in

---

[7] Ordnance Office file O.O. 474.6/160.

[8] Ordnance Office file, Small Arms Division R.474.6/154.

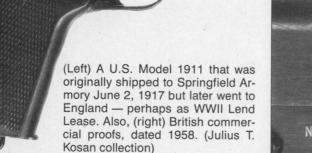

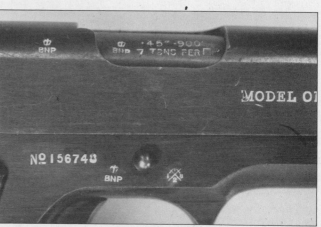

(Left) A U.S. Model 1911 that was originally shipped to Springfield Armory June 2, 1917 but later went to England — perhaps as WWII Lend Lease. Also, (right) British commercial proofs, dated 1958. (Julius T. Kosan collection)

the W91500 range, essentially a continuation of the previous War Office serial range, to wit:

Date Shipped	Qty.	Serial Range
Oct. 2, 1917	300	W91500-W100000
Nov. 2, 1917	200	W91600-W100100
Total	**500**	

Production on the new contract began in December, 1917, with the first shipment on January 22, 1918. As with earlier pistols, they were commercially blued, but most were later refinished with a soft satin blue finish.

The contract for 5000 pistols was completed in November, 1918, but in the meantime another contract, No. U.S. 6755-MM264, had been signed on May 7, 1918 for 10,000 additional pistols and 30,000 extra magazines, "exactly similar" to contract No. U.S. 1139-MM67. The order, granted priority class "A1" by the War Industries Board on May 1, was to be delivered at the rate of 600 pistols per month. Production began in December, 1918, eventually exceeding the required rate of delivery, but the contract was canceled prior to completion. The final shipment was made on April 28, 1919, after a total of 5000 pistols and 24,000 spare magazines were delivered.

The British Air Service/Royal Air Force received 500 interim pistols in 1917, and 10,000 contract pistols from January, 1918, through April, 1919, for a grand total of 10,500. The lowest serial was in the W91100 range; the highest serial number delivered was W110696. However, W113174, completely out of sequence and possibly posted in error, was shipped on April 15, 1919.

British Military Inspection Marks

Colt pistols procured by the British government for official use were normally stamped with standard British military inspection and acceptance marks. British War Office pistols shipped to the London Armoury Company, and the first British Air Service pistols, were inspected and accepted at the Royal Small Arms Factory at Enfield Lock, a suburb of London. They were stamped with the broad arrow government ownership mark, crossed pennant military proofmark (with split-tail pennants), and the individual Enfield inspector's mark. Several Enfield inspector's marks have been observed, of which the following are representative:

His Majesty's crown
Inspector's number
Enfield

The government ownership mark and military proofmark consisted of the following:

Broad arrow   Crossed pennant (with split-tails)

Some pistols were not stamped with military inspection marks, which indicates that they were sold commercially to individual officers, or sold through government outlets before they were inspected. Perhaps some pistols were set aside specifically for such sales.

The first Air Service pistols were inspected by R. Nevin[9], British Army Inspector of Small Arms at

---

[9] The spelling of the name is not certain, as the signature is almost unreadable.

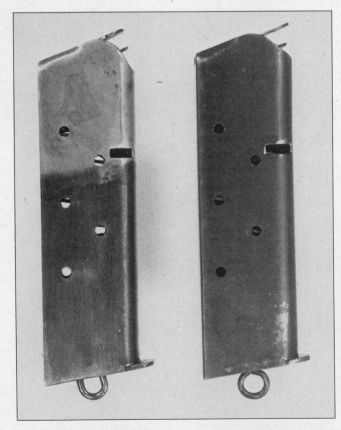

455 magazines, standard Colt's manufacture on the left and an "RAF magazine" on the right. (Author's collection)

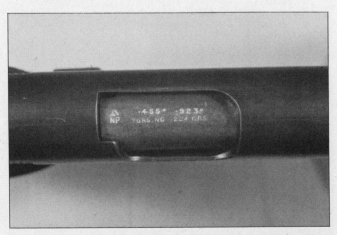

Post-1955 barrel proofs on a 455 pistol. (Paul M.R. Breakey collection)

Colt's. He signed the "Contractors' Invoice and Inspection Note," certifying that the pistols were inspected, but no marks have been observed to indicate his inspection. In fact, those pistols were inspected and marked at the Royal Small Arms Factory at Enfield Lock. The cartridges used for testing the pistols were shipped from England and may not have arrived at the Colt plant in time for his definitive testing, or perhaps the steel inspection stamps were not yet in hand. On April 1, 1918, concurrent with the formation of the Royal Air Force, British inspector G.W.R. Stedman was assigned to Colt's and thereafter, all pistols procured under British contract were inspected and stamped at Colt's by Stedman. His inspection symbol was stamped on the left side of the frame above the magazine catch:

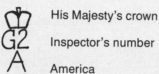

His Majesty's crown

Inspector's number

America

(Note: The G2 inspector's alpha-numberic number may have indicated that he was the second inspector at Colt's. If so, Nevin's number would have been G1.)

In addition to the standard broad arrow government ownership mark, the crossed pennant military proof-mark stamped at Colt's consisted of single-tail pennants, to wit:

Some pistols inspected and stamped at Colt's by Stedman are also marked with an Enfield inspector's mark, signifying later inspection at Enfield after a subsequent inspection or overhaul.

Beginning in April, 1918, at about serial number W100000, most of the pistols were hand stamped R.A.F. or RAF. That marking was most likely added by individual units receiving the pistols, apparently in compliance with "Instructions to Armourers" which established standards for the marking of arms. That assumption also accounts for the fact that some pistols are not RAF marked.

The following markings are typical of early 1918 Royal Air Force pistols:

Enfield inspected, and the earliest observed example with RAF markings.

[10] D.J. Penn, Imperial War Museum.

The earliest observed example inspected at Colt's by British inspector G.W.R. Stedman. It is also Canadian ownership marked.

Inspected by British inspector G.W.R. Stedman, but not RAF marked.

Magazines

Magazines furnished with the 45-caliber pistols were standard, unmarked, commercial, lanyard-loop-type magazines. The 455 magazines were made exactly like 45 ACP magazines, except they were slightly wider to accommodate the larger size cartridges. All 455 magazines were marked with the caliber designation, CAL.455 ELEY. Some magazines were also marked with the serial number of the pistol, but the quality of the hand stamping indicates the serial numbers were stamped in England by British armorers. Magazines that were inspected and issued as military equipage were normally stamped with the broad arrow government ownership mark. So called "RAF magazines" (era and manufacturer unknown) were presumably manufactured in England. These are unusual in that cartridge counting holes are only punched through one side, a round screw-eye-type lanyard loop is affixed to the bottom of the baseplate, bodies are completely blued, and they are marked simply 455. They could be World War II replacement magazines, though there is no evidence supporting that theory.

Summation

When the Armistice was signed in November, 1918, the RAF consisted of 200 squadrons, 22,647 aircraft, 103 airships, and some 27,000 officers, making it the world's largest air force. In the years that followed the war, officer ranks dwindled to 1065, with a corresponding decrease of aircraft and other equipment. The Colt 455 automatic pistols remained in service with the RAF through World War II, although many were transferred to the Royal Navy about 1942 for issue to air/sea rescue units.[10]

As an additional note, some Colt 45 and 455 automatic pistols sold commercially in the United Kingdom bear the letters JJ on the beveled edge above the left front trigger guard. In view of certain evidence, it appears that the letters were applied at the London Armoury Company. D.J. Penn, Keeper of the Department of Exhibits and Firearms, Imperial War Museum, London, comments that the same marking has been noted on many non-military Colt pistols beginning with the 1902 models, and is therefore not considered a British military marking.

British Commercial Proof

The Gun Barrel Proof Act of England specified that commercial firearms could not be offered for sale, exchanged, or exported until they were properly proved in accordance with the British Rules of Proof. Those rules were amended several times since the inception of British proof in the 17th century. Although proof laws of certain other countries were recognized in England, the U.S. did not have official proof regulations, and consequently all U.S. commercial pistols exported to England were subject to British proof. Military weapons, including foreign weapons procured for the British armed forces, were exempt from commercial proof laws until released by the British government.

Proof certification was performed at the London Proof House, also known as the Gunmakers' Company; and at the Birmingham Proof House, also known as the Guardians' Company. The testing procedures were identical at both houses, although each had its own distinctive proofmarks. Pistols and revolvers that were proved during the World War I period were subject to the Rules of 1904. Proof firing consisted of a powder charge sufficient to give a pressure of 25 to 40 percent over normal, after which the barrel was stamped with a definitive proofmark. The viewmark signified a visual inspection. The following symbols are presented as a guide for determining the time and place of proof on Colt automatic pistols; however, pistols were not always marked in strict observance of regulations:

1904 - 1925

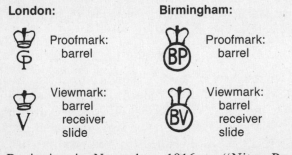

London:

Proofmark: barrel

Viewmark: barrel receiver slide

Birmingham:

Proofmark: barrel

Viewmark: barrel receiver slide

Beginning in November, 1916, a "Nitro Proof" mark was stamped on barrels proved with smokeless nitro powder in addition to the proof and viewmarks. The London mark was described as, "The letters NP surmounted by an arm dexter in armour, embowered, holding a scimitar," thus:

The Birmingham mark was described as, "The let-

ters NP surmounted by a crown," thus:

Beginning in 1925, in compliance with new Rules of Proof, foreign arms were impressed with the words NOT ENGLISH MAKE and the proofmarks were enclosed within a circle:

1925 - 1955

London:

Proofmark: barrel

Viewmark: barrel receiver slide

Nitro proof: barrel

Birmingham:

Proofmark: barrel

Viewmark: barrel receiver slide

Nitro proof: barrel

Beginning in 1921, in addition to the standard proof and viewmarks, the Birmingham Proof House used a "crossed sceptre" viewer's mark to indicate the viewer and date of proof. The letter B designated Birmingham, the other letter represented the year of proof, and the number identified the viewer. The following marks are examples of the code system utilized since 1950:

(1952)[11]   (1953)   (1958)[12]

British Lend-Lease
World War II

In May, 1940, American government officials devised a scheme to sell obsolete or surplus arms, ammunition, and equipment to England and France to bolster their defenses against the Germans. The plan did not go into effect until after the defeat at Dunkirk and the surrender of France; the British Army had left enough stores in France to equip eight to 10 divisions. By the end of 1940, the American-based British Purchasing Commission had placed several billion dollars worth of contracts with U.S. firms, the volume of which limited production capacity for badly-needed American defense items, and which was one of the factors that brought about the Lend-Lease Act of March 11, 1941.

The Lend-Lease Act gave unlimited aid to American

---

[11] The letter B was normally on the right side of the sceptres, but the pattern was sometimes reversed.

[12] It has been reported that the letter I was not used because of the similarity to the letter J, but it is this writer's observation that I was used instead of J.

allies short of war, authorized American aid in the form of grants rather than loans, empowered Congress to transfer materials and equipment from government stocks, and transferred foreign orders to the control of the American government. The War Department administered and controled the type of equipment to be manufactured, usually common to both England and the U.S.

The first lend-lease appropriation of March 27, 1941 authorized transfers from government stocks and current production by random requisitioning; some refurbished weapons were included. Model 1911 and Model 1911A1 pistols were distributed under the lend-lease program as follows:[13]

British Empire	39,592
Canada	1515
China	2266
French Forces	19,325
U.S.S.R.	12,997
American Republics	2890
Other countries	40
Total	78,625

Most lend-lease Model 1911A1 pistols were shipped to England from U.S. military inventory, and included pistols manufactured by Colt's, Ithaca, Remington Rand and Union Switch & Signal Company. They were declared obsolete by the British government beginning in 1952, and were thus subject to English proof law requirements before they could be offered for sale or exported. Most of the pistols released during 1952 were stamped RELEASED BRITISH GOVT. 1952.

The British Rules of Proof were introduced in 1955, and several changes were initiated at that time:

1. The inscription NOT ENGLISH MAKE was eliminated.
2. The viewmarks were eliminated.
3. The Birmingham proof and nitro proofmarks were combined into a single BNP stamp.
4. Barrels were marked with the caliber or bore measurement in decimal parts of an inch, the nominal length of the cartridge case in inches, and the pressure of the proof charge in long tons per square inch.

Colt pistols commercially proved in England since 1955 were marked in the following manner:

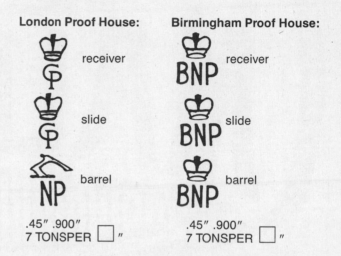

London Proof House:
- receiver
- slide
- barrel

.45″ .900″
7 TONSPER ☐ ″

Birmingham Proof House:
- receiver
- slide
- barrel

.45″ .900″
7 TONSPER ☐ ″

455-Caliber Barrel Marks: .455 .923″. 7 GRS. NC 224. grs.[14] (With appropriate London or Birmingham proofmarks.)

This article has been excerpted from the "Foreign Sales" chapter of a book on the history, development and distribution of the Colt U.S. service pistol that the author has been preparing and expects to publish in the very near future. ●

---

[13] Table LL-14 — quantities of selected items included in War Department lend-lease shipments, United States Army in World War II — Statistics Office of the Chief of Military History, Special Staff, U.S. Army.

[14] Apparently 455 proof cartridges were not available after the ammunition was declared obsolete in about 1952. The standard load was seven grains of nitrocellulose powder and a 224 grain bullet, which was exhibited on the barrels rather than a proof charge. Of course, variations may be found.

455 magazine bottom markings, far left to right: Commercial, with British broad arrow ownership mark, same but serial numbered to the gun, "RAF magazine."

COLLECTING

MAUSER

NON-GUN

by JOSEPH J. SCHROEDER

Collectibles

As ANYONE who has read *System Mauser** knows, I've been an avid Mauser collector for a long time — long enough to have acquired some very interesting Broomhandles, as well as a good selection of other Mauser pistols and revolvers, and even a few rifles. To supplement my "iron" collection, I've also managed to put together a pretty good reference library of original Mauser literature — factory manuals and catalogs.

However, this article is about another kind of gunmaker-related collectible, one that's a lot harder to find than most rifles and pistols. A collectible, when it is found, is often very inexpensive . . . but just as interesting as a new gun variation. In my case, of course, it's Mauser; however, the same collecting opportunity exists with many other gun collecting specialties, as well.

I'm referring to Mauser's "non-guns" — not the model guns they make in Japan of pot metal, but the variety of tools, promotional items, and other things made by Mauser (or at least Mauser marked) at the same time Mauser was also making guns. During the years I've been collecting Mausers, I've handled literally thousands of Mauser small arms, but I've managed to collect only a handful of Mauser "non-guns" — and have seen only a few others.

---

*Handgun Press, Glenview, Illinois

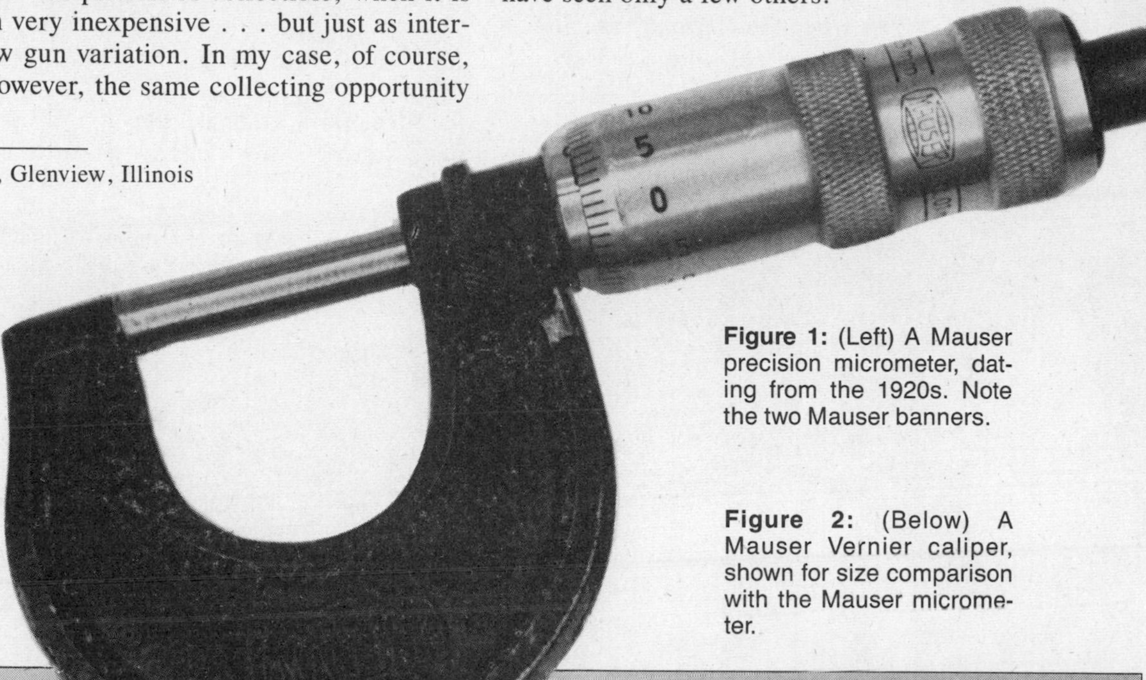

Figure 1: (Left) A Mauser precision micrometer, dating from the 1920s. Note the two Mauser banners.

Figure 2: (Below) A Mauser Vernier caliper, shown for size comparison with the Mauser micrometer.

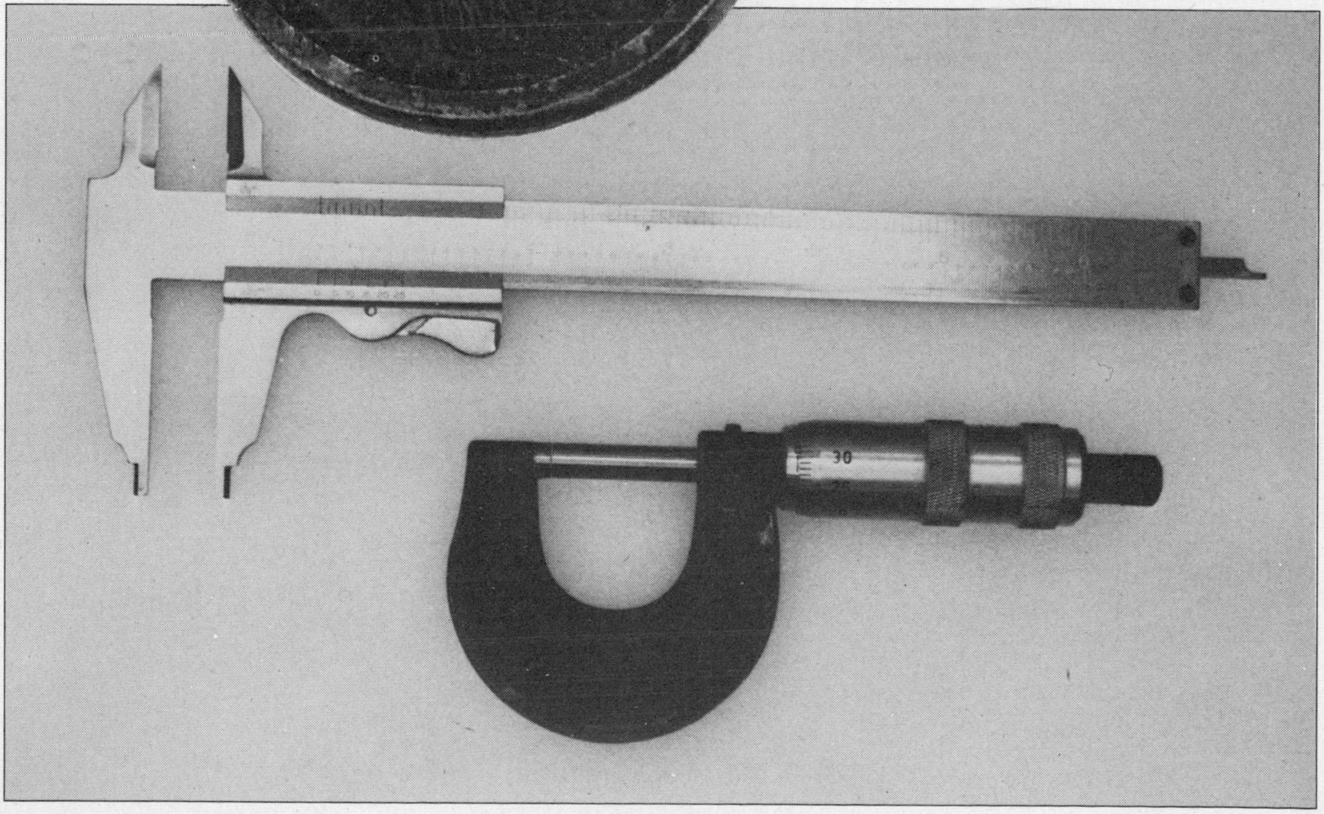

The Mauser banner logo that leads off this article is a prime example of such a collectible. Full size, it is actually black with a gold background, painted on the back of some sort of thin, transparent plastic material. It is supposed to have been brought back from WWII by a G.I. who pried it off a door in a liberated Mauser facility. It has an air of legitimacy about it, but whatever its provenance, it provides a striking highlight to any Mauser display.

Moving on to some genuine Mauser hardware, the micrometer shown in Figure 1 is a Mauser instrument made during the 1920s, when the German arms industry was severely restricted by the Treaty of Versailles. At that time, Mauser was manufacturing precision instruments, tools, office machines and even — briefly — automobiles in order to keep its plants open. The micrometer is beautifully made and sports the Mauser banner on both bridge and handle; it was found in a group of gunsmith's tools at a local gun show, and was very inexpensive.

Another Mauser measuring instrument of the same vintage is shown in Figure 2, along with the Mauser micrometer. It's a Vernier caliper made of stainless steel and calibrated in both inches and millimeters. In addition to the Mauser banner, it bears the legend "Made in Germany for George Scherr Co. New York." An identical Vernier caliper as well as a very similar micrometer is shown in another current Mauser book,

Figure 3: Mauser ''Englander'' adjustable wrench, with a unique quick adjustment feature.

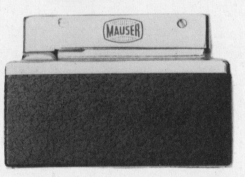

Figure 4: A variety of Mauser non-gun items, mostly promotional. From left: cigarette lighter, penknife, and soldier's or sportsman's knife. At right is a pre-WWII Mauser flashlight.

Mauser, From Gunsmith to World Enterprise* by Wolfgang Seel. This caliper came from a gun collecting friend who had actually used it himself when he was an inspector for a machine toolmaker.

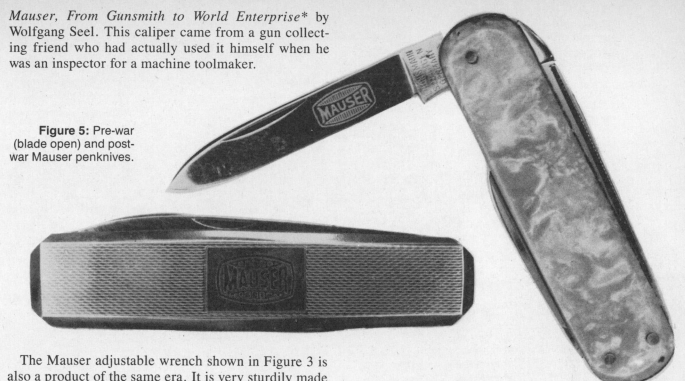

Figure 5: Pre-war (blade open) and post-war Mauser penknives.

The Mauser adjustable wrench shown in Figure 3 is also a product of the same era. It is very sturdily made and well fitted, but is most intriguing for its unique quick adjustment feature. The knurled pushbutton on

*Handgun Press, Glenview, Illinois

Figure 6: The Mauser "Einspur" looked like a motorcycle with training wheels and was introduced in 1922.

Figure 7: (Right) The more conventional Mauser Model 28 PS automobile went into production in 1923. Both Mauser autos were on the market for only a few years. Also, (below) a close-up of a Mauser banner radiator ornament.

Figure 8: A Mauser adding machine made during the 1930s.

the back of the movable jaw releases the adjustment worm gear, permitting the jaw to slide freely up and down. A partial turn of the knurled worm gear provides the final adjustment. A group of four identical "Englander" wrenches in various sizes are also pictured in Seel's book. This example was purchased by a Colt collecting friend at a garage sale for $1, and presented to the author "With Compliments" at the next gun show!

Figure 4 shows a group of Mauser-marked items, most probably used for promotional purposes and all but one post-WWII. At the top is a cigarette lighter, below it a penknife, and at the bottom, a soldier's or sportsman's knife actually made by the well-known Swiss Army knife maker Victorinox. In addition to the Mauser banner on its olive-drab side panel, the bottom knife also bears the legend "Name Unter Lizenz der Mauser-Werke Oberndorf GmbH," along with the Mauser banner etched on one blade.

The unusual flashlight on the right surely dates pre-WWII, as it uses a battery style no longer available. The Mauser banner deeply etched into its chrome-plated case is identical to the banner pictured earlier — black with a gold background.

Figure 5 shows two Mauser promotional penknives, one pre-war, the other post-war. The pre-war knife with the Mauser banner etched into its blade has very attrac-

Figure 9: A Mauser adding machine set up for bookkeeping.

tive rose-colored imitation mother-of-pearl handles and was made by E. Bonsmann of Solingen. The postwar version is all metal and was made by Kaufmann.

Any collector fortunate enough to visit Oberndorf, Germany will have the opportunity to see not only a fantastic collection of rare Mauser arms, but what is perhaps the world's most complete collection of Mauser non-arms as well. This collection is in the City Museum of Oberndorf, which is in turn located in an old Mauser factory building (Schwedenbau).

In the arms section of the museum you will find not only examples of the tools and measuring instruments previously described, but a large selection of fascinat-

ing other Mauser non-guns as well. For example, perhaps Mauser's most unusual product of the 1920s was the "Einspur" — a motorcycle-like vehicle with training wheels and an enclosed frame (Figure 6). In the same time period, Mauser even built a few full-sized cars such as the one shown in Figure 7. Either of these would certainly be a find for the dedicated Mauser — or motor vehicle — collector!

In addition, the museum has both large and small Mauser adding machines (Figures 8 and 9), a variety of Mauser sewing machines (Figures 10 and 11), and even Mauser hair clippers (Figures 12 and 13)! It's surely a "must visit" for any dedicated Mauser buff who finds

Figures 10 (left) and 11 (right): Mauser sewing machines were introduced in the late 1920s.

Figure 12: The original box for Mauser hair clippers.

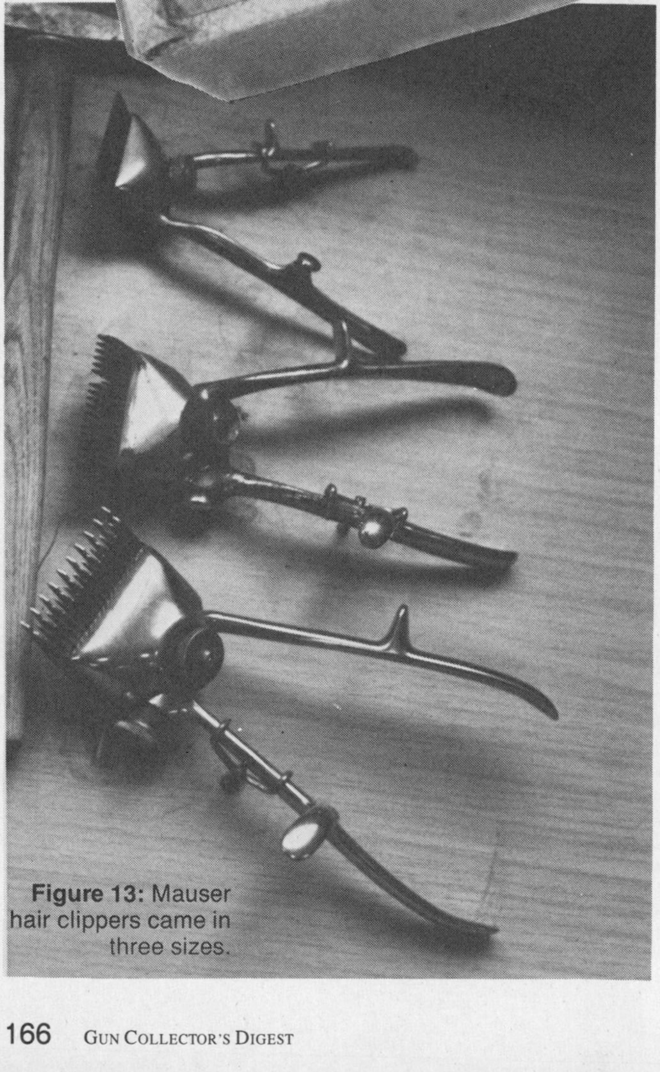

Figure 13: Mauser hair clippers came in three sizes.

himself in southern Germany.

A word of warning, however; the museum is only open a few hours a week — at this writing, Wednesday and Saturday afternoons, and Sunday mornings — so it is best to call ahead to be sure it'll be open when you're there. The telephone number is (07423) 3044, and if your schedule doesn't coincide with the regular open hours, you still may be able to arrange a special visiting time by calling ahead.

A collector who decides to collect only gun company non-gun items has set himself a tough, frustrating course. However, for the collector who keeps his eyes open and whose friends know of his interest, a gem will surely turn up from time to time. In general, only the larger gunmakers invested in promotional items, and in my own field of handgun collecting such items from Colt and Walther are not unusual. In addition, many smaller companies as well as some of the larger ones were also active in fields other than guns, so their names may turn up in unexpected (to a gun buff) places.

One of those larger American gunmakers whose name seems to turn up on practically everything is Winchester, and as a result, there has developed over the years an active interest in collecting Winchester non-guns. If nothing else, perhaps this article will stimulate some *Gun Collector's Digest* readers to look at something besides guns on the tables at their next show.

Now, if someone out there just happens to know where there's a Mauser sewing machine or hair clipper available cheap for an avid "non-gun" collector . . . ●

MADE COLLECTIBLE BY VALOR:

THE STEVENS MODEL 77E MILITARY SHOTGUN

Broadside of military 77E with later-style front sling swivel.

by ERIC H. ARCHER

Bombardier Phillip Harding of the Australian Army Training Team Vietnam, getting the feel of a riot gun at the American Advisor School, Di An, June, 1970. (Australian War Memorial negative number FA1/70/423/VN)

FROM 1963 to 1969, a total of 69,079 Stevens Model 77E riot shotguns were procured by the U.S. Army from Savage Arms Corp. of Westfield, Massachusetts. These guns were intended for distribution to friendly countries, either through foreign military sales or military assistance programs.

More than 88 percent of the G.I. Model 77Es went to the Republic of Vietnam. The Stevens was the most commonly encountered scattergun during the Vietnam conflict and therefore is of special interest to firearms enthusiasts who served with U.S. forces in Nam. The homely Model 77Es are highly-prized collectibles because so many of them went overseas and are unlikely to return.

The Stevens shotguns and about 20,000 Ithaca Model 37s purchased during the same time were expected to be issued to relatively untrained auxiliary troops for local defense. The only skills users had to master were loading the magazine, charging the gun with the slide handle and bolt release, manipulating the push-button safety located in the rear of the trigger guard bow, and pulling the trigger. Disassembly was not expected nor encouraged, except for repair.

Model 77E shotguns were employed by all the U.S. services and by our Australian allies in Vietnam, although they were intended for use by indigenous personnel. Some who served in Vietnam were fond of shotguns because of dispersion characteristics and brush-cutting abilities. Others chose shotguns over more sophisticated weapons because of familiarity gained through previous hunting experience. A few cited a religious reason for preferring shotguns—the teachings of the Lord Buddha hold that souls of dismembered corpses are condemned to wander the earth, forever denied attainment of the blessed state of *nirvana* (heaven). Since the shotgun produces more gruesome wounds than other personal weapons, scatterguns were particularly feared by our Buddhist foes.

There was nothing fancy about the Model 77E military shotgun. Barrels were not removable for cleaning. There was a rudimentary bead front sight, but no bayonet adapter or handguard. For durability, all major external metal parts of the 77E were Parkerized, except the trigger guard assembly and the body of the bolt, which were anodized black. Military markings on the 77E consist of U.S. on the receiver and the proofmark P on both the barrel and receiver.

G.I. 77Es were evidently numbered in a serial range separate from civilian production. The highest and lowest serials of 77Es reported to the author in 8 years of research range from 10892 to 61792.

As a concession to allies of smaller stature than the average American, all military 77Es had terra-cotta red Savage recoil pads with distinctive T-shaped vent holes. Most 77E riot guns appear to have been fitted with the shorter stock assembly (Federal Stock Number 1005-957-4001) for use by the "little people." Length of pull was about 12¾ inches, about ⅝-inch less than the standard Savage-Stevens stock, which appears on occasional specimens. The short buttstock placed the user's thumb uncomfortably close to the right cheekbone when the gun was fired by an average-sized American.

Military 77Es were stocked with inexpensive domestic hardwoods finished with a black alcohol-based stain to keep costs down. Walnut pump handles were common on 77Es, and they were also stained black. A military oil finish was applied on top of the stain. As a result of continued use, the stain eventually wore off, giving the stocks a mottled black and yellow appearance.

Every military 77E was fitted with formed sheet-

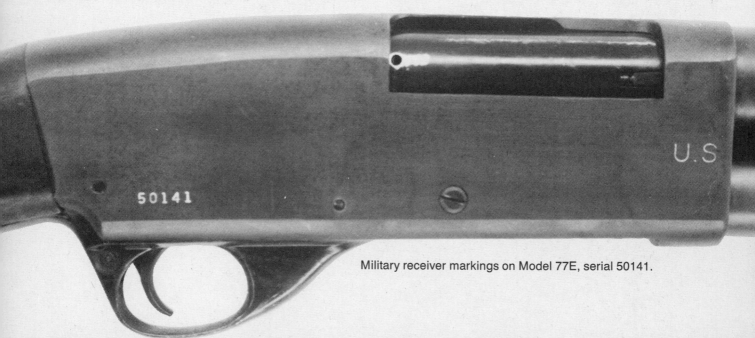

Military receiver markings on Model 77E, serial 50141.

metal sling swivels. The front sling swivel on early production 77Es was suspended from a sheetmetal barrel band. Later, the front swivel was pinned to the lug which retained the magazine plug. So few 77Es are available for inspection that it has not been possible to determine when the design of the front swivel changed. The later swivels have been reported on guns in the 17,000 serial range, but the earlier swivel has been observed on one shotgun with a serial over 20,000.

Two accessories were distributed with each military 77E: one SLING, SMALL ARMS (FSN 1005-654-4058), and one ROD, CLEANING, SMALL ARMS (FSN 1005-630-1446). The web sling was almost identical to that developed during WWII for the M-1 rifle.

Another Vietnam-era accessory suitable for use with the Stevens 77E was the CASE, AMMUNITION, SHOTGUN, COTTON DUCK, O.D., (FSN 8465-261-8944). Each of these pouches held 12 rounds of 12-gauge ammunition in individual loops to prevent rattling or abrasion. The limited capacity of the G.I. shotshell pouch may never have handicapped troops in combat, for this writer has yet to hear from any shotgunner who was issued one of the 12-round pouches for use in Vietnam.

In July, 1963, a manual titled *Field Maintenance Instructions, Repair Parts and Equipment for 12 Gage Stevens Shotgun Model 77E* was published in a manner which confirms that these guns were intended for overseas distribution. Each left-hand page is headed with "THIS PAGE LEFT BLANK FOR TRANSLATION PURPOSES." The cover is generic white in contrast to the customary G.I. manila stock. There is no military form number on the cover, and no U.S. agency took credit for authorship or publication. The Federal Stock Number assigned to the Stevens 77E riot-type shotgun

(1005-00-952-4063) does not appear in the manual, although stock numbers were furnished for 18 replacement parts, which presumably were available through military assistance channels.

The Stevens 77E was not well-suited for rough duty due to a structural flaw. The stock bolt screwed into a thin, tapered extension at the rear of the brittle alloy trigger guard assembly. "The butt would bust right off if you bashed a dink over the head with a 77E," remarked a U.S. Army ordnance technician assigned to shotgun overhaul in Vietnam.

An official Air Force account of air base defense in The Republic of Vietnam contains unfavorable comments on the 77E's ability to chamber and eject ammunition corroded by exposure to the tropical climate. The failure of the Stevens shotguns in the hands of Air Force Security Police was actually due to improper storage of WWII-vintage M19 brass-cased buckshot

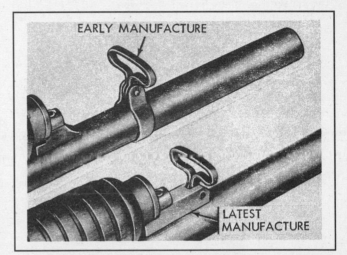

Illustration from ordnance maintenance manual highlighting early and late production Model 77E front sling swivels.

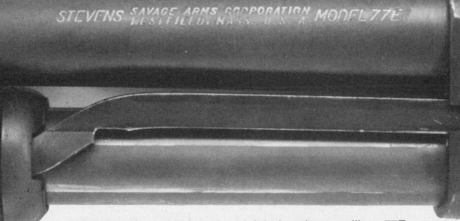

Manufacturer's markings and model designation on military 77E.

M19 brass-cased buckshot round being chambered in 77E. Note military proofs on shoulder of receiver and top of barrel.

Transfers of Stevens Model 77E Through Foreign Military Sales and Military Assistance Programs

COUNTRY:	QUANTITY:
Iran	4
Korea (Rep. of)	1483
Panama	42
Phillippines	59
Thailand	3146
Vietnam (Rep. of)	60,990
Total	65,724

Shotgun rarities: XM257 No. 4 Special buckshot ammunition as manufactured by Western Cartridge Corp. in subdued coloring; shotshell pouch manufactured by NORDAC on a 1969 contract; experimental Olin beehive rounds, each containing 20 flechettes similar to those at right foreground.

Vietnam combat shotgun fodder: WWII-vintage Remington brass-cased M19 00-buckshot; unbuffered XM162 00-buck made by Remington in January, 1964; Federal Cartridge Corp. XM162 ammo from May, 1970; experimental Olin 1305-A011A beehive rounds from February, 1966, assembled in unmarked but headstamped Western commercial shotshell casings.

then employed in Vietnam. The corrosion problem was later avoided by adoption of the newer plastic-cased shotshells for combat use.

Experimental lots of commercial nine-pellet 00 Buck ammunition with primer pockets sealed by lacquer were procured as early as 1963 under the XM162 designation. Later XM162 rounds contained granular buffering to minimize shot distortion. Other 12-gauge ammunition used in Vietnam included the 27-pellet XM257 No. 4 Special buckshot round and experimental beehive cartridges containing 20 cadmium-plated flechettes.

Since the Model 77E remains in service with U.S. military and law enforcement agencies, very few of these G.I. shotguns have become available to firearms enthusiasts. Reported prices of 77Es acquired by collectors confirm how highly-prized these guns have become. Recent sales prices for select specimens range to three times the value of a comparable civilian riot gun.

The Savage-Stevens shotguns of Nam have also been the subject of the first military shotgun commemorative. In early 1989, The American Historical Foundation of Richmond, Virginia announced unique Model 69 Series E shotguns serialed from VN001 to VN750. The guns in this series were the final slide-action shotguns produced by Savage. The deluxe Museum Edition, issued at $1595, featured an ornate hand-engraved receiver, select wood sealed with seven coats of hand-rubbed lacquer, engine turning on the bolt, and gold plating to highlight key parts such as the trigger and safety. The Collector's Edition, issued at $995, had the same mirror-blue finish on the metal but boasted an etched receiver which was also gold-gilt filled. The wood of the Collector grade commemoratives had a special black finish reminiscent of the military originals.

The notion of a commemorative fighting shotgun may seem pretentious to some. However, shotguns

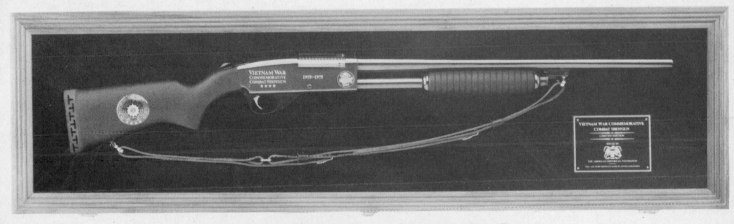

Collector's Edition commemorative scattergun from The American Historical Foundation with texturized stock.

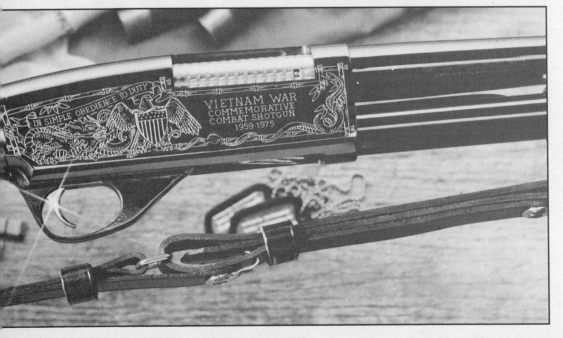

Detail of hand-cut scroll-engraved receiver on Deluxe Museum Edition Vietnam Commemorative Shotgun from The American Historical Foundation.

Spec. 4 Kenneth M. Purvis, a/k/a "California Kid," of Bravo Company, 2nd Battalion, 34th Armored Regiment, 1st Infantry Division, with a 77E atop the 90mm main gun of a M48A3 tank. This photo, originally captioned "Hunting for Cong," was taken near Ben Cat in September, 1967. (Courtesy Ken Purvis)

were used by many who distinguished themselves in the cause of freedom in Southeast Asia. Guns such as the Stevens 77E were highly favored for ambush and counter-ambush use by point men, advisors, and company officers who were particularly exposed by reason of their leadership style on the battlefield. The five-round capacity of the 77E and many other G.I. shotguns was a disadvantage in a prolonged engagement, but the shotgun's multiple-projectile loads gave high hit probabilities at close range.

In March, 1967, just a few kilometers south of the Demilitarized Zone, a recently-commissioned Marine officer earned distinction as the most highly-decorated shotgunner of the Vietnam War. John Paul Bobo, born in 1943 in Niagara Falls, New York, enlisted in the United States Marine Corps Reserve a few days before his graduation from Niagara University. Bobo completed Marine Officer Candidate School and was commissioned in the Marine Corps Reserve on New Year's Eve, 1965. Second Lieutenant Bobo was ordered to the Republic of Vietnam following completion of The Basic School at Quantico in May, 1966. He was eventually assigned to command the Weapons Platoon, Company I, 3rd Battalion, 9th Marine Regiment, 3rd Marine Division (Reinforced).

At 0700 hours on 29 March 1967, Item Company began platoon-sized patrols in an area of low hills covered with dense brush near Con Thien in Quang Tri Province. At 1140 hours on 30 March, the decomposed bodies of two North Vietnamese regulars (NVA) were

Cpl. C.G. McMahon of Hotel Company, 2nd Battalion, 5th Marines, 1st Marine Division, with a Model 77E at the Troui River Bridge, south of Phu Bai, May, 1968. McMahon and Cpl. R. Wade are sitting atop an ARVN M24 tank used as a pillbox. (Photo courtesy Charles McMahon)

found. Nothing more was recorded in the 3rd Battalion, 9th Marines Command Chronology until 1800 hours when the company was preparing to set up a night ambush. The progress of Item Company had not gone unnoticed, and the outfit was bested by a reinforced company of NVA regulars by nightfall.

As platoons 1-2, 1-3, 1-4 and the command group came under heavy mortar and automatic weapons fire, Lieutenant Bobo hastily organized the defense of the company Command Post. Bobo moved from position to position through "murderous hostile fire" encouraging outnumbered Marines. He recovered a 3.5-inch rocket launcher from among friendly casualties and organized a new launcher team to take out enemy machineguns. Bobo's contributions to the defense of his unit as the enemy drew closer were summarized in a recommendation for award of the Medal of Honor as follows:

. . . An exploding mortar round severed Lieutenant Bobo's right leg below the knee and he asked the First Sergeant to tie off his leg with a web belt. He refused to be evacuated and insisted he be given his shotgun and additional ammunition and be pulled to a position on top of the ridge where he could cover the withdrawal of the command group to a covered position. He jammed his leg in the dirt to curtail the bleeding, and remained in this position delivering devastating fire into the ranks of the enemy trying to overrun the Marine position. At least five enemy dead were seen killed by the Lieutenant. He saved the life of the Company First Sergeant who lay on the ground severely wounded and out of ammunition by killing a North Vietnamese soldier

2nd Lt. John P. Bobo, USMCR, born February 14, 1943, killed in action March 30, 1967. (USMC photo)

standing over him. Lieutenant Bobo was last seen alive in a half-sitting position at the main point of the enemy's attack firing his shotgun. He died as a result of the many wounds received at about 2145, 30 March 1967.

Total Item Company losses at Hill 70 were 16 killed and 62 wounded, contrasted with 52 NVA known dead, and two NVA captured.

March 30, 1967 was a bad day for American arms, but a day made forever remarkable through the glorious deeds of shotgunner John Paul Bobo. As long as Lieutenant Bobo's defense of his fellow Marines is remembered, men will comment on what a humble weapon he chose, but no one can question Bobo's dedication or the results he achieved.

Through skillful employment by men of valor, the utilitarian Stevens Model 77E shotgun has surely earned its place in American history.

ACKNOWLEDGEMENTS

This article would not have been possible without the gracious cooperation of Col. Burton P.C. Bacheller II, USAF, Chief, Weapons Systems Division, Defense Security Assistance Agency/Plans; Robert A. Buerlein, President, The American Historial Foundation; Roe S. Clark, Savage Historian; Col. L.A. Hergenroeder, GS, USA, Director for Program Management, U.S. Army Security Assistance Center; Maj. Terence R. Johnston, USAR; Kenneth L. Smith-Christmas, Assistant Officer in Charge, USMC Museums Branch Activities, Quantico; and the staff of the Reference Section, Marine Corps Historical Center.

The author welcomes correspondence from anyone with first-hand information to contribute to a military shotgun book now being prepared. Please write to Eric H. Archer, c/o Old West Gun Room, 3509 Carlson Boulevard, El Cerrito, CA 94530.

The successful fabricant, Fabriques D'Armes Unies de Liege, sold under the world-wide brand name Centaure and filled a great many shooters' needs.

FABRIQUES D'ARMES UNIES DE LIÉGE
SOCIÉTÉ ANONYME
ANCIENNES FIRMES
FABRIQUES D'ARMES RÉUNIES
FABRIQUE D'ARMES DE LIÉGE
F^{AND} HANQUET

Bulldogs and Puppies

Turn-of-the-Century Belgian Revolvers

by EDOURD BENET

Plate 1: Top left is a classic Lefaucheux pinfire of the 1850s. A similar but not identical pistol was given to Stonewall Jackson. Middle and right examples follow the Webley Motif, while the top-break of the Smith & Wesson style has an added thumb safety. Bottom left is the style renowned as "British Bulldog," even when made in Belgium or by Forehand Arms in the U.S.

THE dreaded disease of the 19th century was the infected bite of the mad dog — hydrophobia, or rabies. So searing on the mind of the young scientist Louis Pasteur was the treatment for a rabies bite — cauterizing it with a hot iron — that it turned him on a search for healing and sterilization. Though today rabies is a small, but sometimes serious, problem, "pasteurization" has made the world safer. Safer, too, was the world when the roaming wild dogs of Europe, attacking the new vogue of bicycling in the country, were pacified by a bullet from a whole new breed of short, stubby revolvers appropriately termed Bulldogs.

To fill what was for more than a half-century a widespread need for such pistol protectors, gunsmiths of Liege, Belgium labored by hand and machine. Of the many fabricants, none was more successful in variety of output than the Fabriques d'Armes Unies de Liege,

(F.A.U.L.), the United Arms Factories selling under the world-wide brand name, Centaure.

Their trademark is a rampant centaur firing — you guessed it — a revolver. The symbol expresses the century-old link between the establishment of the gunmaking family Hanquet in Liege, and Sam Colt. American arms men have long made their pilgrimage to Liege, that mecca of guns. Sam Colt arrived in 1849 and licensed production of his revolvers, marked Colt Brevete. One licensee was the firm of Hanquet, founded in the middle 1700s and still active today.

Another American arrived about 50 years later and made the revolver world shift on its axis — John Moses Browning, the automatic pistol inventor. When John Browning stepped off the train at the Gare des Guillemins, he climbed aboard a little white-painted tram car. Leisurely, it rattled out the Rue and along the Boulevard D'Avroy, through the flowered lawns and quiet trees of the park. If Browning had gotten off where the D'Avroy joins the curving Boulevard de la Sauveniere, and walked west along the Rue St. Gilles, he would have come to a busy bar and brasserie, Au Revolver, where gunmaking foremen gathered to take their leisurely 2-hour noonday repast. At that corner begins the Rue Trappe, where at No. 22, now, then, and for much

Plate 2: Folding trigger revolvers are commonly seen, but this group shows rare varieties. The ring trigger pistol has a Webley-pattern ejector rod. The white-gripped pistol in the left column is hammerless, facing is another white-gripped pistol, both are of hinged-frame Smith & Wesson style. The second gun, far right column, seems to have a 10-shot cylinder.

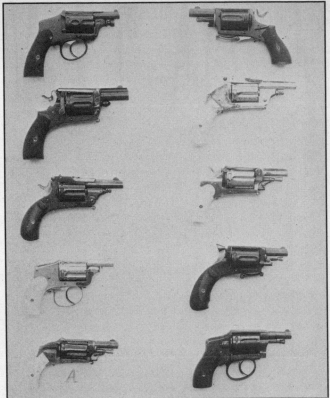

Plate 3: In this lineup, if you have seen one, you definitely have not seen all. Fourth in the left column is a Saturday Night extra finish on a pistol also shown in Plate 6, but the bottom right column hammerless has the same cylinder, barrel, and side-swing as the one in Plate 4 with a white grip, except for the regular trigger and guard. Most of these appear to be of Velodog caliber.

of the century preceding, the Hanquet factory is located, one of the major revolver makers of the world.

Today, the company is not a manufacturing facility. The boss, Nicole Hanquet, direct descendant of the founding family, manages wholesale sporting goods distribution under the classic name Centaure. It is a hand-me-down from the days when Colt's arms made in Paterson, New Jersey from 1836 to 1842, bore the stamp of a centaur on their cylinders.

The company name, United Arms Factories, refers to the horde of small makers whose revolvers were sold by Centaure. Toward 1910, the Hanquets recognized what had happened when Browning passed them by and took his new automatic pistol to the suburb of Herstal and the new industry of the Fabrique Nationale d'Armes De Guerre, the FN.

As the 20th century developed, Browning's influence stimulated the manufacture of many types of automatic pistols. F.A.U.L. even marked one of its revolvers with Browning, and issued a few semiautomatic pistols of a unique design before WWI.

But preserved in their office archives were photos of their revolvers assembled as catalog page illustrations. The arms pictured here could be bought as single examples, or by the hundreds — all alike or assorted.

The automatic pistol's "charisma" then was such that contemporary gun expert Major H.B.C. Pollard wrote that he foresaw the automatic superseding the revolver by 1950. Pollard was, of course, quite wrong, but the arms illustrated in the accompanying pictures are no longer made, and so are of increasing collector interest today.

Most of the revolvers shown are of the type called Bulldog for large bore, and Velodog for 5.5mm, or Puppy for in-between calibers. Mostly unmarked, they were made to sell to merchants all over the world who, in turn, might put their own shop stamps on them. All were safe arms of the kind, bearing the internationally respected stamps of the Banc d'Epreuve, the proof house of Liege — an oval/ELG, and the arrow-shaped water tower in the city square, the "Perron de Liege."

About midway in this production period, F.A.U.L. turned out simulations of the Colt New Army and Navy Revolver, 1892 to 1907, or "left wheeler" arms. Their

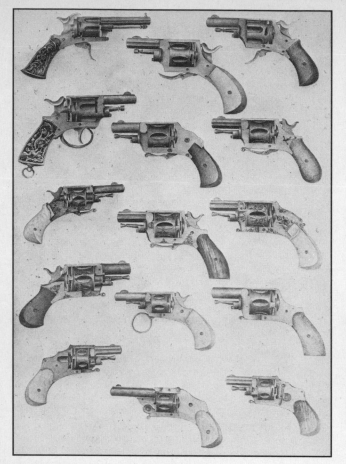

Plate 4: Artists' renderings of many revolvers reveal a choice of moulded hard rubber decorative grips as well as ivory or pearl. Engraving touches set these pistols a class above the ordinary. Fourth down in the right column seems to lack front sight and hammer — did the artist fail to finish it before catalog printing deadline? It is possible these drawings were preliminary stages in catalog makeup, and replaced by actual photos as they appear to duplicate some of the photographed guns.

Plate 5: Webley-type constabulary revolver (center, top line) has round butt, but the pistol below with moulded S&W-style grips has a belted cylinder like many Nagants. Upper left, third down with white grip, and bottom left are all right-side-swing cylinders released by swinging the loading gate back. Small pistols with white grips and folding triggers are probably 5.5mm Velodog caliber. In the middle row, the white-gripped pistol is a side swing and has early Colt-style latch, while the lower right gun has a hinged frame. The original early Lefaucheux pinfire pistol is at upper right.

earliest follow the pioneer design of Lefaucheux, often made in Liege on subcontract. As the accompanying photos show, their production fits into several categories.

The most easily discernible are those evolved from the 1850-type Lefaucheux pistols with folding triggers. Originally with removable barrels, open-top style, their design influenced solid-frame small pistols as well.

The bicycle was then king-of-the-road transportation. Ladies and gents formed cycling clubs for touring country roads on Sunday afternoons, or riding in the fine city parks which foreigners noted as attractions of the great capitals of the continent. Unfortunately, the parks also attracted large numbers of stray dogs, the

Society for the Prevention of Cruelty to Animals and neutering not yet having become fashionable. For these logical reasons, some of these small revolvers came to be named after the canine breed. Thus, big 44 pistols were known as Bulldogs. In England, such arms were even marked "British Bulldog," while in America, Forehand Arms Co. imitated the British imitation of the Continental Bulldog revolvers and so marked them. The spirit has been in a way brought to the present, with the large caliber 44 snub guns of Charter Arms classically known as Bulldogs.

A special high-velocity, long 5.5mm centerfire cartridge was used in smaller-framed pistols. They were directed right at the cyclists, giving rise to to the trade term Velodog, velo being short for the French term for

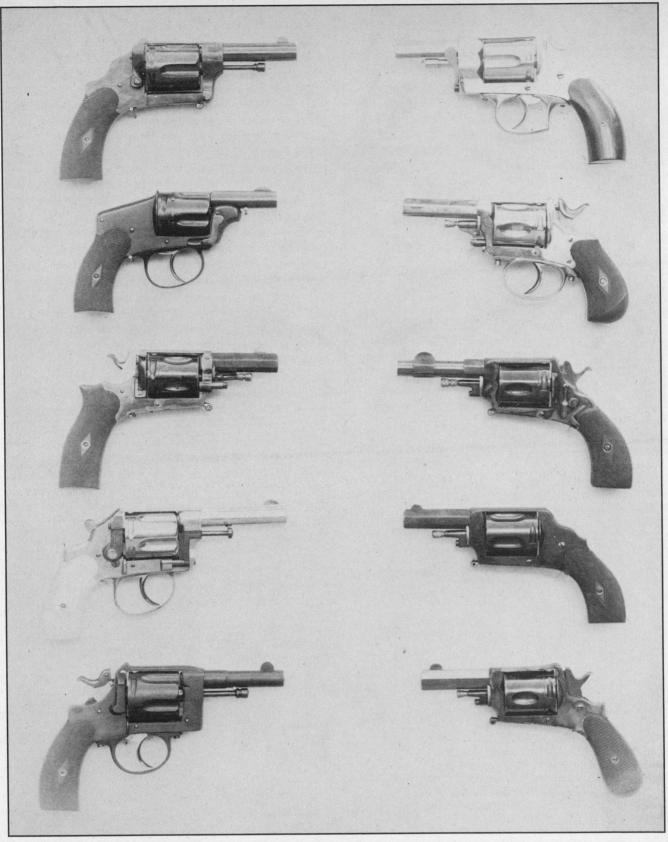

Plate 6: Side-swing and side-lever ejection is shown in this set of 10 different pistols. Hammerless, second from top left, has a lever on the right side hinged to push out empties. Below, nickel and pearl pistol frame profile suggests DA 1878 Colt Army shape, though smaller. Lowest, left, is also a side swing with the ejector rod head copied from the Colt DA 38 series. Third gun in the right column with the front sight set back may have been built with an extended barrel to suit some police regulation on length.

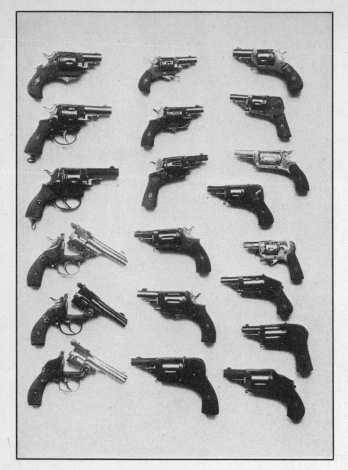

Plate 7: The top left Puppy and a couple of Bulldogs vie with top-break S&W substitutes and an array of Velodog hammer and hammerless models, all with folding triggers.

Plate 8: In Liege, with government proof house testing assuring safe construction, cheap is good; here, variety of low-cost pistols offer a choice of folding trigger Velodogs, including hammerless and deluxe side swings for fast reloading. A long cylinder version, upper right, chambered a long cartridge; a long handle, lower left, assured better grip.

bicycle — velocipede — which literally translates to moving by means of the feet.

To bridge the gap, 32s, and some chambered for the then-new 6.35mm (25 ACP) Browning automatic pistol cartridge, were advertised as "Modele Puppies." Despite their trade names in the days when they were sold, it seems likely that most of these pistols were carried as private defense arms rather than "taking arms" against a sea of stray dogs and by so doing, ending them.

The Smith & Wesson top-break system, which appeared about 1868, inspired a number of imitations including hammerless models. In several models, the top-break was combined with the Lefaucheux-style folding trigger.

The pull-out and side-swinging rod ejector of the Lefaucheux was continued on the Nagant-style revolvers. Original inventions of Emile and Leon Nagant, their best-known design is probably the model made for the Czarist Russian service, "Sans deperdition de gaz," the reciprocating-cylinder seven-shot gas-seal type most often found in 7.62mm Nagant Russian calibers.

Though an exact copy of the Nagant does not appear in the Hanquet pictures, pieces quite similar in style are shown. Obviously, they were for sale in some exclusive Russian sport shop in St. Petersburg or Moscow when French-style products were so vogue, before 1917.

Other arms, especially side-swinging cylinder patterns, reflect the French ordnance revolvers of 1870 to 1890; others show close parity with the style of the famous Montenegrin Gasser, huge 11mm handguns. Although the grips do not show the Swiss Cross, some pieces are intended to amuse and confuse the Swiss buyer.

The style of Webley pistols—with trigger guards or folding triggers, some with square butts and some with round — suggests marketing into Africa. There, the British service revolvers from P. Webley & Sons

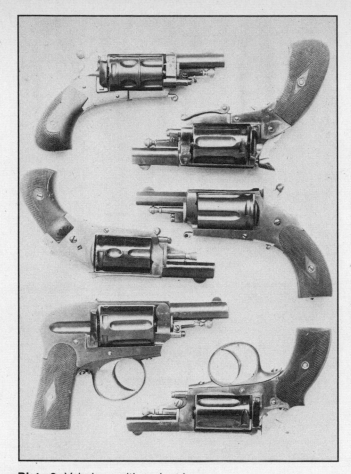

Plate 9: Velodogs with variant hammer forms, hammerless, or as at bottom right, of the basic Webley style except for the long cylinder. All were safety tested by Banc d'Epreuve in Liege.

Plate 10: Some Nagant-style guns, but the middle row second and third guns are of Montenegrin Gasser style in small, non-military caliber. Nickel-plated pistol center, fourth, is a Colt 1877 copy with square butt, the "Texas Ranger" mail-order pattern. At right, a side-swing modified Nagant is below a similar military-type revolver with a quick-change cylinder for fast reloading.

through the Webley & Scott models would be the standard. Against these, Centaure offered its creative simulations to be judged.

One style of hideaway pistol was sold to those who were not quite certain about the new 1905 Browning 25s, but who still wanted novelty. What was novel was the styling—a grip like a pocket automatic, a safety on the left side revealing the word "Feu" for fire, slab sides like an automatic, and the stamping for caliber introducing the buyer to a hitherto unknown "C Browning" stamped on the left of the barrel. As the full stamp reads **C BROWNING 6**^{35}, it is possible the intent (if one had to explain it in a court of law in a trademark infringement suit, for example) was to indicate "Caliber Browning 6.35mm."

The example pictured is clearly a long-pull double-action with revolving chambered cylinder. Mysteriously, the butt appears to shelter a heel-catch detach-

able magazine, as does the folding trigger example above it. An action screw appears to preclude any innovative design of mechanically feeding from a magazine into a cylinder. If there was a clip fitted, we suppose it held five spare rounds to go into the cylinder one by one, when needed.

Most provocative for Americans, and especially Colt collectors who must have one of everything, are the Hanquet takeoffs on the double-action M1877 Colt's "Lightning Model," shown here with a square SAA-style grip. These arms in one form continued to be sold in the U.S. as late as the 1930s by Johnson Smith & Co., a novelty mail-order firm once famous for its pistol offerings, and still in business with sneezing powder and Chinese back scratchers. These arms, sometimes dubbed "Texas Rangers," can occasionally be seen at gun shows.

Very, very rare at present are the solid-frame Cen-

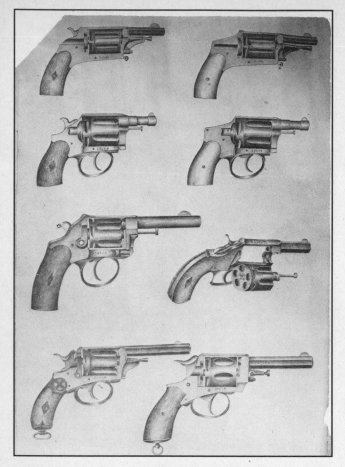

Plate 11: Superb wash drawings reveal details sometimes obscured in photos. This swing-out cylinder gun is stamped "CAL 7.5mm" and the serial 24555 appears to be die-struck in spite of the whole picture being just a drawing, as distortion of the cylinder notches reveals. Tiny grips on the Colt-latch side swings helped concealability, always a valued aspect of these personal defense guns. The S&W-shaped butt on the gun with lanyard loop (lower left) was a frank appeal to the Latin American police buyer.

Plate 12: Military-sized revolvers were usually 8mm Lebel, Nagant Swedish, or 9mm/38 revolver calibers. Top left is a takeoff from the French Ordnance pattern while the second and lockwork-open-view at bottom resembles the Swiss type. Lockwork seems to be famous Chamelot & Delvigne style with rebound lever acting on cylinder-turning pawl, later copied in the Colt Army and Navy Special and Official Police when patents expired. Upper right is a close copy of the Webley Military & Police Model of 1867-80; second is Nagant form but with normal cylinder.

taure copies of the Colt New Army and Navy Special Revolvers, the Police Positive Specials, and the Pocket Positive small 32 frames.

The guns pictured show the swelled breech barrels of the Army Special and later issue, but are clearly on the "left wheeler" lockwork using two kinds of cylinder stop cuts on the outside of the cylinder. The large-framed pistols seem to be frank copies of the Colt New Army and Navy with the late type of barrel, including the circle/Centaure stamp on the heel of the left frame side, simulating the rampant Colt trademark.

Also virtually unknown to American collectors are the smaller sizes, simulating the Police Positive Specials, and the early-style 32 Police Positives. At least two different lockworks may have been used. Grip frames also varied, one large pistol seeming to be a Detective Special scaled up to New Army and Navy Special proportions. One barrel is stamped CART. 38

LONG for caliber, and on another, the appropriate proofs for "Rifled Bore Gun" are impressed. The rampant Centaure trademark appears both plain and surmounting the curved word "Centaure," and the revolver the rampant centaure is shooting may be pointing right or left, although the moulded rubber grip centaure always points "forward" on the right or left grip. The white-handled revolver (ivory?) with lanyard loop is stamped with a circle motif, which suggests the Colt and Centaure stamps, but is an entirely different unknown marking.

These pistols were always well-finished. Rust blue in full or combined with color case-hardened frames were usual. Sometimes hammers were hardened in colors; others were high-polish bright. The Colt imitations copied the Colt style of full blue, with side-polished hammers. Fancy engraving of quite good quality was commonly available, though of course, for an extra

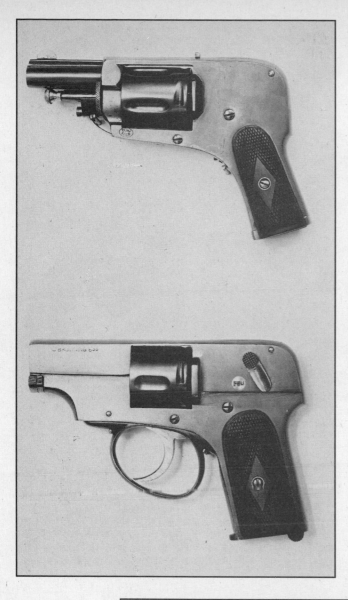

Plate 13: (Left) The Velodog hammerless revolver had an extendible grip to improve holding, and a very long trigger folded flush under the frame. The bottom revolver is chambered for the new 25 ACP cartridge and is marked "C BROWNING 6.35" on the barrel. The original photo bears a 1908 date.

Plate 14: (Above) Velodog-caliber hammerless has thumb safety on the back of the frame. The hole in the folded-trigger tip was often used to attach a chain to avoid loss in a rough and tumble encounter. Barrel shows Liege proofmarks. This photo dates from 1908.

Plate 15: (Below) Colt copies vary the M1877 Lightning model style by adding a single-action-shaped square grip (upper left). This style was sold in the U.S. well into the 1930s. Action design of side swings seems to copy the Colt New Army and Navy of 1892 with variations. Center is a 38, but the frame was also fitted up as 44-40 caliber. The thumb latch is the later style. Upper right is a copy of the Police Positive Special frame; bottom left is a copy of the New Police small frame. Various barrel lengths were offered; widespread manufacture of Colt copies may have ended with the start of WWII.

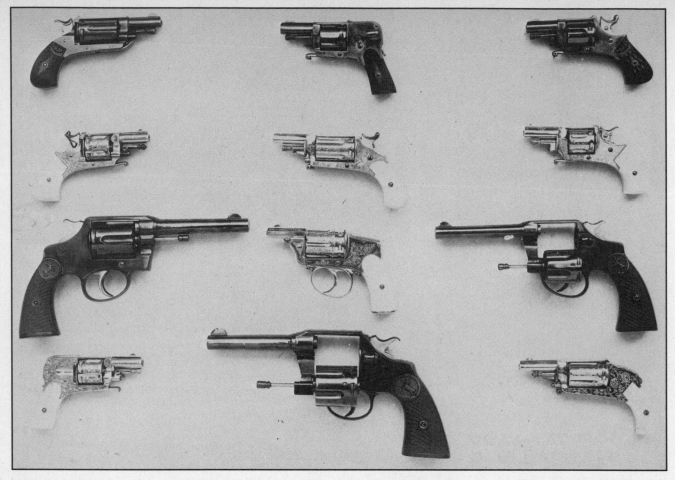

Plate 16: Velodogs, Puppies, and frontier service "Colts" — the tiny engraved and plated pistol second at the left has a cutaway hammer for attachment to a watch fob chain. Deluxe engraving shows roses and scroll patterns, the plating and ivory grips contrasting with the nice blue and color case-hardening of other frames. The Colt copy in the left column has a thickly-reinforced barrel nipple for heavy-caliber 44-40 bullets, and uses a removable left sideplate similar to the Police Positive style in the right column, shown with its cylinder swung out, its frame stamped 32W at the barrel for the 32-20 cartridge then becoming popular. Center, bottom, is a lockwork copy to the New Navy 1892 with sideplate on the right side, but with the late-type barrel ring at the frame.

price; such pieces must have been few. As for survival, until today, engraved "gingerbread" pistols — gold- and silver-plated, with ivory grips — might have avoided destruction or the wear and tear of cops' and robbers' games in the Paris underworld. It is these small, easily-concealed, often inexpensive revolvers with their fancy finish and extra-quality engraving which gave rise to the complimentary term "Saturday Night Special."

Saturday night, of course, is when you take a bath, put on your best clothes, and go steppin' with yo' best gal on your arm.

A pistol for Saturday night was thus an arm of extra-high quality, deluxe style and finish, not something for ordinary wear, but suitable for that special night of the week — Saturday.

In the days when ladies relied on their gentlemen to protect them from the riffraff of the streets, the junkies, the winos, and the panhandlers, the little Saturday Night Specials from Liege with their proud "Perron de Liege" arrow-like proofmarks symbolizing the highest quality of world arms making, did the job. With the social dislocations of the Great War, women, their men serving at the Front, had to stride out into the great world and make a living. These tidy little blue steel bundles of pistol protection allowed independent women to "go a long way" toward equal opportunity in a male-dominated world, protecting them from stray wild dogs or just plain sons of bitches.   ●

To aid collectors the group photos in this article have been arbitrarily labeled Plates 1 through 16. Not until the postage stamp catalogs, with pictures of stamps you could really collect, got published did philately become organized. So it is with these revolvers. By citing an example's location in one of these photos, collectors may identify their prizes and distinguish them from other similar arms. Then you can collect a whole kennel full of Bulldogs, Velodogs and Puppies. Perhaps this system will be of use until a better one comes along. Woof!

Some classic American single shot match target pistols, plus a non-qualifier that deserves recognition in its own right. Clockwise from upper right — Colt Camp Perry match target pistol, First Model; Stevens No. 10 Target Pistol; Harrington & Richardson Model 195/U.S.R.A. match target pistol, Second (last) Walter Roper Model, 1934-1942; Harrington & Richardson 22 Handy Gun, produced 1933-1935; Smith & Wesson Straight Line match target pistol; Hopkins and Allen match target pistol.

The Single Shot Target Pistol in the U.S. 1870-1940

by ALLEN W. TEREK

THE PERIOD more or less from 1870 to 1940 is what I consider the time span most interesting to the serious student of the history and development of American firearms.

It witnessed, to a degree approaching perfection, the evolution of the self-contained metallic cartridge. The development of American hand firearms of breech-loading, single shot, manually-operated magazine, and self-loading magazine types produced a veritable spectrum of arms that are now cherished by students, collectors, and shooters alike. The rapid advance of the technical state of the art, plus the efforts of manufacturers, designers, and highly-skilled hand workmen and machine tool operators — dedicated men who took real pride in their skills and creations — combined to give Americans production-line firearms whose equivalents, despite all the technical advances made in the meantime, are all too often not to be had today except from highly-skilled custom artisans at very high prices.

One of the more interesting categories of handguns produced in the United States during this period is the single shot match target pistol. At least until recently, these pistols have largely been ignored by students and collectors, except in a limited context as the products of their individual manufacturers. In contrast, their counterparts — the classic single shot rifles, particularly the long-range "Creedmoor" and the offhand, or "Scheutzen" models — have received far more attention and, thanks to Roberts, Waters, Grant, Sellers, DeHaas, Kelver, and others, extensive and well-authenticated literature about them is available. Perhaps as a result, the prices asked for such pieces in even passable condition are frequently beyond the financial reach of many, if not most, students and would-be collectors.

The single shot match target pistols made in the U.S. are in their own way equally interesting and of equally fine quality. They were made to satisfy the requirements of a class of competitive shooters as demanding as any. For the most part, however, these pistols have been less well researched and documented; surprisingly few specialized articles and books have been devoted to this category of classic American firearms. This is much to be regretted, as they constitute a part of the American firearms heritage that may largely be lost if the men who designed and built these pistols — the custom gunsmiths who modified and improved them, the marksmen who shot them in competition, even the manufacturers whose names they bear — are to be allowed to pass unrecognized and unrecorded.

Some really significant work already has been done in this direction. Jerry Landskron's *Remington Rolling Block Pistols* is so monumental a work that, in all probability, very little more than specific supplementary detail remains to be added to the material covered by this volume. Also very good is *Stevens Pistols and Pocket Rifles*, by Kenneth L. Cope. DeWitt Sell, in *Handguns Americana*, devotes considerable space to at least basic coverage. The Smith & Wesson single shot match target pistols and the Colt Camp Perry models have been described, all too briefly, and illustrated in the general company histories written for Smith & Wesson by McHenry/Roper and Neal/Jinks, and Colt by Haven/Belden and by Serven. The older American firearms authorities — Gould, Himmelwright, Hatcher, and Roper — are of great, if uneven, value.

But much still remains to be done. This writer feels that this category of handguns — the classic American single shot match target pistols — deserves at least one large, thick, amply illustrated, well researched, scholarly, and comprehensive reference volume, before it is too late . . .

From about 1870 onward, a number of American firearms manufacturers, notably Frank Wesson, Remington, Stevens, and Bay State, produced "pocket rifles" (long-barreled single shot pistols with detachable skeleton shoulder stocks) and single shot pistols qualified for general sporting use and plinking or — marginally, owing to a unanimous lack of properly adjustable sights — for target use. The real history of the American single shot match target pistol dates from 1880, the year of introduction by J. Stevens and Company (later the J. Stevens Arms and Tool Company) of two models of single shot pistols specifically intended for match target shooting.

Previous to 1880, several factors contributed to what was to become a national interest in slow-fire match pistol shooting in the U.S. One of these was the traditional custom of the duel with pistols, dying out but not quite extinct by 1880. For many years, the ability to shoot a pistol accurately while under stress was considered one of the necessary accomplishments of anyone who laid claim to the status of gentlemen and who lived along the Mississippi River, in the South, or in the Southwest. Despite the frequency of laws enacted against the custom of the duel, the practice was widespread and apparently deeply rooted in these sections of the country. And some of these dueling gentlemen could shoot very competently. Alexander Keith McClung, known romantically as the "Black Knight," a noted and notorious pistol duelist active along the Mississippi River in the 1830s and '40s, is recorded as having called and delivered a decisive shot to a dueling opponent's front teeth at a range of 100 feet, well beyond the normal pistol dueling distance.[1]

A second contributing influence appears to have been the popularity of the "pocket rifles," the long-barreled pistols with detachable shoulder stocks previously mentioned, for hunting small game and for informal recreational shooting. A third can be seen as the prevalence and popularity of shooting galleries in American cities. The Stevens "Conlin" model target pistol was named for James S. Conlin, the proprietor of the White Elephant, a well-known shooting gallery in New York City.[2] A topical public interest in competitive rifle shooting, first at long ranges and later in mid-range and Scheutzen, or offhand, rifle competition, from the mid-1870s onward, played an important role. The unlooked-for victory of the American long-range rifle team over the Irish, who had been considered the finest long-range riflemen in the world, at the Creedmoor range on Long Island in 1874, initiated a sustained interest in competitive shooting in the U.S., and a pride in the achievements of American marksmen in interna-

[1]Hamilton Cochran, *Duels and Hostile Encounters* (Philadelphia: Chilton Co., 1963), p. 234.

[2]Arthur G. Gould, *Modern American Pistols and Revolvers* (Boston: Thomas G. Samworth, 1946), pp. 9-11.

tional and later in Olympic competition.

As an example of top-level professional pistol marksmanship in the U.S. in 1860, consider a public challenge match fired by one Captain John Travers — the targets were 9-inch china plates at a distance of 100 feet. Travers, one of the best-known pistol marksmen of his day, broke 11 out of 15; his challenger broke nine.[3] The first great American pistol shot in the modern tradition was Ira A. Paine, active during the 1880s. For years he toured the United States and Europe, giving demonstrations of his skill with a Stevens Lord model single shot target pistol and with Smith & Wesson New Model Number Three single-action break-open target revolvers, first in 44 Russian centerfire caliber, later in 38-44 and 32-44 calibers, these latter two developed specifically for target shooting, as well. The King of Portugal was so impressed by Paine's marksmanship that he conferred upon him membership in an order of knighthood,[4] so that Paine was afterward referred to, in some circles at least, as the *Chevalier* Ira Paine.

Two decisive turning points in the formative period of the history of competitive slow-fire pistol shooting in the U.S., and of the development of the single shot match target pistols themselves occurred in 1880 and 1887, the J. Stevens Company of Chicopee Falls, Massachusetts being responsible for both. The Stevens Lord model and Conlin model target pistols were introduced in 1880 and were specifically intended for match competition and furnished with rear sights adjustable for windage and elevation. The Lord model, named for Frank Lord, a famous pistol shot of New York City, a man of "Herculean frame"[5] with unusually large and strong hands, was based on the Stevens "Hunter's Pet," the largest and heaviest of the three "pocket rifle" models offered by the company. Produced from 1880 until 1911, the Lord model pistol was made available in a number of calibers ranging from 22 Short rimfire to 44 Russian centerfire, at first with the option of 10-inch or 12-inch barrel lengths. About 3500 of these pistols were manufactured. The Stevens Lord pistol is a massive handgun, typically weighing about 3 pounds. Its grip is very long, necessitating a large hand to hold it steady and to shoot it effectively; there is a projecting spur at the rear of the trigger guard, intended to provide

The last of an illustrious line: Stevens No. 35 Offhand single shot pistol in 22 Long Rifle. This was the final descendant of the Stevens Conlin Model of 1880.

a hold for the second finger of the pistol hand.

The other of the two single shot match target pistols introduced by Stevens in 1880 is the Conlin model based on the frame of the "New Model" pocket rifle, the intermediate in size of Stevens' three pocket rifles. The Conlin pistol is essentially a smaller and lighter version of the Lord, weighing about 2¼ pounds, and is normally found with a 10-inch barrel. Like the Lord, the Conlin model is characterized by a spur at the rear of the trigger guard. The Conlin pistol appears to have been the dominant arm in its class on American firing ranges until the turn of the 20th century; about 6500 were sold between 1880 and 1903. It is found in two major variations, the first of which has the parent pocket rifle's spur trigger covered by a trigger guard, while the second and much more common version has a conventional trigger, the trigger guard in both instances having the characteristic spur at its rear.

The Stevens Gould model match target pistol, the Conlin with a conventional trigger guard without the spur, was made at the request of Arthur C. Gould, the foremost American authority and writer on matters pertaining to firearms of his time. It was less popular than the Conlin, only about 1000 being made from 1889 until 1903. However, the basic conformation of the Gould lived on in the post-1900 Stevens Number 35 "Offhand" target and sporting/utility pistols made in first version, with cast trigger guard, (*ca.* 35,000) from 1907 until 1916, and second version, with stamped trigger guard, (43,357) from 1923 until 1942.[6] These Stevens "Offhand" models are not match target pieces, nor were they ever intended to be such. Lacking certain

[3]A.L.A. Himmelwright, *Pistol and Revolver Shooting* (New York: The Macmillan Co., 1928), p. 241.

[4]*Ibid*, p. 242.

[5]Gould, p. 6.

[6]Kenneth L. Cope, *Stevens Pistols and Pocket Rifles* (Ottawa, Canada: Museum Restoration Service, 1971), pp. 35-45.

[7]Gould, pp. 15-16, p. 180.

refinements of the more expensive Stevens pistols, notably the finely-adjustable rear sights, they were intended to answer the requirements of those who wanted a pistol for plinking and small game, or for informal target practice, for all of which they served very well.

Mention should be made here of the Stevens "Diamond" No. 43 model pistols, First and Second Models, produced from 1888 until 1916, to an estimated total of over 100,000. Initially intended as a very light "pocket rifle," a "fun gun" based upon a small pocket-pistol frame, with a tiny detachable skeleton shoulder stock and a choice of 6-inch or 10-inch barrel and sights (V-notch open rear with bead front or aperture rear with globe front, both rear sights being stampings and adjustable for elevation only), this 10-ounce spur-trigger pistol saw amazingly effective use in top-level match competition at the shorter indoor ranges during the 1890s.[7]

All of the above models, although based on frames of three different sizes, shared the following characteristics: a tip-up action designed by Joshua Stevens himself and shown in his 1864 patent, locked by a crosswise sliding bolt pushed from left to right by a thumb-piece on the left side of the standing breech frame, which engaged a lug beneath the barrel at the breech; barrels of consistently excellent quality which delivered fine accuracy; with the exception of the Diamond model, a U-notch rear sight elevation and windage adjustment; and, again with the exception of the very small and light Diamond model, a truly "man-sized" and comfortable grip.

Stevens' reputation as a manufacturer of fine match target pistols was much enhanced when, in 1887, the company introduced the 22 Long Rifle rimfire cartridge, developed by the Union Metallic Cartridge Company at the request of Stevens (according to G.O. Kelver, *100 Years of Shooters and Gunmakers of Single Shot Rifles*, this cartridge was advertised by UMC as early as May, 1885).[8] In 1888, at the Walnut Hill, Massachusetts range, Arthur C. Gould, author of *Modern American Rifles and Modern American Pistols and Revolvers*, tested a Stevens target pistol chambered for the new 22 Long Rifle cartridge in a rest at a range of 50 yards. He found that at that distance it was capable of placing a group of 10 shots in a rectangle 1⁵/₈ inches across by 1-inch high.[9] Very impressive, this performance, by the standards of that day, and a revelation to the competition shooters of the time who had not been willing to give target pistols credit for anything approaching this level of accuracy. In fact, a number of the currently most famous American offhand rifle marksmen, C.W. Hinman and J.B. Fellows among them, intrigued by the inherent accuracy capability of these pistols, discovered a new challenge and joined the ranks of the slow-fire match pistol enthusiasts. In some instances, these men set new records with the pistol as well as with the rifle,[10] and slow-fire match pistol competition flourished as never before.

Very different from the pre-1900 match target pistols based on the "pocket rifle" frames is the Stevens Target No. 10 model, produced from 1919 until 1933, in three variations. The standard version, most frequently encountered, is blued with hard rubber grip plates. At some point before serial number 6000, the standing breech frame was furnished case-hardened in colors, the tipping breech retaining the blued finish. And the so-called "deluxe" version, featuring browned frame, blued barrel, nickel-plated trigger, barrel release cam, and cocking piece, plus checkered aluminum grips, is very rare indeed.[11]

This pistol was designed for Stevens by George S. Lewis — he held patents both for the design of the pistol and for its Patridge-type rear sight adjustable for windage and elevation.[12] After leaving Stevens, he was the "Lewis" of the Page-Lewis Arms Company, manufacturer of 22-caliber boys' single shot rifles, its vice-president, general manager, and chief designer. Still later, he went to Winchester and, according to Michael McIntosh in *The Best Shotguns Ever Made in America*, was chiefly responsible for the design of the glorious Winchester Model 21 double shotgun.[13] It looks for all the world like an autoloader, with a bulky, well-angled slab-sided grip and a heavy 8-inch barrel, giving a weight of 36 ounces. What appears to be the cocking knob for a straight-drive firing pin actually is a cocking piece connected by a link to a concealed internal pivoted hammer. Like its predecessors, the Stevens Target No. 10 pistol is a single shot break-open type. The crosswise locking bolt of the previous models is replaced in the Target No. 10 by a spring-loaded cam, located on the left side of the standing breech, also functioning as a thumb latch, which locks the standing breech to the tipping breech. This is a clever design, essentially simple and self-compensating for wear, but in practice it is no more than marginally satisfactory. First, it acts on one side of the standing breech only, with the at least theoretical objection of an asymmetric lock and corresponding stresses. Second, while there normally exist no problems with standard velocity or low pressure match-specification 22 Long Rifle ammunition, high-velocity 22 Long Rifle cartridges — or even some of the hotter match ammunition — will gen-

---

[10]*Ibid*, pp. 177-183.

[11]Cope, p. 42.

[12]*Ibid*, pp. 15-16.

[13]Michael McIntosh, *The Best Shotguns Ever Made in America* (New York: Charles Scribner's Sons, 1981), p. 134.

[8]Gerald O. Kelver, *100 Years of Shooters and Gunmakers of Single Shot Rifles* (Fort Collins, CO: 1975), p.65.

[9]Gould, p. 175.

erate enough additional pressure and recoil inertia to disengage the cam lock and blow the gun open. Although the Stevens Target No. 10 pistol holds very well, having perhaps the best "feel" in the hand of any American single shot match target pistol (in out-of-the-box form, at least) yet (1919) produced, it did not, according to Walter Roper, achieve any real popularity among serious American slow-fire match pistol shooters despite the fact that 7131 were manufactured.

It should be noted of all the Stevens pistols that they do not stand up well to long-term use and handling. The locking mechanisms are not particularly strong, and the materials of which these pistols are made are not always of the most suitable. The standing breech frames of the early issues of the pre-1900 models are of cast brass and those of the later issues are soft machined iron castings, both being provided with hardened steel breech face inserts, as is the Target No. 10 model. The No. 35 "Target Offhand" and "Offhand" models of post-1900 manufacture, which are utility pistols rather than arms intended for serious match target use, are not furnished with such inserts. All these models of the Stevens single shot pistols are frequently found today with noticeable wear, and consequent lost motion, in the barrel hinge, locking bolt, and extractor. Even the Target No. 10 pistol shares this shortcoming, a consideration which may help to explain its failure to achieve popularity among top-level match pistol shooters. Significantly, the last year in which a slow-fire "any pistol" U.S. Revolver Association match at national championship level was won by a Stevens single shot match target pistol was 1904.[14]

The pre-1900 Stevens single shot match target pistols were well thought of in Europe, and extensively copied by European gunmakers. Some of the European Stevens copies that this writer has examined appear to be, if anything, better made than the originals, always with the possible exception of the barrels, which in the original Stevens models were invariably carefully bored and rifled and, by the standards of their time at least, very accurate. Certainly the ultimate European copy of any model of Stevens target pistol must be the cased replica of a Lord model made by Master Gunmaker (*Hofbuschenmacher*) H. Leue of Berlin and presented in 1894 by Kaiser Wilhelm II to "Capitaine Leon Martin, First Marksman of the World." The frame of this pistol is solid 22-karat gold and is most elaborately engraved with figures from Greek mythology in high relief, in the best classic German tradition . . .[15] But in

Smith & Wesson Second Issue, Model 1905 single shot match target pistol. This is a somewhat modified version of Smith & Wesson's first such pistol, the Model of 1891. The Second Issue was produced from 1905 until 1909.

the U.S. by the turn of the 20th century, the Stevens single shot match target pistols increasingly were giving way on the firing lines to those of other makers, particularly Smith & Wesson.

Smith & Wesson brought out its first single shot match target pistol in 1893, calling it the Model 1891 because it was based on the frame of the Third Model 38-caliber Single Action Pocket Revolver, which dated to the earlier year. (This writer is of the opinion, and the sentiment is not original with him, that a better foundation for a single shot match target pistol would have been the old large-framed New Model No. 3 single-action target revolver.) In any event, the target pistol barrel, furnished with "Paine-type" target sights (U-notch rear, fine bead front), was first offered as part of a cased set with the pocket revolver, the pistol barrel being interchangeable with the barrel/cylinder assembly of the break-open single-action revolver.

Demand for the target pistol per se soon grew sufficiently enough that it was offered as a separate item,[16] and by 1900, or not long afterward, the Smith & Wesson single shot match target pistol appeared to have overtaken the Stevens models as the dominant arm of its class on American firing lines. In 1905, the Smith & Wesson single shot match target pistol appeared in a second issue, strictly in its single shot form, without the feature of interchangeability with the revolver components that had characterized the original model of 1891. Where the Model 1891 has the recoil shields behind the cylinder recess necessary to the revolver, the Second Issue of 1905 lacks them, having instead shallow-milled channels.[17] The single-action revolver frame on which these single shot target pistols are based is small and light, with a small grip and a short reach between grip and trigger. The oversized hard-

[14]Himmelwright, p. 344, 362.

[15]Cope, pp. 22-23.

[16]Roy C. McHenry and Walter F. Roper, *Smith and Wesson Hand Guns* (Huntington, WV: Standard Publ. 1945), pp. 81-82.

[17]Robert J. Neal and Roy G. Jinks, *Smith and Wesson 1857-1945* (S. Brunswick, NJ: A.S. Barnes, 1966), pp. 29-31, 37.

Smith & Wesson Straight Line single shot match target pistol, 1925-1936. It came with cleaning rod and screwdriver in a unique stamped-metal case. The barrel turns on a vertical pivot; the design of its lockwork prevented its being the overwhelming success that Smith & Wesson had anticipated.

rubber grips provided for the target pistols by Smith & Wesson are an aid to the shooter, but do not constitute a wholly satisfactory answer to the problem of a comfortable hold; the frame is too small, the reach from grip to trigger too short, and no provision is made to support the second finger of the pistol hand.

The adjustable rear sights mounted on these Smith & Wesson target pistols are a source of problems; the adjustments, particularly for windage, are difficult to make and are less than positive. Moreover, the sight itself is mounted on the clutch joint that locks the tipping breech to the standing breech, so that care must be taken when closing the pistol that the latch is completely home. If it is not, the rear sight will be high and the ensuing shot likewise. The barrel is very light, and the pistol does not lend itself to an easy or comfortable hold. Despite these shortcomings, the Smith & Wesson models of 1891 (1251 pistols plus 1947 extra barrels, in 6-inch, 8-inch, and 10-inch lengths and chambered in 22 Long Rifle, 32 Smith & Wesson centerfire, and 38 Smith & Wesson centerfire, with the option of blued or nickel finish) and 1905 (4617 manufactured) were very successful, being finely fabricated in the best Smith & Wesson tradition, and sufficiently accurate so that they dominated American slow-fire match pistol competition until 1909, the year of introduction of the Smith and Wesson Third, or Perfected, model single shot match target pistol.

The Smith & Wesson Third model single shot match pistol, produced from 1909 until 1923, proved to be the most popular of the Smith & Wesson single shot target pistols, a total of 7023[18] being manufactured.[19] In its later refined "Olympic" variation, with tighter chamber and bore dimensions, it retained its dominant status in American slow-fire match pistol competition for years after its replacement by Smith & Wesson with the "Straight Line" model. This Perfected model Smith & Wesson single shot match pistol was based, once more, on one of the currently available revolver frames made by the company, in this instance that of the Perfected model of 1909 break-open double-action revolver. Curiously, the match pistol retained the double-action lockwork of the parent revolver; many match shooters removed the "fly" from this mechanism to do away with the double-action pull, for which they had no use and, hopefully, to achieve a quicker lock time in the single-action mode.

Unfortunately, this Perfected model revolver, like the third model single-action pocket revolver, had a small frame and a grip that did not properly support the second finger of the pistol hand. Again, an oversized grip provided by Smith & Wesson for the target pistol, this time in checkered walnut rather than in hard rubber (a real improvement) was a help, but not really a solution

[18]According to Neal and Jinks, *Smith & Wesson 1857-1945*, p. 39, serial numbers 9442-9518 were omitted, making a total production of 6949.

[19]Neal and Jinks, pp. 37-39.

to this problem. The screw that held the barrel-to-frame hinge joint together wanted watching, as it tended to work loose — at least potentially a problem in many break-open gun designs.

In some individual pistols, at least, ignition with cartridges having all but the most sensitive of priming mixtures could be uncertain.[20] The Paine-type sights of the earlier models had been replaced by sights of the Patridge type (square notch in the leaf of the rear sight, combined with a square-topped blade at the front, named for E.E. Patridge, a match pistol shooter prominent in the 1890s; this is the type almost universally used by match pistol shooters at the present time), but the rear sight is still mounted on the clutch joint at the rear of the frame of the pistol. And the weight of the 10-inch barrel is as before; steel rods held by electrician's tape in the grooves formed by the undercuts beneath the rib atop the barrel, to add weight "out front," were frequently seen on the firing line.

For all this, the Smith & Wesson Third, or Perfected, model single shot match target pistol was considered to be the best and most accurate gun of its kind by top-line American slow-fire match pistol shooters, particularly in its "Olympic" version developed by Major Roy D. Jones in the early 1920s.[21] These three Smith & Wesson single shot match target pistol models largely dominated American, and to a great degree international and Olympic, slow-fire match pistol competition from the turn of the century until the early 1920s.

But the American match pistol marksman was still not completely satisfied. In 1920, Smith & Wesson published a questionnaire that was circulated among American slow-fire match pistol enthusiasts.[22] The subject of this questionnaire was, in essence, "What do you, the match pistol shooters and experimenters of this country, consider to be the ideal in a single shot match target pistol?" According to the answers received, the following characteristics were considered most essential: first, a heavier barrel for a steadier hold on the target; second, a quicker lock time than that afforded by the pivoted-hammer revolver-type mechanisms currently in use; third, that the hammer or striker and the trigger should move in straight lines parallel to the lines of bore and sight, rather than in arcs; and finally, that the barrel should be mounted lower on the action of the pistol and closer to the pistol hand, so that there might be less leverage exerted by the recoil of the pistol and less muzzle jump. The sum total of these considerations seemed to rule out any pistol based on a revolver frame, so Smith & Wesson designed and engineered their new single shot match target pistol from scratch, intending that it should be the finest slow-fire piece of its kind that the world had yet seen. They released it to the American shooting public in 1925, and called it the "Straight Line" model.

The Straight Line 22 single shot target pistol constituted an absolutely new design in American target handguns. First, it looked like a semi-automatic pistol (as did the Stevens Target No. 10 model), with a slab-sided grip and a trigger guard design that gave support to the second finger of the pistol hand. Second, the lines of bore and sight were much lower and closer to the hand than on S&W's previous single shot designs, which had been based on revolver frames, a definite plus. Third, the barrel was considerably heavier than on any previous Smith & Wesson single shot match pistol model (the Straight Line weighs 34 ounces, as compared to the Perfected model's 25 ounces), another plus for the Straight Line. Fourth, both the front and the rear sights (of a much-improved Patridge type) are solidly anchored to the barrel, still another plus. Fifth, in the design of the Straight Line pistol, the S&W engineers had abandoned the break-top principle; the barrel swings sideways on a vertical pivot at the front of the standing breech. Finally, the pivoted hammer and trigger, indeed the entire revolver-type lockwork of their previous match pistol models, were replaced by a trigger that slid in a straight line, with a vertical sear and a straight-drive firing pin with an external cocking handle, hence the descriptive model designation "Straight Line." Here was S&W's realization of the single shot match target pistol that American competitive slow-fire pistol marksmen had said that they wanted. How could they possibly go wrong . . .?

How indeed? Unfortunately for all concerned, the Straight Line pistol was not well received; complaints were all too numerous. Many shooters found they couldn't accustom themselves to the automatic pistol-type grip. The new firing mechanism gave a very quick lock time but did not permit a consistent sear engagement; the trigger pull, in a given individual pistol, might vary "from several ounces to several pounds" from shot to shot.[23] In cold weather, any fluid lubricant in the firing pin race might congeal sufficiently to freeze the striker and prevent ignition.

Some pistol marksmen, notably Julian S. Hatcher (*Textbook of Pistols and Revolvers*), were of the opinion that the reach from grip to trigger was still too short and that the barrel was still too light for optimum balance in deliberate aimed fire.[24] This writer has examined one Straight Line pistol that showed a fracture (welded, with the pistol later reblued) that extended from the

[20]Julian S. Hatcher, *Textbook of Pistols and Revolvers* (Plantersville, SC: Small Arms Technical Publ. Co., 1935), p. 168, and Walter F. Roper, *Pistol and Revolver Shooting*, pp. 95-97.

[21]Roper, pp. 97-99.

[22]Jinks, *History of Smith and Wesson* (No. Hollywood, CA: Beinfeld Publ. Co., 1977), p. 119.

[23]Walter F. Roper, *Experiments of a Handgunner* (Harrisburg, PA: The Telegraph Press, 1949), pp. 1-2.

[24]Hatcher, p. 23.

corner of the "water table" at the bottom of the breech face diagonally to the hole for the pin that retains the striker. This misfortune may have been caused by the use of high-velocity ammunition; it is to be noted that Smith & Wesson heat-treated the frames of the Straight Line pistols manufactured from 1928 until the end of production of this model, in 1936.[25] However, from the standpoint of structural strength, the fact remains that the breech frame was not well designed.

Some 1870 Straight Line match target pistols were manufactured between 1925 and 1936; a number of important matches were, in fact, won by shooters using them,[26] but the model was not nearly the success that Smith & Wesson had anticipated. Ironically, the old, discontinued "Perfected/Olympic" model target pistols continued to win matches at national championship levels into the 1930s. The Smith & Wesson people were, understandably, very unhappy about the whole matter; their effort to give the American marksman what he had asked for had cost the company a great deal, and the Straight Line model appears still to be a subject best not mentioned at Smith & Wesson. Again ironically, Walter Roper, that indefatigable American handgun authority and experimenter, modified the lockwork of a Straight Line pistol with the addition of a pivoted hammer that replaced the striker and a new sear of his own design, and stated that this pistol, as modified, was the most consistently accurate slow-fire match target pistol that he had yet shot.[27]

According to Roper (*Pistol and Revolver Shooting*), during the years immediately preceding WWII, S&W was in the process of developing an entirely new single shot match target pistol, once more of hinged-frame tip-up design, considerably heavier than the old Perfected model, and embodying numerous improvements in the lockwork and in the barrel-to-frame locking mechanism.[28] This writer has never seen an example, nor even a picture, of this pistol, nor does he know, or know of, anyone who has.

While the majority of the top-ranking slow-fire match pistol marksmen in the United States preferred the Smith & Wesson single shot match target pistols during the 1900 to 1930 period, there were, inevitably, at least a few dissidents. Of these rugged individualists, a number favored the Remington single shot rolling block pistols based on the military models that Remington had under development from 1865 onward, the "Navy" model and, more particularly, the "Army" model of 1871.

Essentially simple in its conception, this action, as finally offered by Remington in its definitive models of rifles and pistols, is quite surprisingly refined in detail. From 1869 onward, Remington had offered various models of sporting pistols and pocket rifles on these military-model pistol actions; these "commercial" pistols culminated in the fixed-sight sporting or "plinking" model of 1887.

Remington's first real effort to produce a single shot match target pistol was, however, the model of 1891. This was offered on both "Navy" and "Army" frames, the latter being much more common, with a 10-inch half-octagon barrel. The calibers included 22 Short, 22 Long Rifle, 25 Stevens rimfire, 32 Smith & Wesson centerfire, 32-20 WCF and, perhaps surprisingly, the old 50-caliber centerfire Army pistol cartridge[29] (of which James J. Grant, famed authority on American single shot cartridge rifles, once said was "very handy for digging post holes with no effort whatever"[30]). The number of these pistols actually manufactured has been a matter of some dispute, but Jerry Landskron (*Remington Rolling Block Pistols*), citing convincing evidence, concludes that as many as 800 may have been produced.[31] With its 10-inch barrel, the Remington Model 1891 single shot target pistol typically weighs nearly 3 pounds, and is provided with a German silver blade front sight and a step-adjustable-for-elevation "Rocky Mountain" rear with V-notch.

Much more of a serious effort to provide the American match pistol marksman with a suitable single shot target gun was the Remington Model 1901, based on the "Army" (1871) pistol action. Like the Model 1891, this gun had a 10-inch half-octagon barrel, typically not quite as heavy as that of the older model pistol. Several front sights were available; the type most frequently found on surviving examples is a Lyman bead. The rear sight, mounted on the action rather than on the barrel, is adjustable for windage and elevation, and may be found with either a V-notch or a square Patridge notch. The action body of the Model 1901 target pistol is normally blued, rather than case-hardened, as is that of the Model 1891. The trigger of the Model 1901 is knurled to afford better finger contact and control. And the walnut grip and forend of the Model 1901 are checkered, rather than left plain as on the Model 1891.

The Remington Model 1901 match target pistol was offered in 22 Short, 22 Long Rifle, 25 rimfire, and 44 Russian centerfire. As many as 750 of these pistols may have been made between 1901 and 1911.[32] There also

---

[25]Neal and Jinks, pp. 39-40.

[26]Himmelwright, pp. 365-366.

[27]Roper, *Experiments of a Handgunner*, pp. 2-3; *Pistol and Revolver Shooting*, p. 102.

[28]Roper, *Pistol and Revolver Shooting*, p. 113.

---

[29]Jerry Landskron, *Remington Rolling Block Pistols* (Buena Park, CA: Rolling Block Press, 1981), pp. 131-135, 202-204.

[30]James J. Grant, *Single Shot Rifles* (New York: William Morrow & Co., 1947), p. 138.

[31]Charles Lee Karr, Jr. and Carroll Robbins Karr, *Remington Handguns* (Harrisburg, PA: The Telegraph Press, 1956), p. 204.

[32]Landskron, pp. 214-221.

exists the possibility of finding more or less similar Remington target pistols based on the surplus Model 1871 Army pistols sold through retail outlets such as Schuyler, Hartley, and Graham of New York City, and Sears, Roebuck, or even on the Remington No. 2 small rifle action. These basic, small Remington rolling block actions have been subjected to all mannner of custom modifications and "improvements" by all manner of gunsmiths and experimenters, ranging from basement tinkerers to artist-artisans of the caliber of A.O. Niedner and Harry Pope.[33]

The Remington single shot match target pistols saw much service on the firing line long after their production was discontinued, winning "any pistol" slow-fire matches at national championship level into the middle 1920s,[34] in competition with pistols technically far more sophisticated. Arthur C. Gould said of these Remington target pistols (*Modern American Pistols and Revolvers*, published 1894), these pistols "possess great strength and wearing qualities . . . are well-balanced, and have such excellent handles that there is a feeling of firmness and steadiness which is verified when the shooter attempts to sight it on a small object."[35] Less positive attributes include the following: a line of sight that is well above the hand; a trigger pull that cannot, with the existing mechanism, safely be reduced to much below 3 pounds; a slow lock time and a heavy hammer fall, so that the shooter must pay special attention to his "follow-through" if he is to shoot one of these pistols effectively.

Some years ago, Navy Arms Company offered a rolling block pistol made for them in Italy that is nearly a replica of the Remington Model 1891 target model. If the single shot pistol enthusiast of today wishes to have the enjoyment of shooting a "classic" single shot target pistol without having to pay the price asked for one of the original Remingtons, I recommend that he acquire one of these Navy Arms replica pieces. He may then either enjoy it as is, or make a project of it, having the lockwork hand-fitted, the trigger pull regulated to about 3 pounds, and new sights and even a new barrel installed. The sum total of all this will not even come close to the cost of a fine original piece in proper shooting condition, and if the marksman does his part, such a pistol will do gratifyingly well for him at a local 22 *silueta* match or turkey shoot. The expressions of the

No, not a Remington, but a much-modified Navy Arms rolling block pistol in 22 Long Rifle. These were made in Italy for Navy Arms as a virtual replica of the Remington Model 1891 rolling block target pistol. Note the heavy barrel (not original), Bo-Mar rear sight and Redfield globe front sight. The lockwork has been hand fitted and the trigger pull regulated to 3 pounds. Scarcely a classic single shot match pistol, but a splendid toy. It shoots well, too.

shooters to either side can in themselves be worth the price of admission, particularly when the silhouettes fall with any reasonable degree of regularity.

From about 1884 until after the turn of the century, William Wurfflein of Philadelphia, better known for his fine tip-up-action target rifles, made, apparently to order, a small number of match target pistols. These pistols were built on his light single shot rifle action, which was notable for its simplicity and solidity. As rifle actions go, the Wurfflein break-open was a relatively small and light one, but it made for a substantial pistol that weighed as much as $3\frac{1}{2}$ pounds, according to a Wurfflein catalog dated 1889. It was available with interchangeable barrels chambered for cartridges ranging from 22 Short to 44 Russian, and was furnished with a rear sight adjustable for both windage and elevation.[36]

These Wurfflein pistols are well-made and finished, and very strong and solid, utilizing a locking bolt that protrudes horizontally from the bottom of the standing breech, engaging a lug on the underside of the barrel. It is fair to state that this Wurfflien pistol is probably the strongest, and in that sense, if in no other, the best of the American break-open single shot match target pistol designs. On the basis of targets shot with them and recorded,[37] these guns appear to have been inherently as accurate as any of their competitors, at least before 1900. However, the Wurfflein single shot target rifles, like the pistols, despite their fine quality, did not

[33]*Ibid*, pp. 250-251, 266-267.

[34]Himmelwright, p. 345.

[35]Gould, p. 24.

[36]Grant, p. 245.

[37]Gould, p. 154, 174.

Stevens No. 10 Target Pistol, 1919-1933. This was Stevens' last effort to produce a competitive top-level single shot match target pistol. The gun holds and balances very well in the hand, but never achieved any real popularity among serious American match shooters. The tipping-breech-to-standing-breech lock, accomplished by a spring-loaded cam, is characteristically weak and not up to its job.

Hopkins and Allen Target Pistol, 1906-1915, a commendable effort to provide the out-of-pocket match pistol enthusiast with an at least potentially competitive gun. Despite several attractive features, including a notably quick lock time and an excellent grip, it never became popular among American slow-fire-match pistol shooters of any note.

achieve much more than regional popularity, as they are very scarce today. The Wurfflein, in my opinion, is a design that should be revived and brought up to date by the use of captive coil springs, as its virtues are numerous.

Between 1906 and 1915, Hopkins and Allen Arms Company, of Norwich, Connecticut, better known for its inexpensive boys' 22 rifles, "Suicide Special" revolvers sold under a variety of trade names, small-frame double-action revolvers, and shotguns of various patterns, featured as its finest handgun a break-open single shot match target pistol. This pistol, with single-action lockwork, was based on the frame of the best revolver then made by Hopkins and Allen, the double-action (called by the company in its advertisements "triple-action" for its very ingenious and effective built-in safety mechanism) "Safety Police" model.

The gun was offered in 22 Long Rifle only, but options of blued or nickel finish and of 6-, 8- or 10-inch barrel lengths were cataloged.[38] Light in weight for a target pistol at 20 ounces, this gun never achieved popularity among serious slow-fire match shooters, although about 2500 were manufactured before the company was

[38]DeWitt E. Sell, *Handguns Americana* (Harrisburg, PA: The Telegraph Press, 1963), pp. 80-81.

sold in 1917.[39]

Nobody prominent in the world of American match pistol shooting seems to have taken the Hopkins and Allen pistol seriously; the reputation of the company's products — mediocre quality at a low price — was against it. Unfortunately, quality control was not outstanding — this pistol sold for $10 when its well-known competitors cost $15 to $18 — and its performance on the range was handicapped by a deplorably crude rear sight furnished with the by-now-obsolete V-notch.

However, it should be noted that it incorporated several worthwhile features in its design. First, the tipping-breech-to-standing-breech lockup was accomplished by two spring-loaded hooked levers mounted horizontally in the top of the tipping breech frame (the arrangement reminds one of the old "ice-tong" Pryse-type lock used on some English revolvers of the 1870s, translated from the vertical to the horizontal), more positive than a clutch joint and at least partially self-adjusting for wear. Second, a well-shaped "man-sized" walnut grip, affording a reach from grip to trigger long enough to be comfortable, was furnished as standard equipment. This gun feels, in this respect at least, better in the hand than any of the pre-1909 Smith & Wesson single shot match target pistols. Third, the lockwork, utilizing a stout leaf mainspring, makes possible a crisp trigger pull and a short and very quick hammer fall, virtually a "speed action." Walter Roper has stated that the Harrington & Richardson Model 195/U.S.R.A. single shot match target pistol incorporated the first "speed action" available in a production target pistol to the American match shooter; this writer is of the opinion that a case in favor of the Hopkins and Allen target pistol may be argued in this context.

As a postscript to this account of the Hopkins and Allen single shot match target pistol, the assets of Hopkins and Allen were purchased in 1917 by the Marlin-Rockwell Corp. At some time between 1921 and 1923 the Marlin Firearms Corp., which had in the meantime been divorced from the Rockwell syndicate, had assembled from parts on hand 25, more or less, of the Hopkins and Allen target pistols, and marked them on the top of the barrel The Marlin Firearms Corp., New Haven, Conn., U.S.A. Twelve of these Marlin-marked pieces are known to have survived, all in blued finish with 10-inch barrels.[40]

At some time prior to 1920, Colt, who for much of the period under consideration had not offered a single shot match target pistol, began to develop such a piece, using as its foundation the frame of their Officer's Model Target revolver. Instead of the double-action lockwork of the parent revolver, the Colt "Camp Perry," as it was to be titled, model single shot target pistol incorporated a much-simplified single-action mechanism actuated by a coil rather than by a leaf mainspring. The solid-frame, side-swing principle of the revolver was retained in the target pistol, with this difference: whereas in the revolver the crane carries the cylinder outward from the left side of the solid frame, in the Camp Perry pistol the barrel is screwed into a fluted rectangular block that takes the place of the cylinder, and the complete assembly swings outward on the crane when released by the catch.

As with the revolver, extraction/ejection of the fired case is accomplished manually rather than automatically. Again as in the case of the revolver, the breech-block-barrel-crane assembly is locked to the frame of the target pistol at one point only, by a horizontal tapered bolt at the breech face. This arrangement, in terms of theoretical long-term accuracy at least, is by definition immediately suspect, as any degree of looseness between the crane and the frame must inevitably affect the accuracy of the pistol. This consideration is potentially even more serious in the case of the Camp Perry model than in that of Colt's parent revolver. Whereas in the revolver the crane has merely to carry the weight of the cylinder, in the single shot pistol it must bear the combined weight and mass of breech-block and barrel; care must be taken in shooting and handling a Colt Camp Perry pistol to make sure that no undue strain is placed on the crane and its pivot while opening and closing the piece. However, it must be said that examination of any Colt Camp Perry pistol that has not undergone obvious mishandling or abuse will show no looseness between crane and frame, despite the absence of any lock at this point, and these pistols typically shoot very accurately indeed.

The Camp Perry target pistols, like all Colt products of this period, were made with an absolute dedication to quality. As this writer recalls, a distinguished authority concerning matters pertaining to classic motorcars once termed the Rolls-Royce Silver Ghost model, ". . . a triumph of materials and workmanship over design," and he feels that the sentiment of this quotation may be applied, with equal justice, to the Colt Camp Perry target pistols.

Although series production of the Camp Perry pistol was not initiated until 1926, pre-production examples of this arm appeared on the firing line as early as 1920, when T.K. Lee won the U.S. Revolver Association (U.S.R.A.) national 50-yard slow-fire championship match with a "Colt S. S. 10 in."[41] pistol which, in the opinion of this writer, was a pre-production Camp Perry. At the National Matches at Camp Perry, Ohio in 1921 and 1924, pre-production Colt single shot match target pistols were reported as being used by members of the United States Marine Corps pistol team. These pre-production examples, and the initial production

---

[39]As of 1915, the H&A manufacturing facilities were devoted to the production of Belgian-contract Mauser rifles. In 1917, they were purchased by the Marlin-Rockwell Corp.

[40]George A. Carr, "A 'Marlin' Single Shot Target Pistol" (Aledo, IL: The Gun Report, 1983).

[41]Himmelwright, p. 345.

Colt Camp Perry single shot match target pistols: First Model (top), Second Model (bottom). Note the shorter and heavier (8-inch as compared to 10-inch) barrel and lighter, straighter trigger of the Second Model.

version manufactured from late 1925 until the end of 1933, are characterized by slender 10-inch barrels, deeply curved triggers, and lockwork that affords a very fine trigger pull, but that incorporates a long hammer fall with attendant slow lock time.

The second, or improved version, of the Camp Perry target pistol has a slightly heavier 8-inch barrel, which renders this pistol's weight nearly equal to the 34 ounces of the earlier model, a lighter trigger with less curve, and — most importantly — a reworked lock mechanism that affords a length of hammer fall about two-thirds that of the early model, with much quicker lock time. Both versions share Patridge-type sights, the front being adjustable for elevation, the rear for windage. These sights are visually very clear, but are condemned by Roper for the inability to hold a given setting.

The total production of both versions is said to be 2525, with between 440 and 450 being of the second, or improved type.[42] Such study as I have been able to make of the serial numbers of pieces that have been made available to me leads me at least tentatively to dispute this latter figure; I believe that at least 850 of the improved versions may in fact have been manufactured, provided that the line of demarcation between the first version and the second was strictly observed by Colt at the beginning of 1934. The Camp Perry pistols were assigned their own block of serial numbers by Colt, and examples of the second, or improved, version serially numbered as low as the 1670s are known to me. Considerable additional research is called for, as published figures pertaining to the numbers of first and second versions actually produced, and to the breakdown by calendar year of the serial numbers of pieces

manufactured, tend not to correspond with the serial numbers of individual pistols actually examined and noted in dealers' advertisements.

Arguably the finest, certainly the most highly evolved and developed single shot match target pistol produced in the United States during the period 1880 to 1940, is the Harrington & Richardson Model 195/U.S.R.A. From 1930 (the original, admittedly rather crude version had come on the market in 1929) until WWII the basic design underwent continuous and extensive evolutionary development at the hands of Walter F. Roper. Roper, a tireless experimenter and perfectionist, took particular care to make certain that **a.)** the pistol as a "shooting machine" would be capable of optimum accuracy and that **b.)** the pistol as made available to the individual marksman would be so constituted that he would be able to take the best advantage of all of the accuracy of which the pistol was capable.

Contrary to what appears to be a widespread impression, Walter Roper was, in fact, not responsible for the basic design of the 195/U.S.R.A. pistol; in its original form it had been in production for about a year before Roper's services were engaged by the company.[43] Roper was, however, responsible for the numerous modifications and improvements that were to render the Model 195/U.S.R.A. target pistol dominant in American slow-fire pistol matches from the early 1930s until the outbreak of WWII.

The Harrington & Richardson Model 195/U.S.R.A. target pistol is still another example of such an arm based upon the frame of a double-action break-open revolver, specifically that of the Model 944 introduced in 1925, which was locked by a clutch joint and provided with a specially-designed single-action lockwork. In this instance, the lockwork incorporates a particularly strong coil mainspring and an unusually small and light hammer with a very short fall. This combination gives a lock time quicker than that of any other American single shot match target pistol yet produced before WWII, with a minimum of the disturbance normally associated with the fall of the hammer. This is a genuine "speed action" (according to Roper, the first available to the American match pistol marksman) that will,

---

[42]R.L. Wilson, *Colt's Dates of Manufacture, 1837-1945* (Coburg, Australia, 1983).

[43]Roper, *Pistol and Revolver Shooting*, p. 106.

with the original light hammer, pass the classic test of keeping a dime balanced on the front sight during the dry-firing cycle. This "speed action" constituted the single feature of the original pistols that really commended itself to Roper, and that persuaded him to undertake his extended program of development and improvement of the piece.[44]

The inherent accuracy capability of this pistol in its original form was mediocre; at best it would shoot 1 1/2-inch groups from rest, at a range of 50 yards.[45] The grip was not particularly well designed or comfortable (it incorporated a bulky spur at the top),[46] and no provision had been made to support the second finger of the pistol hand. The sights, in Roper's words, ". . . left much to be desired."[47] Despite all this, however, fine match scores had been recorded with this original version of what was to become the Harrington & Richardson U.S.R.A. model single shot match target pistol, and there was much genuine potential for improvement. Confronted with this challenge, Walter Roper set to work.

The first consideration was that of inherent accuracy. With the aid of a sliding-rail machine rest[48] that he developed specifically for this purpose, Roper initiated an extended series of experiments and trials to determine the particular combination of barrel contour, rifling specification, and bore and chamber dimensions that would yield the smallest and most consistent groups with the then-new non-corrosive smokeless 22 Long Rifle ammunition. He found, as had Colonel Roy Jones in his earlier development of the "Olympic" version of the Third Model Smith & Wesson single shot match target pistol, that a smaller diameter (.213- to .215-inch, measured on the lands) bore and a tight chamber so cut that the bullet actually impinged upon the lands for about 1/32-inch gave the best results,[49] and that a heavier and more rigid barrel afforded additional improvement. During the production span of the Model 195/U.S.R.A. pistol three different (in cross-section) barrel forms were employed. The first was the "hourglass" or flat-topped figure eight. The second was that of a circle with a heavy rib, and the last, heaviest, and definitive form was the so-called "truncated teardrop." Each addition of weight made for a heavier, more rigid, and more consistently accurate barrel. All pistols were tested for accuracy from the machine rest before being released for sale. With the final barrel form, five-shot machine rest groups at a range of 50 yards were typically about 3/4-inch center to center with selected am-munition,[50] and 1/2-inch five-shot test groups were not unknown.

Other improvements and modifications initiated and developed by Roper that appeared on the production-line pistols were the addition of a trigger guard spur that acted as a "filler" and supported the second finger of the pistol hand; the replacement of the original fixed front sight by a type positively adjustable for elevation; replacement of the original L-shaped stamped-metal adjustable rear sight by a more substantial type that shaded the sight notch from side light; replacement of the original plunger extractor by a lever-type; a heavier hammer, following reports of less-than-certain ignition with some brands of cartridges with the original very light hammer (many match shooters, however, preferred the original light hammer, as its fall was less disturbing to the hold and aim),[51] replacement of the original deeply-curved trigger by one nearly straight, with a beveled finger engagement surface; modification of the trigger so that it incorporated well-separated notch surfaces for half-cock/hammer rebound and full-cock engagement (the original arrangement of engagement surfaces had not permitted a trigger pull of less than 2 pounds without risk of damage to the cocking notches caused by mechanical interference; the redesign allowed a trigger pull as light as 1-pound, so that the pistol could be used in ISU — International Shooting Union — "free pistol" matches as well as those conducted according to U.S.R.A. rules);[52] the substitution of enlarged, rectangular, and undercut grasping surfaces on the clutch joint latch for the original smaller round version, which rendered opening the breech much easier; and — perhaps the innovation most popular with American slow-fire match pistol marksmen — Roper took advantage of the circular-section profile of the rear of the grip frame, designing a series of differently-shaped one-piece checkered walnut grips, each held firmly in place by a single screw into the rear of the frame, that might readily be interchanged.

As of 1936, 11 different grip shapes were available, plus — for the really finicky or experimentally-minded marksman — a solid block of walnut, inletted and ready to be attached, that he could carve to suit his own ideas of what a proper grip should be. Originally the Model 195/U.S.R.A. pistol was available with a 10-inch barrel only, but in 1931 the option of a 7-inch barrel was offered. This shorter barrel, which some marksmen found easier to control, was listed as an option after Julian S. Hatcher had won an important match at the English Bisley range with an 8-inch barreled pistol given to him by Roper to try out, which Hatcher had stowed with his traveling gear more or less as a last-

---

[44]*Ibid.*

[45]Himmelwright, p. 44.

[46]*Ibid.*

[47]Roper, *Pistol and Revolver Shooting*, p. 106.

[48]Roper, *Experiments of a Handgunner*, p. 124.

[49]Roper, *Pistol and Revolver Shooting*, p. 108.

---

[50]Roper, *Experiments of a Handgunner*, pp. 125-128.

[51]Hatcher, p. 30.

[52]Roper, *Pistol and Revolver Shooting*, p. 109.

minute inspiration.[53] To the best of this writer's knowledge, the 8-inch barrel was probably cataloged only as a very late production-line option. A number of new American records were set by these pistols as improved by Roper and, in 1936, a Model 195/U.S.R.A., in the hands of E.A. Hatmaker of Florida, set a new ISU free-pistol record (60 shots 50-meters) of 563×600.[54]

Any attempt to determine well-defined variations in the evolution of the Model 195/U.S.R.A. pistol is rendered quite difficult by a number of considerations. Those writers who have ventured opinions on this subject have usually restricted themselves to ". . . two (or '. . .at least two') major variations," and let the matter rest at that, without any further attempt at specification. Even the total number manufactured is at this time uncertain; DeWitt Sell, in *Handguns Americana*, offers "between 2000 and 2500,"[55] while Ladd Fanta ("Old Timers" column, *Guns Magazine*, August, 1984) estimates "less than 3500." Factory records are now of no help in this matter because **a.)** Harrington & Richardson is no longer in business, and **b.)** the older factory records were destroyed by fire in 1940. One writer, M.D. Waite, in his article "The Harrington and Richardson 22 Single-shot Pistols" (*American Rifleman*, September, 1974) has dated the option of the 7-inch barrel to 1931, and the straight trigger, lever-type extractor, and rectangular barrel-catch grasping surfaces all to 1934.

For the benefit of the student and/or collector of these pistols, this writer herewith offers his judgment (based, admittedly on meager hard data): there can be identified three versions of the Harrington & Richardson Model 195/U.S.R.A. single shot match target pistols sufficiently distinct to be termed models, plus a range of transitional variations sharing one important characteristic that is not nearly as easily sorted out. This nomenclature, assignment of characteristics, and all errors pertaining thereto are the writer's responsibility; he only hopes that the following classification may serve as a base for additional research and for more definitive conclusions by those interested.

1.) The Early Production or "Pre-Walter Roper" model, 1929-1930, not yet termed the "U.S.R.A." model and known simply as the "H&R Single Shot Pistol:" Identifying characteristics are the 10-inch "hourglass" barrel with deeply undercut rib; Patridge sights, the front being fixed and the rear a rather fragile L-shaped metal stamping adjustable for windage and elevation; plunger extractor; clutch joint surfaces round/convex/checkered; trigger thin and deeply curved; trigger pull not screw adjustable; trigger having the original arrangement of half-cock/hammer rebound and full-cock notches; small, light hammer; grip incorporating spur at top; trigger guard lacking spur or "filler" for support of the second finger of the pistol hand; the bore and chamber dimensions marginally larger than later models.

2.) The "First Walter Roper Model," 1930-1931: The 10-inch "hourglass" barrel, the sights, plunger extractor, clutch joint grasping surfaces, trigger, and hammer are all as on the "Early Production" model; the trigger pull is (in the later examples) adjustable, regulated by a screw; the trigger guard now has the spur or "filler" that supports the second finger of the pistol hand; the tighter bore and chamber dimensions determined by Roper's experiments are now standard; a limited selection of optional grips designed by Roper is now available; and the inscription U.S.R.A. Model is now stamped on the left side of the tipping breech frame.

3.) The "Second Walter Roper Model," 1934-1942: This is the last, definitive production model of the Harrington & Richardson Model 195/U.S.R.A. single shot match target pistol, with all production-line modifications and improvements. Distinguishing characteristics are the third version, or "truncated teardrop" barrel cross section; the second-type rear sight; a front sight positively adjustable for elevation by a screw with a four-sided point that bears upon the under side of the spring-loaded front sight blade; rectangular grasping surfaces on the clutch joint latch; the straight beveled trigger with relocated cocking surfaces; the lever-type extractor; a larger selection of optional walnut grips which are attached by a screw through the frontstrap horizontally into a bushing in the rear of the grip; and, on a few of the last production examples, the spur at the rear of the trigger guard is made wider, so as to afford additional support for the second finger of the pistol hand.[56]

Chronologically between 1931 and 1934, between the First and Second "Walter Roper" Models, there falls a range of variations that share the common characteristic of the number two barrel cross section that I feel may best collectively be termed the "Walter Roper transitional" pieces. As the crucial identifying factor, any Harrington & Richardson U.S.R.A. pistol with a barrel of this configuration is by definition such a "transitional" piece. (Note: Occasionally an earlier pistol fitted by the factory with this barrel may be found, and it is possible that a few pistols with the first barrel contour but with "transitional" features may have been made. I have never seen such a piece, but am of the opinion that this would be a logical, evolutionary variation.) Late examples of the "transitional" type

---

[53]Hatcher, pp. 32-33.

[54]Roper, *Experiments of a Handgunner*, p. 16.

[55]Sell, p. 79.

[56]M.D. Waite, "The Harrington & Richardson Single-Shot Pistol" (Washington, DC: National Rifle Association, *The American Rifleman*, December, 1974).

will show nearly all, or all Second Model characteristics except for the "truncated teardrop" barrel configuration; earlier pistols will typically show fewer of these identifying features. Unfortunately, this is a generalization only, as individual pistols with serial numbers higher in the "transitional" range may actually show fewer "Second Model" characteristics than their predecessors.

To determine definitive dates of introduction of individual modifications in the Model 195/U.S.R.A. pistols is not easy, in large part for this reason. For example, Waite has assigned 1934 as the year of introduction of the lever-type extractor, but study of the serial numbers of pistols made available to him leads me to believe that the date of change may well have been a year or two earlier. The "transitional" 195/U.S.R.A. pistols constitute a fascinating, albeit exasperating, minor study in their own right, particularly because the factory records no longer exist. The study and research necessary for even a working understanding of the history and development of the Model 195/U.S.R.A. match pistol in all of its variations, including some known to have been made up by Roper that never saw the production line, have scarcely even been properly begun. This pistol may well be worthy of a book devoted specifically to it.

In conclusion, I feel that a piece which, technically speaking, may not properly belong in this select list of match-qualified American single shot target pistols at all, deserves to be considered — the Harrington & Richardson Handy Gun, manufactured in 22 Long Rifle from 1933 until 1935. The Handy Gun is best remembered, and most frequently seen, as a 410-gauge pistol-shotgun (a few were also made in 28-gauge). In fact, this gun was based on the action of an inexpensive, lightweight, small-gauge, single-barrel, break-open external-hammer shotgun, the H&R No. 5, furnished with a pistol grip, and offered with the option of an 8-inch or a 12¼-inch barrel. According to the provisions of the National Firearms Act of 1934, these pistol-shotguns were assigned to the same heavily-restricted category as machineguns, and their manufacture was soon discontinued.

However, the Handy Gun had also been cataloged in 22 Long Rifle and 32-20 calibers, apparently intended as a trapper's or woods runner's companion. Very little concerning the 22 Handy Gun has appeared in print; at least one scribe has seen fit summarily to dismiss it as no more than a marginally serviceable plinking and small game gun.[57] This writer wishes to take issue with this evaluation. While the Harrington & Richardson Handy Guns in shotgun chambering that I have examined appear to have been fitted and finished to the standards normally expected in an inexpensive production-line single-barrel utility shotgun, the 22 Long Rifle Handy Gun in my collection is another matter. This piece shows considerable indication of careful manufacture and hand fitting, and — a most pleasant surprise in a gun based upon such an action — it closes and locks with a silky solidity reminiscent of a fine double shotgun. The trigger pull is light, the let-off crisp and positive, the hammer fall quick, the sights surprisingly good (the rear sight has two spring-loaded leaves, permitting an instant choice of Patridge or aperture), and the accuracy is excellent. For a 22, the bore is unusually tight, and the rifling appears to be of the same form as that found in the U.S.R.A. match target pistols. It is my opinion that the barrels of the 22 Handy Guns may well have been bored and rifled on the same machinery responsible for the finely-finished and splendidly-accurate barrels furnished on the more expensive match pistols.

With its break-open shotgun action and top-snap lever release, the spur at the rear of the trigger guard to support the second finger of the pistol hand, its 12¼-inch barrel and the pistol grip seemingly added as an afterthought, the 22 Handy Gun looks as if it must be ill balanced and impossibly muzzle heavy for good shooting. This appearance is misleading. The barrel is no less than .875-inch thick at the breech, but tapers rapidly to .495-inch at the muzzle, so that the 42-ounce weight is balanced very favorably for deliberate shooting, particularly so with a two-hand hold. If this pistol, with its 12¼-inch barrel, was qualified for the smallbore pistol silhouette matches under the current rules, it would be this writer's choice, given his option of the fine iron or optical sights now available for competition shooting. When November rolls around and Thanksgiving turkeys are to be shot (metal turkey-shaped silhouettes giving the effective equivalent of about a 3½-inch circle, at a range of 50 yards, 22 rifle or handgun, offhand), the 22 Long Rifle Handy Gun is the piece that makes the pilgrimage to the range, even in preference to the Smith & Wessons, the Camp Perrys, and the U.S.R.A.s. If the reader, having come this far, feels that he may have reason to suspect that this writer entertains a strong personal bias in favor of the Handy Gun, he is absolutely correct.

Unfortunately, few examples of this "poor relation" among fine American single shot 22 handguns were manufactured; 22 Handy Guns are far less frequently encountered now than, for instance, the much better known Model 195/U.S.R.A. target pistols. A letter of inquiry to H&R several years ago as to the number of Handy Guns in 22 Long Rifle actually manufactured, yielded only the answer that the Handy Gun in 22 Long Rifle had been made from 1933 until 1935, and is "considered extremely rare." If this writer were to be pressed for an estimate as to how many of these pieces actually were manufactured (they are known in both 8-

[57]Pete Dickey, "American Single Shot Target Pistols" (Washington, DC: National Rifle Association, *The American Rifleman*, November, 1979).

A selection of classic Harrington & Richardson single shot pistols, from top: Handy Gun in 22 Long Rifle; First Walter Roper Model 195/U.S.R.A., produced 1930-1931; Walter Roper Transitional Model 195/U.S.R.A., produced 1931-1934; Second Model 195/U.S.R.A., produced 1934-1942. Note the difference in barrel contour, rear sight, hammer, and trigger. Note also that the three grip shapes illustrated represented but a small part of a much larger selection offered as factory options by H&R to the American slow-fire match pistol shooter.

inch and 12¼-inch barrel lengths, despite at least one published statement to the contrary)[58] his reply, and it could be no more than a guess, would be, "Almost certainly fewer than 500, and very possibly considerably fewer."

This, then, constitutes the honor roll of the fine single shot match target pistols actually produced in any considerable numbers by well-known American firearms manufacturers between 1870 and 1940. A number of these pistols have, at one time or another, been more or less modified or customized to suit the requirements of individual shooters. Other single shot pistols intended for match, or at least for informal target competition, have been individually built by gunsmiths and enthusiastic designers, but typically these efforts have been based on existing foundations, most often a re-

volver frame or small rifle action, but very infrequently a unique, one-of-a-kind piece of high quality is to be encountered)[59]. And finally, single shot match target pistols of European make, built for and sold by such firms as A.F. Stoeger of New York City,[60] will on occasion appear.

One definite conclusion concerning the factory-produced American single shot match target pistols in a collective sense may immediately be drawn from this account: All of these models were low-production prestige items, perhaps even "loss leaders" for their respective manufacturers. The two such pistols manufactured in the greatest numbers were the Stevens Target

---

[58]Sell, p. 70.

[59]Richard C. Marohn, M.D., "Alonzo Crull, Indian Gunsmith" (Aledo, IL: *The Gun Report*, November, 1979).

[60]Hatcher, p. 38.

No. 10 (7131 from 1919 until 1933; these are not nearly as "rare" as some writers and dealers have stated, but examples in really fine original condition are not at all common), and the Smith & Wesson Third, or Perfected model (7023 — or 6949 as previously stated — manufactured between 1909 and 1923). Several of the most famous described saw a total production of fewer than 1000 units. The market for these fine pistols was always sharply limited, if demanding, and during the great days of American slow-fire match pistol competition, the rivalry among the concerned manufacturers was intense. And the advent, in the 1920s, of the National Rifle Association matches, with their course of fire incorporating timed- and rapid-fire stages, as well as slow-fire, did much to ensure that the single shot match target pistols would be replaced on the firing line by target revolvers and semi-automatic pistols, despite the inherently superior accuracy of the fine single shots.

From the beginning of the period under consideration, the manufacturers of the American single shot match target pistols went to ingenious lengths to provide their customers with arms of the high quality and the standard of accuracy required, without incurring undue expense. Ideally, such pistols should have been designed and manufactured "from the drawing board" as the superlative European "free pistols" long have been. Only two models of the American single shot match target pistols described in this account were in fact so conceived, designed, and manufactured — the Stevens No. 10 Target and the Smith & Wesson Straight Line. Ironically, while both of these pistols showed promise and incorporated genuinely worthwhile ideas and features, neither were really successful in competition against the other American single shot match target pistols which were in reality improvisations and adaptations. The pre-1900 Stevens match target pistols were based on existing break-open "pocket rifle" frames of three sizes. The Wurfflein single shot match pistol utilized as its foundation a small, but still substantial, break-open target rifle action. The Smith & Wesson First, Second, and Third (Perfected) models were all based more or less closely upon production-line break-open revolver frames, as were also the Hopkins and Allen and the Harrington & Richardson U.S.R.A. models. The Remington rolling block single shot match target pistols, Models 1891 and 1901, were built upon frames intended for U.S. contract single shot military pistols that were, in fact, obsolete at their time of introduction. The Colt Camp Perry pistols used as their foundation the frame of Colt's already well-known Officer's Model double-action solid-frame target revolver. And the Harrington & Richardson 22 Handy Gun was based on the unlikely foundation of a light, single-barrel, break-open, utility shotgun action.

With all their limitations and shortcomings, the American single shot match target pistols constituted a noble breed, vindicated by sheer excellence of quality,

but in the long run events were against them. From 1900, the year of its inception, the United States Revolver Association had instituted a program of matches that catered to a variety of handgun interests — slow-fire matches for "any pistols" and for "any revolvers" at 20 and 50 yards, plus timed- and rapid-fire individual matches (and team matches as well) for military handguns and pocket revolvers, plus matches specifically for novice competitors.[61]

The "any pistol" slow-fire matches at 20 and 50 yards had a prestige, a special status, all their own. And American slow-fire pistol marksmen, shooting American-made match target pistols, largely dominated the international and Olympic slow-fire pistol events until 1924,[62] when it became all too evident that the Europeans had developed a secret weapon. This "weapon" was the "free pistol," so called because the only significant limitation placed upon it was that the barrel might be no longer than 500mm, or a bit less than 20 inches (!). The weight, the distance between sights, and the let-off of the trigger pull were unrestricted.[63] In contrast, the regulations imposed by the United States Revolver Association upon the "any pistols" used in its sanctioned matches had long specified that the barrel of the "any pistol" might be no longer than 10 inches, that the sights must be strictly open and situated forward of the hammer of the pistol, that the distance between them must be no more than 10 inches, and that the pistol's trigger pull must be no less than 2 pounds.[64] American pistol shooting authorities felt that the European regulations encouraged the design of absurdly specialized match pistols good for no practical purpose, and dismissed the free pistols themselves as "freaks."[65]

The U.S. Revolver Association retained its established regulations with respect to the "any pistols" eligible for its slow-fire matches. In 1925, a special match for "free pistols" was instituted,[66] but this innovation did not stimulate the development of any new American single shot match target pistol designs. The essential point that the Americans had missed was that the new generation of single shot match target pistols inspired by these liberal European regulations was designed with their use by human beings foremost in mind. These pistols could be held steadily with less effort and fired with less disturbance, hence more accurately, than the traditional European and American

---

[61]Himmelwright, pp. 337-368.

[62]*Ibid*, pp. 248-260.

[63]Hatcher, p. 36.

[64]Himmelwright, p. 268.

[65]*Ibid*, p. 260.

[66]*Ibid*, p. 366.

slow-fire match target pistols. The free pistol was adapted ergonomically to the shooter, so that he would not be distracted by the necessity of coming to terms with a gun with which he did not feel naturally comfortable and that did not properly fit his hand. The free pistol is, in fact, the handgun counterpart of the highly-specialized Scheutzen, or offhand match, rifle familiar to European and American marksmen during the late decades of the 19th century and the early years of the 20th, and currently enjoying an at least minor revival.

The only American experimenter/designer who appears to have understood and digested the essence of this lesson was Walter F. Roper. He successfully developed a rather elementary and not outstandingly accurate single shot pistol based on a break-open revolver frame, with unfavorably high lines of bore and sight, non-adjustable trigger, and crude sights into a production-line match target handgun capable of a standard of accuracy not exceeded by the finest custom-made arms. And as far as this pistol's basic form and production costs permitted, Roper saw to it that it was pro-vided with numerous ingenious features and options calculated to give the individual pistol marksman every opportunity to make the most of this inherent accuracy. It is fascinating to speculate that if the NRA had seen fit to institute a comprehensive program of slow-fire pistol matches to conform both to European and to American regulations, there might have existed an incentive to American firearms manufacturers sufficient to ensure the further development of lines of American single shot match target pistols of quality and "shootability" such as to give American slow-fire pistol marksmen the chance that they deserved against the European free pistols. Indeed, the Harrington & Richardson U.S.R.A. model, as developed by Walter Roper, came very close to doing so. The decision of the NRA to specify that its pistol matches incorporate three stages of fire, plus the Great Depression and WWII, combined to bring to an end the Golden Age of the American single shot match target pistol at a point in history that also, in a larger sense, marked the end of much else as well. ●

Bibliography

Carr, George. "A 'Marlin' Single Shot Target Pistol." *The Gun Report*. August, 1983.

Cochran, Hamilton. *Noted American Duels and Hostile Encounters*. Phil.: Chilton Co., 1963.

Cope, Kenneth L. *Stevens Pistols and Pocket Rifles*. Ottawa, Canada: Museum Restoration Service, 1971.

Dickey, Pete. "American Single Shot Target Pistols." *The American Rifleman*. November, 1979.

Fanta, Ladd. "Old Timers" feature, *Guns Magazine*. August, 1984.

Fanta, Ladd. "The H&R Free Pistol." *Gun Digest*. 1976.

Gould, Arthur G. *Modern American Pistols and Revolvers*. Boston: Bradlee Widden, 1894; republished by Thomas G. Samworth, Plantersville, SC: 1946.

Grant, James J. *Single Shot Rifles*. New York: William Morrow & Co., 1947.

Hatcher, Julian S. Major U.S.A. *Textbook of Pistols and Revolvers*. Plantersville, SC: Small Arms Technical Publ. Co., 1935.

Haven, Charles T., and Frank A. Belden. *A History of the Colt Revolver and the Other Arms Made by Colt's Patent Fire Arms Manufacturing Company from 1836 to 1940*. New York: Bonanza Books, 1940.

Himmelwright, A.L.A. *Pistol and Revolver Shooting*, New Revised Edition. New York: The Macmillan Co., 1928.

Jinks, Roy G. *History of Smith & Wesson*. No. Hollywood, CA: Beinfeld Publ. Co., Inc., 1977.

Kane, Harnett T. *Gentlemen, Swords, and Pistols*. New York: Bonanza Books, 1951.

Karr, Charles Lee, Jr., and Carroll Robbins Karr. *Remington Handguns*, 3rd ed. Harrisburg, PA: Stackpole Co., The Telegraph Press, 1956.

Kelver, Gerald O. *100 years of Shooters and Gunmakers of Single Shot Rifles*. Fort Collins, CO: Robinson Press, Inc., 1975.

Landskron, Jerry. *Remington Rolling Block Pistols*. Buena Park, CA: Rolling Block Press, 1981.

Marohn, Richard C., M.D. "Alonzo Crull, Indian Gunsmith." *The Gun Report*. November, 1979.

McHenry, Roy C., and Walter F. Roper. *Smith and Wesson Hand Guns*. Huntington WV: Standard Publications, 1945.

McIntosh, Michael, *The Best Shotguns Ever Made in America*. New York: Charles Scribner's Sons, 1981.

Neal, Robert J., and Roy G. Jinks. *Smith and Wesson 1857-1945*. S. Brunswick, NJ: A.S. Barnes & Co., 1966.

Perkins, Jim. *American Boys' Rifles, 1890-1945*. Koppel, PA: ARA Corp., 1976.

Roberts, Ned H., and Kenneth Waters. *The Single-Shot Breechloading Match Rifle*. Princeton, NJ: Van Nostrand, 1967.

Roper, Walter F. *Experiments of a Handgunner*. Harrisburg, PA: Stackpole & Heck, Inc., The Telegraph Press, 1949.

Roper, Walter F. *Pistol and Revolver Shooting*. New York: The Macmillan Co., 1945.

Sell, DeWitt E., Ph.D. *Collector's Guide to American Handguns*. Harrisburg, PA: Stackpole Co., The Telegraph Press, 1963.

Sell, DeWitt E., Ph.D. *Handguns Americana*. Alhambra, CA: Borden Publ. Co., 1972.

Serven, James E. *Colt Firearms from 1836*. Santa Ana, CA: The Foundation Press, 1967.

Stepien, R.P. "Fred Adolph's Gem." *Gun Digest*. Northbrook, IL: DBI Books, Inc., 1985.

Terek, Allen W. "A Modern Replica, More or Less, of the Remington Model 1901 Target Pistol." (Unpublished)

Terek, Allen W. "A Rare One from Hopkins and Allen." (Unpublished)

Waite, M.D. "The Harrington & Richardson Single-Shot Pistol." *The American Rifleman*. December, 1974.

Wilson, R.L. *Colt's Dates of Manufacture, 1837-1938*. Coburg, Australia: Maurie Albert, 1983.

Periodicals

JOSEPH J. SCHROEDER

for the

Arms Collector

To be truly worthwhile, collecting requires understanding the history and evolution of the arms collected. Though much of that knowledge can be derived from studying the arms themselves, at least as much is available from a variety of printed sources.

Most collectors boast a basic arms library of books on their chosen subject — Colt, Mauser, Webley, U.S. martials, Civil War carbines, and even "Suicide Specials" have all had books written about them that have become key references for the collectors in those respective fields.

However, too many collectors have ignored another fruitful source of information about their specialties — the arms periodicals. It's likely that at one time or another every arms collectible, no matter how obscure, has been discussed and pictured in one or another arms journal. The problem is, of course, determining which of the dozens of arms periodicals did indeed publish an article on a specific subject, when it was published, and — in many cases — where the desired copy can be found.

This directory of collecting-related arms periodicals was started in the 3rd edition of GUN COLLECTOR'S DIGEST. Since then we've discovered quite a number of appropriate publications to add to our listings, many of them from overseas. During the years since that first directory, they, along with the "old reliables," have published many hundreds of excellent articles on arms-related subjects. In this, our second revision of the original directory, we have added a dozen new entries, while dropping many because their content was rarely, if ever, of collector interest or because they have since ceased publication.

Another source of very valuable information that is being included in this directory for the first time is the various special-interest collector organizations. It should go without saying that those interested in Colts, Rugers, Brownings, automatic pistols, Japanese militaria, and a myriad of other collecting interests should belong to the groups dedicated to those specialties.

Some of these organizations have simple photocopied newsletters, while others publish slick-paper publications that rival general-circulation magazines in appearance and content. But what they all have in common is first-rate information on their collecting areas. If yours is a collecting interest served by one of these groups, you should be a member and receive their mailings. This new listing will help you do that.

Finally, thanks to Ernie Lang for his invaluable assistance in this directory revision. Ernie reviews a dozen or more magazines each month for articles of interest to readers of *Auto Mag,* the monthly journal of the National Automatic Pistol Collectors' Association. For a $25 a year membership, it's an excellent example of the special-interest organization described above.

worth including in this listing. Format 8x11″

Bi-monthly: $14.75/year. 591 Camino de la Reina, Suite 200, San Diego, CA 92108.

American Rifleman

Comes with membership in the National Rifle Association, and every U.S. gun or shooting enthusiast should be an NRA member. Expect a first-class collecting article in almost every issue, but even without that benefit, NRA membership should be a must! Format 8x11″

Monthly: $20/year, $55/3 years, $85/5 years. National Rifle Association of America, 1600 Rhode Island Ave., Washington, D.C. 20036.

l'Amateur d'Armes

French language. Very well-done general gun magazine with good coverage of firearm collectibles as well as current military and civilian small arms. Outstanding photography. Format 8¹/₂x11³/₄″

Monthly: Contact publisher for rates. 1. place Mendes-France, 91025 Evry Cedex, France.

American Firearms Industry

Though a trade publication as the name suggests, *American Firearms Industry* has frequent write-ups on new developments that will interest collectors of modern arms. It is also good on commemoratives, gun politics and legal matters, especially for FFL holders. Format 8¹/₄x11″

Eleven issues annually: $15/year. National Association of Federally Licensed Firearms Dealers, 2801 E. Oakland Park Blvd., Ft. Lauderdale, FL 33306.

American Handgunner

A shooter's magazine rather than one for collectors, but often includes enough of collector interest to make it

American Survival Guide

Directed toward individuals interested in protecting life and property, this 5-year-old magazine does have an occasional article of interest to arms collectors. Format 8x11″

Monthly: $21.98/year. McMullen Publishing Co., 2145 West LaPalma Ave., Anaheim, CA 92801.

Armas

Spanish language. Nicely done, covering rifle, pistol, shotgun and crossbow shooting plus some collecting subjects. Note: our letter received no response, but the magazine is believed to still be available. Format 8¹/₄x11¹/₂″

Monthly: Contact publisher for rates. Hobby Press, S.A., Apartado de Correos 54.062 de Madrid, Spain.

Armas y Municiones

Spanish language. Strong emphasis on shooting and current military matters, but usually includes one or two first-rate articles on collectibles. Format 8x11³/₄″

Monthly: Contact publisher for current rates. C/ Oruro, 11 - 1.o A, 28016 Madrid, Spain.

Armes International

French language. Very attractively done, with much in-depth collector arms coverage along with current subjects. Some excellent color photography. Format 8¼x11″

Monthly: Write for U.S. subscription rate. 19, Quai Le Gallo, 92100 Boulogne, France.

Armes Militaria

French language. Devoted to all kinds of historical militaria, including uniforms, insignia, and vehicles, but with some coverage of small arms. Much excellent large-scale color. Format 8¼x12″

Monthly: Contact U.S. distributor for rates. Bill Dean Books, Ltd., 151-49 Seventh Ave., Box 69, Whitestone, NY 11357.

ARMI

French language. Covers both antique and modern arms plus a wide range of militaria, all of it very well indeed. Very well done, with much color. Format 8½x11¾″

Monthly: Contact publisher for current rates. Euro-Editions, Boulevard du Triomphe 132, B-1160 Brussels, Belgium.

ASE

Finnish language. Covers all phases of military history with special emphasis on small arms, by some of the least-known but most thorough arms researchers in the world. Every issue is a fascinating study, even if you don't know the language! Format 8x11¾″

Monthly: Contact publisher for rates. Roihuvuorentie 1 B 12, 00820 Helsinki, Finland.

The Backwoodsman Magazine

Covers all aspects of primitive living including weapons, with some coverage of antiques and a lot of coverage of their use.

Bi-monthly: $13.50/year. Charlie Richie, Backwoodsman Press, P.O. Box 627, Westcliffe, CO 81252.

The Blade Magazine

Handsomely-done magazine on all facets of knife collecting and knives in general, both current and antique. Many well-researched articles on collecting. Format 8½x11″

Bi-monthly: $12.95/year (U.S.); $23.95/year (overseas). 2835 Hickory Valley Rd., Chattanooga, TN 37422.

Cibles

French language. Heavily collector oriented, though some articles on current arms and shooting. Good coverage of both antique and 20th century collectibles. Format 8¼x10¾″

Monthly: Contact publisher for rates. Crepin-Leblond et Cie Editeurs, 12, rue Duguay-Trouin, 75006 Paris, France.

Combat Handguns

Almost entirely shooter/user oriented, but some articles do touch on subjects pertinent to collectors.

Bi-monthly: $15/year. Harris Publications, 1115 Broadway, New York, NY 10010.

Deutsches Waffen-Journal

German language. One of the world's top arms magazines, *DWJ* has several outstanding, well-illustrated and researched collector articles in every issue. Excellent coverage of current arms developments as well. Format 9x11½″

Monthly: About $60/year. Journal-Verlag Schwend GmbH, Postfach 100340, D7170 Schwäbisch Hall, West Germany.

Diana/ARMI

Italian language. Excellent general-coverage arms

book, with a good deal of attention to collecting subjects. Ample illustration makes it worthwhile, even without a knowledge of the language. Format 7³/₄x10¹/₂″

Monthly: Contact publisher for current rates. Editoriale Olympia S.p.A, 50129 Firenze, Viale Milton, 7, Italy.

Gazette des Armes

French language. Very well done, covering military and sporting arms, ancient through current, with plenty of emphasis on collecting. Format 8¹/₄x11¹/₂″

Monthly: Contact publisher for current rates. Revue publiee par Argout-Editions, 138 rue Montmartre, 75002 Paris, France.

Gun

Japanese language. Though not at all a collector magazine, every collector should have a traveling friend bring him a copy from Japan just for the pictures. Entirely in color, with gun photography that's simply incredible! Very good coverage of Japan's extensive "non-gun" replica industry, as well. Format 7¹/₄x10″

Monthly: About $100/year. Kokusai Publishing Co., Ltd., Showa Building, 3-25 Nakano 5-Chome Nakano-Ku, Tokyo 164, Japan.

Gun List

A publication devoted entirely to gun advertising, but organized by maker and/or field of interest (e.g., air guns, military weapons, gunsmith services) to facilitate locating a specific need. Format 12x14″

Monthly: $16.95/year, $31.95/2 years, $45.95/3 years, foreign $42.95/year. 700 E. State St., Iola, WI 54990.

The Gun Report

One of the first and surely one of the best all-collector-oriented monthlies. Features well-researched historical articles on guns, edged weapons and cartridges, plus one of the best gun show calendars. Format 8¹/₂x11″

Monthly: $29/year, $55/2 years, $75/3 years (U.S.), add $6/year elsewhere. Box 111, Aledo, IL 61231.

Gun Show Calendar

As the name suggests, *Gun Show Calendar* is entirely devoted to gun show listings and gun show ads.

Quarterly: $12.95/year. 700 E. State St., Iola, WI 54990.

Gun Week

Unquestionably the best source available for late-breaking gun news, *Gun Week* was bought by the Second Amendment Foundation in early 1985. At the time of purchase, SAF said its ownership would not influence the paper's traditional independence, and that position has been maintained. Some collector-oriented articles and an excellent gun show calendar, but for news alone *Gun Week* is a must for every gun owner concerned with the future of gun ownership. Format 11¹/₂x17″

Weekly: $27/year (U.S.), $33/year (elsewhere). Box 488, Station C, Buffalo, NY 14209.

Gun World

Another general-coverage gun magazine, with frequent articles on collecting subjects. A monthly column on collecting topics is a bonus. Format 8x11″

Monthly $20/year, $36/2 years (U.S.), $28/year (elsewhere). Gallant Publishing, 34249 Camino Capistrano, Capistrano Beach, CA 92624.

The Gunrunner

Published in Canada, *The Gunrunner* is primarily an ad paper like *Shotgun News* and *The List* but does have some worthwhile editorial material. Format 11¹/₂x17″

Monthly: $20/year (U.S. third-class). Box 565, Lethbridge, Alberta T1J 3Z4, Canada.

Guns Magazine

Guns has been on the scene since the '50s, and has always had a nice balance of current guns and shooting vs collecting editorial coverage. Format 8x10³/₄″

Monthly: $14.95/year, $24.85/2 years, $33.45/3 years (U.S.), add $6/year for overseas. 591 Camino de la Reina, Suite 200, San Diego, CA 92108.

Guns & Ammo

Good general arms and shooting coverage, with frequent well-done collecting features. Above average "Q & A" columns on collecting as well as current subjects. Format 8x11″

Monthly: $19.94/year (U.S.), $29.94/year (elsewhere). Petersen Publishing Co., 8490 Sunset Blvd., Los Angeles, CA 90069.

Guns & Ammo Action Series

Special-interest periodical with each issue targeting a specific gun field, for example pocket pistols. Generally includes some worthwhile collector-oriented material as well as the usual shooter reports and market updates. Format 8x10¹/₂″

Six issues/year, newsstand only: $2.95/copy. Petersen Publishing Co., 8490 Sunset Blvd., Los Angeles, CA 90069.

Guns Review

Excellent coverage of the English (and European, to a degree) gun scene, shooting, collecting and regulatory. GUN COLLECTOR'S DIGEST contributors John Walter and Tony Carter appear regularly in *Guns Review*. Format 8¹/₂x11″

Monthly: About $30/year (surface). Ravenhill Publishing Co., Ltd., Standard House, Bonhill St., London EC2A 4DA, England.

Knife World

This tabloid is a really first-class source of material on edged weapons, current and antique, military and civilian. Format 11¹/₂x14³/₄″

Monthly: $12.50/year, $21/2 years (U.S.), $25/year (elsewhere). Price Brothers Co., 730 N. Broadway, Knoxville, TN 37927.

Magnum

Portuguese language. A very nicely done journal that does a good job on both current and collector small arms. Format 8¹/₄x11″

Bi-monthly: $35/year. Editoria Magnum Ltda., Av. Alfredo Egidio de Souza Aranha, 75, 5.o andar — CEP 04726 — Sao Paulo, SP, Brazil.

Man At Arms

Completely devoted to collecting topics, with some excellent articles on various phases of arms and accoutrement collecting in every issue. Well illustrated, with some fine color work. Format 8¹/₄x10³/₄″

Bi-monthly: $20/year (U.S.), $27/year (overseas). Box 460, Lincoln, RI 02865.

Military

Covers general military matters from WWII through the present, with fascinating first-person combat stories. Some weapons coverage of collector interest. Format 8¹/₂x11″

Monthly: $12/year, $23/2 years, $33/3 years, add $10/year overseas. MHR Publishing, 2122 28th St., Sacramento, CA 95818.

Military Illustrated

Military equipment of all vintages, with some coverage of small arms and lots of good information on accoutrements. Some nice color illustrations. British. Format 8x11³/₄″

Bi-monthly: $30/year to U.S. Bill Dean Books Ltd, 151-49 7th Ave., Whitestone, NY 11357.

Muzzle Blasts

Membership magazine of the National Muzzle Loading Rifle Association, providing historical and shooting information on muzzleloaders of all eras. Format 8¹/₂x11″

Monthly: $25/year (included with NMLRA membership) NMLRA, Box 67, Friendship, IN 47021.

NRA Action

Newspaper of the NRA's Institute of Legislative Action, *NRA Action* does a good job of keeping on top of both local and national anti- (and pro) gun happenings. Highly recommended for those concerned with the future of gun ownership. Format 11¹/₂x14¹/₂″

Bi-monthly: $6/year. NRA/ILA, Box 2019, Washington, D.C. 20013.

Petersen's Handguns

Mostly aimed at the shooter, with an occasional collector-oriented offering. Format 8x10¹/₂″

Bi-monthly: $12.96/year, foreign $17.95/year. Petersen Publishing Co., 8490 Sunset Blvd., Los Angeles, CA 90069.

Rifle

"The Magazine for Shooters" is its subtitle, and though that's what it is mostly about, long gun collectors will frequently find worthwhile articles in their fields. Format 8x11″

Bi-monthly: $19/year, $35/2 years, $50/3 years (U.S.), $25/year elsewhere. Wolfe Publishing Co., 6471 Airpark Dr., Prescott, AZ 86301.

SAM Wapenmagazine

Dutch language. Holland has some of the strictest gun laws in the world, yet SAM manages to provide excellent articles on arms history while covering its homeland's limited competition shooting activities plus current military and police small arms developments. Format 8x11³/₄"

Bi-monthly: Contact publisher for rates. Keppelseweg 28, 7001 CG Doetinchem, Netherlands.

Schuss und Waffe

German language. Somewhat of a re-creation of the famous pre-WWI German arms periodical, but much more elegant than its namesake. Strong historical/collector orientation, though some modern gun coverage as well. Format 9¹/₄x11³/₄"

Semi-annual: Contact publisher for current price. Verlag Stocker-Schmid AG, Postfach 66, CH-8953 Dietikon, Switzerland.

Schweizer Waffen-Magazine

German language. A very nicely done general-interest arms magazine, with some collector interest subjects included along with the usual coverage of shooting events and new arms. Format 8¹/₄x11"

Ten issues/year: Contact publisher for current rates. Dietzingerstrasse 3, CH-8036 Zürich, Postfach, Switzerland.

Shooting Industry

Another gun-industry-oriented periodical, but does cover the latest arms developments in a manner useful to

Format 8x10³/₄"

Monthly: $16.97/year, $29.97/2 years, $42.97/3 years, add $6/year overseas. PJS Publications, News Plaza, Box 1790, Peoria, IL 61656.

Shotgun News

Shotgun News tends to establish the marketplace, with about 200 pages of gun and accessory ads every 10 days. Lots of discounted current guns in every issue, but plenty of collector's items as well. Next to visiting lots of gun shows, perhaps the best place to get a good feel for the current gun market. Format 11x13"

Three issues/month: $18/year, $35/2 years, $52/3 years. Snell Publishing Co., Box 669, Hastings, NE 68902.

Soldier of Fortune

Not a gun magazine per se, but its excellent coverage of new and unusual military small arms developments makes it a valuable source for collectors of modern military arms. Format 8x11"

Monthly: $26/year (U.S.), $33/year (elsewhere). Box 348, Mt. Morris, IL 61054.

Střelecká Revue

Czech language. Very interesting general arms publication with an Eastern European viewpoint. Much information on shooting sports, but also some fascinating articles

the collector of modern guns. Format 8¹/₂x11"

Monthly: $25/year. Publishers' Development Corp., 591 Camino de la Reina, Suite 200, San Diego, CA 92108.

Shooting Times

Shooting, handloading, current arms evaluations and some collector arms articles are all featured. Excellent regular columns on a variety of firearms-related subjects.

on little-known but fascinating collector's arms. Format 8¹/₄x11³/₄"

Monthly: Contact foreign trade distributor for rates. Artia, podnik zahranicniho obchodu, Ve Smeckach 30, 110 00 Praha 1, Czechoslovakia.

TACARMI

Italian language. Very attractively done with a great deal of well-illustrated collector oriented editorial material. Format 8x11½"

Monthly: Contact publisher for current rates. Editrice Leone srl, Via E. De Amicis, 25, I - 20123 Milano, Italy.

Tradition

French language. Covers military arms, uniforms and figurines, with outstanding color photography. Extremely good directory of European gun shows. Format 8½x11¾"

Monthly: Contact publisher for rates. Histoire et Collections, BP 316-09; 75425 Paris Cedex 09, France.

Visier

German Language. Another very well done general-interest gun magazine that usually includes some good collector-oriented material as well as the standard shooting, new product and reloading fare. Format 8½x11"

Monthly: About $40/year to U.S. Pietsch & Scholten Verlag GmbH, Boblinger Strasse 18, 7000 Stuttgart 1, West Germany.

Special Interest Collector Organizations

Browning Collectors Association, Mrs. Judy Rogers, 4928 Merrick Ave., Grand Island, NE 68801

Colt Collectors Association, Box 11464, St. Paul, MN 55111

Garand Collectors Association, Box 181, Richmond, KY 40475

Harrington & Richardson Gun Collectors Association, George L. Cardet, 525 N.W. 27th Ave., Suite 201, Miami, FL 33125

International Cartridge Collectors Association, Charles Spano, 570 Memorial Circle, Suite D, Ormond Beach, FL 32074

International Military Arms Society, Robert Jensen, 3021 Benjamin Dr., Wichita, KS 67204

The Mannlicher Collectors Association, Rev. Don L. Henry, Box 7144, Salem, OR 97303

Marlin Firearms Collectors Association, Dick Paterson, 407 Lincoln Bldg., 44 Main St., Champaign, IL 61820

Miniature Arms Collectors/Makers Society, Joseph Macewicz, 104 White Sand Lane, Racine, WI 53402

National Automatic Pistol Collectors Association, Box 15738, Tower Grove Station, St. Louis, MO 63163

Remington Society of America, Gordon Stanley, P.O. Box 40, Fulton, TX 78358

Ruger Collectors Association, Box 1778, Chino Valley, CA 86323

Sako Collectors Association, Karen Reed, 1725 Woodhill Lane, Bedford, TX 76021

Smith & Wesson Collectors Association, George Linne, 133 S. Eleventh St., Chouteau Center, Suite 400, St. Louis, MO 63102

The Society of American Bayonet Collectors, Box 44021, Baton Rouge, LA 70804-4021

The Webley & Scott Collectors Association, R. Guy Sizer, 1261 Marywood Lane, Apt. 230, Richmond, VA 23220

Winchester Arms Collectors Association, Richard Berg, Box 6754, Great Falls, MT 59406

CURIOS & RELICS

Revised Listings

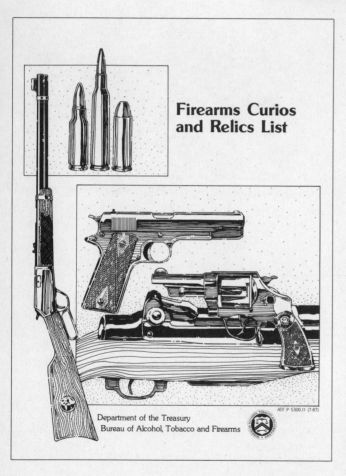

Firearms Curios and Relics List

Department of the Treasury
Bureau of Alcohol, Tobacco and Firearms

ATF P 5300.11 (7-87)

As THIS 5th edition of GUN COLLECTOR'S DIGEST goes to press, private gun ownership in the United States is under the most concentrated attack ever. This follows in the wake of several tragedies in which disturbed individuals used firearms in attacks on school children. As a result, the anti-gun forces are holding great sway with local, state and federal lawmakers and additional restrictions on gun ownership and transfer are a likely certainty. Indeed, some communities, and even a few states, have already rushed new gun control measures into law, particularly with respect to "assault rifles." Unfortunately, entire classes of firearms have fallen into the banned category in some areas.

For federally licensed gun collectors, though, there is still one positive glimmer. Many lawmakers are following in the footsteps of the Morton Grove, Illinois village trustees, who signed an ordinance banning handguns — the country's first real gun ban — but who exempted "federally licensed gun collectors" from the law. In other words, any resident of Morton Grove can continue to own, buy and sell guns providing he holds a collector's FFL.

This naturally gives the collector's license — and thus the curio and relics firearms it covers — far greater importance that it ever had. Now, even the most casual collector will find it to his advantage to sign up for the $10-per-year, 3-year FFL. To get an application, just call the nearest office of the Bureau of Alcohol, Tobacco and Firearms; you'll find it listed in every major city's phone book under United States Government — Treasury Department.

Every previous edition of *Gun Collector's Digest* has included both information on the Gun Control Act of 1968 and the Firearms Curios and Relics List current at the time of publication. Prior to the recent upsurge in anti-gun activity we'd decided not to run the complete list again, but only the guns newly added since the last *Gun Collector's Digest* was published in 1985. However, since it now appears likely that a far higher percentage of our readers might have or be getting the collector's FFL in order to legally continue their collecting activities, we felt it was necessary to publish the entire current list, just updated by the BATF as we went to press. Also included is the BATF's introductory material; all is being reproduced exactly as published by the Treasury Department to avoid any chance of error or omission.

In order to do this without taking any more pages than necessary from our other collecting articles, we've greatly reduced the size of the print in this edition's listings. We hope this does not cause too much difficulty to our readers and that it still proves to be a valuable reference.

Finally, a few words of explanation about the meaning of "curios and relics" and what is covered and what is not.

● Ammunition — in 1986 Congress dropped the GCA '68 controls on ammunition, so cartridge collectors no longer need an FFL to deal across state lines and the curios and relics cartridge list is no longer significant. Though the pre-1986 curios and relics cartridge list is still included in BATF publications as "Section I," we are dropping it from *Gun Collector's Digest* as unnecessary.

● Definition of curio and relic — a curio and relic is any gun more than 50 years old, and/or one that is more valuable as a collector's item than as a weapon. Read the more detailed definitions under "Curios or Relics" in the BATF text very carefully, so you *understand perfectly* what they mean.

There are a great many arms that are on the curios and relics list that are covered automatically under the "more than 50-year-old" definition. Furthermore, the BATF has also included some expanded *general* listings of military arms that would not automatically be covered. These include:

● All original military bolt-action and semi-automatic rifles manufactured between 1899 and 1946.
● All properly marked and identified semi-automatic pistols and revolvers used by, or manufactured for, any military organization prior to 1946.
● All shotguns, properly marked and identified as having been manufactured for any military organization prior to 1946 and in their original military configuration only.

Section III of the list includes a variety of arms, mostly shoulder-stocked pistols or short-barreled rifles, that were formerly under the same limitations that apply to machine-guns and sawed-off shotguns. These arms have specifically been taken out of that category but — *note carefully* — are still subject to the laws that pertain to ordinary rifles and pistols.

Section IIIA is a listing of firearms that were previously considered "National Firearms Act Weapons" and thus subject to the NFA controls, but which have been determined to be "antiques" under the terms of GCA '68 and thus are no longer subject to any federal limitations on transfer or ownership. Unlike the Section III guns, these are no longer "guns" for federal purposes.

Section IV includes the machineguns and other ordnance that may, by virtue of their inclusion on the list, be acquired across state lines by licensed collectors. However — and a *very crucial however* — all Section IV arms are still under rigid federal control and require BATF approval and the payment of appropriate transfer tax before they can be acquired.

— *Joseph J. Schroeder*

FIREARMS CURIOS AND RELICS LIST (1972 - 1986)
1987 Edition
INDEX

COMPILER'S NOTES:

1. "*" indicates a new entry;
2. In the *Marlin* entries, "Rd" indicates a round barrel and is not part of a firearm serial number;
3. "S/N" and "S/Ns" mean "serial number" and "serial numbers;"
4. "Cal." and "cals." mean "caliber" and "calibers."

This List is Composed of Four Major Sections:

SECTION I. Ammunition Classified as Curios or Relics: "Ammunition (as now defined in 18 U.S.C. 921(a)(17)(A)) has been *deleted* as items to be classified as curios or relics by the Congress during 1986. *(Though BATF still includes this section in their current list of curios and relics, as stated previously, we have opted not to include it in this 5th edition of GUN COLLECTOR'S DIGEST. Editor)* "Ammunition" is not to be confused with "armor piercing ammunition", defined during 1986 in Section 921(a)(17)(B).

SECTION II. Firearms Classified as Curios or Relics Under 18 U.S.C. Chapter 44: Licensed collectors may acquire, hold or dispose of these firearms as curios or relics. However, they are still "firearms" as defined in 18 U.S.C. 921(a)(3) and are, therefore, subject to all Chapter 44 controls. Generally, this category includes commemorative handguns, semiautomatic pistols, revolvers and rifles.

SECTION III. National Firearms Act Weapons Removed From the National Firearms Act as Collectors' Items and Classified as Curios or Relics Under 18 U.S.C. Chapter 44: Weapons in this Section are excluded entirely from the provisions of the National Firearms Act. Thus, approval from ATF to transfer these weapons is not required. They need not be registered in the national Firearms Registration and Transfer Record; there is no transfer tax liability. These weapons are still "firearms" under Chapter 44, and remain subject to regulation under Part 178. Licensed collectors may receive these weapons in both intrastate and interstate commerce, and may transfer them intrastate to both licensees and nonlicensees and interstate to licensed collectors and other licensees. While transfer may be made interstate to another licensee, they cannot be shipped interstate to a nonlicensee. **NOTE:** Certain antique firearms are discussed and listed in a new Section IIIA.

SECTION IV. National Firearms Act Weapons Classified as Curios or Relics Under 18 U.S.C. Chapter 44: These weapons (e.g., machineguns), are firearms within the scope of the National Firearms Act (NFA) [26 U.S.C. Chapter 53], and are subject to all the Act's provisions. Accordingly, these weapons cannot be lawfully transferred or received unless they are registered in the National Firearms Registration and Transfer Record, at ATF Bureau Headquarters. Once the registration requirements have been met, transfer may be made either intrastate or interstate to licensed collectors on ATF Form 4, **"Application For Tax Paid Transfer and Registration of a Firearm."** In each instance, the appropriate transfer tax must be paid and ATF must first approve the transfer application. The application to transfer must be accompanied by an individual transferee's fingerprints and photograph as prescribed on the form. The form also contains a law enforcement official's certification which must be completed.

Unserviceable weapons are still subject to the provisions of the National Firearms Act, except that they may be transferred free of transfer tax on ATF Form 5, **"Application For Tax Exempt Transfer and Registration of a Firearm."**

Questions concerning the lawfulness of transactions in these weapons should be directed to the Bureau of ATF, National Firearms Act Branch, Washington, DC 20226.

Questions concerning the criteria for rendering a specific weapon unserviceable should be directed to the Firearms Technology Branch at the same address.

Federally Licensed Firearms Collectors

A collector of curios or relics may obtain a collector's license under the Gun Control Act of 1968 (Chapter 44 of Title 18, United States Code) and the Federal firearms regulations, 27 CFR Part 178. The privileges conferred by this license extend *only* to curio or relic transactions, as discussed in detail below. In transactions involving firearms not classified as curios or relics, the licensed collector has the same status as a nonlicensee.

A person *need not* be federally licensed to collect curios or relics. However, the individual must be licensed in order to lawfully receive curios or relics by shipment from outside his or her State of residence. Federal law, regulations, and general information pertaining to licensed collectors and curios or relics can be found in ATF Publication 5300.4, "(Your Guide To) Federal Firearms Regulation." Recordkeeping requirements for licensed collectors are discussed in detail in Part 178 of Title 27, Code of Federal Regulations.

The Licensed Collector's Activities

Subject to other applicable provisions of the law and regulations, a collector's license entitles its holder to transport, ship, receive and acquire curios or relics in interstate or foreign commerce, and to dispose of curios or relics in interstate or foreign commerce to any other Federal firearms licensee.

However, ATF has recognized only assembled firearms as curios or relics. Moreover, ATF's classification of surplus military firearms as curios or relics has extended only to those firearms in their original military configuration. Frames or receivers of curios or relics and surplus military firearms not in their original military configuration are not generally recognized as curios or relics by ATF since they are not of special interest or value as collectors' items. Specifically, they do not meet the definition of curio or relic in Section 178.11 as firearms of special interest to collectors by reason of a quality other than is ordinarily associated with sporting firearms or offensive or defensive weapons. Those collectors having questions concerning the importability of specific curio or relic firearms should contact the Bureau of ATF, Firearms and Explosives Imports Branch, Washington, DC 20226.

The principal advantage of a collector's license is that the collector can acquire curios or relics from both licensees and nonlicensees without regard to his/her State of residence. A licensed collector may acquire and dispose of curios or relics at any location, the only limitation being that a disposition made to a nonlicensee is to be made to a resident of the same State in which the collector is licensed.

Restrictions on the Licensed Collector's Activities

The collector's license covers *only* transactions in curios or relics. A licensed collector has the same status as a nonlicensee with respect to transactions in firearms that are not curios or relics. While a licensed collector may acquire curios or relics and dispose of same from a personal collection, the collector is not authorized to engage in a firearms dealing business in curios or relics pursuant to their collector's license. "If the acquisition and disposition of curios and relics by a collector bring the collector within the definition of a manufacturer, importer or dealer under this part, he shall qualify as such." For example, if a collector acquires curios and relics for the purpose of a sale rather than to enhance a collection, the collector would have to be licensed as a dealer in firearms under Chapter 44. Additionally, if the curios and relics acquired were to include National Firearms Act weapons, the collector would be liable for the special (occupational) tax prescribed by the National Firearms Act. *The sole intent and purpose of the collector's license is to enable a firearms collector to enhance a collection of curios or relics.*

Curios or Relics

As set out in the Federal regulations (27 CFR 178.11), curios or relics include firearms which have special value to collectors. These firearms have special value because they possess some qualities not ordinarily associated with firearms intended for sporting use or as offensive or defensive weapons. To be recognized as curios or relics. firearms must:

1. Have been manufactured at least 50 years prior to the current date, but *not* including replicas thereof; *or*
2. Be certified by the curator of a municipal, State or Federal museum which exhibits firearms to be curios or relics of museum interest; *or*
3. Derive a substantial part of their monetary value from the fact that they are novel, rare, or bizarre, or from the fact of their association with some historical figure, period, or event.

Collectors Wishing to Obtain A Determination

Collectors wishing to obtain a determination whether a particular firearm qualifies for classification as a curio or relic in accordance with 27 CFR 178.11, 178.26 or 179.11, should submit a written request for a ruling. The letter should include:

- A complete physical description of the item;
- Reasons the collector believes the item merits the classification;
- Data concerning the history of the item, including production figures, if available, and market value.

In some cases, actual submission of the firearm may be required prior to a determination being made. Please submit your request to: Bureau of Alcohol, Tobacco and Firearms, Firearms Technology Branch, Room B230, 1200 Pennsylvania Avenue, NW, Washington, DC 20226. *The list of curios or relics following is not all inclusive.*

Section II
Curios & Relics — Title I Firearms

FIREARMS CLASSIFIED AS CURIOS OR RELICS
UNDER 18 U.S.C. CHAPTER 44

The Bureau has determined that the following firearms are curios or relics as defined in 27 CFR 178.11 because they fall within one of the categories specified in the regulations.

Such determination merely classifies the firearms as curios or relics and thereby authorizes licensed collectors to acquire, hold, or dispose of them as curios or relics subject to the provisions of 18 U.S.C. Chapter 44 and the regulations in 27 CFR Part 178. They are still "firearms" as defined in Chapter 44 of Title 18, U.S.C.

All Original military bolt action and semiautomatic rifles manufactured between 1899 and 1946.
All properly marked and identified semiautomatic pistols and revolvers used by, or manufactured for, any military organization prior to 1946.
*All Shotguns, properly marked and identified as having been manufactured for any military organization prior to 1946 and in their original military configuration only.
Alkartasuna, semiautomatic pistol cal .32.
Armand Gevage, semiautomatic pistols, .32ACP cal. as manufactured in Belgium prior to World War II.
Astra, model 400 pistol, German Army Contract, cal. 9mm Bergmann-Bayard, S/N range 97351-98850.
Astra, model 400 semiautomatic pistol, cal. 9mm Bergmann-Bayard, second German Army Contract, in S/N range 92851 through 97350.
Astra, model 1921 (400) semiautomatic pistols having slides marked Esperanzo Y Unceta.
Astra, M 800 Condor model, pistol, cal. 9mm Parabellum.
Auto Ordnance, West Hurley, NY, World War II Commemorative Thompson Semiautomatic rifle cal .45.
Auto Ordnance, West Hurley, NY, Korean War Commemorative Thompson Semiautomatic rifle, cal. .45.
Baker Gun and Forging Company, all firearms manufactured from 1899 to 1919.
Bannerman model 1937, Springfield rifle, cal. .30-06.
Bayard, model 1923 semiautomatic pistol, cal. 7.65mm or .380, Belgian manufacture.
Beretta, model 1915 pistols, cal. 6.35mm, 7.65mm, and 9mm Glisenti.
Beretta, model 1915/1919 (1922) pistol (concealed hammer), cal. 7.65mm.
Beretta, model 1919 pistol (without grip safety), cal. 6.35mm.
Beretta, model 1923 pistol, cal. 9mm Glisenti.
Beretta, model 1932 pistol, having smooth wooden grips w/"PB" medallion, cal. 9mm.
Beretta, model 1934 pistols, cal. 9mm post war variations bearing Italian Air Force eagle markings.
Beretta, model 1934 pistols, cal. 9mm produced during 1945 or earlier and having S/Ns within the ranges of 500000 - 999999, F00001 - F120000, G0001 - G80000, 00001AA - 10000AA, or 00001BB - 10000BB. This classification does not include any post war variations dated subsequent to 1945 or bearing post war Italian proof marks.
Beretta, model 1934 pistol, light weight model marked "Tipo Alleggerita" or "All" having transverse ribbed barrel, cal. 9mm.
Beretta, model 1935 pistol, Rumanian Contract, marked "P. Beretta - cal. 9 Scurt - Mo. 1934 - Brevet." on the slide, cal. 9mm.
Beretta, model 1935 pistol, Finnish Home Guard Contract, marked "SKY" on the slide, cal. 7.65mm.
Beretta, model 1935 pistols, cal. 7.65mm, produced during 1945 and earlier and having S/Ns below 620799.
Beretta, M1951 pistol, Egyptian Contract, cal. 9mm Parabellum.
Beretta, M 1951 pistol Israeli Contract, cal. 9mm parabellum.
Bergmann-Bayard, M1908 pistol, cal. 9mm Bergmann-Bayard.
Bernardelli, model 1956, experimental pistol, cal. 9mm Parabellum.
Bern Arsenal, Experimental Gas Locked pistol, cal. 9mm Parabellum.
Bern Arsenal, Experimental 16 shot pistol, cal. 9mm Parabellum.
*Brazilian copy of German G43 semiautomatic rifle, M954, cal. .30, manufactured at the Itajuba Arsenal, S/Ns G43-1 to G43-95.
FN Browning, model 1902 (usually known as the model 1903) semiautomatic pistol, cal. 9mm Browning long.
Browning, Centennial model High Power Pistol, cal. 9mm Parabellum.
Browning, Centennial model 92 lever action rifle, cal. .44 Magnum.
Browning, Superposed Centennial, consisting of a 20 gauge superposed shotgun, supplied with an extra set of .30-06 cal. superposed barrels.
Browning, M1935 Hi Power pistol, Canadian, Congolese, Indian and Nationalist Chinese Contracts, cal. 9mm Parabellum.
Browning, "Baby" model pistol, Russian Contract, cal. 6.35mm.
Browning, model 1906 Pocket Pistol if more than 50 years old.
Browning, model 1922 pistol, cal. 7.65mm, bearing German NSDAP or RFV markings.
Browning, model 1922 pistol, cal. 7.65mm or 9mm Kurz, marked "C.P.I.M." denoting issue to the Belgian Political Police.
Budischowsky, model TP70, semiautomatic pistol, cal. .25 ACP, with custom S/N DB1.
Campo-Giro, model 1913 and 1913/16 pistol, cal. 9mm Largo.
Chinese Communist, types 51 and 54 (Tokarev) pistols, cal. 7.62mm.
Chinese, Peoples Republic of China, copy of Japanese Type Sigiura Shiki semiautomatic pistol, cal. 7.65mm.
Chylewski, semiautomatic pistol manufactured by S.I.G. Switzerland, cal. 6.35mm (.25 ACP)

Clement, pistol, Belgian manufacture, cal. 5mm Clement.
Colt, .22 cal. Lord and Lady Derringer as manufactured by Colts Patent Firearms Manufacturing Co., Hartford, CT.
Colt, Ace Service model semiautomatic pistol, cal. .22, manufactured by Colt from 1935 to 1945, S/N range from SM1 to SM13803 including those marked "UNITED STATES PROPERTY" on the right side of the frame.
Colt, Ace semiautomatic pistol, cal. .22, manufactured by Colt from 1931 to 1947, S/N range from 1 to 10935 including those marked "UNITED STATES PROPERTY" on the right side of the frame.
Colt, Aircrewman revolver produced between 1951 and 1959, cal. .38 Special, marked "Property of U.S. Air Force" on back strap, having Air Force issue numbers of 1 - 1189 and in the S/N range 1902LW - 90470LW.
Colt, American Combat Companion, General Officers model, cal. .45ACP pistol marked "1911 American Combat Companion 1981, 70 Years at America's Side," S/Ns 1 STAR, 2 STAR, 3 STAR, 4 STAR, and 5 STAR.
Colt, ATF Special Edition, Deluxe model automatic pistol, cal. .45 ACP.
Colt, ATF Special Edition, Python Revolver model automatic pistol, cal. .357 magnum.
Colt, ATF Special Edition, standard model automatic pistol, cal. .45 ACP
Colt, Abilene, .22 (Kansas City-Cow Town).
Colt, Age of Flight 75th Anniversary semiautomatic pistols, cal. .45.
Colt, Alabama Sesquicentennial, .22.
Colt, Alamo, .22 and .45.
Colt, American Combat Companion, Enlisted Man's model, cal. .45ACP pistol marked "1911 American Combat Companion 1981, 70 Years at America's Side."
Colt, American Combat Companion Officers model, cal. .45ACP pistol marked "1911 American Combat Companion 1981, 70 Years at America's Side."
Colt, Appomattox Court House Centennial, .22 and .45.
Colt, Argentine D.G.F.M.-(F.M.A.P.) System Colt model 1927, cal. 11.25mm commercial variations.
Colt, Argentine model 1927, pistols, cal. .45, commercial variations.
Colt, Arizona Ranger model commemorative, .22 Revolver.
Colt, Arizona Territorial Centennial, .22 and .45.
Colt, Arkansas Territory Sesquicentennial, .22.
Colt, Army model double action revolver, any cal., manufactured between 1899 and 1907.
Colt, Bat Masterson, .22 and .45 (Lawman Series).
Colt, Battle of Gettysburg Centennial, .22.
Colt, Belleau Wood, .45 Pistol (World War I Series).
Colt, Border Patrol model Revolver, .38 Special Heavy Duty, Police Positive (D) style frame, S/Ns within the range 610000 through 620000.
Colt, Buffalo Bill Historical Center, Winchester Museum, Special Issue, Colt Single Action Revolver, cal. .44-40, S/N 21BB.
Colt, California Bicentennial, .22.
Colt, California Gold Rush, .22 and .45.
Colt, Camp Perry Single Shot Target Pistols, .22 long rifle or .38 Special cal.
Colt, Carolina Charter Tercentenary, .22 and .22/.45.
Colt, Chamizal Treaty, .22 and .45.
Colt, Chateau Thierry, .45 Pistol, (World War I Series).
Colt, Cherry's Sporting Goods 35th Anniversary, .22/.45.
Colt, Chisholm Trail, .22 (Kansas Series-Trails).
Colt, Civil War Centennial Single Shot, .22.
Colt, Coffeyville, .22 (Kansas Series-Cow Town).
Colt, Colorado Gold Rush, Colt, Colonel Samuel Colt, Sesquicentennial, .45.
Colt, Colt's 125th Anniversary, .45.
Colt, Columbus (Ohio) Sesquicentennial, .22.
Colt, Custom Gun Shop's "Custom Edition Sheriff's model" Single Action Revolver, cal. .45 Colt, S/N 1 to 35.
Colt, DA .38, New Army and Navy Revolver, made from 1899 to 1907.
Colt, Dakota Territory, .22.
Colt, Des Monies, Reconstruction of Old Fort, .22 and .45.
Colt, Detective Special model Revolver, cal. .38, S/N 418162, owned by Colonel Charles A. Lindbergh.
Colt, Dodge City, .22 (Kansas Series-Cow Town).
Colt, "Duke," Commemorative, .22 cal. revolver.
Colt, European Theater, .45 Pistol (World War II Series).
Colt, First model, Match Target Woodsman, .22, semiautomatic pistol, manufactured from 1938 to 1944, S/Ns MT1 to MT15,000.
Colt, Florida Territory Sesquicentennial, .22.
Colt, Fort Findlay (Ohio) sesquicentennial, .22.
Colt, Fort Hays, .22 (Kansas Series-Forts).
Colt, Fort Larned, .22 (Kansas Series-Forts).
Colt, Fort McPherson (Nebraska) Centennial Derringer, .22.
Colt, Fort Scott, .22 (Kansas Series-Forts).
Colt, Fort Stephenson (Ohio) sesquicentennial, .22.
Colt, Forty-Niner Miner, .22.
Colt, Fourth model Derringer, cal. .22 short rimfire, cased as a set of two pistols in a leather book titled "Colt Derringer, Limited Edition, by Colt," on the spine of the book and "A Limited Edition by Colt," on the cover.
Colt, General George Meade, Pennsylvania Campaign, .22 and .45.
Colt, General Hood, Tennessee Campaign Centennial, .22.
Colt, General John Hunt Morgan, Indiana Raid, .22.
Colt, General Nathan Bedford Forrest, .22.
Colt, Genesco (Illinois) 125th Anniversary, Derringer, .22.
Colt, Golden Spike Centennial, .22.

Colt, Government model pistols in cal. .45 ACP, BB series.
Colt, H. Cook, "1 to 100," .22/.45.
Colt, Idaho Territorial Centennial, .22.
Colt, Indiana Sesquicentennial, .22.
Colt, J frame, Officer's model Match, .38 Special revolver manufactured from 1970 - 1972, identified by J S/N prefix.
Colt, Joaquin Murrieta, "1 of 100," .22/.45.
Colt, John M. Browning Commemorative, .45 cal., semiautomatic pistol, S/Ns JMB 0001 - JMB 3000, and numbers GAS O JMB, PE CEW JMB, and 0003JMB.
Colt, John Wayne, Commemorative .45 long Colt cal., revolver.
Colt, Kansas Centennial, .22.
Colt, Lightning model double action revolver, any cal. manufactured between 1899 and 1909.
Colt, Los Angeles Police Department (L.A.P.D.) Special Edition .45 cal. Government model Semiautomatic pistol.
Colt, Maine Sesquicentennial, .22 and .45.
*Colt, Mark IV, Government Model, commemorative "Michigan State Police 60th Anniversary," 1917-1977. The left side of slide engraved with scroll pattern and depicts 4 modes of transportation; Horse, Motorcycle, Auto and Helicopter, S/Ns 1 to 1608.
Colt, Match Target Woodsman Semiautomatic Pistol, cal. .221r, S/N 128866S, owned by Ernest Hemingway.
Colt, Meuse Argonne, .45 Pistol, (World War I Series).
Colt, Missouri Sesquicentennial, .22.
Colt, Mk IV Series 70 semiautomatic pistols in all cals., which were incorrectly marked at the factory with both Colt Government model markings and Colt Commander markings.
Colt, Montana Territory Centennial, .22 and .45.
Colt, NRA Centennial, Gold Cup National Match pistol, in cal. .45.
Colt, NRA Centennial, single action revolver, in cals. .357 Magnum and .45.
Colt, Nebraska Centennial, .22.
Colt, Ned Buntline Commemorative, cal. .45 revolver.
Colt, Nevada Centennial, .22. and .45.
Colt, Nevada Centennial "Battle Born," .22 and .45.
Colt, New Frontier .22 LR Revolvers, "Kit Carson" Commemorative, Colt model GB275.
Colt, New Frontier, .357 magnum cal., single action revolver, barrel length 4 3/4" S/N 4411NF.
Colt, New Frontier, .45 cal., Abercrombie and Fitch, "Trailblazer."
Colt, New Frontier and Single Action Army model revolvers originally ordered and shipped with factory engraving, accompanied by a letter from the manufacturer confirming the authenticity of the engraving.
Colt, New Jersey Tercentenary, .22 and .45.
Colt, New Mexico Golden Anniversary, .22.
Colt, New Service revolvers as manufactured between 1899 and 1944, all variations, all cals.
Colt, Officers model Match (1953-1969), .22 and .38 cal. revolvers.
Colt, Officers model Special (1949-1952), .22 and .38 cal. revolvers.
Colt, Officers model Target (1930-1949), .32 and .38 cal. revolvers.
Colt, Officers model (1904-1930), .38 cal. revolver.
Colt, Officers model (1930-1949), .22 cal. revolver.
Colt, Official Police Revolver, cal. .38, S/N 583469, Silver Inlaid and Engraved by Wilbur A. Glahn.
Colt, Oklahoma Territory Diamond Jubilee, .22.
Colt, Oregon Trail, .22 (Kansas Series-Trails).
Colt, Pacific Theater, .45 Pistol (World War II Series).
Colt, Pat Garrett, .22 and .45 (Lawman Series).
Colt, Pawnee Trail, .22 (Kansas Series-Trails).
Colt, Peacemaker Commemorative, .22 and .45 revolver.
Colt, Pocket Positive revolver, .32 cal.
Colt, Pocket Positive revolver, S/N 6164.
Colt, Pony Express Centennial, .22.
Colt, Pony Express, Russell, Majors and Waddell, Presentation model .45.
Colt, Python Revolver, cal. .357 Magnum, engraved and inlaid with the Crest of the United Arab Emirates.
Colt, Revolver, cal. .38, Police Positive, S/N 139212.
Colt, Rock Island Arsenal Centennial Single Shot, .22.
Colt, Santa Fe Trail, .22 (Kansas Series-Trails).
Colt, Second (2nd) Marne, .45 Pistol (World War I Series).
Colt, Shawnee Trail, .22 (Kansas Series-Trails).
Colt, Sheriff's model revolver, cal. .44 and .45.
Colt, Sheriff's model revolver, cal. .44 and .45.
Colt, Single Action Army revolver, cal. .45, S/N 85163A, engraved and inlaid with a bust of President Abraham Lincoln.
Colt, Single Action Revolvers, cal., .45, engraved and silver inlaid for presentation to Chuck Connors, S/Ns CC1 and CC2.
Colt, St. Augustine Quadricentennial, .22.
Colt, St. Louis Bicentennial, .22 and .45.
Colt, Texas Ranger, .45.
Colt, "The Right to Keep and Bear Arms" commemorative, .22 cal. Peacemaker Buntline, single action revolver having a 7 1/2" barrel with the inscription "The Right to Keep and Bear Arms" inscribed on the barrel and a S/N range of G0001RB - G3000RB.
Colt, United States Bicentennial Commemorative, Python revolver, cal. .357.
Colt, United States Bicentennial Commemorative single action army revolver cal.45.
Colt, West Virginia Centennial, .22 and .45.
Colt, Wichita, .22 (Kansas Series-Cow Town).
Colt, Wild Bill Hickok, .22 and .45 (Lawman Series).
Colt, Woodsman, cal. .22, semiautomatic target pistol, manufactured from 1915 to 1943, S/Ns 1 to 157000.

Colt, Wyatt Earp, .22 and .45 (Lawman Series).
Colt, Wyatt Earp, Buntline Special, .45 (Lawman Series).
Colt, Wyoming Diamond Jubilee, .22.
Colt, 1873 Peacemaker Centennial 1973, single action revolver, .44/.40 or .45.
Colt, model 1900 semiautomatic pistol, cal. .38, in original configuration.
Colt, model 1902 semiautomatic pistol, military model, cal. .38, in original configuration.
Colt, model 1903 Pocket (hammerless), semiautomatic pistol, cal. .32.
Colt, model 1911 Commercial Semiautomatic pistols, cal. .45 ACP, S/Ns C1 - C130000.
Colt, model 1902 semiautomatic pistol, sporting model, cal. .38, in original configuration.
Colt, model 1903 Pocket (exposed hammer), semiautomatic pistol cal. .38 ACP.
Colt, model 1908 Pocket (hammerless) semiautomatic pistol cal. .380.
Colt, model 1908, cal. .25 ACP, hammerless semiautomatic pistol, having a grip safety, in S/N range 1 - 409061.
Colt, model 1911-A, commercial model, in cal. .45 and bearing Egyptian inscriptic meaning police, on the upper forward right-hand side of the trigger guard and having S/Ns within the range of C186000 to C188000.
Colt, model 1911-A-1, .45 cal. pistol, manufactured by Union Switch and Signal Company, prototype model, with S/Ns US & S Exp. 1 to US & S Exp. 100.
Colt, single action Army (Bisley, Standard, and target variations), all original, manufactured from 1899 to 1946, S/N range from 182000 to 357869.
Colt, the Liege Number 1 Colt Single Action Army Revolver, cal. .45, S/N Liege No. 1.
Czechoslovakian, model CZ 27, 7.65mm semiautomatic pistol with Nazi markings.
Czechoslovakian, CZ38, pistol cal. .380ACP.
Czechoslovakian, CZ50 pistol, cal. 7.65mm.
Czechoslovakian, CZ52 pistol, cal. 7.62mm.
Czechoslovakian, model 1952 and 1952/57, 7.62 x 45mm and 7.62 x 39mm cal., semi-automatic rifles.
Danish, M1910/1921 Bayard, pistol, cal. 9mm Bergmann-Bayard.
Davis Warner, Infallible, semiautomatic pistol, cal. .32.
Dreyse, Military model 1910 pistol, cal. 9mm.
Egyptian, Hakim (Ljungman) 7.92mm semiautomatic rifle as manufactured in Egypt.
*Egyptian Raschid, semiautomatic rifle, cal. 7.62 x 39mm, original Egyptian military production.
Esser-Barratt, English manufacture, slide action rifle, cal. .303.
Fabrique Nationale, model SAFN49 semiautomatic rifle, any cal.
French, model 1949/56 (Fusil Mle (MAS 7.5mm)) semiautomatic rifle.
French, model 1949, cal. 7.5mm, semiautomatic rifle (Fusil Mle. 1949 (MAS) 7.5mm)
Geha and Remo, shotguns made from Mauser rifles after World War I prior to 1946.
German, P38 pistols, cal. 9mm Parabellum manufactured prior to 1947.
German, model 1916 Grenatenwerfer original spigot type mortars.
Gustloff, semiautomatic pistol in cal. 7.65mm manufactured by Gustloff Werke, Suhl, Germany.
Hammond or Grant Hammond, pistols, all models, variations or prototypes, made by Grant Hammond Corporation, New Haven, CT.
Hammond/Hi-Standard, semiautomatic pistols, in cal. .45.
Harrington & Richardson, Abilene Anniversary, .22 revolver.
Harrington & Richardson, Centennial Officer's model Springfield rifle .45-70 Govt
Harrington & Richardson, Centennial Standard model Springfield rifle .45-70 Govt.
*Harrington & Richardson, model 999, revolver, cal. 22 Long rifle, barrel 6," 110th year commemorative, S/Ns from 001 to 999.
Harrington & Richardson, self loading semiautomatic pistol, cal. .32.
Hartford Arms and Equipment Company, single shot target pistol, cal. .22LR.
Hartford Arms and Equipment Company, repeating pistol, cal. .22LR.
Hartford Arms and Equipment Company, model 1928 pistol, cal. .22LR.
High Standard, Crusader Commemorative, Deluxe Pair, .44 Magnum and .45 Colt cal. revolvers.
Hi-Standard, experimental electric free pistol, cal. .22 long rifle.
Hi-Standard, experimental electric free pistol, cal. .38 special.
Hi-Standard, experimental electric free pistol, cal. .38 special.
Hi-Standard, model P 38, semiautomatic pistol, cal. .38 SPL.
Hi-Standard, experimental model T-3 semiautomatic pistol, cal. 9mm Luger.
Hi-Standard, experimental ISU rapid fire semiautomatic pistol, cal. .22 short.
High Standard, model A pistol, cal. .22LR.
High Standard, model B pistol, cal. .22LR.
High Standard, model C pistol, cal. .22Short.
High Standard, model D pistol, cal. .22LR.
High Standard, model E pistol, cal. .22LR.
High Standard, model H-A pistol, cal. .22LR.
High Standard, model H-B pistol, first model, cal. .22LR.
High Standard, model H-B pistol, second model, cal. .22LR.
High Standard, model H-D pistol, cal. .22LR.
High Standard, model H-E pistol, cal. .22LR.
High Standard, model USA-HD pistol, cal. .22LR.
High Standard, model HD-Military pistol, cal. .22LR.
High Standard, model G-380 pistol, cal. .380.
High Standard, model G-B pistol, cal. .22LR.
High Standard, model G-D pistol, cal. .22LR.
High Standard, model G-E pistol, cal. .22LR.
High Standard, model G-O (First model Olympic) pistol, cal. .22 Short.
High Standard, Supermatic Trophy model 107 .22 pistol Olympic Commemorative model
Holland and Holland, Royal Double Barrel Shotgun, .410 Gauge, S/N 36789.
*Hopkins and Allen, model 1901, "FOREHAND," cal. .32 S&W model.
Hopkins and Allen, Revolver, .32 cal., S/N G 9545.
Italian, Brixia, M1906, pistol, cal. 9mm Glisenti.
Italian,Glisenti, M1910, pistol, cal. 9mm Glisenti.

Ithaca, double barrel shotguns actually manufactured in NY by the Ithaca Gun Co. Ithaca, NY. All gauges and all models, having barrels at least 18" in length and an overall length of at least 26," manufactured before 1950.
Ithaca Gun Co., single barrel trap guns, break open all gauges, all models actually manufactured at Ithaca, NY, before 1950.
Ithaca, St. Louis Bicentennial, model 49, .22 Rifle.
Iver Johnson Arms, Pistol, cal. .380, U.S. Border Patrol 60th Anniversary commemorative, serial USBP 0001 to USBP 5000.
*Iver Johnson Arms, model M 1 Carbine, cal. .30, Korean War commemorative, S/Ns KW0001 to KW2500.
*Iver Johnson Arms, model M 1 Carbine, cal. .30, Airborne commemorative, S/Ns KW0001 to KW2500.
Jieffeco, pistol, Belgian manufacture, cal. 7.65mm.
Jieffeco, semiautomatic pistol, in cal. .25 ACP, marked "Davis Warner Arms Corp., N.Y."
Kimball, pistols, all models, all cals.
Kolibri, pistols, cals. 2.7mm and 3mm Kolibri.
L. C. Smith, Shotguns manufactured by Hunter Arms Co. and Marlin Firearms Co. from 1899 to 1971.
Lahti, L-35 pistol, Finnish manufacture, cal. 9mm Parabellum.
LeFever, shotguns made from 1899 to 1942.
Luger, pistol, all models and variations manufactured prior to 1946.
Luger, Mauser commercial manufacture, semiautomatic pistol, 70 Jahre, Parabellum -Pistole, Keisereich Russland, commemorative, cal. 9mm.
Luger, Mauser commercial manufacture, semiautomatic pistol, 75 Jahre, Parabellum -Pistole, 1900-1975, commemorative, cal. 7.65mm.
Luger, Mauser commercial manufacture, semiautomatic pistol, 75 Jahre, Parabellum -Pistole, Konigreich Bulgarian, commemorative, cal. 7.65mm.
Luger, Mauser Parabellum, semiautomatic pistol, 7.65mm or 9mm Luger, 4 and 6" barrel, Swiss pattern with grip safety and the American Eagle stamped on the receiver; made from 1970 to 1978.
MAB, model R pistol, cal. 9mm Parabellum.
Makarov, pistol, Russian and East German, cal. 9mm Makarov.
Mannlicher, pistol, M1900, M1901, M1903 and M1905, cal. 7.63mm Mannlicher.
*Marlin, Model 336 TS carbine, cal. 30-30, Powell Wyoming 75th anniversary commemorative, having PW S/N prefix.
Marlin, 90th Anniversary, model 39-A, .22 rifle.
Marlin, 90th Anniversary, model 39-A, .22 Carbine.
Mauser, semiautomatic pistols manufactured prior to 1946, any cal.
Mauser, Congolese model 1950 rifles marked FP 1952 on the receiver, cal. .30/06.
Mauser, model 1935 rifle 7 x 57mm cal. with Chilean Police Markings.
Mauser, P 38, Pistols cal. 9mm, marked SVW46.
Mauser, rifles, bolt action and semiautomatic any cal., commercially produced by Waffenfabrik Mauser, Oberndoff, Germany prior to 1945.
*MBA Gyrojet Carbine, S/N B5057.
Menz, Liliput, German manufacture cal. 4.25mm.
Menz, PB III, in cal. 7.65mm, manufactured by August Menz, Suhl, Germany.
Menz, PB IIIA, in cal. 7.65mm, manufactured by August Menz, Suhl, Germany.
Menz, PB IV, in cal. 7.65mm, manufactured by August Menz, Suhl, Germany.
Menz, PB IVa, in cal. 7.65mm, manufactured by August Menz, Suhl, Germany.
Menz, Special, in cal. 7.65mm, manufacture by August Menz, Suhl, Germany.
Mexican, Obregon, pistol, cal. .45 ACP.
Mugica, model 120, pistol, cal. 9mm Parabellum.
Navy Arms, Oklahoma Diamond Jubilee Commemorative, Yellow Boy Carbine.
North Korean Type 1964, pistol, cal. 7.62mm Tokarev.
Ortgies, semiautomatic, cal. .25, with S/N 10073.
Ortgies, semiautomatic, cal. .32, with S/N 126314.
OWA, semiautomatic, pistol, cal. .25.
PAF, "Junior" semiautomatic pistol, cal. .25, manufactured by the Pretoria Arms Factory Ltd. of South Africa.
PAF, pistol, marked "BRF," cal. .25, manufactured by the Pretoria Arms Factory Ltd. of South Africa.
Parker, shotguns, all grades, all gauges, produced by Parker Brothers, Meridan, CT, and Remington Arms, Ilion, NY, from 1899 through 1945.
Phoenix, (U.S.A.), pistol, cal. .25 ACP.
James Purdey, Over & Under shotgun, 12 guage, S/N 26819, engraved and gold inlaid.
Reising, .22 cal., semiautomatic pistol.
Remington, over/under Derringer, cal. .41 rim fire, Remington Arms Company, Ilion NY, made between 1898 and 1935.
Remington, Canadian Territorial Centennial, model 742, Rifle.
*Remington, model 12, rifle, cal. .22 short, long rifle, and 22 Remington Special manufactured by Remington Arms, Union Metallic Cartridge Co., Remington Works, Ilion, NY from 1909 to 1936.
Remington, model 51, semiautomatic pistol, cals. .32 ACP or .380 ACP.
Remington, 150th Anniversary model 1100SA semiautomatic shotgun, cal. 12 gauge.
Remington, 150th Anniversary model 870SA slide action shotgun, cal. 12 gauge.
Remington, 150th Anniversary model 742ADL semiautomatic rifle cal. .30/06.
Remington, 150th Anniversary model 760ADL slide action rifle cal. .30/06.
Remington, 150th Anniversary model 552A semiautomatic rifle, cal. 221r.
Remington, 150th Anniversary model 572A slide action rifle, cal. .221r.
Remington, 150th Anniversary model Nylon 66 semiautomatic rifle, cal. 221r.
Remington, Montana Territorial Centennial, model 600, Rifle.
*Rhode Island Arms Co., Morrone Model 46, Shotgun.
Roth Steyr, 1907, semiautomatic pistol, cal. 8mm.
Ruger, Blackhawk .44 with 6 1/2" barrel, revolver with S/Ns 1 to 29860.
Ruger, Blackhawk .44 with 7 1/2" barrel, revolver with S/Ns 17000 to 29860.
Ruger, Blackhawk .44 with 10" barrel, revolver with S/Ns 18000 to 29860.
Ruger, Blackhawk .357 with 4 5/8" barrel, revolver with S/Ns 1 to 42689.
Ruger, Blackhawk .357 with 6 1/2" barrel, revolver with S/Ns 20000 to 42689.
Ruger, Blackhawk .357 and 9mm stainless steel revolver with S/Ns 32-56000 - 32-59000.
Ruger, Blackhawk .357 magnum w/10" barrel, revolver with S/Ns 20000 - 38000.
Ruger, Canadian Centennial, Matched No. 1 Rifle Sets, Special Deluxe.
Ruger, Canadian Centennial, Matched No. 2 Rifle Sets.
Ruger, Canadian Centennial, Matched No. 3 Rifle Sets.
Ruger, Canadian Centennial, model 10/22, Carbine.
Ruger, 10/22 Canadian Centennial, carbine with S/Ns C1 to C4500.

Ruger, Falling Block Long Range Creedmore rifle, cal. .45 (Sharps), S/N 130-06888, The Amber Silver - Jubilee.
Ruger, flattop, "Blackhawk" revolvers, cals. .44 Magnum & .357 Magnum, all barrel lengths, made from 1955 through 1962.
Ruger, flattop, single-six, .22 cal. revolvers with flat side loading gate, all barrel lengths, made from 1953 through 1956.
Ruger, Hawkeye, pistol with S/Ns 1 to 3296.
Ruger, Lightweight Single Six, Revolver with S/Ns 200000 to 212530.
Ruger, Mark I "U.S." stamped medallion, pistol with S/Ns 76000 - 79000.
Ruger, Single Six, engraved revolver with S/Ns 5100 - 75000.
Ruger, Standard Auto with red eagle, pistol with S/Ns 1 - 25000.
Ruger, Super Black Hawk, revolver with S/Ns 24000 - 77000.
Ruger, Super Single Six stainless with 4" barrel, revolver with S/Ns 62-07500 - 64-650000.
Ruger, Super Single Six stainless with 9," revolver with S/Ns 62-07500 - 63-40000.
Ruger, Super Single Six chrome with 4 5/8" barrel, revolver with S/Ns 504000 - 505000.
Ruger, "21 Club" No 1, rifle with random S/Ns.
Ruger, 44 Deerstalker, carbine with S/Ns 1 to 5000.
*Russian (U.S.S.R.), Nagant revolver, model 1895, cal. 7.62 Nagant & .22 cal. all variations, manufactured by the Tula Arsenal, Tula, Russia, after 1898.
*Russian (U.S.S.R.), Tokarev, model TT, 1930, pistol, cal. 7.62, manufactured at the Tula Arsenal, Tula, U.S.S.R., from 1939 through 1956.
*Russian (U.S.S.R.), Tokarev, model TT, 1933, pistol, cal. 7.62, manufactured at the Tula Arsenal, Tula, U.S.S.R., from 1933 through 1956.
*Russian (U.S.S.R.) Tokarev, model TT R-3, .22 cal., pistol.
*Russian (U.S.S.R.), Tokarev, model TT R-4, .22 cal., pistol.
*Russian (U.S.S.R.), Tula Korovin, Tk, .25 ACP cal., semiautomatic pistol.
*Russian (U.S.S.R.), model 1891, Mosin-Nagant rifles, cal. 7.62 x 54R & .22 cal, all models and all variations, manufactured after 1898 (i.e., M1891/30, M1910, M1938, and M1944).
*Russian (U.S.S.R.), Tokarev, semiautomatic rifle, model 1938 (SVT38), cal. 7.62 x 54R, of Soviet manufacture.
*Russian, (U.S.S.R.), Tokarev, semiautomatic rifle, model 1940 (SVT40), cal. 7.62 x 54R, of Soviet manufacture.
*Russian (U.S.S.R.), Tokarev, semiautomatic carbine, model 1932 (nonstandard), cal. 7.62 x 54R, of Soviet manufacture.
*Russian (U.S.S.R.), Tokarev, semiautomatic carbine, model 1940 (SVT40), cal. 7.62 x 54R, of Soviet manufacture.
*Russian (U.S.S.R.), Simonov, semiautomatic rifle, model SKS, cal. 7.62 x 39, of Soviet manufacture.
*Russian (U.S.S.R.), Dragunov, semiautomatic rifle, model SVD, cal. 7.62 x 54R, of Soviet manufacture, Soviet military issue only.
*J. P. Sauer & Sohn pistols, manufactured prior to 1946.
Sauer, 38(h), pistol, cal. 7.65mm marked with Third Reich police acceptance stamps of Eagle C,F,K, or L.
Savage Arms, semiautomatic pistols, cal. .45 ACP, all models.
Savage Arms Co/Corp. model 99, lever action, centerfire rifles, manufactured in Utica, NY prior to World War II with S/Ns below 450000.
Savage, Prototype pistols cal. .25, .32 and .38 made between 1907 and 1927.
Savage, model 1907 Pistols, cal. .32 and .380.
Savage, model 1915 Pistol, cal. .32 and .380.
Savage, model 1917 Pistol, cal. .32 and .380.
Schwarzlose, pocket model 1908 in 7.65mm, pistol manufactured by A.W. Schwarzlose, G.m.b.h., Berlin, Germany and those assembled or made by Warner Arms.
Smith & Wesson, 125th anniversary Commemorative, model 25, revolver, cal. .45, marked "Smith & Wesson 125th Anniversary" and manufactured in 1977.
Smith & Wesson, 150th anniversary Texas Ranger Commemorative model 19 revolver.
Smith & Wesson, 1st model, Ladysmith revolver, cal. .22 rimfire long.
Smith & Wesson, .22/32 Kit Gun, cal. .22 LR, S/Ns 525670 - 534636 (no letter).
Smith & Wesson, 2nd model, Ladysmith revolver, cal. .22 rimfire long.
Smith & Wesson, 2nd model, single shot pistol, cals. .22 rimfire, .32 S&W & .38 S&W.
Smith & Wesson, .32 Double Action Top Break, cal. .32 S&W, S/Ns 209302 & higher.
Smith & Wesson, .32 Safety Hammerless Top Break (New Departure), cal. .32 S&W, S/Ns 91401 & higher.
Smith & Wesson, .357 Magnum Hand Ejector, cal. .357 Magnum, S/Ns 45768 to 60000 (no letter).
Smith & Wesson, .38 Double Action Top Break Perfected model, cal. .38 S&W.
Smith & Wesson, .38 Double Action Top Break, cal. .38 S&W, S/Ns 382023 & higher.
Smith & Wesson, .38 Hand Ejector Military and Police, cal. .38, S/Ns 1 to 241703 (no letter).
Smith & Wesson, .38 Safety Hammerless Top Break (New Departure), cal. .38 S&W, S/Ns 119901 and higher.
Smith & Wesson, .38/44 Outdoorsman & Heavy Duty, cal. .38, S/Ns 36500 - 62023 (no letter).
Smith & Wesson, 3rd model, Ladysmith revolver, cal. .22 rimfire long.
Smith & Wesson, 3rd model, single shot pistol, cals. .22 rimfire, .32 S&W & .38 S&W
Smith & Wesson, .44 Hand Ejector, all cal., S/Ns 1 - 62488 (no letter).
Smith & Wesson, .455 Mark II Hand Ejector, cal. .455.
Smith & Wesson, California Highway Patrol Commemorative model 19 revolver, cal. .357.
Smith & Wesson, City of Los Angeles 200th Anniversary Commemorative model 19 revolver, cal. .357.
Smith & Wesson, K-22 Hand Ejector, cal. .22 LR, S/Ns 632132 - 696952 (no letter).
Smith & Wesson, K-32 Hand Ejector (K-32 Masterpiece), cal. .32 S&W Long, S/Ns 653388 to 682207 (no letter).
Smith & Wesson, Mercox Dart Gun, cal. .22 rimfire, blank.
Smith & Wesson, model 16 (K-32 Masterpiece), cal. .32 S&W Long, "K" S/N series.
Smith & Wesson, model .22/32 Hand Ejector (Bekeart model), cal. .22 LR, S/Ns 138220 to 534636 (no letter).
Smith & Wesson, model 39, steel frame pistol, cal. 9mm Parabellum.
Smith & Wesson, model 39-1 (52-A), pistol, cal. 9mm Parabellum.
*Smith and Wesson, model 53, Remington Jet Center Fire Magnum, cal. .22.
Smith & Wesson, model Straight Line, single shot pistol, cal. .22 rimfire long rifle.

Smith & Wesson, pistol, cal. .32 ACP.
Smith & Wesson, pistol, cal. .35, all variations.
Smith and Wesson, U.S. Border Patrol 50th Anniversary Commemorative, model 66, stainless steel, cal. .357 Magnum, revolvers.
Sosso, pistols, manufactured, by Guilio Sosso, Turin, Italy, or Fabrica Nationale D'Armi, Brescea Italy, cal. 9mm.
*Springfield Armory, Inc., Korean War Commemorative .30 cal., M1 Garand Rifle S/Ns from KW0001 to KW1000.
Standard Arms Co., rifle/shotgun combination, U.S., model "Camp," slide action cal. .50.
Standard Arms Co., rifle model G, slide action or gas operated, cal. unknown.
Standard Arms Co., rifle model M, slide action cal. .25 - .35, .30 Rem. and .35 Rem.
Steyr, model 1909, .25 ACP cal. semiautomatic pistol.
Steyr-Hahn, M1912, pistol, cal. 9mm Steyr.
Steyr-Hahn, M1912, pistol, cal. 9mm Parabellum marked with Third Reich police acceptance stamps of Eagle C,R,K, or L.
*Swiss Schmidt Rubin, Model 1911, rifle made into a harpoon gun, cal. 12mm.
*Swiss self loading rifle, test 1947, cal. 7.5mm, all variations.
Tauler, model military and police pistol.
*Thompson Center Contender Pistol, cal. .30 Herrett, Steve Herrett Commemorative, Serial Number SH-001 to SH-500.
*Thompson Center Contender Pistol, cal. 7mm TCU, IHMSA 10th anniversary commemorative, Serial Number IHMSA 10-001 to IHMSA 10-200.
Tokagypt 58, pistol, cal. 9mm Parabellum.
*Uberti, Single action revolver, cal. .45, General George S. Patton Commemorative, S/Ns P0001 to P2500.
U.S., model 1911-A1, semiautomatic, pistol, cal. .45, manufactured by the Singer Manufacturing Company in 1942, S/N range from S800001 to S800500.
U.S., model 1911-A1, semiautomatic pistol, cal. .45, manufactured by Remington Rand, bearing S/N prefix of ERRS.
U.S., model 1911-A1 semiautomatic pistol, cal. .45, produced as original factory cut-a-ways.
U.S., Rifle, cal. .30 M1, original military issue only, produced prior to 1956.
U.S., cal. .30, MC-1952, equipped with telescopic sight mount MC, telescopic sight MC1, marked U.S.M.C. or kollmorgan.
*UZI, Model A, semi automatic carbine, cal. 9mm, having a satin nickel finish applied at the factory, S/Ns SA 0001 to SA 0100.
Walther, Olympic bolt action single shot match rifle, in cal. .22 made by Wafenfabrik Walther, Zella-Mahlis (thur.) prior to World War II.
Walther, pistols, Manufactured at Zella-Mahlis prior to 1946, all models any cal.
Walther, model PP & PPK semiautomatic pistols, in all cals., manufactured in France and marked "MANHURIN".
Walther, Rifles, model 182, cal. .22 made by Waffenfabrik, Walther, Zella-Mahlis (thur.) prior to World War II.
Webley, model 1909, pistol, cal. 9mm Browning Long.
Webley and Scott, model 1910 and 1913 high velocity pistols, cal. .38 ACP.
Webley and Scott, M1913, Navy or Commercial, self loading pistol, cal. .455.
Webley-Fosbury, semiautomatic revolvers, all cals., all models.
Whitney, "Wolverine" and "Lighting" .22 cal. automatic pistols as manufactured by Whitney Firearms Company, Hartford, CT between 1855 - 1962.
Winchester, Apache Commemorative carbine, commemorative edition of model 1894 Winchester with S/N prefix of AC.
Winchester, Comanche Commemorative carbine, commemorative edition of model 1894 Winchester with S/N prefix of CC.
Winchester, "Ducks Unlimited" shotgun, model 12, bearing S/Ns DU-001 through DU-800 (Commemorative).
Winchester, "Matched Set of 1000," a cased pair consisting of a Winchester model 94 rifle, cal. .30-30 and a Winchester model 9422 rifle, cal. .22.
Winchester, Northwest Territories Centennial rifle.
*Winchester, model 12, Shotgun, 12 gauge, prototype, for Ducks Unlimited Commemorative, S/N Y2002214.
Winchester, model 21 Grand American Double Barrel Shotgun, cal. 20 and 28 gauge, S/N 32984, Engraved Custom Built by Winchester for Philip S. Rane.
Winchester, model 52, rifle, bearing S/Ns 1 to 6500.
Winchester, model 53, all original, manufactured from 1924 to 1947 with 16" or longer barrel, and 26" or longer overall length.
Winchester, model 54, rifle, speed lock variation, cal. .270.
Winchester, model 63, self loading rifles, cal. .22 rimfire.
Winchester, models 64 and 65, lever action rifles.
Winchester, model 1866, Centennial, Rifle.
Winchester, model 1866, Centennial, carbine.
Winchester, model 70, Ultra Match Target Special Grade rifle, cal. .308.
Winchester, model 70, rifle, cal. .308 rifle, 19" barrel and Mannlicher type stock, made from 1968 to 1971.

Winchester, model 70, rifles, .308, .270 Winchester, and 30-06 cal., 19" barrel and Mannlicher type stock, made from 1968 to 1971.
Winchester, model 71, all original, manufactured from 1936 to 1958, with 16" or longer barrel and 26" or longer overall length.
Winchester, model 1873, all original, manufactured from 1899 to 1925, with 16" or longer barrel and 26" or longer overall length.
Winchester, model 85, (single shot rifle), all original, manufactured from 1899 to 1920, with 16" or longer barrel and 26" or longer overall length.
Winchester, model 86, all original, manufactured from 1899 to 1935, with 16" or longer barrel and 26" or longer overall length.
Winchester, model 88, carbine, cal. .243, .284, .308, or.358 manufactured by Winchester Western Division, Olin Corporation, New Haven, Connecticut.
Winchester, model 92, all original, manufactured from 1899 to 1947, with 16" or longer barrel and 26" or longer overall length.
Winchester, model 94, 150th Anniversary Texas Ranger Commemorative, carbine.
Winchester, model 94, Alaskan Purchase Centennial, carbine.
Winchester, model 94, American Bald Eagle Commemorative Carbine.
Winchester, model 94, Bat Masterson commemorative.
Winchester, model 94, Bicentennial 76, carbine.
Winchester, model 94, Buffalo Bill, carbine.
Winchester, model 94, Buffalo Bill, rifle.
Winchester, model 94, C.M. Russell, Great Western Artist Commemorative Carbine.
Winchester, model 94, Calgary Stampede Commemorative, carbine, cal. .32 Winchester Special.
Winchester, model 94, Canadian 1967, Centennial carbine.
Winchester, model 94, Canadian 1967, Centennial rifle.
Winchester, model 94, "Chief Crazy Horse," commemorative lever action rifle, cal. .38-55, manufactured by U.S. Repeating Arms Co., New Haven, CT.
Winchester, model 94, Colt Commemorative Set, Winchester Signature model "Oliver F. Winchester" carbine, cal. 44-40, Lever Action, as manufactured by U.S. Repeating Arms Co., New Haven, CT.
Winchester, model 94, Cowboy Commemorative, carbine.
Winchester, model 94, Frederick Remington, Great Western Artist Commemorative Carbine.
Winchester, model 94, Illinois Sesquicentennial, carbine.
Winchester, model 94, John Wayne Commemorative (Canadian Issue), carbine, cal. .32-40.
Winchester, model 94, John Wayne commemorative, cal. .32-40, carbine.
Winchester, model 94, Klondike Gold Rush Commemorative carbine.
Winchester, model 94, Legendary Frontiersman rifle, cal. .38-55.
Winchester, model 94, "Limited Edition I".
Winchester, model 94, "Limited Edition II" rifle, cal. .30-30.
Winchester, model 94, Limited Edition, carbine, cal. .30-30, S/Ns 77L1 - 77L1500.
Winchester, model 94, Little Big Horn Centennial, carbine.
Winchester, model 94, Lone Star Commemorative, carbine.
Winchester, model 94, Lone Star Commemorative, rifle, .30-30.
Winchester, model 94, Mounted Police, carbine.
Winchester, model 94, NRA Centennial rifle, .30-30.
Winchester, model 94, Nebraska Centennial, carbine.
Winchester, model 94, One of One Thousand European Rifle commemorative.
Winchester, model 94, Royal Canadian Mounted Police Centennial carbine.
Winchester, model 94, Saskatchewan Diamond Jubilee Carbine commemorative.
Winchester, model 94, The Oliver F. Winchester commemorative.
Winchester, model 94, Theodore Roosevelt, Rifle.
Winchester, model 94, Theodore Roosevelt, carbine.
Winchester, model 94, United States Border Patrol Commemorative carbine cal. .30-30.
Winchester, model 94, Wells Fargo and Company Commemorative, carbines.
Winchester, model 94, Wyoming Diamond Jubilee, carbine.
Winchester, model 94, Yellow Boy Indian, carbine.
Winchester, model 94, cal. .30-30, Antlered Game Commemorative, carbine.
Winchester, model 94, cal. .30-30, Legendary Lawman Commemorative, carbine.
Winchester, model 94, carbine, Canadian Pacific Centennial, cal. .32 Winchester Special.
Winchester, model 94, carbine, Oklahoma Diamond Jubilee Commemorative.
Winchester, model 94, in cal. .38/55.1980, Alberta Diamond Jubilee Commemorative, carbine
Winchester, model 94, model NRA Centennial, carbine.
Winchester, model 94, rifles and carbines manufactured prior to January 2, 1964, and having a S/N of less than 2,700,000, provided their barrel length is at least 16" and their overall length at least 26".
Winchester, model 95, all original, manufactured from 1899 to 1938, with 16" or longer barrel and 26" or longer overall. length.
Winchester, model 1894, Golden Spike, carbine.
*Winchester, model 1894, Texas Sesquicentennial rifle and carbine, cal. .38-55.
Winchester, model 9422, Annie Oakley Commemorative Carbine .22 cal.

Section III
Curios & Relics — Former NFA Firearms

NATIONAL FIREARMS ACT WEAPONS
REMOVED FROM THE ACT AS COLLECTOR'S ITEMS AND
CLASSIFIED AS CURIOS OR RELICS UNDER 18 U.S.C. CHAPTER 44

The Bureau has determined that by reason of the date of their manufacture, value, design and other characteristics, the following firearms are primarily collector's items and are not likely to be used as weapons and, therefore, are excluded from the provisions of the National Firearms Act.

Further, the Bureau has determined that such firearms are also curios or relics as defined in 27 CFR 178.11. Thus, licensed collectors may acquire, hold or dispose to them as curios or relics subject to the provisions of 18 U.S.C. Chapter 44 and 27 CFR Part 178. They are still "firearms" as defined in Chapter 44 of Title 18, U.S.C.

Any military bolt action or semiautomatic rifle manufactured prior to 1946 and

accompanied by a "cup type" grenade launcher designed for the specific rifle.
Belgian, Pre-war manufactured Hi Power pistols, in cal. 9mm having tangent sights graduated to 500 meters, slotted for shoulder stock, having S/Ns of less than 47,000 without letter prefixes or suffixes and accompanied by original Belgian manufactured detachable wooden flat board type shoulder stocks.
Beretta, model 1918/1930, semiautomatic carbine, cal. 9mm, having a barrel length of 12.5" and a magazine capacity of 25 rounds.
Beretta, model 1923, semiautomatic pistol, in cal. 9mm Kurz (.380), accompanied by original Italian detachable leather and metal holster/shoulder stock.
Bergmann-Bayard, model 1908, Pistol, 9mm Bergmann-Bayard with shoulder stock and 4" barrel.
Bergmann, Mars model 1903, self loading pistol, with accompanying shoulder stock.
British PIAT (Projector, Infantry, Anti-tank).
Browning, model 1903, Pistol, 9mm Browning Long, with shoulder stock and 5" barrel.
Browning Hi power pistols, 9mm having tangent sights graduated to 500 meters, slotted for shoulder stock, having S/Ns less than T200,000 etched vertically on the right side of slide, barrel or frame and bearing crest of Emirates of Muscat & Oman, or mirror image of such crest, accompanied by original detachable wooden flat board shoulder stocks.

*Canadian, Inglis No. I, Chinese Contract, Hi Power pistols, cal. 9mm Parabellum, having a tangent rear sight adjustable from 50 to 500 meters, slotted for shoulder stock, and having the letters CH in the S/N and accompanied by original Canadian manufactured detachable wooden holster/shoulder stock.
Clement, Pistol Carbine, cal. 9mm.
Chinese manufactured copies of the Mauser model 1896, semiautomatic pistol, produced prior to 1945, any cal., accompanied by original Chinese manufactured detachable wooden holster/shoulder stocks.
Colt, New Service Revolver, cal. 44/40, w/original smooth bore barrel, S/N 326596.
Colt, Officers model, .38 Special cal., double action revolver, with 6" barrel and a detachable, experimental skeleton shoulder stock and holster combination.
Colt, Single Action Army revolver, cal. .45, with original smoothbore barrel, S/N 325085.
Colt, Single Action Army revolver, S/N 354096, cal. .44/40 having a smooth bored barrel and a barrel length of $7\ ^{1}/_{2}$".
Colt, lightning rifle, original cutaway demonstrator produced by Colt.
Colt, model 1905, Pistol, .45 rimless, with leather holster/shoulder stock and 5 inch barrel.
Colt, model Woodsman, .22 Long Rifle cal., semiautomatic pistol with an experimental 10" barrel and an experimental wooden detachable shoulder stock.
Colt, model Woodsman, .22 Long Rifle cal., semiautomatic pistols, manufactured between 1915 and 1943, together with the original leather detachable holster stocks, manufactured by the N&S Corporation, Ventura, CA.
*Colt, semi automatic pistol, cal. .22 Rimfire, S/Ns 49551 and 49712, accompanied by an original Rifle-ette shoulder stock as originally manufactured by Monarch Arms & Mfg Co, Los Angles, CA in the 1920s.
Czechoslovakian, model C724, semiautomatic pistol, in cal. 9mm Kurz (.380) accompanied by original Czechoslovakian detachable wooden holster/shoulder stock.

Fiala, model 1920, repeating pistol, cal. .22LR in all barrel lengths with accompanying detachable shoulder stock; original copies of the Fiala repeating pistol, marked Schall, Columbia or Botwinick Brothers, cal. .22LR, with accompanying original detachable shoulder stock.
Finnish, model L-35, Lahti, Semiautomatic pistol, in cal. 9mm Parabellum, accompanied by original Finnish detachable wooden holster/shoulder stock.
*Flashlight Revolver, cal. .22 Rimfire, having a rifled barrel, patented on July 10, 1923 and originally manufactured by S. P. Cottrell & Son, Buffalo, NY.
Frommer, model 1912, semiautomatic pistol w/Benke-Thiemann folding shoulder stock.

German, model 1918, (WWI) anti-tank rifle (PzAgew 1918), cal. 13.25mm.
German, (Nazi) Belt Buckle Gun, .22 rimfire, marked "DRP Ausl Pat, Louis Marquis, W. Elberfeld."
German, (Nazi) Belt Buckle Gun, 7.65mm, marked "D.R.P. Angem."
German, Kamphpistole, cal. 26.7mm.
German, Leuchpistole, 26.7mm, Walther pattern, manufactured in or before 1945, with original 23mm rifle grenade launching adapter sleeve.
German, VGl-5 (Volksgewehr), semiautomatic rifle, cal. 7.92mm Kurz, having a barrel length of 14.9" and an overall length of 34.8".
Greener Cattle Killer (Original model) No. B1201, .310 cal.
Greener Cattle Killer (Pocket Pattern) No. B1203, .310 cal.
Greener Safti Killer No. B1216, .22 cal.
Greener Universal Safti Killer No. B1217, .310 cal.

Hamilton, model 7, Rifle.
Hamilton, model 11, Rifle.
Hamilton, model 15, Rifle.
Hamilton, model 19, Rifle.
Hamilton, model 23, Rifle.
Hamilton, model 27 and 027, Rifle.
Hamilton, model 31, Rifle.
Hamilton, model 35, Rifle.
Hamilton, model 39, Rifle.
Hamilton, model 43, Rifle.
Heal, Rifle No. 10, cal. .22
Heal, .22 rimfire cal. rifles, all models, manufactured prior to 1908, by the Heal Rifle Company or the Detroit Rifle Company.
High Standard, model C/S, smoothbore .22 cal. shot semiautomatic pistols, bearing S/Ns 59279 59473 59478 59460 59469
High Standard, model S, smoothbore .22 cal. shot semiautomatic pistols having slides marked: "HI-STANDARD MODEL "S" .22 L.R. SHOT ONLY," & bearing S/Ns 48142 48143 48144 48145 48146 59474 59496 59458 59459
"JGA" (J.G. Anchutz, Ulm, Germany), .22 Flobert single shot pistol.
*Kennedy Repeating Rifle, cal. .44, with 14" barrel, S/N C329.
Krupp, models 1902 & 1906, 50mm Mountain Cannons as produced for the Siamese Government.
Luger, Artillery model, pistols having chamber dates of 1914 through 1918 or 1920, having German Weimar Navy markings consisting of the letter M over an anchor & a German Navy property number accompanied by original Artillery Luger flat board stocks, bearing German Weimar Navy markings of the letter M over an anchor with or without Navy property numbers.
Luger, the 1920 Commercial Artillery model, pistols as manufactured by DWM or Erfurt, having undated chambers, commercial proofmarks, & bearing the inscription Germany or Made in Germany on the receiver & accompanied by original, German manufactured, artillery type, detachable wooden shoulder stocks.
Luger, DWM Pistol, model 1900, 1902, or 1906, in 7.65 Luger or 9mm Parabellum cal., having the American Eagle chamber crest, & barrel lengths of either 4" or $4\ ^{3}/_{4}$" with original detachable Ideal shoulder stocks & Ideal frame grips.
DWM Luger, Original models 1904, 1906, 1908, 1914 & 1920. Naval pistols in 9mm Parabellum or 7.65mm cal., in both the Commercial & Naval military vars.; in both altered & unaltered barrel lengths in the model 1904 & in both altered & unaltered safety markings in the model 1906; w/original board-type detachable shoulder stocks bearing brass or iron discs, with or without markings, or, if without brass or iron discs, being of the Navy flat board-type. This exemption applies only to the listed Naval Luger pistols if mated to the Naval Luger stock & will not apply if the Naval Luger pistol is mated to the Artillery stock. The Naval stock has an overall dimension of $12\ ^{3}/_{4}$," a rear width of $4\ ^{5}/_{8}$," a front width of $1\ ^{1}/_{2}$," a rear thickness of $^{9}/_{16}$," & a front thickness of $1\ ^{3}/_{16}$".

Luger, DWM Stoeger model 1920 & 1923, semiautomatic pistols in 7.65mm or 9mm Parabellum cal., in barrel lengths of 8, 10, 12, & $12\ ^{1}/_{2}$," having either American Eagle chamber crests &/or Stoeger frame &/or upper receiver marks, having either standard, Navy or artillery rear sights, having extractors marked either "Loaded" or "Geladen" & having frame safety markings of either "Gesichert" or "Safe," together w/original commercial flat board stocks of the artillery type, which bear no S/Ns or military proof marks; may include a "Germany" marking.
Luger, DWM Pistol-Carbine, model 1920, 7.65mm or 9mm Parabellum cal., with accompanying original commercial type shoulder stock, with or without forearm piece, having barrel lengths of $11\ ^{3}/_{4}$" to less than 16".
Luger, German model 1914, Artillery model pistol, manufactured by DWM or Erfurt, having chambers dated 1914 through 1918, bearing Imperial German military proofmarks and accompanied by original, German manufactured, artillery type, detachable wooden shoulder stocks.
Luger, model 1902, Pistol-Carbine, 7.65mm Luger with original commercial type shoulder stock and forearm and $11\ ^{3}/_{4}$" barrel.
Luger, Persian (Iranian) Artillery model, pistols, as manufactured by Mauser prior to 1945, accompanied by the original artillery type, detachable wooden shoulder stock, bearing a S/N in Farsi characters stamped into the wood on the left side.
Luger, semiautomatic pistol, certain variations with Benke-Thiemann folding shoulder stock.

MBA, Gyrojet Rocket Guns, cal. 13mm, semiautomatic version only, produced in 1968 or earlier, S/N ranges A0001 through A0032, A001 through A085, B010 through B411, and B5059 through B5692.
Manville, 18-shot-drum, 25mm, semiautomatic tear gas gun.
Marlin, model 93 carbine, cal. .32-40 WCF, with 15" barrel, S/N 426311
*Marlin, model 94, carbine, cal. .32-20, with $15\ ^{1}/_{4}$" barrel, S/N 376900
Marlin, model 94, carbine, cal. .38-40 WCF, with 15" barrel, S/Ns 384186 397215
Marlin, model 94, baby carbine, cal. .44-40 with 15" barrel, S/Ns 324137 401404 401374
Marlin, model 94, carbine, cal. .44-40 with $15\ ^{1}/_{4}$" barrel, S/N 396987
Marlin, model 94, carbine, cal. .44 W.C.F., with $15\ ^{1}/_{4}$" barrel, S/Ns 396987 423099
Marlin, model 1893C, cal. .25/36 with a 15" barrel, S/Ns 193134 284957 320283
Marlin, model 1893C, cal. .30 with a 15" barrel, S/Ns 164888 199669 199690 203990 204585 208526
Marlin, model 1893C, cal. .30/30 with a 15" barrel, S/Ns 228856 237681 244372 256559 256568 256577 256583 256611 258853 261889 261901 269397 269636 281802Rd 281810 291358 336467 336478 336504 336610 338883
Marlin, model 1893C, cal. .32 with a 15" barrel, S/Ns 176656 285305 285331
Marlin, model 1893C, cal. .32/30 with a 15" barrel, S/N 194786
Marlin, model 1893B Carbine, cal. .32/40 with a 15" barrel, S/Ns 336651 336964
Marlin, model 1893C, cal. .38 with a 15" barrel, S/N 167090
Marlin, model 1893, cal. .38/40 with a 15" Rd. barrel, S/N 323928
Marlin, model 1893C, cal. .38/55 with a 15" barrel, S/Ns 194783 246363 275896 336529
Marlin, model 1893 B/C., cal. .38/55 with a 15" barrel, S/N 316309
Marlin, model 1894C, cal. .25 with a 15" barrel, S/Ns 190958 190962 190976
Marlin, model 1894, cal. .25/20 with a 12" Rd. barrel, S/Ns 283149 328901 328925 328928 328937 328958
Marlin, model 1894C, cal. .25/20 with a 15" barrel, S/Ns 211087 280125 280128 280141 280147 283330 287748 294716 328910 337955
Marlin, model 1894, cal. .32/20 with a 15" Rd. barrel, S/N 314652
Marlin, model 1894C, cal. .32/20 with a 15" barrel, S/Ns 190944 190950 190963 190972 217948 282898 282904 287741 287745 287753 287755 287762 287764 287769 287770 287772 294666 294732 301560 325609 328807 328837 328933
Marlin, model 1894C, cal. .32/40 with a 15" barrel, S/N 335434
Marlin, model 1894C, cal. .38 with a 15" barrel, S/Ns 195570 199975 200007 200022 215011 216412 282004 282936 282997
Marlin, model 1894, cal. .38/40 with a 14" Rd. barrel, S/N 324849
Marlin, model 1894, cal. .38/40 with a 15" Rd. barrel, S/Ns 310864 316798 324195 324238
Marlin, model 1894C, cal. .38/40 with a 14" Rd. barrel, S/N 326718
Marlin, model 1894C, cal. .38/40 with a 15" barrel, S/Ns 285870 285974 285979 285990 286281 287729 300626 318000 321957 321970 321973 321985 321986 321990 322025 322035 322037 322053 322077 322079 322082 322095 325732 325740 326143 326726 330543
Marlin, model 1894C, cal. .38/40 with a 15" Rd. barrel, S/Ns 322514 323672 323688 323785 323810 323846 323925 326206
Marlin, model 1894C, cal. .44/40 with a 14" Oct. barrel, S/N 322641
Marlin, model 1894 rifle, cal. .44/40 w/a 15" Rd. barrel, S/N 302059
Marlin, model 1894, cal. .44/40 with a 15" Rd. barrel, S/Ns 305795 324290 324855 324864
Marlin, model 1894, cal. .44/40 with a 15" barrel, S/N 317706
Marlin, model 1894C, cal. .44/40 with a 15" Rd. barrel, S/Ns 323752 323776 323803 323822 324056

Section III (cont.) Marlin through Winchester

Marlin, model 1894C, cal. .44 with a 15" Rd. barrel, S/N 185174

Marlin, model 1894C, cal. .44 with a 15" barrel, S/Ns 169854 181852 181863
181911 181967 182048 182068 182093 182205 182219 182226 182321 182322
182344 183374 183376 183379 183400 183401 183403 183408 183413 183418
183428 183432 183433 185128 185129 185133 185145 185150 185155 185165
185167 185175 185185 185186 185187 185192 191033 191006 191097 191098
191099 191100 191101 191104 191105 191106 191424 195823 195840 195842
196827 197867 200830 200903 200906 200922 200928 200929 200930 200958
203760 203761 203763 203766 203767 203769 203771 203772 203773 203774
203778 203780 203781 203782 203784 203785 203787 203788 203789 203796
203798 203806 203811 203812 203813 203818 203822 203824 203826 204395
204398 204403 204404 204407 204411 204414 204415 204419 204421 204426
204427 204428 204429 204430 204499 205727 210260 210269 211064 215017
215019 215020 215030 215037 215043 215054 215058 215063 215068 215070
215071 215079 216340 216348 216357 216363 216366 216368 216416 216423
216424 216425 219240 219253 219254 219273 219288 232678 232950 232999
232981 233240 233299 233344 233403 233519 233535 233543 233549 233592
233712 276239 282927 282945 283260 285999 286011 286018 286019 299662
299689 300800 300629 300634 322126 322135 322112 322116 322185 322209
325635 325667 325677 325779 325850 325857 325867 325881 326003 333635

Marlin, model 1894, cal. .44/40 with a 14" Oct. barrel, S/Ns 316617 316628
316632 316645 316649 316654 316656 316739 316772 316803 317427 317449
317466 317470 317499 317559 317573 317578 317582 317587 317596 317646
317687 317690 317693 317697

Marlin, model 1894C, cal. .44/40 with a 15" Rd. barrel, S/Ns 271131 271328
271330 271331 276170

Marlin, model 1894C, cal. .44/40 with a 15" barrel, S/Ns 215023 215059 216350
219291 219295 232948 232964 232997 233001 233010 233281 233355 233369
233396 233481 233530 233600 233632 233695 233733 233781 233798 234308
238716 238720 276129 276138 276156 276162 276177 276183 276189 276195
276218 276226 276228 276249 276254 276255 276258 276262 276264 276265
279683 285876 285943 285946 285961 286250 295694 295725 297384 297473
297598 297639 299635 299643 299648 299670 299676 300302 300656 300685
300690 300698 300705 300709 300719 300738 300744 300754 300777 300780
300793 300806 300832 300834 300850 300904 300905 300917 300918 300927
300931 300936 300951 300955 300967 301844 301857 301863 301866 301867
301896 301924 301942 301961 301976 301981 302015 302102 302149 302209
302224 302239 302246 302341 304526 306179 307210 312344 312358 312367
312370 312371 312377 312378 312382 312384 312387 312391 312393 312403
312415 312419 312420 312423 312425 312427 312435 312437 312438 312443
312445 312446 312451 313218 317710 317713 317723 317726 317728 317742
317744 317750 317751 317761 317796 317802 317817 317832 318000 318012
318023 318029 318042 318043 318044 318045 318046 318048 318054 318792
321954 321955 321956 321962 321972 321974 321975 321977 321978 321979
321988 321994 322002 322015 322019 322021 322028 322046 322048 322065
322066 322076 322087 322088 322103 322114 322123 322140 322144 322147
322149 322154 322157 322162 322175 322176 322178 322181 322182 322183
322184 322186 322187 322189 322190 322191 322192 322194 322195 322197
322198 322202 322203 322205 322208 322210 322211 322212 322222 322226
322231 322244 322249 322259 322260 322261 322269 322273 322274 322279
322283 322285 322311 323918 323968 324030 324144 325036 325048 325622
325653 325700 325817 325861 325896 325908 325965 326047 326060 326108
326116 326121 326130 326139 326187 326214 330307 330308 330310 330311
330312 330313 330314 330316 330317 330318 330319 330320 330321 330324
330325 330327 330332 330333 330336 330337 330339 330341 330429 330446
330465 330466 330468 330476 330478 330479 330480 330481 330487 330491
330492 330494 330496 330599 330614 330616 330621 330624 330625 330628
330644 331269 331298 338420 338450 338593 338598 338665

Marlin, model 1895C, cal. .38/56 with a 15" barrel, S/N 167406

Marlin, model 1895C, cal. .40/65 with a 15" barrel, S/Ns 313644 315054

Marlin, model 1895C, cal. .45/70 with a 15" barrel, S/Ns 313669 313673 313683
313684 313688

Mauser, commercial Luger Artillery model semiautomatic pistols cal. 9mm, Mauser banner marked, produced under contract for the Royal Thai Police accompanied by original, German manufactured, detachable wooden shoulder stocks.

Mauser, model 1896 semiautomatic pistol accompanied by original German manufactured detachable wooden holster/shoulder stocks, all semiautomatic German manufactured variations produced prior to 1940, any cal.

Mauser, Pistol-Carbine, model 1896, 7.63mm, with shoulder stock and 11 $^{3}/_{4}$" to 16" barrel.

Mauser, model 1902, 6 and 10 shot magazine capacity, semiautomatic pistols in cal. 7.63 x 25mm (.30 Mauser), having the distinctive hammer safety, barrel lengths of either 3.9 or 5.5," and accompanied by an original detachable wooden holster/shoulder stock.

Mauser, model 1912/14, Pistol, 9mm Mauser short or .45 ACP, with original detachable wooden holster/shoulder stock and 5" barrel.

E. Mayer single shot handgun, no S/N, cal .38-55 smoothbore, barrel length 14 $^{1}/_{2}$"

Military type Nambu pistol, model 1904, cal. 8mm Nambu with an accompanying original detachable telescoping wooden holster/shoulder stock.

One Pocket Creedmores and other original pocket rifles with extension shoulder stocks, cal. .22, made by Samuel Watson Johnson (1838-1903).

OSS Glove Pistol, cal. .38 S&W or .38 special.

OSS "Liberator" pistol, .45 ACP or 9mm.

Remington Flare (Very) Pistol, Mark III, 10 gauge.

Royal, semiautomatic pistol, cal. 7.63 x 25mm (.30 Mauser) having an integral 10 or 20 round magazine, 5 $^{1}/_{2}$," 6 $^{1}/_{4}$," or 7 $^{1}/_{8}$" barrel, and accompanied by an original Spanish manufactured detachable holster/stock.

Sedgley, Mark V, 10 gauge, signal pistol.

The Shatuck "Unique" palm gun in .22 and .32 cal. rimfire.

Smith & Wesson, model Military and Police revolver, cal. .38, S/N 112037, with original Ideal holster/shoulder stock.

Smith & Wesson, model 40, Light Rifle, cal. 9mm Parabellum.

Spanish Star, model A, semiautomatic pistol in cals. 7.63 Mauser, 9mm Parabellum, 9mm Long, .38 ACP and .45 ACP, accompanied by original Spanish manufactured detachable wooden holster/shoulder stock.

Spanish manufactured copies of the Mauser, model 1896, semiautomatic pistol produced prior to 1946 in cal. 7.63mm or 9mm and having either integral or detachable magazines; accompanied by original Spanish manufactured detachable wooden holster/shoulder stock.

Stevens, Rifle, No. 20, with smooth bore barrel for .22 and .32 rimfire shot cartridges.

Stevens, Reliable Pocket Rifle, second issue, cal. .22 long rifle or .22 Stevens-Pope.

Stevens, New model Pocket Rifle, first issue, cal. .22.

Stevens, New model Pocket Rifle, second issue, cal. .22 short, long or long rifle rimfire, .22 WRF, .32 long centerfire.

Stevens, New model Pocket Rifle No. 40, cal.: .22 long, rifle, .22 WRF, .22 Stevens-Pope, and .32 long centerfire.

Steven, Hunter's Pet No. 34 Pocket Rifle, cal. .22 short rimfire to .44-40 WCF.

Stevens, Vernier Hunter's Pet No. 34 $^{1}/_{2}$ Pocket Rifle, cal. .22 short-.44-40 WCF.

Stevens, Vernier New model Pocket Rifle 40 $^{1}/_{2}$, cal. .22 long rifle, .22 WRF, .22 Stevens-Pope, .32 long centerfire.

Stevens, 1898 New model Pocket Shotgun, in cals. .38-40 and .44-40.

Stevens, Number 39, New model Pocket Shotgun, in cals. .38-40 and .44-40.

Stevens, 44 $^{1}/_{2}$ rifle, .22 cal. S/N 11006 with two piece barrel owned by A.O. Neidner, Malden, MA.

Steyr Hahn, model 1911/12, semiautomatic pistol, cal. 9mm Steyr or 9mm Parabellum w/5" barrel & accompanied by an original European detachable holsterstock.

Strong, Breech Loading Salute Cannon, 10 gauge, manufactured by Strong Firearms Co., New Haven, CT after 1898.

Swedish, model P-40 Lahti, semiautomatic pistol, in cal. 9mm Parabellum, accompanied by original Swedish detachable wooden holster/shoulder stock.

The Taylor "Fur Getter" manufactured by the F.C. Taylor Fur Company, St. Louis, MO, .22 cal. rimfire.

U.S., Mark II, 10 gauge signal pistols.

Walther, model 1937, Pistol, "Armee Pistols," 9mm Parabellum, with original detachable shoulder stock and 4.9" barrel.

Webley & Scott Pistol, Mark I, No. 2, .455 cal., with original detachable shoulder stock.

Winchester, model 36, shotgun, 9mm rimfire.

Winchester, model 1873, carbine, cal. .32-20 WCF, w/14" barrel, S/N 695081B

Winchester, model 1873, carbine, cal. .44-40 WCF, w/14" barrel, S/N 719510B

Winchester, model 1873, carbine, cal. .44-40 WCF, w/15" barrel, S/N 579080B

*Winchester, model 1873, carbine, cal. .44-40 w/14" barrel, S/N 710976B

Winchester, model 1885, single short rifle, cal. .25/35, w/15" number 3 round barrel, shotgun butt, plain pistol grip & Winchester Express sight, S/N 104783

Winchester, model 1892, carbine, cal. .25-20 WCF, w/14" barrel, S/Ns 575644
765952 818777 859912 903891 940986

Winchester, model 1892, carbine, cal. .25-20 WCF, w/15" barrel, S/Ns *512237
692609 846245

Winchester, model 1892, carbine, cal. .32-20 WCF, w/15" barrel, S/N *475520
490150 *807957

Winchester, model 1892, carbine, cal. .32-20, w/14" barrel, S/N 615287 808290
826022 837181 *850556 960471

Winchester, model 1892, carbine, cal. .38-40 WCF, w/14" barrel, S/Ns 288562
*475736 *653874 679709 847750 848745 848873 850811 887641 998845

Winchester, model 1892, carbine, cal. .38-40 WCF, w/15" barrel, S/Ns 179252
408307 804878 *832039 842788 843000

Winchester, model 1892, carbine, cal. .44-40 WCF, w/14" barrel, S/Ns 268828
*319250 320567 *323300 *323428 324318 *340471 *349471 446526 475736 495045
583403 600903 710267 743634 820170 *823943 *842679 852636 *861856 895062
898838 898938 921643 948932 *976596 977351 977828 978462 *979227 979429
*980097 981212 982483 984073 987239 *987305 989144 993799 999398

Winchester, model 1892, carbine, cal. .44-40 WCF, w/15" barrel, S/Ns 381573
*414906 518748 659700 *756846 816422 881573 896494 905158 954796 977103
*997305 988160 990107 994171 998059 998419 998461 998679 998761 998852
998844

Winchester, model 1894, carbine, cal. .25-35 WCF, w/14" barrel, S/N 865268

Winchester, model 1894, carbine, cal. .25-35 WCF, w/15" barrel, S/Ns 542097
589609

Winchester, model 1894, carbine, cal. .30-30 WCF, w/14" barrel, S/Ns 505307
793359 805815 864415

Winchester, model 1894, carbine, cal. .30-30 WCF, w/15" barrel, S/Ns 273691
315250 318257 324318 360587 *368971 433426 444269 *447421 464604 467286
481877 *495342 593839 662192 701730 758406 794467 806780 820101 820375
*839880 840123 862245 868769 870637 *871276 883055 884272 885975 887409
910758 938370 952507 959421 973001 973063 986621 990851 991114 *995540
*995578 995675 998829 1004615 1004958 1009373*1013465 1013515 1017305 1017946
1017950*1021495 1032798 1033898 1033973 1034037 1040905 1046737 1051727 1052211
*1052749 1052851*1052982 1059318 1066951 1068292 1072755 1090460

Winchester, model 1894 carbine, cal. .32 WSPL, w/14" barrel, S/N 781211

Winchester, model 1894 carbine, cal. .32 Winchester Special w/ 15" barrel, S/N
437440 860098 880845 1006715

Winchester, model 1894 carbine, cal. .32-40, w/15" barrel, S/N 807261

Winchester, model 1894 carbine, cal. .38-55 WCF, w/15" barrel, S/N 247646

Winchester, 1902, pistol made from a rifle, cal. .22, produced at factory, having no S/N, but having a decorated stock & accompanied by documents denoting its use by Mr. Ned Tupperwein.

Section IIIa
Former Curios & Relics
(Former NFA Firearms Now Classified as Antiques)

ANTIQUES: NATIONAL FIREARMS ACT WEAPONS
REMOVED FROM THE ACT AS COLLECTOR'S ITEMS --
ALSO REMOVED FROM CHAPTER 44 OF TITLE 18, UNITED STATES CODE

The following firearms were removed from the National Firearms Act as collector's items and classified as curios or relics under 18 U.S.C. Chapter 44. However, since they are antiques as defined in Chapter 44, they should not have been classified as curios or relics. Since they are no longer NFA weapons and are antiques under Chapter 44, they are not subject to GCA provisions:

Any pistol or revolver, manufactured in or before 1898, originally designed to accept a shoulder stock, and accompanied by an original shoulder stock.
Belgian, Cane Gun, 41 cal. rimfire.
Bergmann, model 1897, cal. 7.65mm (7.8mm) pistol with accompanying shoulder stock.
Borchardt, model 1893, cal. 7.63mm pistol with accompanying shoulder stock.
Chicago, palm pistol, cal. .32 rimfire extra short.
Frank Wesson, Bicycle Rifle with accompanying shoulder stock.
Gaulois, palm squeezer, 8mm short "Little All Right" palm pistol, .22 cal. rimfire patented by Edward Boardman and Andrew Peavey, January 18, 1876.
Mannlicher, Pistol-Carbine, model 1896, 7.63mm Mannlicher, with rifle type shoulder stock and forearm and 11 3/4" barrel.

Marlin, model 1889C, cal. .32 with a 15" barrel, S/Ns   45952   69571   70624
```
70678   70729   70737   70738   80884   85429   96169
```
Marlin, model 1889C, cal. .38 with a 15" barrel, S/Ns   53545   63448   63476
```
63478   69566   69568   69569   69657   69660   73133   73715   73742   83805
83875   83892   83949   83957   83984   83986   88942
```
Marlin, model 1889C, cal. .44 with a 15" barrel, S/Ns   40013   40021   40074
```
40083   40084   40089   44305   44306   44313   44324   44327   44430   44432
44335   44336   44338   44343   44345   44347   44348   44351   44360   44366
44369   44372   46621   46641   46709   46743   46765   46876   48997   49009
49012   49016   49019   49026   49029   49031   51902   51912   52022   52023
52029   52031   52038   52039   52043   53304   53318   53360   53376   53392
53393   55365   55820   59140   59792   61252   61265   61347   61350   61903
61904   61929   61932   31935   61972   61982   61985   63440   63458   63???
63735   63747   63761   63763   65070   66071   66329   66415   66819   66841
66842   66910   66852   66888   67397   67402   67403   67406   67433   67436
67454   67457   67460   67513   67518   68599   68612   68620   70779   70784
70821   70830   70832   72848   73049   73083   73085   73090   73151   73159
73160   73181   73195   73208   73216   73218   73713   73729   73733   73735
73749   73750   73751   73764   73768   73772   73774   73776   73789   73814
73824   73838   73842   73848   73853   81046   81052   81063   81077   81084
81092   81099   81119   81187   81194   83456   83471   83472   83484   83493
83499   83501   83513   83514   83515   83520   83533   83542   83543   83554
83559   83632   83679   83691   83859   83870   83930   83933   83937   83950
83953   83954   83964   83969   86458   86506   86674   86697   86745   86746
86782   86786   86795   88938   89484   89485   89491   89503   89523   89534
89535   89541   89562   89584   89587   89609   89818   89823   89831   90012
90013   90016   90021   90037   90053   90055   90072   90075   90706   91389
91496   91520   91657   91672   91819   91842   91869   91887   91889   91918
91949   91962   91974   91981   91983   91984   91990   91995   92009   92010
92011   92012   92030   92044   92061   92074   92078   92079   92104   92106
92116   92133   92137   92142   92144   92154   92170   92172   92178   92193
92197   92198   92213   92218   92224   99751   99753   99758   99766   99819
99820   99869   99885   99967   99972   99974   99992   99994   100003  100009
100021  100086  100228  108487  108513  108517  108526  108532  108537  108541
108546  108554  108555  108557  108567  108570  108571  108572  108575  108577
                                                    108579  108581  108585
```
Marlin, model 1893C, cal. .25/36 with a 15" barrel, S/N   124940
Marlin, model 1893C, cal. .30/30 with a 15" barrel, S/Ns   161903   162931
Marlin, model 1893C, cal. .32 with a 15" barrel, S/Ns   107944   107948   107950
```
                                                        107958   107970   176191
```
Marlin, model 1893C, cal. .32/40 with a 15" barrel, S/Ns   103641   103643   124405
```
                                    131030   142050   147669   162785   162810
```
Marlin, model 1893C, cal. .32/50 with a 15" barrel, S/N   96935
Marlin, model 1893C, cal. .38/40 with a 15" barrel, S/N   147644
Marlin, model 1893C, cal. .38/55 with a 15" barrel, S/Ns   96930   96938   96942
```
103642   103648   103660   103661   103666   103670   133880   147658   147638
```
Marlin, model 1894C, cal. .25/20 with a 15" barrel, S/Ns 148157   148173   148183
```
                                                                            148217
```
Marlin, model 1894C, cal. .25 with a 15" barrel, S/Ns   137247   137248   137250
```
137252  137256  137261  140941  146754  146755  146756  146757  146758  146759
147678  147681  147682  147688  147694  147699  147700  147701  147703  151981
                                                                            174745
```

Marlin, model 1894C, cal. .32 with a 15" barrel, S/Ns   47431   84993   126545
```
129211  129221  129227  130657  134113  134118  134126  135406  135407  137124
137125  137129  137130  137131  137133  137136  137137  137138  137139  137145
137146  137147  137149  137151  137156  140876  140877  140892  140899  140903
140907  140909  140921  140922  140924  140927  140931  140934  140942  140943
140945  142038  142039  147206  147704  148147  148153  148155  148158  148178
148183  148184  148194  148197  148200  148201  148207  149209  148212  148214
```
Marlin, model 1894C, cal. .38 with a 15" barrel, S/Ns   109874   111674   115770
```
115772  126799  126858  126907  126953  127093  127180  127382  133190  133260
133491  134348  133645  134363  134364  134446  134495  134526  134565  137669
142371  142374  142379  142389  145783  145784  145787  145788  145789  145790
145792  145793  145794  145796  145798  145799  145800  145806  145813  147629
147630  147631  147632  147633  147634  150482  150483  150486  150576  151586
151594  151651  151721  151726  151737  151746  151748  151751  151753  151761
151923  151987  152004  152043  152057  152066  152070  169850  169851  169852
                                                            169856  169855
```
Marlin, model 1894C, cal. .44 with a 15" barrel, S/Ns   109588   111398   111696
```
111789  111794  111813  115362  115363  115365  115378  115383  115385  115388
115392  115393  115400  115403  115407  115408  115412  115413  115414  115418
115419  115421  115433  115436  115438  115439  115449  115451  115453  115457
115458  115459  115473  115476  115487  115489  115496  115499  115616  115622
115644  115649  115651  115662  115710  115723  115743  115822  120065  120094
120107  120115  120118  120119  120126  120133  120137  120139  120145  120146
120149  120161  120213  120227  120228  120239  120243  120270  120273  120276
120292  120296  120469  120496  120504  120505  120523  120534  120549  121549
121933  124704  124651  124662  124671  124725  124734  126787  126843  126851
127149  127251  127300  133605  134090  134376  134543  137725  137734  137765
137495  137614  142367  142368  142373  142376  142377  142380  142390  142402
144194  144197  144198  144272  144296  145687  145689  145693  148154  150568
150181  150260  150369  150371  150380  150384  150385  150406  150420  150421
150430  150462  150471  150568  151047  151074  151082  151086  151087  151091
151092  151094  151096  151097  151101  151107  151113  151134  151137  151140
151144  151145  151151  151158  151187  151193  151106  151214  151227  151242
151243  151619  151600  151031  151632  151698  151723  151724  151730  151733
151735  151744  151756  151757  151760  151764  151790  151792  151797  151994
151997  152020  152022  152075  169854  169914  169940  169971  169972  169986
                                                            170002  170025  170138
```

Marlin, model 1894, cal. .44, with a 15" barrel, S/N   151743
Merveilleux, squeezer pistol, 6mm and 8mm short.
Peavey, A.J., Knife Gun, .22 short rimfire.
Protector palm gun, .32 rimfire extra short, patented by Jacques Tubiaux, Patent No. 732644.

Quackenbrush Bicycle Rifle, with telescopic wire stock, .22 cal.
Remington, Cane Gun, model 1, .22 rimfire.
Remington, Cane Gun, model 2, .32 rimfire.
Stevens, Old model Pocket Rifle, .22 short or long rimfire.
Stevens, Reliable Pocket Rifle, first issue, cal. .22 short, long or long rifle.
Stevens, New Model Pocket Rifle, first issue, in cal. .32 short or long rimfire.
Stevens, New Model Pocket Rifle, 2nd issue, in cals. .25 Stevens or .32 long rimfire.
Stevens, New Model Pocket Rifle No. 40, in cal. .25 Stevens or .32 long rimfire.
Stevens, New Model Pocket shotgun, in cal. .44-50 Everlasting.
Stevens, Vernier, New Model Pocket Rifle, cal. .22 short, .22 long rifle, .22 WRF, 32. long rimfire.
Stevens, Vernier, New Model Pocket Rifle, No. 40 1/2, in cal. .25 Stevens or .32 long rimfire.
Tribuzio, "Squeezer" invented by Catello Tribuzio of Turin, Italy, cal. 8mm short.
Winchester, model 73 carbine, cal. .44 WCF, w/15" barrel, S/Ns   92842A   127884
```
198040B  235014B  247094B  263826B  336514B  336549  380061  486139B  520569
```

Winchester, model 1873 carbine, cal. .32-20-WCF, w/original 15" barrel, S/N
382027
Winchester, model 1873 carbine, cal. .38-40 WCF, w/original 14" barrel, S/N
514709

Winchester, model 1885 cal. .38-40 WCF, w/15" barrel, S/N   79085
Winchester, model 1885 carbine, cal. .44-40 WCF, w/original, 15" barrel, S/Ns
79256   83304

Winchester, model 92 carbine, cal. .38-40 WCF, w/15" barrel, S/N   43844
Winchester, model 92 carbine, cal. .44-40 WCF, w/15" barrel, S/Ns   51976   95516
158145

Winchester, model 1892 carbine, cal. .32-20 WCF, w/14" barrel, S/N   50480
Winchester, model 94, cal. .30-30 WCF, w/15" barrel, S/N   42771

Section IV
Curios & Relics — NFA Firearms

NATIONAL FIREARMS ACT WEAPONS CLASSIFIED AS
CURIOS OR RELICS UNDER 18 U.S.C. CHAPTER 44

The Bureau has determined that the following National Firearms Act weapons are curios or relics as defined in 27 CFR 178.11 because of their dates of manufacture. These National Firearms Act weapons, classified as curios or relics, are still subject to all the controls under the National Firearms Act. However, licensed collectors may acquire hold or dispose of them as curios or relics subject to the provisions of 18 U.S.C. Chapter 44 and 27 CFR Part 178. They are still "firearms" as defined in the National Firearms Act and Chapter 44 of Title 18, U.S.C.

Alarm Pistol, S/N IRS-3591, cal. .22 rimfire, marked Patent Pending about 1883, which rings an alarm bell and also fires a cartridge when set to do so.
*Armalite, AR 10, 1955, cal. 7.62mm NATO submachinegun, made by the Armalite Div. of Fairchild Engine & Airplane Co., Costa Mesa, CA prior to 1961.
Astra, model 901, selective fire pistol, cal. 7.63mm (.30 Mauser).
Astra, model 902, selective fire pistol, cal. 7.63mm (.30 Mauser).
Astra, model 903, selective fire pistol, cal. 7.63mm (.30 Mauser).
Astra, model F, selective fire pistol, cal. 9mm Bergmann.
Azul, selective fire pistol, cal. 7.63mm (.30 Mauser), copy of Mauser model 1896 pistol.
Australian, Austen MK I and MK II Submachineguns, cal. 9mm, manufactured in Australia prior to 1946.
Australian, Owen MK I and MK II Submachineguns, cal. 9mm, manufactured in Australia prior to 1946.
Austrian, Swartzlose machinegun, model 1905 & 1907/1912, cal. 8mm.
Austrian, Steyr-Solothurn model MP-30 and MP-34 submachineguns as originally manufactured by Steyr-Daimler-Puch of Steyr-Austria, prior to 1946.
Auto Ordnance, WWII commemorative Thompson model 1928, cal. .45.
Auto Ordnance, Korean War Commemorative Thompson model 1928, cal. .45.
Benet Mercie, machine rifle, model 1909 (French and American manufacture), cal. 8mm Lebel or .30.
Boys, MK1, cal. .55 , anti-tank rifle.
*Brevettata, model F.N.A.- B 1943, submachinegun, cal. 9mm Parabellum, with an 8" barrel, S/N 5391.
*Browning automatic rifle (BAR), model 1918A2, manufactured by New England Arms Corporation prior to 1946.
Bren, light machineguns, any model, any cal., British Commonwealth manufacture.
British, Lanchester (Lancaster) Mk 1 and Mk 1, 9mm, submachineguns manufactured in England, during World War II.
British, STEN submachineguns Mk. I, Mk. II, Mk. III, Mk. IV & Mk. V, cal. 9mm, original British Commonwealth Military issue only.
Canadian, EX1 and EX2 experimental series of the FN FAL in cal. 7.62mm NATO, as manufactured by Fabrique Nationale, Herstal, Belgium, for the Canadian Government.
Cane Gun, cane with horn handle, silver tipped, wood covered steel, breech loading, smooth bore barrel, S/N IRS-5834, cal. .32 centerfire.
Cane Gun, English walking stick, bamboo covered steel rifled barrel with horn handle, S/N IRS-3589, cal. .38 centerfire.
Cane Gun, S/N IRS-3587, cal. .410 centerfire.
*Chinese manufactured copy of the U.S. 60mm mortar manufactured prior to 1946.
Chinese, Type 24 (Maxim) machinegun, cal. 7.92mm, Chinese manufacture.
Chinese, Type 26 light machinegun.
Colt, machinegun, model 1895, any cal.
Colt, machinegun, model 1914, any cal.
Colt, model MG38 and MG38B, water cooled machinegun any cal. manufactured by Colt.
Colt, model 1919 auto rifle.
Colt, Monitor model machine rifle, cal. 30-06, commercial version of the BAR, 18" barrel, vertical pistol grip, Cutts compensator, manufactured by Colt.
Crescent, Certified Shotgun .410 gauge, w/12 $1/4$" barrel and pistol grip.
Czechoslovakian, model ZB 26 and ZB 30 light machinegun.
Danish, Madsen machineguns, all models produced prior to 1946; all cals.
Danish, Madsen, model 1946, submachineguns.
Danish, Madsen, model 1950, submachineguns.
Degtyarev-PTRD 1941, 14.5mm anti-tank rifle.
Enfield, military bolt action rifle cut-a-ways, having barrels of less than 16".
Fabrique Nationale, model BAR, full automatic rifle, all cals., as manufactured by Fabrique Nationale, Herstal, Belgium.
Federal Laboratories, 12 Gauge Gas Billy, all variations.
French, 25mm anti-tank cannon SA-L mil. 1937, commonly known as French models 34 SA and 37A.
French, Chatellerault model 1924/29 machineguns, cal. 7.5mm.
French, C.S.R.G. (Chauchat) machinegun model 1915, cal. 8mm Lebel.
French, C.S.R.G. (Chauchat) machinegun, model 1918, cal. .30.
French, model MAT 49, submachinegun, cal. 9mm.
French, model 37, 50mm (1.97 in.) mortar - also designated as a German, model 203(f), 5cm (1.97 in.) mortar.
French, model 34 SA & 37A, antitank cannon 1937 in 25mm.
French, model 1934 M39 (Mle 34 K39), cal. 7.5 x 54mm, aircraft machinegun.
Franchi, model 1962 Semiautomatic carbines, cal. 9mm.
French, St. Etienne machinegun, model 1907, cal. 8mm. Lebel.
Finnish, Tampella (original), model 1938, cal. 81mm mortars.
German, assault rifles selective fire, produced during 1941 through 1945, in cal. 7.92mm Kurz (7.92 x 33mm) including MP - 43 per EMO.
German, Bergmann model 1915 water cooled machinegun, cal. 7.92mm.

German, Bergmann model 1915, an air cooled machinegun cal. 7.92mm.
German, Bergmann, MP-34, 9mm, machine pistol.
German, Bergmann, MP-35/I, 9mm, machine pistol.
German, BUCO hand firing device, cal. 12mm (.44 cal.).
German, Dreyse model 1918 water cooled machinegun, cal. 7.92mm.
German, Erma (EMP), or MPE, 9mm, machine pistol.
German, Gast machinegun, cal. 7.9mm.
German, FG42 Parachutists rifle, cal. 7.92mm, manufactured prior to 1946.
German, MG 15 anti aircraft machinegun 7.92mm made before 1945.
German, MG 15 machineguns, cal. 7.92mm, made prior to 1945.
German, 15cm Nebelwerfer, 41 (150-mm) Rocket Launcher.
German, Parabellum machinegun, model 1913, 1914 and LMG 14/17, cal. 7.9mm.
German, Raketenpanzerbuchse 43 (8.8cm, RPzB43), German model 43, 88mm Rocket Launcher.
German, Raketenpanzerbuchse 54 (8.8cm, RPzB54), German model 54, 88mm Rocket Launcher.
German, Schmeisser, MP-28/II, 9mm, machine pistol.
German, Steyr-Solothurn, 9mm, machine pistol.
German, submachinegun, model MP18-1, cal. 9mm Parabellum.
German, MG 34 light machinegun, cal. 7.92mm.
German, MP38 submachinegun, cal. 9mm Parabellum, manufactured by B. Geipel (Erma) prior to 1941.
German, MP40 submachinegun, cal. 9mm, manufactured from 1940 - 1945 for the German military forces.
German, MG 42 light machinegun, produced prior to 1946, cal. 7.92mm.
German, 7.5cm Pak 40 anti-tank gun (75mm).
German, 7.5cm Pak 39 anti-tank gun (75mm).
German, 7.5cm Stuk assault gun (75mm).
German, 7.5cm Kw.K 40 tank gun (75mm).
German, 8mm MG 81 and MG 81Z aircraft Machineguns.
German, 15/20mm MG 151 Aircraft Machineguns (all variations).
German, 30mm MG 108 Aircraft Machineguns/Cannons.
German, 13mm Rheinmetal-Borsig model 131, Aircraft Machineguns (all variations).
H & A A. Company, 16 gauge, set gun.
Harrington & Richardson (H&R), .410 gauge, "Handy Gun," with a 12 $1/4$" barrel.
High Standard, USA model HD, .22 1r cal. pistols, originally equipped with silencers for issue to the OSS & other military agencies, S/N range 109110 - 153890.
Hotchkiss, light machinegun, British model 1909 Mark 1 and Mark 1, cal. .303.
Hotchkiss, models 1897, 1900 & 1914 machineguns of French manufacture in all cals.
Italian, Breda model 1930 machineguns, all cals.
Italian, Breda Safat, model 1935, 7mm aircraft machinegun, manufactured by Societa Anonima Ernesto Breda, Brescia, Italy, prior to 1946.
Italian, Breda model 1937 heavy machinegun, cal. 8mm.
Italian, Cannone anticarro e d'accompagnamento 47/32 M1935, cal. 47mm, all variations and manufacturers.
Italian, model 38A, 9mm Parabellum submachinegun, manufactured by Pietro Beretta SpA, Gardone-val Trompia, Italy, prior to 1946.
Italian, model 38/42, 9mm parabellum, by Beretta SpA, Gardone-val Trompia, Italy prior to 1946.
Italian, Fiat Revelli model 1935 machinegun, cal. 8mm.
Italian, Revelli model 1914 machinegun, cal. 6.5mm.
Italian, Villar Perosa submachinegun, model 1915, 1916 & 1917, cal. 9mm Parabellum.
Ithaca, "Auto and Burglar Guns," manufactured by Ithaca Gun Company from 1922, to 1933, all original guns.
Japanese, experimental submachinegun "Bullpup" cal. 8mm Nambu.
Japanese, model 38 Field Cannon.
Japanese, (model 1921 Browning Type), aircraft fixed machinegun, cal. 12.7mm.
Japanese, model 94, 37mm gun manufactured prior to 1946.
Japanese, modified Bergmann (SIG), submachinegun, cal. 7.63mm, featuring bayonet mounting lug.
Japanese, Type 1 (1941), aircraft flexible machinegun, cal. 7.92mm, twin barrel type Japanese, Type 3 (1927), heavy machinegun, cal. 6.5mm. twin barrel type.
Japanese, model 10 & 89, 50 mm grenade dischargers.
Japanese, Type 11 (1922) light machinegun, all variations, cal. 6.5mm.
Japanese, Type 38 (1905) machinegun (Hotchkiss) cal. 6.5mm.
Japanese, Type 89 (1929) Vickers pattern machineguns, cal. 7.7mm.
Japanese, Type 91 (1931), tank machineguns (modified Type 11), cal. 6.5mm.
Japanese, Type 92 (1932), heavy machinegun, Hotchkiss pattern cal. 7.7mm.
Japanese, Type 92 (1932), light machinegun or aircraft machinegun, Lewis pattern, cal. 7.7mm.
Japanese, Type 92 (1932), tank machinegun, cal. 13.2mm.
Japanese, Type 93 (1938), aircraft machinegun cal. 7.29mm.
Japanese, Type 94, 37mm gun, manufactured prior to 1946.
Japanese, Type 96 (1936), light machinegun, cal. 6.5mm.
Japanese, Type 97 (1937), tank machinegun, cal. 7.7mm.
Japanese, Type 98, 7.92 aircraft machinegun, Japanese manufactured prior to 1946.
Japanese, Type 99 (1939), light machinegun, all vars., cal. 7.7mm.
Japanese, Type 100 (1940), aircraft flexible machinegun, cal. 7.92mm, twin barrel type.
Japanese, Type 100 submachinegun, cal. 8mm Nambu, all vars.
Japanese, 12.7 (13)mm Browning HO-103 Machineguns.
Japanese, 20mm Browning Aircraft HO-5 Machineguns/Cannons.
Japanese, 30mm Browning Aircraft HO-155 Type 1, Machineguns/Cannons.
Japanese, 30mm Browning Aircraft HO-155 Type 2, Machineguns/Cannons.
Japanese, 37mm Browning Aircraft HO-204 Machineguns/Cannons.
Japanese, 40mm Caseless Aircraft Machineguns/Cannons.

Japanese, 20mm Oerlikon model 99, Machineguns/Cannons.
Japanese, model 94, 37mm gun, manufactured prior to 1946.
Lahti, model 39, cal. 20mm anti-tank rifle.
Lewis, Light machinegun (American or British manufacture), cal. .303 or .30.
Luger, Mauser commercial manufacture, semiautomatic pistol, 75 Jahre, Parabellum
  -Pistol, Mod. Karabiner, Commemorative, cal. 9mm, accompanied by a carbine type
  shoulder stock.
*M1918 and 1918A2 BAR, manufactured by Colt, Winchester, Marlin Rockwell, New
  England Small Arms, IBM, Royal Typewriter.
2 Browning, .30 cal. machineguns (AN-M2), as manufactured by various U.S.
  Government contractors prior to and during WWII.
Marble's Game Getter, Firearms, with a combination of .44 cal. or .410 gauge
  smooth bore and .22 cal. barrels, both 1st and 2nd models, with barrel lengths
  of less than 18," manufactured by the Marble Arms Corporation of Gladstone,
  Michigan, prior to 1943.
Marlin, aircraft machinegun, model 1917 and 1918, cal. .30.
Marlin, U.S. model 1917, ground machinegun, cal. 30/06.
Marlin, tank machineguns, model 1918 cal. .30.
Mauser, manufactured Schnellfeuer selective fire pistols and all original proto-
  types, cal. 7.63mm Mauser.
Maxim, machineguns of German manufacture, all models and cals.
Maxim, machineguns produced by Maxim Nordenfeldt and Vickers Sons and Maxim from
  approximately 1885 through 1908, all cals.
Maxim, machineguns, Russian model 1905, Russian manufacture having a brass water
  jacket in cal. 7.62mm, Russian rimmed.
Oerlikon, 20mm Automatic Cannon, all variations manufactured in the United States
  prior to 1946.
Pipe Pistol, S/N 420, cal. .22 rimfire (word "pipe" means smoking tobacco type).
Pipe Pistol, S/N IRS-3579, cal. 7mm centerfire, marked drgm Bucksom (word "pipe"
  means smoking tobacco type).
Reising, Submachineguns U.S. model M-50, .45 cal., Harrington & Richardson Arms,
  Worchester, MA, USA Pat Pending.
Royal, selective fire pistol, cal. 7.63mm (.30 Mauser), copy of Mauser model 1896
  pistol.
Russian, Degtyarev, machineguns, models DA, DP, DPM, DT, and RP46, cal. 7.62mm.
Russian, model 1910 (Maxim), machinegun, any cal., Russian manufacture.
Russian, model PPD 1943/38 and PPD 1940, submachineguns, cal. 7.62mm, original
  Russian manufacture.
Russian, 50mm Mortar Launcher.
Russian, PSH41, 7.62mm submachineguns & all copies/variations produced in the
  Communist Bloc countries prior to mid 1950's.
Russian, PPS 42, submachineguns, cal. 7.62mm.
Russian, PPS43 submachineguns, cal. 7.62 mm manufactured in the Soviet Union
  prior to 1946.
Russian, model SG43 heavy machinegun, cal. 7.62mm, Russian manufacture.
*Russian (U.S.S.R.), Federov, automatic rifle, model 1916 AVF (Avtomat), cal.
  6.5 x 50.5SR (6.5mm Japanese) of Russian manufacture.
*Russian (U.S.S.R.), Simonov, automatic rifle, model 1936 AVS (AVS36), cal.
  7.62 x 54R, of Soviet manufacture.
*Russian (U.S.S.R.), Tokarev, automatic rifle, model 1940 AVT (AVT40), cal.
  7.62 x 54R, of Soviet manufacture.
*Russian (U.S.S.R.), Stechkin, automatic pistol, model APS, cal. 9 x 18
  (Makarov), of Soviet manufacture.
Sedgley, Glove Pistol .38 centerfire, S/N IRS-3580, single shot, marked MK2S,
  manufactured by Sedgley, Philadelphia, for the U.S. Marines.
Simonov-PTRS 1941, 14.5mm anti-tank rifle.
Solothurn, models S18-100 S18-1000 & S18-1100 20mm semiautomatic, antitank rifle.
Springer, .32 cal., Knife-Pistols, marked "C-16" and "C-12" on the left & right
  extractors, respectively, with "BAZAAR" marked on the left side of the blade.
  Some devices are marked "Solingen" on the left side of the blade and "Made in
  Germany" on the other.
STAR, model AD, Selective Fire Pistol, any cal., produced prior to 1953.
STAR, model BD, Selective Fire Pistol, any cal., produced prior to 1953.

*STAR, model MD, Selective Fire Pistol, any cal., produced prior to 1953.
*STAR, model PD, Selective Fire Pistol, any cal., produced prior to 1953.
Stevens, Offhand Number 35, .410 gauge shot pistols.
Stevens, Auto Shot Number 35, .410 gauge shot pistols.
*Stoner, model 63 and 63A, rifles.
*Suomi, model 26 and 31 sub machinegun.
*Swedish, model 37 and 39 sub machinegun.
Swedish, model M-42 20mm recoilless anti-tank rifles.
Swedish, 3.7cm Bofors anti-tank guns produced prior to 1946, including the
  following variations or designations: Swedish Bofors, 37mm, anti-tank cannon,
  German 3.7cm, Pak 30 anti-tank gun (designation unconfirmed), German 3.7cm, Pak
  157(b) anti-tank gun (captured Danish guns), Polish 37mm, Armata Przeciwpancerna
  Wz 36, British Ordnance O.F. 37mm, Mk 1, anti-tank gun.
Swedish, models 21, 6.5mm, auto rifles manufactured prior to 1946.
Swedish, model 37, 6.5mm, auto rifles manufactured prior to 1946.
Thompson, model 1927, semiautomatic carbine, cal. .45 ACP.
Thompson, submachineguns including all models, prototypes, and variations actually
  manufactured in or before 1945.
Thompson, model 1928, Korean War Commemorative. submachineguns, cal. .45
  produced by Auto Ordinances, West Hurley, N.Y.
Umbrella Gun, 6 shot pepper box revolver with dagger attachment extending from
  muzzle, combined with handle and umbrella, S/N 16, cal. .22 rimfire, with
  markings Brevette PT, manufactured by Marquis de Fabrique, France.
*United Defense Supply Corporation, model U.D. 42, submachinegun, cal. 9mm
  Parabellum, as manufactured by Marlin Firearms Company, New Haven, CT.
U.S. Arms Company, knife pistol, cal. .22, manufactured prior to 1934.
U.S. 37mm Antitank guns M3 and M3A1, produced by various U.S. Government
  contractors prior to 1946.
U.S. M6 Survival rifle/shotgun, cal. .22/410 gauge, having 14 $1/2$" barrels,
  produced by various U.S. Government contractors.
U.S. Browning machineguns (original), cal. .30, M1917 and M1917A1, manufactured
  by Colt's Patent Firearms Company, New England Westinghouse Company, Remington
  Arms-Union Metallic Cartridge Company, Rock Island Arsenal, High Standard
  Company, Savage Arms Corporation, Buffalo Arms Corporation, Frigidaire, AC
  Spark Plug, Brown-Lipe-Chappin, Saginaw Steering Gear Division, and Kelsey
  Hayes Wheel Company.
U.S. Browning model 1919, cal. .30, machineguns, produced by various U.S. Gov't.
  contractors prior to 1946, all variations.
U.S. Browning model 1919A4 air cooled machinegun, produced by various U.S. Gov't.
  contractors prior to 1946, cal. .30.
U.S. Carbine, cal. 30, M2, original U.S. Military issue, manufactured prior to
  1946, and marked "M-2" on the receiver.
U.S. Johnson models 1941 and 1944 light machineguns, cal. .30.
U.S. Mortar (original), cal. 60mm, M1 and M2, with mount M2.
*U.S. M 4 Survival Rifle, cal. .22 Hornet, as issued by the gov't., manufactured
  in the United States and Canada by Harrington & Richardson Arms Company.
U.S. Maxim machinegun, model 1904, cal. .30.
U.S. models 1915 & 1918 Vickers machineguns manufactured by Colt in cals. 30/06
  or 11mm.
U.S. models M1, M9 and M18, cal. 2.36" Rocket launcher (Bazooka) and variations
  thereof.
U.S. 3" Anti-tank Gun, model M5.
U.S. model M6, 37mm, gun, produced prior to 1946.
U.S. model T-48 assault rifles, cal. 7.62mm, manufactured by Harrington &
  Richardson.
U.S. Small Arms Company knife pistol, cal. .22 original manufacture produced
  prior to 1934.
Vickers commercial water cooled machinegun, any configuration, any cal.,
  British manufacture.
Vickers original military machineguns, all variations, all cals., manufactured
  prior to 1946.
Winchester model 92 Trapper carbines having barrel lengths of less than 16"
  (original Winchester manufacture only).

The Astra Model 902, left and right sides.

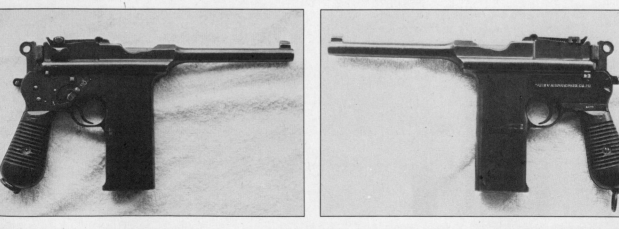

Section V
Curios & Relics Update

Members of the Firearms Industry and Others Concerned

The following listed firearms have been classified as curios and relics during the period January 1987 through December 1988. This list is an addendum to the Firearms Curios and Relics List, ATF Publication 5300.11 (7/87).

SECTION II

British Lee Enfield, Number 9, training rifles, caliber .22.

British SMLE XL42E1 Bolt action sniper rifle, caliber 7.62 NATO.

Chinese, Peoples Republic of China, copy of German Walther PPK .32 ACP caliber with Chinese proof marks, Type I and II.

Colt Buffalo Bill Wild West Show single action army .45 caliber.

Colt Missouri Sesquicentennial single action army .45 caliber.

Colt Texas Sesquicentennial Standard and Premier model single action army, .45 caliber.

Colt Theodore Roosevelt single action army .44-40 caliber.

Colt 150th Anniversary single action army buntline, .45 caliber.

French Military Rifle Model 1949/56, in 7.62 x 51mm (NATO) caliber.

Lahti Swedish Model M40 pistols, caliber 9mm, all variations, manufactured prior to 1968.

Smith & Wesson Registered Model 27 revolvers, caliber .357 magnum, 50 Year Commemorative, 5 inch barrel, serial numbers REG0001 through REG2500 inclusive.

Winchester Model 1897 or 97 riot guns, 12 gauge, 20 inch barrels, with original RIC (Royal Irish Constabulary) markings.

Winchester Model 9422 "Eagle Scout Commemorative," rifle, .22 caliber.

SECTION III

Colt .22 rimfire caliber semiautomatic pistol, serial number 49712 accompanied by an original "Rifle-ette" shoulder

stock as originally manufactured by the Monarch Arms and Manufacturing Company, Los Angeles, California, in the 1920's.

Marlin Model 1893 Carbine, caliber .25-36, serial number 387186, with 15 1/4 inch barrel.

Marlin Model 1893 Saddle Ring Carbine, caliber .32-40, with a 15 1/4 inch barrel, serial number C3967.

Winchester Model 1892 Carbine, caliber .25-20 WCF, serial number 766291, with 14 inch barrel.

Winchester Model 1892 Carbine, caliber .32 WCF, serial number 772706, with 14 inch barrel.

Winchester Model 92 Carbine, caliber .32-20 WCF, serial number 850460, with 14 inch barrel.

Winchester Model 1892 Carbine, caliber .44 WCF, serial number 897282, with 14 inch barrel.

Winchester Model 1892 Carbine, caliber .44 WCF, serial number 897168, with 14 inch barrel.

Winchester Model 1892 Carbine, caliber .44 WCF, serial number 650991, with 15 inch barrel.

Winchester Model 1892 Carbine, caliber .44 WCF, serial number 511099, with 15 inch barrel.

Winchester Model 94 Trapper Carbine, caliber .25-35, serial number 814142, with 14 inch barrel.

Winchester Model 1894 Saddle Ring Carbine, caliber .25-35, serial number 812956, with a 15 inch barrel.

Winchester Model 1894 Carbine, caliber .25-35 WCF, serial number 444585, with 15 inch barrel.

Winchester Model 1894 Carbine, caliber .30 WCF, serial number 559831, with 15 1/8 inch barrel.

Winchester Model 1894 Carbine, caliber .30 WCF, serial number 820413, with 15 inch barrel.

Winchester Model 1894 Carbine, caliber .30 WCF, serial number 868912, with 15 inch barrel.

Winchester Model 1894 Carbine, caliber .30-30 WCF, serial number 638701, with 15 inch barrel.

Winchester Model 1894 Carbine, caliber .30-30 WCF, serial number 923215, with 15 inch barrel.

Winchester Model 94 Trapper Carbine, caliber .30-30, serial number 1057043, with 15 inch barrel.

SECTION IIIA

German Minenwerfers, old and new models, manufactured prior to 1919, utilizing a radial, straight pull friction primer ignition system

Winchester Model 1873 carbine, serial number 131762A, caliber .44 WCF, with a 15 inch barrel.

SECTION IV

Armalite AR-15, .222 Remington or .223 calibers, produced by Armalite.

Armalite AR-15, Model 601, .223 caliber, manufactured by Colt. Must be marked "Armalite."

Colt, Model 1921, Model 1921A1, Model 52, and Model 52A, .50 caliber, water-cooled machinegun, as originally manufactured by Colt and bearing the original serial number with the letter "C" prefix.

Danish HOVA M1949, 9mm Parabellum caliber, produced in Denmark.

Egyptian "Port Said" version of the Swedish Model 45B, 9mm caliber, produced in Egypt.

German Flak 30, 2cm antiaircraft machinegun.

German Minenwerfers, having fixed firing pins, spring or hammer actuated striker, any caliber, any model, manufactured prior to 1919.

Ingram Models 6 and 7, various calibers, produced by Police Ordnance Company.

Ingram Models 8 and 9, various calibers, produced in Thailand.

M3 submachinegun, caliber 9mm Parabellum as originally produced by the United States Government, having no manufacturers name or serial number and originally marked U.S. 9mm SMG on the left side of the magazine housing. Original production only.

Smith and Wesson, Model 76 submachinegun, caliber 9mm parabellum, serial number range from U100 to U6100.

Solothurn Maschinengewehr, Model 38 (MG38), 7.92 mm machinegun, manufactured between 1930 - 1935, by Waffenfabrik Solothurn AG, Solothurn, Switzerland.

Swedish Model 45, and Model 45B 9mm Parabellum caliber, produced in Sweden.